THE MUTE IMMORTALS SPEAK

A volume in the series

MYTH AND POETICS

edited by Gregory Nagy

A list of titles appears at the end of the book.

THE MUTE IMMORTALS SPEAK

Pre-Islamic Poetry and the Poetics of Ritual

SUZANNE PINCKNEY STETKEVYCH

CORNELL UNIVERSITY PRESS

ITHACA AND LONDON

First published 1993 by Cornell University Press.

International Standard Book Number 0-8014-2764-9
Library of Congress Catalog Card Number 93-18173
Printed in the United States of America
Librarians: Library of Congress cataloging information appears on the last page of the book.

♾The paper in this book meets the minimum requirements of the American National Standard for Information Sciences–Permanence of Paper for Printed Library Materials, ANSI Z39.48-1984.

To Julian, Qays, and Khalid

Contents

Foreword, by Gregory Nagy ix

Preface xi

PART ONE: PRESENTING THE RITUAL PARADIGM

1 Voicing the Mute Immortals: *The Muʿallaqah of Labīd* and the Rite of Passage 3

2 Eating the Dead / The Dead Eating: Blood Vengeance as Sacrifice 55

PART TWO: THE PARADIGM OF PASSAGE MANQUÉ

3 Taʾabbaṭa Sharran and Oedipus: A Paradigm of Passage Manqué 87

4 Archetype and Attribution: Al-Shanfarā and the *Lāmiyyat al-ʿArab* 119

PART THREE: ORALITY AND GENDER IN THE ELEGY

5 The Obligations and Poetics of Gender: Women's Elegy and Blood Vengeance 161

6 Memory Inflamed: Muhalhil ibn Rabīʿah and the War of al-Basūs 206

Foreword

Gregory Nagy

The Mute Immortals Speak: Pre-Islamic Poetry and the Poetics of Ritual is a vital new entry in the Myth and Poetics series, which is committed to the exploration of interaction between myth and ritual in the poetics of traditional societies. Combining various approaches derived from anthropology and literary theory, this book examines from a comparative perspective one of the most difficult and challenging genres in Arabic literature, the pre-Islamic *qaṣīdah*. Suzanne Stetkevych's application of a wide range of reading and research in this area has made it possible for specialist and nonspecialist alike to grasp the mythic dimension of Arabic poetics—a dimension largely overlooked in previous scholarly writings on the subject. What is more, the author succeeds in showing the importance of the tradition of the Arabic *qaṣīdah* for comparative research on the nature of lyric.

Preface

The pre-Islamic ode (*qaṣīdah*) has traditionally been regarded as one of the twin foundations of Arab-Islamic literary culture, the other being the Qurʾān. And just as the Qurʾānic text, as the word of God, was held to be inimitable, so too the poetry of the pagan pre-Islamic era (the Jāhiliyyah or "Age of Ignorance") was considered to be of a quality unattainable by the poets of the Islamic period. The rich history of classical Arabic literature stretches from the deepest recesses of the Jāhiliyyah (roughly the late fifth century A.D.) into the first half of the twentieth century. From the advent of Islam, traditionally dated from the Hijrah (when Muḥammad and a small group of Muslims migrated from Mecca to Medina in A.D. 622 = 1 H.), the qaṣīdah played profane antitext to the Qurʾānic sacred text. This dynamic tension formed the generative core of a vast body of literature, sacred and secular, poetry and prose. Not only are the literary texts themselves informed by this dialectic, but it is everywhere present in the vast exegetical and hermeneutical production of the scholiasts, so that pre-Islamic poetry and the extensive body of lore that accompanies it constantly appear in Qurʾānic commentary, and vice versa.

Despite the general recognition of the esteem in which Arabs have traditionally held the poetry of their pagan past, modern critics from both East and West have yet to formulate a poetics through which to analyze and evaluate this body of verse. Orientalist studies, whether well or ill disposed toward pre-Islamic poetry, have tended to read the recurrent themes of this originally oral tradition as purely descriptive of bedouin life and to attribute the paratactic juxtaposition of themes within the qaṣīdah to the illogic or prelogic of the bedouin.

In the present book I undertake to bring together findings in the fields of literary criticism, anthropology, and history of religions to create a poetics suitable to a body of bedouin tribal poetry that was oral in composition and, until its collection and compilation some time in the second or third Islamic century, in preservation. I propose, first, that this poetry is ritual in both form and function and offer the patterns of rites of passage and of sacrifice as a basis for interpretation. Second, I propose to employ the extensive body of lore, legend, and myth which accompanies pre-Islamic poetry in the classical commentaries and literary compendia of the Islamic period as an exegetical tool for reading the qaṣīdah. Finally, I suggest a distinct inter- and intratextual aesthetics for originally oral poetry which is intimately derived from the exigencies of oral composition and preservation and of ritual obligation and function. At the same time, however, I attempt to address the paradoxical identity of the pre-Islamic qaṣīdah, which, although oral and pagan in origin, was codified and institutionalized as one of the twin foundations of a preeminently literary Arab-Islamic culture. In no way do I intend to suggest that the ritual paradigmatic approach to pre-Islamic poetry is exclusive or exhaustive; rather, I want to explore a hitherto neglected aspect of the complex and multifaceted poeticity of the Arabic qaṣīdah.

In Part I, "Presenting the Ritual Paradigm," I argue that the tripartite classical Arabic ode (qaṣīdah), consisting of the *nasīb* (description of the ruined abode and lost mistress), *raḥīl* (desert journey and camel description), and *fakhr* (praise for self and tribe), is not a series of arbitrary and unrelated descriptive passages, as has been asserted by both Arab and Orientalist critics, but rather reflects a ritual pattern. Taking as its model Arnold van Gennep's formulation of the rite of passage/initiation, Chapter 1 is an analysis of *The Muʿallaqah of Labīd* in light of archetypal, structuralist, and poststructuralist literary theory. Further, I show that the *akhbār* (biographical anecdotes) concerning Labīd in the classical Arab-Islamic sources form a literary construct or persona that in archetypal terms parallels the structure of the qaṣīdah. Chapter 2 adds to the theoretical framework of Chapter 1 the theories of sacrifice propounded by Henri Hubert and Marcel Mauss, Edmund Leach, and René Girard and the work on blood vengeance among the Arabs by Henri Lammens and Joseph Chelhod to establish that the pre-Islamic poem of blood vengeance likewise reflects a ritual pattern. It establishes that the taking of blood vengeance as depicted in the akhbār, as well as the poetry, constituted a blood sacrifice that marked the passage from childhood to adulthood, and that the institution of blood vengeance served, along the lines of Mauss's theories of the gift, as a ritual exchange of sacrificial victims.

The purpose of Part II, "The Paradigm of Passage Manqué," is to demonstrate that the poetry of the *ṣaʿālīk* (brigands), although it does not exhibit the tripartite structure of the classical qaṣīdah, can nevertheless be interpreted in light of the same ritual paradigm as the full form, as a *rite de passage manqué*, that is, a failed or aborted rite of passage, in which the passenger/poet remains perpetually in the "liminal" antisocial phase that corresponds to the raḥīl section of the qaṣīdah. Drawing on the work of the Classical (Greek) scholars Marie Delcourt, Paul Diel, Pierre Vidal-Naquet, and Jean-Pierre Vernant, the studies of Taʾabbaṭa Sharran and al-Shanfarā in Chapters 3 and 4 demonstrate that these two ṣaʿālīk exhibit in both their akhbār and their poetry the characteristics of the passenger manqué: the irregular gait, the deviation from or perversion of social norms, the use of ruse and trickery, and the like, and that the *ṣuʿlūk* poem, lacking the section of aggregation or praise of the tribe, can, in effect, be termed a qaṣīdah manqué.

Taking as its working proposition the ritual nature of pre-Islamic poetry as demonstrated in the preceding chapters and its oral-formulaic character as established in the studies of James Monroe and Michael Zwettler, Part III, "Orality and Gender in the Elegy," defines an aesthetics appropriate to this sort of verse. Referring to the studies of orality and literacy by Eric Havelock and Walter Ong, I focus on the mnemonic imperative of oral poetry—that is, whatever is not remembered/memorized is lost. Chapter 5 investigates the production and perpetuation of meaning in the closed oral-formulaic system of pre-Islamic women's elegiac verse. It deals in particular with the concepts of polysemy and intertextuality in the repetition of formulaic phrases. Chapter 6 concludes from its analysis of five poems of blood vengeance by Muhalhil ibn Rabīʿah that, in the absence of reliable prose akhbār and commentaries, the body of oral-formulaic and ritual verse serves an intertextual exegetical function through which variations on a particular motif from poem to poem serve to explicate one another. Within the poem a similar intratextual exegesis operates, whereby, through the repetition of the same message by means of a variety of metaphors and images, the preservation of meaning is guaranteed. In the course of the analysis of the poems in these two chapters, it becomes increasingly clear that a gender differentiation is operative in the ritual obligations of men and women to fallen kinsmen and in the formal and thematic requirements of its ritual poetic expression. Finally, these two chapters demonstrate that the composition of both men's and women's elegies was perceived as an act of sacrifice and redemption.

In Part IV, "The Master Poem," the concluding chapter, "Regicide and Retribution," takes as its subject what has traditionally been regarded as the best achieved qaṣīdah in the Arabic language, *The Muʿallaqah of Imruʾ al-Qays*. This chapter begins with an analysis of the akhbār of Imruʾ al-Qays, which reveals two fundamental components: first, the prodigality or "arrested development" of the poet's youth, and second, the domination in the later parts of the theme of exaggerated blood vengeance for the poet's slain royal father. I then proceed on the principle of the exegetical value of the akhbār to argue that Imruʾ al-Qays's masterpiece can be read as a "sublimated" poem of blood vengeance, that is, one in which the metaphorical expression has so displaced the literal that it is no longer even stated. In this interpretation of the master poem of the Arabic qaṣīdah tradition, I add a final ritual paradigm to the rite of passage and rite of sacrifice: Theodor Gaster's "seasonal pattern" of rite and myth. The effect of what I have termed the "sublimation of imagery" is to raise Imruʾ al-Qays's *Muʿallaqah* above the level of the individual poem of blood vengeance, such as those of Muhalhil in Chapter 6, to a more mythic expression of pollution and purification and of the hero's accession to power, one that shares the same form-determining structure as ancient Near Eastern ritual, myth, and drama.

Far from being a purely theoretical work, *The Mute Immortals Speak* presents close readings of a selected body of poems and the lore that surrounds them. These are presented in original translations in such a way as to form a subcorpus from which the reader of English can get a sense of the dense intertextuality, the thematic canon, and even the distinct poetic lexicon of the pre-Islamic Arabic qaṣīdah. Above all, the contemporary English idiom of the poetry translations is meant to convey with directness and immediacy the power and beauty of the originals. In attempting to accomplish this goal, however, the translations are often at a considerable remove from the "literal." So, for the reader of Arabic, the original poetic texts have been provided in an appendix keyed by bracketed numbers to the English text.

In the transliteration of Arabic proper names, terms, and phrases I have used the Library of Congress system with some modifications for long vowels and with the addition of case endings for phrases of poetry.

In the various stages of its evolution this book has benefited from the kindness and expertise of many friends and colleagues. Deserving of particular thanks are Basima Berzirgan, Olga Davidson, Hassan el-Banna Ezz el-Din, Allen Douglas and Fedwa Malti-Douglas, Aḥmad ʿAbd al-Majīd Harīdī, James Monroe, Consuelo Lopez-Morillas, Gregory Nagy, Michael A. Sells, Nazif Shahrani, and Elizabeth Sherman. A special category of thanks is reserved for Jaroslav Stetkevych, the first to make the mute immortals speak.

I am grateful as well for the generous financial and institutional support I have received: an American Schools of Oriental Research–sponsored National Endowment for the Humanities Research Fellowship allowed me to spend 1983–1984 in Jordan, and the Department of Arabic Literature of Yarmūk University served as my host that year; a Fulbright Foundation Islamic Civilization Fellowship supported my research in Egypt in 1988; and at Indiana University, Bloomington, the Office of Research and Graduate Development awarded me a Summer Faculty Fellowship in 1988 and an Outstanding Young Faculty Award in 1990 in support of my research, and the Middle Eastern Studies Program awarded me a Faculty Research Grant for technical support.

I would like too to express my appreciation to the editors and publishers who have granted permission to reprint some of the materials in this book. These include my articles "Ritual and Sacrificial Elements in the Poetry of Blood-Vengeance: Two Poems by Durayd ibn al-Ṣimmah and Muhalhil ibn Rabīʿah" and "Structuralist Analyses of Pre-Islamic Poetry: Critique and New Directions," which appeared in the *Journal of Near Eastern Studies* 45, no. 1 (1986): 31–43, and 42, no. 2 (1983): 85–107 © 1983 and 1986 by The University of Chicago. All rights reserved. "Ritual and Sacrificial Elements" appears in revised form as parts of Chapters 2 and 5. The theoretical conclusions and some sections of "Structuralist Analyses" appear, largely rewritten, in parts of Chapters 1 and 7. My article "Archetype and Attribution in Early Arabic Poetry: Al-Shanfarā and the *Lāmiyyat al-ʿArab*," which appeared in the *International Journal of Middle East Studies* 18 (1986): 361–90, appears in revised form as Chapter 4. My article *The Rithāʾ of Taʾabbaṭa Sharran*: A Study of Blood-Vengeance in Early Arabic Poetry," which appeared in the *Journal of Semitic Studies* 31, no. 1 (1986): 27–45, appears in revised form as part of Chapter 2. My article "The Ṣuʿlūk and His

Poem: A Paradigm of Passage Manqué," which appeared in the *Journal of the American Oriental Society* 104, no. 4 (1984): 661–78, appears in revised form as Chapter 3. Finally, some brief passages from my book *Abū Tammām and the Poetics of the ʿAbbāsid Age*, published by E. J. Brill, Leiden, in 1991, appear with some revision in Chapters 2, 3 and 5.

SUZANNE PINCKNEY STETKEVYCH

Bloomington, Indiana

PART ONE

PRESENTING THE RITUAL PARADIGM

CHAPTER I

Voicing the Mute Immortals: *The Muʿallaqah of Labīd* and the Rite of Passage

The outstanding characteristic of classical Arabic poetry is the perpetuation of a single dominant poetic form, the qaṣīdah, or ode, throughout its fifteen-hundred-year history—that is, from its pre-Islamic beginnings around 500 B.C. until our own century, which witnessed its final neoclassical flowering in the poetry of Aḥmad Shawqī[1] (d. 1932) and, in midcentury, the advent of a new poetic form, the first in a millennium and a half potent enough to compete for domination with the traditional form, Arabic "free verse" (*al-shiʿr al-ḥurr*).[2] The qaṣīdah, in the broadest terms, is a metered poem in monorhyme, usually of fifteen to eighty lines. In its full traditional form it comprises three thematic units:[3] the

1. For a study of the neoclassical qaṣīdah form in the hands of Aḥmad Shawqī see Jaroslav Stetkevych, "Sīniyyat Aḥmad Shawqī wa ʿIyār al-Shiʿr al-ʿArabī al-Kilāsīkī," *Fuṣūl* 7 (Oct. 1986/Mar. 1987): 12–29.

2. This is not to deny the development of other forms, the *ghazal*, the *muwashshaḥ*, etc., but rather to point out that they developed in the shadow of the qaṣīdah, are fundamentally off-shoots or derivatives of it, and never achieved its influence and preeminence. They reflected and supplemented the qaṣīdah, but never seriously challenged it. *Al-shiʿr al-ḥurr*, on the other hand, represents a radical departure from, or abandonment of, the classical tradition. That it has challenged and even displaced the qaṣīdah, and with it *al-shiʿr al-ʿamūdī* (which subscribes to the prosodic requirements of the qaṣīdah), as the major vehicle for poetic expression since the 1950s is undeniable.

3. The classical formulation of the qaṣīdah is that of Ibn Qutaybah (d. 276/889). See ʿAbd Allāh ibn Muslim Ibn Qutaybah, *Kitāb al-Shiʿr wa al-Shuʿarāʾ*, ed. M. J. de Goeje (Leiden: E. J. Brill, 1904), 14–15, translated in Reynold A. Nicholson, *A Literary History of the Arabs* (Cambridge: Cambridge University Press, 1956), 77–78. In ʿAbbasid times the central raḥīl section tended to fall out, resulting in the prevalence of a bipartite nasīb/madīḥ qaṣīdah. For a description of the major themes and motifs of the pre-Islamic qaṣīdah, see Renate Jacobi, *Studien zur Poetik der altarabischen Qaṣide* (Wiesbaden: Franz Steiner, 1971).

nasīb, consisting of the description of the abandoned encampment and of the poet's beloved mistress who once dwelled there; the *raḥīl*, which describes the poet's journey through the desert and his mount, the she-camel, with comparisons of her to wild creatures, notably the oryx cow or bull, the onager, and the ostrich; and the final section which may be of several sorts—*fakhr*, the poet's praise or boast of himself and his tribe, including the hunt, the feast, combat, the drinking scene, tribal wealth, authority, and generosity; or *madīḥ*, court panegyric in which the praise of the ruler takes the place of fakhr; or *hijā'*, invective, which is, in effect, an inverted form of fakhr.[4]

An explanation of the tenacity of the qaṣīdah form would seem to be in order if we are to understand anything of the essential nature and dynamism of classical Arabic poetry. Recent critical attempts have been largely unsatisfactory, or at least unsatisfying. Coleridgean "organic unity" à la ʿAbd al-Qāhir al-Jurjānī has been proposed, but not established in any unit longer than an image extending over several consecutive verses;[5] no relationship, "organic" or otherwise, is established between the thematic sections of the qaṣīdah. Structuralist analyses have resulted, in Kamal Abu-Deeb's work, in the perception of a series of Lévi-Straussian binary oppositions throughout the qaṣīdah and, in the work of Adnan Haydar, in the application of a Proppian lack → mediation → lack-liquidation formula to the qaṣīdah.[6] Although I have expressed some reservations about these studies elsewhere,[7] they nevertheless introduce ideas that will bear much fruit in our further discussion: first, the establishment of a nature/culture dialectic operating throughout the qaṣīdah and, second, the proposal that an underlying structure generates the qaṣīdah's thematic sections. Also worthy of

4. The structure of the *rithā'*, the elegiac qaṣīdah, differs substantially, as I shall describe later. Nevertheless, the genres share a common thematic ground, as expressed in the dictum repeated by Ibn Rashīq; "All poetry can be summed up in three phrases: . . . when you praise you say 'you are . . . '; when you elegize you say 'you were . . . '; and when you lampoon you say, 'you are not. . . .' " Abū ʿAlī al-Ḥasan Ibn Rashīq al-Qayrawānī, *Al-ʿUmdah fī Maḥāsin al-Shiʿr wa Ādābih wa Naqdih*, ed. Muḥammad Muḥyī al-Dīn ʿAbd al-Ḥamīd, 2 vols., 4th ed. (Beirut: Dār al-Jīl, 1972), 2:147.

5. Kamal Abu-Deeb, "Studies in Arabic Literary Criticism: The Concept of Organic Unity," *Edebiyât* 2, no. 1 (1977): 57–89.

6. Kamal Abu-Deeb, "Towards a Structural Analysis of Pre-Islamic Poetry," *International Journal of Middle Eastern Studies* 6 (1975): 148–84; and Abu-Deeb, "Towards a Structural Analysis of Pre-Islamic Poetry (II): The Eros Vision," *Edebiyât* 1 (1976): 3–69; Adnan Haydar, "*The Muʿallaqa of Imru' al-Qays*: Its Structure and Meaning, I and II," *Edebiyât* 2 (1977): 227–61, and 3 (1978): 51–82.

7. Suzanne Pinckney Stetkevych, "Structuralist Analyses of Pre-Islamic Poetry: Critique and New Directions," *Journal of Near Eastern Studies* 42, no. 2 (1983): 85–107.

mention in this regard is Stefan Sperl's work on the bipartite ʿAbbasid panegyric qaṣīdah, which, he maintains, incorporates elements of ancient Middle Eastern kingship ritual and exhibits a dialectical strophe/antistrophe structure.[8]

Running counter to these attempts is G. J. H. van Gelder's book *Beyond the Line,* which concludes that since the classical critics do not deal with this issue and modern critics have produced no conclusive or convincing argument for the unity of the qaṣīdah, no such unity or cohesiveness exists.[9] This questionable logic leads us back to the earlier and still standard Orientalist estimation of the qaṣīdah as "a string of pearls at random strung," otherwise termed the "atomistic" theory, which proposes that the individual and independent lines of verse bear no semantic connection to one another. The sense of the Arabic pun (*naẓama* means both to string pearls and to compose verse—hence *naẓm* denotes verse—whereas *nathara*, to scatter, disperse, gives *nathr*, prose) is that the "stringing" refers by analogy to rhyme and meter. What this analogy leaves unexplained is why the same themes and motifs, each with its distinctive diction, occur over and over again and, furthermore, largely in the same place and order in poem after poem. Orientalism has regularly attributed the "tediousness" of the convention-bound ordering of traditional themes to a conservatism born of a lack of poetic imagination perceived as a racial characteristic of the Semites.[10] Another avenue of approach, which should eventually lead us to an understanding of the qaṣīdah form is the application of the Parry-Lord theory of oral-formulaic composition to pre-Islamic poetry, as J. T. Monroe and Michael Zwettler have done.[11] These two scholars have established that early Arabic poetry is indeed oral and formulaic, but their treatment is limited to verbal and morphological formulas in individual lines of poetry, to the exclusion of the question of form as formula.

8. Stefan Sperl, "Islamic Kingship and Arabic Panegyric Poetry in the Early 9th Century," *Journal of Arabic Literature* 8 (1977): 20–35; Sperl, *Mannerism in Arabic Poetry: A Structuralist Analysis of Selected Texts (3rd Century A.H./9th Century A.D.–5th Century A.H./11th Century A.D.)* (Cambridge: Cambridge University Press, 1989).

9. G. J. H. van Gelder, *Beyond the Line: Classical Arabic Literary Critics on the Coherence and Unity of the Poem* (Leiden: E. J. Brill, 1982), 194–208.

10. Michael Sells's exposition and indictment of the pervasive Orientalist disparagement of the classical Arabic qaṣīdah and the culture that produced it, make reiteration here redundant. See his "The *Qaṣīda* and the West: Self-Reflective Stereotype and Critical Encounter," *Al-ʿArabiyya* 20 (1987): 307–24.

11. J. T. Monroe, "Oral Composition in Pre-Islamic Poetry," *Journal of Arabic Literature* 3 (1972): 1–53; Michael Zwettler, *The Oral Tradition of Classical Arabic Poetry: Its Character and Implications* (Columbus: Ohio State University Press, 1972).

The obvious place to start looking for a literary-critical explanation of a repeated poetic form or pattern would be archetypal criticism. Such classic works as Maud Bodkin's *Archetypal Patterns in Poetry*, Vladimir Propp's *Morphology of the Folktale*, Marie Delcourt's *Oedipe; ou, La légende du conquérant*, Joseph Campbell's *Hero with a Thousand Faces*, Harry Slochower's *Mythopoesis: Mythic Patterns in the Literary Classics* come to mind. Although all these, and more, should ultimately have some bearing upon the qaṣīdah, their applicability, in the initial stages at least, is hampered by the fact that they all deal with myths or literary (or folk-literary) works that are narrative in form—"stories," if you will, in which a character (or characters) proceeds through a "historically" perceived series of actions; that is, the form is determined by a narrative syntax. The qaṣīdah, by contrast, is eminently nonnarrative; rather, the thematic sections and the *topoi* within them are paratactically juxtaposed.[12] It is above all this lack of a surface narrative syntax, the absence of "plot" or "story," that has led to the accusations of disunity and incoherence in the classical Arabic poem.

In searching for a prospective paradigm, I have therefore found a more apt or obvious analogy in anthropological studies of ritual, the repetition of an ordered series of symbolic actions whose logic or connection lies at a deeper, nonnarrative structural level. What is curious is that despite considerable mention of the "ritual" nature of classical Arabic poetry,[13] little inquiry has been made into the fields, notably anthropology and the history of religions, that specialize in such subjects. Such an inquiry, once undertaken, leads almost inevitably to the van Gennepian tripartite model of the rite of passage.[14] Originally proposed by Arnold van Gennep some eighty years ago, it has enjoyed an extended vogue since the 1960s among anthropologists, historians

12. Despite this apparent difficulty, Jaroslav Stetkevych has succeeded in analyzing the qaṣīdah form by analogy to narrative heroic patterns, notably medieval romance (Chrétien de Troyes). See *The Zephyrs of Najd: The Poetics of Nostalgia in the Classical Arabic Nasīb* (Chicago: University of Chicago Press, 1993), chap. 1.

13. E.g., Andras Hamori, *On the Art of Medieval Arabic Literature* (Princeton, N.J.: Princeton University Press, 1974), 21–27; Abu-Deeb, "Towards a Structural Analysis (II)," 66; Haydar, "Structure and Meaning, I," 228; Sperl, "Islamic Kingship," passim, and *Mannerism in Arabic Poetry*, 9–27.

14. Arnold van Gennep, *The Rites of Passage*, trans. Monika B. Vizedom and Gabrielle L. Caffee (Chicago: University of Chicago Press, 1960) [*Les rites de passage*, 1908]. The application of this ritual formula as a paradigm for the classical Arabic qaṣīdah was first proposed in S. Stetkevych, "Structuralist Analyses," 98–107, and in Suzanne Stetkevych, "Al-Qaṣīdah al-ʿArabiyyah wa Ṭuqūs al-ʿUbūr," *Majallat Majmaʿ al-Lughah al-ʿArabiyyah bi-Dimashq* 60, no. 1 (1985): 55–85.

of religion, and to a limited extent, literary critics. An apt formulation of the rite for our purposes is Victor Turner's:

> Van Gennep has shown that all rites of passage or "transition" are marked by three phases: separation, margin (or *limen*, signifying "threshold" in Latin), and aggregation. The first phase (of separation) comprises symbolic behavior signifying the detachment of the individual or group either from an earlier fixed point in the social structure, from a set of cultural conditions (a "state"), or from both. During the intervening "liminal" period, the characteristics of the ritual subject (the "passenger") are ambiguous; he passes through a cultural realm that has few or none of the of the attributes of the past or coming state. In the third phase (reaggregation or reincorporation), the passage is consummated. The ritual subject, individual or corporate, is in a relatively stable state once more and, by virtue of this, has rights and obligations vis-à-vis others of a clearly defined and "structural" type; he is expected to behave in accordance with certain customary norms and ethical standards binding on incumbents of social position in a system of such positions.[15]

"Liminal entities," Turner explains, "are neither here nor there; they are betwixt and between the positions assigned and arrayed by law, custom, convention, and ceremonial. As such their ambiguous and indeterminate attributes are expressed by a rich variety of symbols in the many societies that ritualize social and cultural transitions. Thus, liminality is frequently likened to death, to being in the womb, to invisibility, to darkness, to bisexuality, to the wilderness."[16] Mary Douglas describes a dangerous antisocietal state:

> Danger lies in transitional states, simply because transition is neither in one state nor the next, it is undefinable. The person who must pass from one to another is himself in danger and emanates danger to others. . . . To say that the boys [in an initiation] risk their lives says precisely that to go out of the formal structure and to enter the margins is to be exposed to power that is enough to kill them or make their manhood. The theme of death and rebirth, of course, has other symbolic functions: the initiates die to their old life and are reborn to the new. The whole repertoire of ideas concerning pollution and purification are used to mark the gravity of the event and the power of ritual to make a man—this is straightforward.
>
> During the marginal period which separates ritual dying and ritual

15. Victor Turner, *The Ritual Process: Structure and Anti-Structure* (Ithaca, N.Y.: Cornell University Press, 1977), 94–95.
16. Ibid., 95.

> rebirth, the novices in initiation are temporarily outcast. For the duration of the rite they have no place in society. Sometimes they actually go to live far away outside it. Sometimes they live near enough for unplanned contacts to take place between full social beings and the outcasts. Then we find them behaving like dangerous criminal characters. They are licensed to waylay, steal, rape. This behaviour is even enjoined on them. To behave anti-socially is the proper expression of their marginal condition. To have been in the margins is to have been in contact with danger, to have been at the source of power.[17]

These explications serve to clarify the position of such concepts as pollution and purification, ritual death and rebirth, and, we should add, sacrifice and redemption within this ritual structure. It should be noted, furthermore, that the effect of this ritual paradigm is to establish a series of dichotomies or binary oppositions between the various sections: parts 1 and 3, both in "society" are thus opposed to part 2 the "extrasocietal" or "antisocietal" margin; in addition, parts 1 and 3, separation from society and reentry into it, proceed in diametrically opposite directions.

The logic of the exercise in which I am engaged suggests an analogy between the qaṣīdah and the rite of passage, hence between the nasīb and separation, the raḥīl and liminality, the fakhr, or madḥ, and aggregation. Further, we should take from the beginning the rather simple step of identifying the stages of the rite of passage or of initiation, at least metaphorically, with the three stages of psycho-social development (perhaps in the Freudian sense)—childhood, adolescence, and adulthood—and with some concept of its narrative embodiment in the heroic quest.

The Muʿallaqah of Labīd

The poet Labīd ibn Rabīʿah is said to have been born in the Jāhiliyyah and at the age of ninety to have converted to Islam. He is counted among the *muʿammarūn* (those granted longevity), living to the age of 145 or 157 and dying sometime in the reign of Muʿāwiyah. It is said that he forswore the composition of poetry upon his conversion to Islam, and his *Muʿallaqah* (one of the canonical seven, or ten, greatest masterpieces of the Jāhiliyyah, the *Muʿallaqāt* "suspended odes") is therefore considered a pre-Islamic composition.[18] Although it should

17. Mary Douglas, *Purity and Danger: An Analysis of Concepts of Pollution and Taboo* (London: Routledge and Kegan Paul, 1966), 96–97.

18. See Fuat Sezgin, *Geschichte des arabischen Schrifttums*, vol. 2: *Poesie bis ca. 430 H.* (Leiden: E. J. Brill, 1975), 126–27.

therefore be considered a rather late product of the Jāhiliyyah, the purity and clarity of its classical formal structure make it an ideal poem with which to begin our analysis of the qaṣīdah form in light of the rite of passage model.[19]

The poem, whose full text follows, opens with a twenty-one-verse nasīb that comprises a description of the ruined abodes (verses 1–11), followed by the departure of the women, among them the poet's inamorata, Nawār. The raḥīl (22–54) exhibits the description of the poet's mount, the she-camel, through similes to the pregnant onager mare and her mate (28–35) and the oryx cow bereft of her calf and pursued by hounds and hunters (36–53). The fakhr (55–88) contains a drinking scene (57–61), a description of the poet's battle mare (63–69), the gambling over the slaughter camel and subsequent feast (73–77), to conclude with a boast about the political might of the poet's tribe (78–88).

The Muʿallaqah of Labīd [1]

1. Effaced are the abodes,
 brief encampments and long-settled ones;
 At Minā the wilderness has claimed
 Mount Ghawl and Mount Rijām.
2. The torrent channels of Mount Rayyān,
 their tracings are laid bare,
 Preserved as surely as inscriptions are
 preserved in rock,
3. Dung-darkened patches over which,
 since they were peopled, years elapsed,
 Their profane months and sacred ones
 have passed away.
4. They were watered by the rain
 the spring stars bring,
 And on them fell the rain of thunderclouds,
 downpour and drizzle

19. The paradigmatic nature of Labīd's *Muʿallaqah* has been recognized, e.g., by Kamal Abu-Deeb who terms it "the key poem." See Abu-Deeb, "Towards a Structural Analysis," 153. Other studies of interest include Gottfried Müller, *Ich bin Labīd und das ist mein Ziel: Zum Problem der Selbstbehauptung in der altarabischen Qaside* (Wiesbaden: Franz Steiner, 1981); Muḥammad Ṣiddīq Ghayth, "Al-Taḥlīl al-Dirāmī lil-Aṭlāl bi Muʿallaqat Labīd," *Fuṣūl* 4 (Jan. 1984): 165–77; Michael Sells's translation with introduction in *Desert Tracings: Six Classic Arabian Odes* (Middletown, Conn.: Wesleyan University Press, 1989), 32–44; and A. J. Arberry's translation and introduction in *The Seven Odes: The First Chapter in Arabic Literature* (London: George Allen and Unwin, 1957), 119–47.

5. From each night-faring rain cloud
and early morning horizon-darkener
And cloud at forenoon
with resounding rumble.
6. The *ayhuqān* thrust up its shoots, and
on the two sides of the valley
Gazelles and ostriches
have borne their young.
7. Wide-eyed oryx cows, newly-calved,
stand above their newborns, motionless,
While on the plain the yearlings
in clusters caper.
8. The torrents have exposed the ruins,
as if they were
Writings whose texts pens have
inscribed anew
9. Or like the tattooer sprinkling lampblack
again and yet again
Over hands on which
tattoos appear.
10. Then I stopped and questioned them,
but how do we question
Mute immortals whose speech
is indistinct?
11. Stripped bare where once a folk had dwelled,
then one morn departed;
Abandoned lay the trench that ran around the tents,
the *thumām* grass that plugged their holes.
12. The clanswomen departing stirred your longing
when they loaded up their gear,
Then climbed inside their howdah frames
with squeaking tents,
13. The howdahs each enclosed with wooden frame,
covered by a woolen carpet,
And shaded by fine veil
and figured drape,[20]
14. In clusters they departed, as if the howdahs bore
the wild cows of Tūḍiḥ

20. There is some confusion among the classical commentarists on the distribution of curtains here. See Abū ʿAbd Allāh al-Ḥusayn ibn Aḥmad al-Zawzanī, *Sharḥ al-Muʿallaqāt al-Sabʿ*, ed. Muḥammad ʿAlī Ḥamd Allāh (Damascus: al-Maktabah al-Umawiyyah, 1963), 209.

And the white does of Wajrah tenderly inclining
over their young.
15. They were urged on, and the mirage
dissolved them till they were like
The windings of the riverbed of Bīshah,
its tamarisks and boulders.
16. What then do you remember of Nawār
when she has gone far off,
And her bonds, both firm and frayed,
are cut asunder?
17. A Murrite woman who alit in Fayd,
then dwelled nearby the people of Ḥijāz,
How then could you hope
to meet with her again?
18. On the eastward slopes of Ṭayy's two mounts
she alighted, or on Muḥajjir's mount,
Then a lone peak contained her,
and its foothills,
19. Then in Ṣuwāʾiq if she headed toward the Yemen,
so that by now
She is most likely in its Wiḥāf al-Qahr,
or in Ṭilkhām.
20. Cut off your love from him
whose bond is not secure,
For the best binder of affection's bond
is he who breaks it.
21. Be generous to him who treats you well,
but only the cutting of bonds remains
When affection falters
and its foundation fails,
22. With a camel mare jaded by journeys
that have reduced her to a remnant,
Till she is emaciate
of loins and hump.
23. When her flesh has dwindled
and she is exhausted,
And after great fatigue her leathern shoe thongs
are cut through,
24. Yet is she as nimble in the reins
as if she were a rose-hued cloud,
Rain-emptied, running with the south wind,
sprightly.

25. Or is she like a she-ass, teats milk-swollen,
pregnant by a stallion white-bellied
And gaunt from repelling rivals,
biting them and kicking.
26. Much scratched and bitten he mounts with her
the hump-backed hills,
Perplexed by his pregnant mate's
recalcitrance and cravings.
27. Above the jagged heights of Thalabūt he scouts
the empty lookout posts,
Fearful of hunters hid behind
the roadmarks made of stone.
28. Until when winter's six months pass,
they live on moisture from the grass,
Long avoiding waterholes,
both he and she.
29. Then they put their trust in resolution,
tightly twisted,
For the success of one's resolve
lies in its firmness.
30. Then the blades of *buhmā* grass
pricked at her pasterns,
And the summer wind picked up,
its passing gusts and fiery blasts.
31. Back and forth they tugged a flowing train
of stirred-up dust
Whose cloud flies up like smoke
when the kindling is lit,
32. Fanned by the north wind, mixed
with the thorny *ʿarfaj* tree's green wood,
Like the smoke of a mighty blaze
with leaping flames.
33. Then he continued driving her before him,
for it was his custom,
When she strayed or lagged behind,
to drive her on ahead.
34. They plunged into the middle
of a rivulet
And cut through to a brimming spring
grown thick with reeds,
35. On all sides surrounded by
a stand of canes

That shaded it with fallen stalks
and stalks still standing.
36. Is my camel mare like this or like the oryx cow,
her calf the wild beasts' prey,
Who, though among the lead bull's wards,
now lagged behind the herd,
37. A snub-nosed cow bereft of calf,
who mid the stony tracts between the dunes
Does not leave off
her roaming and her lowing
38. For a calf half-weaned and white,
its limbs torn back and forth
By ashen predators who never
hunger long.
39. They chanced upon it unawares
and struck;
Indeed fate's arrows never miss
their mark.
40. She waited through the night beneath a cloud
that shed an unremitting rain
And let a ceaseless downpour fall
upon the dense-grown dunes.
41. Uninterrupted raindrops fell
on her spine's track
In a night whose stars
were veiled by clouds.
42. She took shelter in the hollow
of a contorted tree
Set apart upon the edges of the dunes
whose drift-sand slopes.
43. And in the first watch of the night
her lustrous face
Gleamed like the diver's pearl,
its string drawn forth.
44. Till, when the dark dispelled
and dawn shone forth,
Her hoofs slipped on the early morning's
rain-soaked earth.
45. Bewildered, she searched doggedly
among Ṣuʿāʾid's puddles
Seven full nights coupled
with their days.

46. Until, hope's stores exhausted,
and udder, once milk-swollen,
Neither from suckling nor weaning
now gone dry,
47. She heard with dread the buzz
of human voice
That frightened her from unseen side—
For mankind is her bane.
48. Then early in the day she ventured forth,
fearing for head and tail,
Dangers from behind
and from in front
49. Until when the hunters in despair
of bow and arrow
Set on her their rawhide-collared,
flop-eared hounds.
50. They overtook her, and she
returned their charge
With a horn like a Samharī spear
in point and shaft
51. To ward them off,
for she knew
If she did not repel them
she would die.
52. Fetch was first to fall,
smeared all in blood,
Then Blackie was left for dead
where he had charged.
53. On this one when sun's shimmerings
dance in full forenoon light,
And the hillocks don the cloaks
of the mirage
54. I attend my own heart's needs,
not neglecting them for fear
that others will think ill of me
or rebukers blame me.
55. Did Nawār not know
that I am both
He who ties the knots in ropes
and he who cuts them?
56. He who leaves a place
that does not please him,

Unless his own soul's fate
  overtakes him there.
57. And don't you know how many a night
  mild in its weather,
Delightful in its sport
  and in its revelry,
58. I spent as its convivial, and rushed
  to many a merchant's banner
When it was raised
  and the price of wine was high.
59. I paid a dear price for a wine
  in an aged and darkened wineskin,
Or in a pitch-lined jug, ladled into cups,
  its seal broken.
60. And many a morning draught of a pure wine
  and a slave girl with a lute,
Plucking with her thumb
  on its taut strings.
61. My first cup I downed before the cock
  could crow in daybreak
To take a second when
  its sleepers woke.
62. And many a bitter morn of wind and cold
  I curbed,
When its reins were in the hand
  of the north wind.
63. I defended the tribe, my battle gear borne
  by a winning courser,
Her reins my sash when I
  went forth at dawn.
64. Then I mounted a lookout post
  on a narrow, wind-blown peak
Whose dust rose to the banners
  of the foe
65. Until when daylight dipped its hand into
  the all-concealing night,
And darkness veiled the crotches of
  each mountain pass,
66. To the plain I descended and my mare
  held erect her neck
Like the date palm's stripped trunk at which
  the picker's courage fails.

67. I spurred her to a speed
fit for the ostrich chase,
Until when she was heated through
and her bones were nimble,
68. Her light leathern saddle slipped,
sweat flowed from her neck,
And her saddle girth
was soaked with froth.
69. She coursed, head held high and thrusting
in the bridle, racing headlong
Like a thirsting dove to water when
her flock beats urgent wings.
70. And many a chief's domed tent,
where unknown strangers sojourn,
Its favor hoped for,
its displeasure feared,
71. Its men burly-necked, lionlike,
braced for revenge,
As if they were the Jinn of al-Badī,
their feet fixed in the earth.
72. Their false claims I denied,
their due rights recognized,
And no nobleman among them could vaunt
his glory over me.
73. And many a *maysir* players' slaughter camel
its death I called for
By the fate-sealing arrows whose shafts
look all alike,
74. Summoning them to a she-camel,
barren or with foal,
Her meat bestowed on all whom we
have granted refuge.
75. Then for the guest and for the foreign refugee,
it is as if
They had descended to Tabālah Valley,
its lowlands ever green.
76. Every indigent woman seeks the refuge
of my tent ropes,
Emaciated, rag-clad, like a starved she-camel hobbled
at her master's grave.
77. When winter's winds wail back and forth
her orphans plunge

Into streams of flowing gravy which
  my clan crowns with meat.
78. When tribal councils gather
  there is always one of us
Who contends in grave affairs
  and shoulders them,
79. A divider of spoils who gives
  each clan its due,
Demanding their rights for the worthy,
  the rights of the worthless refusing
80. Out of superior might; a man munificent,
  who with his bounty succors,
Openhanded; a winner and plunderer of all
  that he desires,
81. From a clan whose fathers set for them
  their law—
For each tribe has its leader
  and its law.
82. Their honor is not sullied, their deeds
  not without issue,
For their judgment is not swayed
  by passion's flights.
83. Be then content, O enemy, with what the sovereign
  allotted you,
For virtues were allotted us
  by him who knows them.
84. When trusts were apportioned
  to the tribes,
The apportioner allotted us
  the greatest share.
85. He built for us a high-roofed
  edifice,
To which the tribesmen mount,
  both youths and full-grown men.
86. They are the first to act
  when the tribe is stricken;
In war, its horsemen;
  in disputes, its arbiters.
87. They are a springtime
  to those that seek refuge
And to indigent women, their food stores exhausted,
  while the year stretches long.

88. They form a band so tight that none of them
impedes it out of envy,
Nor, out of treachery,
leans toward the foe.[21]

Labīd's *Muʿallaqah* opens with the traditional motif of the poet stopping at the abandoned and ruined abodes (*al-aṭlāl*).[22] The "separation" of the poet from his past as lived in these dwellings is obvious. What we have here, however, is not the individual's separation from a continuous "social structure" but the departure of society itself; it has disappeared. The poet's desolation, thus projected on the ruins, is expressed in terms of a nature/culture dialectic—the encroachment of nature and the concomitant departure of culture—that is pursued through the twenty-one verses of the nasīb. What society, culture, had created—both temporary and permanent encampments—nature has erased; what was once settled, cultivated, is now grown wild (*taʾabbada*). Essential to this dialectic is the ephemeral and transitory quality of all that is cultural or cultivated—that is, human—as opposed to the permanence and perpetuity of the natural. *Taʾabbada*, to become wild, derives from the root *ʾ-b-d*, which means to become wild, unsocial (*ʾabada/u*), but also, to last, to remain, to dwell permanently, as in *abad*, lasting, everlasting, eternity (*ʾabada/i*).[23] Thus *taʾabbada* also conveys at some level the sense of perpetuity or eternity. Its opposite *taʾannasa*, to be sociable, is from *ʾ-n-s*, a root meaning to be social, sociable, tame—hence *ins*, mankind. It appears here in verse 3 in the form *anīsihā* "the time when they were peopled." The effect of this opposition, further suggested by the Arab-Christian use of the term to mean "to become man (son of God)"[24] is to point to the sense of "mortality" that separates man from beast or

21. The translation is based on the recension and commentary of al-Zawzanī, *Sharḥ al-Muʿallaqāt*, 198–234, with reference to that of Abū Bakr Muḥammad ibn al-Qāsim al-Anbārī, *Sharḥ al-Qaṣāʾid al-Sabʿ al-Ṭiwāl al-Jāhiliyyāt*, ed. ʿAbd al-Salām Muḥammad Hārūn, 2d ed. (Cairo: Dār al-Maʿārif, 1969), 505–98.

22. The role of *al-muqaddamah al-ṭalaliyyah* (ruined encampment prelude) in the pre-Islamic qaṣīdah, particularly in light of theories of orality and literacy, is the subject of Ḥasan al-Bannā ʿIzz al-Dīn, *Al-Kalimāt wa al-Ashyāʾ: Baḥth fī al-Taqālīd al-Fanniyyah lil-Qaṣīdah al-Jāhiliyyah* (Cairo: Dār al-Fikr al-ʿArabī, 1988).

23. Lane, *ʾ-b-d*. [Lane = Edward William Lane, *Arabic-English Lexicon*, 8 vols. (New York: Frederick Ungar, 1958) (London, 1863)].

24. Hava, *ʾ-n-s*.[Hava = J. G. Hava, *Al-Faraid Arabic-English Dictionary* (Beirut: Catholic Press, 1964)].

from nature.[25] The opening verse thus tells us that what man makes is ephemeral—abodes for a shorter or a longer stay—but the mountains, untamed nature, are eternal. Labīd expresses the same idea elsewhere with far less subtlety but in a manner that serves virtually as a *sharḥ* (commentary) for this verse:

We vanish but the rising stars
do not;
Mountains remain when we are gone,
and fortresses.
. . . . .
People are just like abodes:
one day filled with folk,
The next day
barren wastes.[26] [2]

The remainder of the nasīb develops this opposition through a reversal of attributes: culture is dehumanized, feralized, whereas nature is described with the attributes of culture. Thus in verse 2 the tracings, outlines of drainage ditches, have been stripped, laid bare (*ʿurriya*)—the opposite of clothing, the preeminent symbol of culture—by the torrents. The results of the ravages of nature are then described in uniquely cultural terms: the man-made ditches worn ever deeper by the torrents have acquired the permanence of writing carved in rock. The theme of nature displacing culture continues in verses 3 and 4. The abandoned encampment, still visibly darkened by the droppings of the animals of its inhabitants in days gone by, is now sustained or watered (*ruziqat*) by rain clouds. The years of the human calendar, with their division into sacred and profane months, have elapsed (*khalawna*), but the verb *khalā/yakhlū* also means to be vacant, empty, hence reinforcing

25. Curiously, this interpretation supports the apparently fanciful etymology of *insān*, man, as a metathesis (*qalb*) from the root *n-s-y* that denotes forgetfulness and oblivion. Hence Ibn ʿAbbās's saying: *Innamā summiya insānan li-annahu ʿuhida ʿalayhi fa nasiya* (He [the first man, Adam] was called man [*insān*] because he was commanded and then forgot [*nasiya*]). See Lane, ʾ*-n-s*; see also Qurʾān 22:114. My argument would be rather that he is *mansī*, forgotten, that is, mortal, ephemeral, condemned to oblivion. Such etymological musings are compounded, or confounded, by the root *n-s-'* associated with delay and postponement, the prolonging of life, hence *nasāʾ*, length of life and *nisāʾ*, women—the latter an especially clear metathesis from ʾ*-n-s* (see Lane, ʾ*-n-s*, *n-s-*ʾ, *n-s-y*). We thus obtain a root that generates two apparently opposite meanings (*min al-aḍdād*).

26. Ibn Qutaybah, *Al-Shiʿr wa al-Shuʿarāʾ*, 151.

the waning of all things human, cultural. Even the word used for "years," *ḥijaj*, is a specifically cultural, that is, ritual one, for it is literally ḥajjes, pilgrimages, that is, the span of time between one pilgrimage and the next, time as measured by human ritual, not natural phenomena. It is the difference between saying "five Christmases ago" and "five years ago".

To the depletion of the cultural in verses 1–3, verses 4–7 contrast the plenitude of nature. Time is now measured by natural phenomena: the human vernal encampments lie abandoned, but the rain-boding stars dwell in their spring abodes (*marābīʿa al-nujūmi*). The sustenance of the ruin is not that which human society provides but that which the rain clouds bring. The days, too, are now measured not by human activity but by the times at which the clouds let down their life-giving burdens (5). The displacement of culture by nature is completed in verses 6 and 7, in which cultural sterility is replaced by natural fecundity depicted in the propagation of flora and fauna where once thrived the tribe of the poet's beloved. But it is the nature of poetry to be ambiguous. Gazelle does and oryx cows are, in Arabic poetry, the conventional simile for the poet's beloved and the women of her tribe. It is thus almost inevitable that we read into these two verses a sublimation of the poet's yearning for lost love, for a love that failed, and see in the parturition and nurturing of the gazelle does and oryx cows a metaphor for what might have been. A subtle personification, perceptible only through a familiarity with the poetic convention, thus emerges from the scene of the maternal serenity of the newly calved oryx cows contrasted with the sprightly capering of their yearlings.

The poet's psychological/metaphorical con-fusion of the natural and cultural comes to a head in verses 8–10. The torrents' ever deeper etching of the ruins is likened to pens' rewriting of a faded text. More telling still is the comparison to the repeated application of lampblack, time and time again, as the tattooed design emerges clearer and clearer. Both verses describe nature in eminently cultural terms; both affirm that with the passage of time and increased devastation the traces of the ruin become not vaguer but more distinct. Moreover, both *zubur* (writings) and *wishām* (tattoos) refer to signs, sign systems, encoded messages that must be read or decoded. The first is related through consonantal shifts to *sifr* (book, sacred book) and *ṣifr* (cipher);[27] the

27. See Jaroslav Stetkevych, "Arabic Hermeneutical Terminology: Paradox and the Production of Meaning," *Journal of Near Eastern Studies* 48, no. 2 (1989): 90.

second, with the instability or variability characteristic of weak roots, is related by both metathesis and consonantal shift to *ism* (name), *sammā* (to name), and *wasama* (to brand, stigmatize, stamp, mark), hence *simah* (mark, sign).[28] The point here is that such marks, signs, writings, and ciphers do not speak for themselves; they bear messages that must be deciphered.[29]

In verse 10, however, the poet stops to query the ruins, only to conclude with a more profound query: How can we question deaf and mute immortals (*ṣumman khawālida*)—that is, insensate rocks (*aṣammu* means deaf, but also dumb, mute, with reference to animate objects; solid, hard, with reference to rocks).[30] The mute rocks, in the context of the qaṣīdah, refer in a specific way to the *athāfī*, the three stones of the campfire which support the cauldron and remain, blackened and bare, as a sign of former habitation.[31] Here, they function as a synecdoche for the ruined encampment. Verse 10 is thus, above all, a riddle, and the answer to it will reveal much about the nasīb, in fact, about the entire qaṣīdah.

The poet has told us thrice (verses 2, 8, and 9) that the passage of time and the ravages of nature have only rendered the message all the more permanent. Then he tells us in verse 10 that this message is borne by deaf, mute rocks whose speech is unclear. To answer this riddle, to make the mute immortals speak, we must first know the proper question. It is not, I would argue, about the geographical whereabouts of the departed mistress and her tribe; for this, the ruins have no answer. Rather it is about the permanence of nature, the impermanence of culture, and thus, ultimately, nature's immortality and man's—espe-

28. See Joseph Chelhod's extensive discussion of this root in regard to the *mawsim*, season of pilgrimage, particularly as concerns his interpretation of these "signs" as signs of consecration. Joseph Chelhod, *Le sacrifice chez les Arabes: Recherches sur l'évolution, la nature, et la fonction des rites sacrificiels en Arabie occidentale* (Paris: Presses Universitaires de France, 1955), 152–57.

29. On the semantics of encoding, recognizing, and decoding signs see Gregory Nagy, *Greek Mythology and Poetics* (Ithaca, N.Y.: Cornell University Press, 1990), chap. 8, "Sêma and Nóēsis: The Hero's Tomb and the 'Reading' of Symbols in Homer and Hesiod," pp. 202–22. Nagy's discussion of the double meaning of *sêma* as "sign" and "tomb" is intriguingly close to the Arabic rocks or ruins as *memento mori* whose message, once decoded, spells heroic (con)quest. It is, furthermore, tempting to see a cognation between the Greek *sêma* and the Arabic *simah*.

30. Lane, *ṣ-m-m*.

31. On the symbolic and mythic dimensions of the *athāfī*, see Jaroslav Stetkevych, "Toward an Arabic Elegiac Lexicon: The Seven Words of the Nasīb," in Suzanne Pinckney Stetkevych, ed., *Reorientations/Arabic and Persian Poetry* (Bloomington: Indiana University Press, 1993).

cially the poet's own—mortality. Once we know the right question, the answer is not hard to find: it appears in the following verse (11). Whereas rocks and ruins are solid, motionless, silent, and unchanging (immortal), human life is transhumant and transient; departure and abandonment are synecdoches for death.

And yet it is only man, the mortal, who can read this message. The text is thus a cipher (*ṣifr/zubur*). The message, the rock that bears it, is mute, voiceless, inanimate, until given voice, breath, spirit—that is, life—by the reader.[32] At this point we can bring our etymological argument full circle to suggest that the root *ṣ-m-m* (deaf, mute, immobile) is also connected to the *ʾ-s-m*, *w-sh-m*, *w-s-m* group, that it thus implies ṣign and message as well as silence, the permanence of the name, tattoo, brand, and scar.[33] Moreover, we should note that in the context of the nature/culture dialectic it is man alone who can read the signs, who can know his own mortality.

It appears moreover, that the message of the stones, like the ancient rock inscriptions so often encountered by the nonliterate bedouin of

32. Voicing or "vocalization" is a necessary complement to the Semitic scripts, including Arabic, for whereas the Greek alphabet, for example, represents all vowels and consonants, the Semitic scripts represent consonants (and long vowels) only. This distinction is made much of, in a decidedly Grecocentric manner, in Eric A. Havelock, *The Muse Learns to Write: Reflections on Orality and Literacy from Antiquity to the Present* (New Haven, Conn.: Yale University Press, 1986), 59–61 and passim; Walter J. Ong, *Orality and Literacy: The Technologizing of the Word* (London: Methuen, 1982), 26–27 and passim.

It is of note that with the development of the Arabic writing system the short (unwritten) vowels came to be termed *ḥarakāt*, movements, as opposed to the immobility of the penned or graven text. It is with this Semitic graphic peculiarity in mind that the metaphor or pun of the biblical "for the letter killeth, but the spirit quickeneth" (2 Cor. 3:6) is to be understood, and likewise, ultimately, the "mute immortals" of Labīd's poem. See Havelock's remark that "the consonants by strict definition are by themselves 'dumb,' 'mute,' 'unpronounceable' (*aphona, aphthonga*—Plato's terms, borrowed he says from previous sources)." Havelock, *The Muse*, 60. Nevertheless, as Jesper Svenbro convincingly demonstrates, even with the fully vocalized Greek alphabetical system, stone inscriptions were considered "voiceless" without a reader, as in Théognis's *líthos áphthongos* (voiceless stone). See Jesper Svenbro, *Phrasikleia: Anthropologie de la lecture en Grèce ancienne* (Paris: la Découverte, 1988), p. 70 and chap. 2, "Le lecteur et la voix lectrice," passim. My thanks to Gregory Nagy for this reference.

33. Once more, see Nagy on the sign (*sêma*) that does not declare or command of or by itself, i.e., is silent, mute, but requires recognition (*nóos*) and decoding. In other words, it is mute to those without *nóos*. Nagy, "Sêma and Nóēsis," 208 and passim. This relation between sign and recognition would suggest, too, that the concept of naming has its origin in a physical sign—a symbol, mark, tattoo, scar, totem—not a verbal one, most likely denoting consecration to a deity or spirit, or membership in a tribe or clan—as Chelhod suggests, a sign of ownership. See Chelhod, *Le sacrifice chez les Arabes*, 152–57. This, in turn, should have something to do with the taboo, common in many tribal societies, against saying/voicing a person's true name, for its "immortality" is associated with the soul.

the pre-Islamic period, is ultimately indecipherable. The message, then, is that the silence of illegibility or indecipherability is death. The poet responds to this memento mori in two ways. On the poetic level, his realization of his own mortality marks the ritual separation and his embarking on the "heroic quest" that is the raḥīl (desert journey) section of the poem, to finally conclude with the fakhr (self-praise) section that celebrates his manly exploits and thus perpetuates his name. On the metapoetic level, we can interpret the entire poetic enterprise as the poet's quest for immortality, for a never-muted voice. For in an oral poetic tradition the poem is, as it were, that very spirit or anima that otherwise has to be read into the written/graven text. It is an unincarnate anima or, inasmuch as it is passed from one man's mouth and memory to another's, perpetually reincarnate and, hence, not mortal.[34]

The image of tribal departure in verse 11 bears deeper dimensions as well. Its connection with death in the personal sense is clear, as indicated by the repeated use of this image in *rithā*ʾ (elegy), but there is also a quite Jungian voice of collective historical experience speaking here—that of the failure of the polity, the destruction of the social order, and the dispersal or scattering of its members. The Arab archetype in this respect is the bursting of the Dam of Maʾrib, the history of a once sedentary and prosperous people scattered and reduced to desperate transhumance. The cautionary tale of the Qurʾān is phrased in terms of "expulsion from the garden":

> For Sheba also there was a sign in their dwelling-place—two gardens, one on the right and one on the left: "Eat of your Lord's provision, and give thanks to Him; a good land, and a Lord All-forgiving." But they turned away; so We loosed on them the Flood of Arim, and we gave them, in exchange for their two gardens, two gardens bearing bitter produce and tamarisk bushes, and here and there a few lote-trees. Then We recompensed them for their unbelief; . . . And we set between them and the cities that We have blessed, cities apparent and well we measured the journey between them: "Journey among them by night and by day in security!" But they said, "Our Lord, prolong the stages of our travel"; and they wronged themselves, so We made them as but tales, and We tore

34. This argument attempts to follow, mutatis mutandis, Svenbro's discussion of the relationship between writer and reader as a form of metempsychosis. See Svenbro, *Phrasikleia*, chap. 7, "La vraie metempsychose," passim. My point is that for the pre-Islamic Arabic poet the indecipherable inscriptions of lost peoples become, as it were, a permanent sign of their mortality or, if you will, a sign of their failed immortality.

> them utterly to pieces. Surely in that are signs for every man enduring, thankful. [Qur'ān 34:15–19][35]

The narrative versions of the bursting of the Dam of Ma'rib suggest an explanation that is more sociopolitical than the Qur'ānic theological one for the disintegration of the network of dams that supported the South Arabian kingdom of Saba', leading to its demise: that is, the failure of the polity, which resulted in the neglect of dam maintenance. The resultant infestation with rats or moles (*khuld*) weakened the dam to the point where it could not withstand the torrential floods. A Weberian interpretation will, of course, reconcile the sociopolitical with the theological. Thus, in the version given by Maḥmūd Shukrī al-Ālūsī, as in the Qur'ān, the image of Saba' is one of consummate civilization and cultivation: habitations (*ʿamārah*) stretched out in measured stages all the way to Sha'm, or so far that fire (a prime symbol of civilization) could be borrowed from one habitation to the next for a distance of a two-month journey. So lush were the date groves that a woman had only to carry a palm basket through them to fill it with their falling fruit. And all this bounty was attributable to divine providence in the form of a masterfully engineered system of dams. With the dispersal of its people, the Ḥimyarite kingdom became a byword for a failed polity, the moral of their story preserved in the idiom *tafarraqū aydiya Sabā*, "they scattered in all directions."[36]

Likewise there come to mind the lost peoples of ʿĀd and Thamūd, which were to become the Qur'ānic paradigm for divine destruction visited upon failed or wicked polities. For the pre-Islamic bedouin, then, the abandoned encampment, like the more majestic ruins such as those of Madā'in Ṣāliḥ or of Petra, was a sign of the failure of culture, the human inability to establish a permanent, sedentary abode. It is not surprising, then, that in Islamic terms, the heavenly garden is termed *dār al-qarār*, the permanent abode, and the Kaʿbah at Mecca (and its heavenly counterpart) given the epithet *al-bayt al-maʿmūr*, the (continuously) inhabited dwelling.[37]

Verses 12–15 constitute the *ẓaʿn*, the description of the departure of the women of the tribe. What is striking within the context of the

35. Here and hereafter I use the translation of A. J. Arberry, trans., *The Koran Interpreted*, 2 vols. in 1 (New York: Macmillan, 1969).

36. Maḥmūd Shukrī al-Ālūsī, *Bulūgh al-Arab fī Maʿrifat Aḥwāl al-ʿArab*, ed. Muḥammad Bahjat al-Atharī, 3 vols., 2d ed. (Beirut: Dār al-Kutub al-ʿIlmiyyah, n.d.), 1:207–8, also 3:283–88.

37. Lane, *ʿ-m-r*.

present argument is how the scene is constructed in such a way as to portray culture as swallowed up by nature or dissolved in it. Verse 12 describes the yearning that stirs in the poet's heart as the women load up their belongings and enter their howdahs; the enclosure and protection of the women, another primary cultural characteristic, is emphasized in verse 13 by their double or triple curtaining (again, cloth or clothing as a preeminent symbol of culture) in a variety of carpets, veils, and drapes. This image thus constitutes an opposition to the "laying bare" of the abandoned dwelling. In verses 14 and 15, however, despite the extravagant layering of cultural stuffs and fabrics, the women (culture) dissolve into nature. First merely in simile: the women are compared to the oryx cows of Tūḍiḥ and the white antelope does with their fawns at Wajrah, the conventional fauna of the nasīb, which here hearken back to verses 6 and 7. Finally, in verse 15, the camel-borne women are completely absorbed in nature as they recede into the distance until their forms are indistinguishable from the trees and boulders of the riverbed of Bīshah. It is worth observing here that the motion of the *ẓaʿn* is depicted not as directional or intentional but as a gradual dissolution from the effect of the refracting light of the mirage.

Where the eye fails, the mind's eye takes over, and it is here, in verses 16–19, having lost sight of the *ẓaʿāʾin*, that the poet reflects upon the possible whereabouts of his former love. Behind this reflection lies the motif of the cutting of bonds (*qaṭʿ al-asbāb*) (cf. verse 16: *wa taqaṭṭaʿat asbābuhā wa rimāmuhā*), that is, the cutting of ties both emotional and social. This nasīb convention admirably fits Turner's description of the separation phase as comprising "symbolic behavior [read "imagery," "diction"] signifying the detachment of the individual . . . either from a fixed point in the social structure, from a set of cultural conditions . . . , or from both."[38] The verses are phrased hypothetically: there is no hope of meeting Nawār again, only of conjecturing where she might now be, depending upon the direction her tribe has taken. The poet's mind's eye roams from place to place where she might have encamped. It is as if the beloved herself were the victim, if you will, of a geographical *sparagmos*, scattered among her possible abodes: Fayd, Ḥijāz, Mount Muḥajjir, Ṣuwāʾiq, Wiḥāf al-Qahr, Ṭilkhām. She is everywhere and nowhere. The poet cuts short his daydreaming, his musings, in verse 20, using diction that is once more as conventional to the nasīb as it is fitting to the separation phase of the rite of passage paradigm, a chiastic

38. Turner, *Ritual Process,* 94.

(abba) pattern of oppositions: *faqṭaᶜ* . . . *waṣluhu* . . . *wāṣilu* . . . *ṣarrāmuhā* (cut . . . joining . . . joiner . . . cutter).

In verse 21 the poet reaffirms in aphoristic terms the necessity of cutting (*ṣarm*) failed bonds of affection, the necessity of separation. The tone, however, has changed from the melancholy yearning of the abandoned encampment and the equally abandoned poet, the passive victim of others' departure. The poet's reflection has revealed to him the nature of mortality (of "the human condition") and the fickleness of the bonds and relationships that he has established up until now. In verses 21 and 22 the poet begins to take the initiative, becomes the actor, not the victim, of separation, and takes his own departure. The journey he undertakes is not like the dispersal and ultimate doom symbolized by the abandoned encampment and departed tribe; rather, it is a well-directed quest, a quest, I believe, for an alternative to the nature/culture dialectic, to doomed mortality, to the temporal and temporary. It is the quest for the permanent abode, for what ultimately could be termed immortality. Thus in the end the poet is not expelled from his lost paradise but, making a virtue of necessity, opts to depart.

With verse 22 the raḥīl (desert journey) section is begun and the poet, according to the dictates of our paradigm, enters the "margin," the "liminal" phase of the rite of passage in which the passenger/poet is an outcast. Recalling Mary Douglas's statement that the marginal period separates ritual dying from ritual rebirth, we might emphasize once more the elegiac tone of the nasīb, the specter of death that haunts the ruined encampment, the message of mortality conveyed by the time- and weather-ravaged remnant of what was once a human dwelling, the poet's intentional departure from death or from the past. With the raḥīl he enters a state characterized by ambiguity, wilderness, and above all, danger. It is a test, the poet's test of his own mortality, overcoming death—or the fear of it—by facing it head on. In the Arabic qaṣīdah the liminality of the raḥīl finds expression in the poet's solitude or self-absorption. Whereas in the nasīb he is traditionally accompanied by two companions or, in any case, is preoccupied with his social relationships (or the failure thereof) to his beloved and her people, in the raḥīl he is alone, his only companion his trusty mount, invariably the she-camel (*nāqah*).[39]

39. On the gender inversion of the departing women *ẓaᶜāʾin* mounted on male camels and the poet on the camel mare, see Jaroslav Stetkevych, "Name and Epithet: The Philology and Semiotics of Animal Nomenclature in Early Arabic Poetry," *Journal of Near Eastern Studies* 45, no. 2 (1986): 112–25.

In practical terms, the choice of the she-camel for the desert journey is perhaps self-evident. The classical commentators take pains to point out that the she-camel was employed for travel, whereas the horse (*faras*, m. or f.) was reserved for battle and the hunt. In the qaṣīdah, therefore, the she-camel is associated with the raḥīl, and hence the liminal phase, whereas the horse is found in the heroic "tribal" exploits of battle and hunt, hence in the fakhr section of the poem, which corresponds to the aggregation phase of the rite of passage.[40] Moreover, the she-camel is poetically and ritually appropriate for a "passage" since it is *par excellence* that beast most suited for surviving the arduous desert crossing. The identification of the poet with his mount thus ensures, as it were, his successful passage. Moreover, for the pre-Islamic Arab, both bedouin and merchant, the camel is the preeminent symbol of culture, the "staff of life." The she-camel provided not only transport for men and goods but also hair for tents and food in the form of meat, milk, and blood (drunk from a slit vein in times of dearth). Wealth was measured in camel herds; even the value of human life, be it blood price or bride price, was measured in camels, one hundred camels being a standard price for both.[41] In addition, the caravan trade of the Arabs, both of the by-this-time defunct caravan empires of Petra and Palmyra and, latterly, of the caravan city of Mecca, depended utterly upon the camel. It is not surprising, then, that the camel, especially the she-camel, became virtually the totemic animal of the pre-Islamic Arabs and thus a sacrificial beast[42]—in poetry especially in the "game" of *maysir*—a symbol of the polity whose apportionment, as Mary Douglas remarks, is an expression of social division within that polity.[43]

All these significations are mythopoeically present in the pre-Islamic and Qurʾānic legend of Nāqat Ṣāliḥ (the She-Camel of Ṣāliḥ, the scorned prophet of the people of Thamūd):

> And to Thamood their brother Salih; he said, "O my people, serve God! You have no other god than He; there has now come to you a clear sign

40. In this light, Renate Jacobi's statement that the camel section constitutes "the nucleus of tribal *fakhr*" reflects a misperception of the structure of the pre-Islamic qaṣīdah and the role of the camel in it. See Renate Jacobi, "The Camel-Section of the Panegyrical Ode," *Journal of Arabic Literature* 8 (1982): 1.

41. The story of ʿAbd al-Muṭṭalib's sacrifice of ʿAbd Allāh (the father of the Prophet Muḥammad) serves as an etiological myth for the customary amount of the bloodwite.

42. See W. Robertson Smith, *The Religion of the Semites: The Fundamental Institutions* (New York: Meridian Books, 1957) [London, 1889], 218, 281–83.

43. Mary Douglas, *Implicit Meanings: Essays in Anthropology* (London: Routledge and Kegan Paul, 1975), 67–68.

> from your Lord—this is the She-camel of God, to be a sign for you. Leave her that she may eat in God's earth, and do not touch her with evil, lest you be seized by a painful chastisement. And remember when He appointed you successors after Ad, and lodged you in the land, taking to yourselves castles of its plains, and hewing its mountains into houses. Remember God's bounties, and do not do mischief in the earth, working corruption." Said the Council of those of his people who waxed proud to those that were abased, to those of them who believed, "Do you know that Salih is an Envoy from his Lord?" They said, "In the Message he has been sent with we are believers." Said the ones who waxed proud, "As for us, we are unbelievers in the thing in which you believe." So they hamstrung the She-camel and turned in disdain from the commandment of their Lord, saying, "O! Salih, bring us that thou promisest us, if thou art an Envoy." So the earthquake seized them, and morning found them in their habitation fallen prostrate. So he turned his back on them, and said, "O my people, I have delivered to you the Message of my Lord, and advised you sincerely; but you do not love sincere advisers." [Qur'ān 7:71–77]

The she-camel here functions as a symbol of fecundity and prosperity, a sign of divine blessing whose improper or forbidden sacrifice marks the disintegration, indeed, extermination, of the polity. In the extra-Qur'ānic versions a certain mythic ambiguity is detectable.[44] The vast proportions of the she-camel suggest that the excessive accumulation of wealth in the hands of one man led to the impoverishment and resentment of his fellow citizens and, ultimately, to the destruction of the polity. In the Qur'ānic version, however, the she-camel serves as an expression of God's blessing upon its owner and his people or, more precisely, as miraculous proof of Ṣaliḥ's prophetic mission (see Qur'ān 17:61). In both cases, however, the hocking of the mythologically proportioned she-camel marks the disintegration of the social order for the people of Thamūd, much as the bursting of the Dam of Ma'rib signals the dispersal of the once prosperous and sedentary denizens of Saba'. Similarly, in the lore of the Jāhiliyyah, the improper slaying of the she-camel of al-Basūs—in what was ultimately a dispute over the relations between clients and clans—signals the breakdown of the tribal polity of the closely related Banū Bakr and Banū Taghlib and instigates the forty-year War of al-Basūs.[45]

44. See Shihāb al-Dīn Aḥmad ibn ʿAbd al-Wahhāb al-Nuwayrī, *Nihāyat al-Arab fī Funūn al-Adab*, 18 vols. (Cairo: al-Mu'assasah al-Miṣriyyah al-ʿĀmmah lil-Ta'līf wa al-Tarjamah wa al-Ṭibāʿah wa al-Nashr, 1964), 13:79–85.

45. Al-Ālūsī, *Bulūgh al-Arab* 2:150–51, and below, Chapter 6.

The point, with respect to the argument at hand, is that the she-camel is the preeminent symbol of prosperity and fecundity and, in particular, of human culture. The proper sacrifice of the she-camel thus constitutes a commensal meal that defines and consolidates the kin group, just as, conversely, her improper sacrifice signals the disintegration and destruction of the polity.[46] Her presence in the raḥīl thus functions semiotically to indicate that the poet, though now alone in the liminal desert, is ultimately a societal being with a societal intention: the tribe (or in panegyric, his patron's court) is his ultimate goal.[47] Furthermore, we can perceive in the she-camel's ambiguous nature—an animal domesticated, nature cultivated—the ideal mediator for the nature/culture dialectic, the appropriate vehicle for liminal passage.

In the raḥīl section of Labīd's *Muʿallaqah*, we find no direct description of the journey or the she-camel, but rather a series of three similes, likening the she-camel to a cloud that has shed its rain, a pregnant onager mare, and an oryx cow bereft of her calf. Each of these, I would argue, details a miniature rite of passage, inasmuch as each deals with images of death and rebirth, sacrifice and redemption, or simply the reaffirmation of life and fertility after life-threatening hardship.

The cloud simile (verses 22–24) begins with the depiction of the she-camel's emaciation after the hardships of the desert journey, together with the assertion that this only leaves her all the more nimble and sprightly. I believe the sacrificial aspect of the camel is intended here, that through the sacrifice of her own flesh the salvation of the poet is accomplished. This aspect is affirmed by the simile of the rose-hued cloud, which is lightened after having let down its life-giving rain.

The second simile (verses 25–35), that of the pregnant she-ass conducted by her mate to the highlands in the rainy season and finally down to a water hole in the dry season, is considerably more extended. The she-ass, bearing the promise of new life, her udder in hormonal anticipation swollen with milk, must nevertheless pass, guided by her mate, through hardships seasonal and geographical before arriving at the life-sustaining pool. The journey, as befits liminal passage, is characterized by trials and dangers. The onager stallion has already been bitten and scarred from fighting off rivals and predators. He heads with his mate to the uplands where, during the winter season, they can sustain

46. See the "improper" sacrifice of the poet's mount in *The Muʿallaqah of Imruʾ al-Qays*, which I discuss in Chapter 7.

47. By contrast, the *ṣuʿlūk* (brigand-poet), who roams perpetually in the desert and never reenters society, never has a she-camel.

themselves on herbage. The fear of hunters is omnipresent and the biological cycle of the pregnant she-ass affects her behavior, her recalcitrance and cravings adding to the burdens of her mate. Thus in verses 25–28 we begin to see a progression through a series of synchronized natural cycles: the instinctive/hormonal, the seasonal/vegetative, and the geographical. The cycles progress: the rainy season comes to an end with the onslaught of the scorching summer heat and winds, forcing the onagers to descend from the highlands to seek water (28–30). The herbage that sustained them in the winter now turns against them with the coming of the dry season as the sharp blades of the *buhmā* grass prick their pasterns. The desperation of their thirst and their desiccation is expressed in verses 31 and 32 by likening the cloud of dust they trail behind them as they race toward the pool of water to the smoke of a blazing fire. In verse 33 we return to the instinctive behavior of the male protectively driving his pregnant mate before him. After the breathless race of verses 31–33, the exultant onagers, not stopping to drink at the edge, plunge headlong into the midst of the pool, the sweet fecundity of its water depicted in its profuse growth of reeds. Yet here, too, in the final verse (35), an essential feature of the cycles, both natural and ritual, is alluded to: that in the "test" or "contest" some survive and others fail, that there are victors and victims. Hence the reeds around the pool are described in distinctly martial diction—some are *muṣarraʿ*, fallen, as in battle, whereas others are *qāʾim*, standing firm (cf. *qawm*, the men of the tribe that stand in battle).

We find then that this ekphrastic extended simile is not by any means a digression but a concise reiteration of the deep semantic structure of the poem. The effect is to tell us that the she-camel subsumes, as it were, the natural cycles of reproduction and fertility in their animal, vegetable, and meteorological aspects. Therefore, although the simile occurs in the raḥīl section and the emphasis is on characteristically liminal trials and dangers—the stallion's vying to mate and protect his mate, the migration to the rocky highlands where hunters lurk, the downward migration marked by thirst dust and scorching winds—the total pattern parallels that of the rite of passage/qaṣīdah and concludes with an image of consummate fecundity.[48] Above all we should be able to see in the onager mare's burden of new life the burden that the she-

48. Jaroslav Stetkevych points out that in general the image of the onagers at the water hole includes the threat of lurking hunters. That Labīd omits this feature suggests his intention to emphasize the sense of success and safety.

camel bears, the poet himself. Indeed, the simile as a whole applies to the poet. In this respect verse 29 is of special importance for its personification of the onagers as succeeding by virtue of their firm resolve. It is important to note here that the parts of the qaṣīdah exhibit a semiotic inter-referentiality, the form or structure of the whole being reiterated in its parts. Thus in the raḥīl of a fakhr qaṣīdah such as Labīd's *Muʿallaqah*, the passenger and reader are not confronted with an utterly wayless desert, but rather there are signs and guideposts along the way which indicate where the poem will end and where the poet/passenger will end up.[49]

The metaphorical reiteration of the deep structure, the "message," if you will, of the poem must be understood, too, in light of the exigencies of oral-mnemonic poetry. The rule of "plenitude" or "redundancy" is at work here, serving first of all as a mnemonic device for the reciter, as a reminder of which direction the qaṣīdah is going, and furthermore ensuring that, should part of the poem be lost, distorted, or misunderstood, its "message" would still, in one form or another, be preserved.

The final nāqah simile (verses 36–52) is even longer. This time the poet's mount is compared to an oryx cow that has lost its calf to the predations of a pack of wolves. Here too we can extract a "qaṣīdah within a qaṣīdah," particularly if we look for the characteristics of the passage pattern rather than, in a literal sense, the traditional *topoi* of the qaṣīdah sections. Thus in verses 36–46 the underlying theme is that of separation, loss, death. First, the oryx cow has lagged behind her herd (36), perhaps a suggestion that the individual without society's protection is exposed to mortal danger.[50] The wolves strike, dismembering and devouring her calf, and the bereft oryx cow is left waiting out the starless night through an unremitting downpour. There are nevertheless subtle signs that point in a hopeful direction: first, she seeks protection in a tree (42), which should be read in a broadly Middle

49. This, no doubt, is the principle to be extracted from al-Jāḥiẓ's (d. 255/969) remark that in fakhr the oryx bull in such scenes is triumphant, whereas in elegy it is slain. See Abū ʿUthmān ʿAmr ibn Baḥr al-Jāḥiẓ, *Al-Ḥayawān*, ed. ʿAbd al-Salām Muḥammad Hārūn, 8 vols. (Cairo: Muṣṭafā al-Bābī al-Ḥalabī, 1965–69), 2:20. A clear case in point is the *marthiyah* of Abū Dhuʾayb al-Hudhalī for his children, *Mufaḍḍaliyyah no. 126*. See Charles James Lyall, ed. and trans., *The Mufaḍḍalīyāt: An Anthology of Ancient Arabian Odes Compiled by al-Mufaḍḍal Son of Muḥammad according to the Recension and with the Commentary of Abū Muḥammad al-Qāsim ibn Muḥammad al-Anbārī* (Oxford: Clarendon Press, 1921), 1:849–84, 2:335–62.

50. This may sound like overreading here, but see Chapters 3 and 4, where I return to this theme.

Eastern "tree of life" context; second, her face is described as shining in the dark of night like a pearl, an object that appears elsewhere in Arabic poetry and the Qurʾān among the symbols of purity, fertility, and immortality.[51]

When daybreak comes we find the oryx cow beginning a dogged search of seven days and nights for her lost calf. It is not difficult to draw an analogy between the oryx cow's search for her lost calf (44–46) and the poet's search with his mind's eye for his lost mistress (16–19). The poet's search, his ultimate realization that his beloved is lost to him, and his resolve to cut his ties to the past and set out on a new quest parallel on the human, psychological level what occurs on the instinctual, hormonal level in the oryx cow's search and abandonment of the search for her own self-preservation. The end of her instinctually determined period of search is marked by the drying up of her udder. Verses 47–52 exhibit a completely different tone as the heroic "test" or "contest" replaces the pathetic search. The ever-present danger of hunters alerts us to the liminality of this passage. Fear of the unseen (47–48) gives way to combat when the hunters sic their hounds on the oryx. Her earlier despair is forgotten in the heroic struggle to the death. It is appropriate too, in this liminal section, that the protagonist is "natural"—the wild oryx cow—whereas the antagonists are "cultural"—the human hunters and their trained hunting dogs (*dawājin*, s. *dājinah*, translated here as "hounds," more precisely means tame, domesticated), their rawhide collars contributing to the effect: they are "natural" animals "cultivated," trained to human service. These roles will be inverted in the horse description of the fakhr section. Verse 52 celebrates the oryx cow's triumph by displaying the bloodied corpses of Fetch and Blackie.

Once again we find a natural cycle—that of loss and redemption—wherein the oryx cow first loses her calf and then, after her instinctually determined period of lowing and searching, turns to self-preservation, again portrayed in biological terms, the instinctive awareness of danger and knowledge that the fight would be to the death. Once again, too, we find a sign that points to the cultural analogue when in verse 50 the oryx cow's horn is likened to the well-known Samharī spear of Arabic

51. See my discussion of the pearl as one of the symbols of immortality in Suzanne Pinckney Stetkevych, "Intoxication and Immortality: Wine and Associated Imagery in al-Maʿarrī's Garden," in Fedwa Malti-Douglas, ed., *Critical Pilgrimages: Studies in the Arabic Literary Tradition* (= *Literature East and West* 25 [1989]), 38–39. Later, I discuss it as a symbol of feminine purity and fecundity. Note too that in medieval Christian symbolism the pearl is associated with the Virgin Mary, likewise a mother whose offspring is a victim or sacrifice.

battle poetry. These two major raḥīl protagonists—the asinine and bovine—appear, in domesticated form, as the ox and the ass in the medieval Christian iconography of the Nativity. In light of this reading of Labīd's *Muʿallaqah*, we can go beyond the facile medieval allegorization of the two as, respectively, the New and Old Testaments, and perceive in them more ancient Middle Eastern symbols of fecundity, and hence, immortality.

The raḥīl concludes with two verses (53–54) that take us back to the she-camel and the poet. Here too, just as in the closing of the *ẓaʿn* scene of the nasīb (15), the prism of the mirage effects a fusion or confusion of the natural and cultural which marks a transition point between the two. Thus in verse 53 the shimmering heat is described as "dancing," the hillocks as "cloaked" in the mirage. The final verse (54) is one of self-affirmation, of return to the first person, which is where the fakhr/aggregation section will begin. If we look back at this point to the beginning of the raḥīl, the journey appears to have been above all an inner one. In verses 21 and 22 we find the transition from the poet, apparently apostrophizing himself in the second person, to the she-camel, and from the she-camel to her similization as rain cloud, onager mare, and oryx cow, which can all be read as expressions of the poet's own inner self, gaining in psychological proximity in measure to their rhetorical distancing. With verses 53 and 54 the reentry from the subconscious, instinctual level to the conscious level is effected first from the oryx cow to the she-camel, then from the she-camel to the poet, and finally (55) back to Nawār. Thus the reentry into society constitutes a precise inversion of the exit: verses 16–23: the memory of Nawār (society failed) → the poet cutting his social bonds → the she-camel; verses 52–56: she-camel → poet → Nawār. Through this extended chiasmus the opposition between, on the one hand, society and the social self of the first and third sections of the qaṣīdah and, on the other, the liminal, isolated, antisocial (inner) self is achieved. What we should now, in accordance with our chosen model, anticipate in the aggregation is a "societal" state opposed both to the "immature" state of the nasīb/separation phase and to the antisocietal isolation and self-absorption of the liminal raḥīl.

Let us first note that, although the fakhr section opens, as the nasīb closed, with a recapitulation of the theme of knotting and cutting ropes, whereas the nasīb ultimately affirms the cutting of failed social bonds, the themes of the fakhr section are, to the contrary, concerned with the knotting of social bonds, the shouldering of societal and communal responsibilities. It is not, the poet takes pains to point out (verse 56), abject submission that brings him to participate in matters communal: his raḥīl has already established his independence and his willingness and ability to strike out on his own should he feel slighted or wronged. Rather, it is through his own will and magnanimity that he both submits and contributes to the polity. The fakhr/aggregation section proper, then, comprises a series of scenes, all of which share the underlying theme of participation in society. The concept of the common weal here subsumes the individual. The boast is not of testing oneself against nature, the quest for identity—this was the domain of the raḥīl—but of the willing sacrifice of the self for the common good, that which, above all, defines manhood and maturity in tribal society. This is the reason that fakhr encompasses the boast for both the self and the tribe, for it is essentially a celebration of the self as an aggregate social entity.

The first scene of the fakhr section is that of the poet as convivial in an all-night drinking party. We should not be misled, however, by the tone of delightful revelry, for it does not imply frivolity. Rather it provides, first of all, the anticipated counter to the loss and despair of the nasīb/separation phase. There the abode is desolate, here alive with jovial celebrants. Likewise it counters the lone quest of the inner and outer wilderness of the liminal raḥīl. Consider also that wine drinking constitutes, above all, a commensal meal, the equivalent, metaphorically and ritually, of a sacrificial feast. Thus the mere fact of participating in such a drinking party is an affirmation of membership in the community, that is, of aggregation.

Of further import is that the poet himself has paid dearly to provide the "sacrament" (and here we should emphasize this word in its Latin etymological sense of oath of allegiance, sacred obligation). The mature man thus sacrifices his own wealth for the common weal. The sacramental implications of wine, moreover, go beyond mere communal membership. It is intimately involved in the symbolism of sacrifice and redemption, death and rebirth, and especially immortality. The Christian sacrament (itself of neighboring origin and known among pre-Islamic tribes both Christian and non-Christian) provides a convenient example of wine as a symbol of blood sacrifice. So too, the pre-Islamic poet al-Aʿshā, a monotheist with Christian leanings,[52] draws a precise analogue between the opening of the wineskin and the slitting of the victim's throat in blood sacrifice:

52. Sezgin, *Poesie*, 130–32.

When the jar is empty, we raise our wineskin,
open up its neck vein,
and it bleeds.[53] [3]

This association is further suggested in verse 59 by the description of the wine as *ʿātiq*, aged, but also implying longevity, and by *adkan*, red-black, and *jawnah*, black, both applicable to blood as well as wine. Finally the term *fuḍḍa* is from *faḍḍa*, to break the seal of a wine jar but also to deflower a virgin—yet another ritualized form of sacrifice in which bloodshed is perceived as producing new life. The use of the word *ṣabūḥ*, morning draught (60), further corroborates the commensal aspect of the drinking scene, as established by the dictum recorded by W. Robertson Smith: "He who has drunk thy morning draught is thy undoubted son."[54] The archetypal iconography of the paradisiac drinking scene is completed here by the houri-like musician slave girl (60).[55] The scene concludes with the crowing of the cock, which signals new day and, as in its medieval Christian employ as a symbol of the Resurrection, new life.

What this agglomeration of symbols suggests in the present context is the association of the community with immortality. It would thus seem that in pre-Islamic poetry we are dealing more with the old Semitic concept of perpetuity through the prosperity of the tribe and the proliferation of progeny than with the Christian and Islamic concept of the immortality of the individual soul. It appears, however, that both concepts of immortality share the same symbols and iconography.

The next scene is that of the poet as tribal warrior mounted on his battle steed (faras), here a mare. The equine imagery of the first line is metaphorical. The poet describes himself as wresting the reins of a bitterly cold morning from the hand of the north wind and curbing it. Al-Zawzanī takes this to refer to the poet's slaughtering a camel and providing meat to feed the destitute during the winter season (taking *wazaʿtu*, "I curbed," as suggesting form II *wazzaʿa*, to distribute).[56] It thus serves as a line of transition from the preceding drinking scene to

53. Maymūn ibn Qays al-Aʿshā, *Sharḥ Dīwān al-Aʿshā* (Beirut: Dār al-Kātib al-ʿArabī, 1968), 43; and see my discussion in S. Stetkevych, "Intoxication and Immortality," 36–37 and passim.

54. From an anecdote from al-Maydānī, cited in W. Robertson Smith, *Kinship and Marriage in Early Arabia* (Oosterhout N.B., Netherlands: Anthropological Publications, 1966) [rpr. of 2d ed., 1907], 138–39.

55. See S. Stetkevych, "Intoxication and Immortality," 42–43.

56. Al-Zawzanī, *Sharḥ al-Muʿallaqāt*, 227.

the horse scene that follows. The image expresses the essential principle of aggregation: man curbing nature to the service of society. On one level it refers to the taming of wild nature, animal or meteorological, domesticating the horse to serve man or countering the hardships of winter by slaughtering livestock to succor the needy, but further, inasmuch as the mare, like the she-camel, is an expression of the poet himself, this image refers to the aggregate man who curbs his personal drives and desires to serve the common good. The passions of youth have been tamed and replaced by the self-possession of maturity. Warrior and horse exist in symbiosis, brought out in verse 63: the poet's mare bears his battle gear; her reins he throws over his shoulder as a sword belt or sash. The crucial element in the context of my argument, however, is that the role of the warrior and his horse is communal, to defend the tribe.

We follow the warrior and his mount through the day—departing at dawn (verse 63), mounting the rugged windblown peaks to scout for the enemy (64), descending at nightfall to the plain (65–66). At this point the poet shifts to the description of his mare. Her neck, held erect, he likens to the stripped trunk of a date palm so tall and smooth that the date picker is afraid to climb it. On the one hand, this is a comparison of the domesticated beast to the domesticated plant—both examples of nature tamed to the service of mankind. The description of the palm trunk as *jardāʾ*, stripped, seems related to the conventional description of the steed as *ajrad*, short-haired, signifying well groomed. What is intended here is not the "laying bare" (*ʿurriya*) of the nasīb (2), nature divesting the ruin of its cultural attributes, but just the opposite, culture trimming or pruning off the "wild" attributes of nature in order to domesticate, cultivate (cf. *hadhdhaba*, to crop, trim a tree, rear a child, etc.). In this image, too, there is an expression of male potency, and I suggest that in this context the tamed horse/stripped palm trunk alludes metaphorically to the circumcised phallus. This would amount, in those societies in which adolescent (as opposed to infant) circumcision constitutes the rite of initiation to full manhood, to the consummate expression of the curbing of personal/"animal" passion to serve the tribe, the "cultivating" or civilizing of untrammeled, untamed nature. It is perhaps of note here that the verb *ʿadhara* in forms I and IV is used to mean both to circumcise a boy and to bridle a horse.[57]

Like the she-camel, the mare embraces both the natural and cultural,

57. Lane, *ʿ-dh-r*.

suggested here by her speed like that of the ostrich, her gallop like the flight of the thirsty dove. The difference is that in the nāqah similes of the liminal raḥīl the protagonist is "natural"—the wild onager or oryx—and the antagonist is "cultural"—human hunters (verses 27, 47) and their trained hounds (49–52), whereas in the aggregate fakhr section, as we would expect from our paradigm, the opposite obtains: the warrior/hunter and his trained steed are "cultural" protagonists, the antagonist/victim the ostrich (67) or, in other poems, the oryx.

In verses 70–72 the poet boasts of his prestige and authority in dealings with tribes other than his own. Even at the chieftains' tents of the most powerful and belligerent tribes his voice is heard and respected. The terms employed—denial of false claims, recognition of due rights—are precisely those of the aggregation phase of the rite of passage paradigm. Recall Turner's words: "The ritual subject . . . has rights and obligations vis-à-vis others of a clearly defined and 'structural' type; he is expected to behave in accordance with certain customary norms and ethical standards binding on incumbents of social position in a system of such positions."[58]

The next section (verses 73–77) is a scene of animal sacrifice and commensal feast, and once again the attributes celebrated are those of the polity and the aggregate male who serves it. In terms of our archetypal interest, it is worth noting that the difference between childhood and adulthood (analogous to parts 1 and 3 of the qaṣīdah form) is that children are nonproductive and nonreproductive—they only consume—whereas adults are expected to produce and reproduce.[59] The transition of the archetype of psychosocial development, and hence of the qaṣīdah, can thus be viewed as that from the child's dependence on society, which is ultimately betrayed (nasīb), to the independence and self-sufficiency of the adolescent (raḥīl), to the adult role of protecting, providing for, and sustaining others, that is, being depended upon. Thus far in the fakhr section the poet has depicted himself as provider of wine, as defender of the tribe in war and in council. Now the imagery

58. Turner, *Ritual Process,* 95.

59. The etymological connection in Arabic between *ṭifl*, child, and *ṭufaylī*, parasite, party crasher, "sponge," is illuminating in this regard and should be added to the discussion. Cf. Fedwa Malti-Douglas, "Structure and Organization in a Monographic *Adab* Work: *Al-Taṭfīl* of al-Khaṭīb al-Baghdādī," *Journal of Near Eastern Studies* 40, no. 3 (1981): 229. See also Bruno Bettelheim's analysis of "Hansel and Gretel." The children feel betrayed and abandoned when their parents cease to provide for them, but to grow up they must ultimately make the transition from consumer to producer. Bruno Bettelheim, *The Uses of Enchantment: The Meaning and Importance of Fairy Tales* (New York: Random House, 1977), 159–66.

culminates in the *maysir* and camel slaughter. Let me note first that the *maysir* must be understood in its original sense, not as an idle pastime or squandering of wealth but as a "game" of chance in which the gaming arrows are in fact divining arrows (*qidḥ*, pl. *qidāḥ*) through which some divine or supernatural will is revealed. The most interesting case in point is that of ʿAbd al-Muṭṭalib's sacrifice of his son ʿAbd Allāh (the father of the Prophet Muḥammad) in which divining arrows are used both for selecting the sacrificial victim and for determining the price of his redemption.

ʿAbd al-Muṭṭalib ibn Hishām vowed that if he were given ten sons and saw them grow to manhood before his eyes, he would sacrifice one of them to the Kaʿbah in thanksgiving to his Lord. He made this vow because he knew that Ibrāhīm had ordered the sacrifice of his son, believing it to be the noblest of deeds. So when ʿAbd al-Muṭṭalib had ten grown sons, he called them before him, and had them write their names on arrow shafts (*qidāḥ*). The arrows were shaken and that of ʿAbd al-Muṭṭalib's favorite son, ʿAbd Allāh, was drawn. So ʿAbd al-Muṭṭalib took his broad knife and lay his son down between the pillars of Isāf and Nāʾilah. He was about to slay him when another of his sons, ʿAbd Allāh's full brother Abū Ṭālib, stayed his hand and called his maternal uncles to their nephew's defense. When ʿAbd al-Muṭṭalib explained that he was fulfilling a vow and that since ʿAbd Allāh's arrow was the one that was drawn he could not substitute another son, the uncles offered to redeem the youth with all their wealth. Finally the elders of Quraysh decided that they should consult the sybil (*kāhinah*) of the Banū Saʿd on how the youth might be redeemed. She advised them that ʿAbd al-Muṭṭalib should present the youth and ten camels and cast the divining arrows over them. If the arrows came out in favor of the camels, he should sacrifice them in place of the youth; if they came out in favor of the youth, then he should add ten more camels and repeat the procedure as many times as necessary. This ʿAbd al-Muṭṭalib did, and finally, when the number of camels reached one hundred, the arrows came out for the camels. ʿAbd al-Muṭṭalib repeated the casting of arrows three more times to ascertain that he had indeed propitiated his Lord and then sacrificed the camels as redemption for ʿAbd Allāh. It was thus that the bloodwite was established as one hundred camels and for this that the Prophet Muḥammad said, "I am the son of the two intended sacrificial victims [*anā ibnu al-dhabīḥayni*]," that is, of Ismāʿīl ibn Ibrāhīm and ʿAbd Allāh ibn ʿAbd al-Muṭṭalib.[60]

60. Al-Ālūsī, *Bulūgh al-Arab* 3:46–49.

Labīd's poem is concerned with the division and distribution, not the redemption of the sacrificial victim, which should remind us of Mary Douglas's statement that the sacrificial animal is a symbol of the polity and its division therefore a reflection of the social structure.[61] Thus the she-camel that functioned as a symbol of society in the raḥīl, as the vehicle that ensured the poet's passage from the immature or failed society of the nasīb through the liminal antisociety of the raḥīl to the mature and successful society of the fakhr, serves too as the totemic animal or sacrificial symbol of that society. I would add that the choice of the totemic she-camel as sacrificial victim has a further significance: that it is above all self-sacrifice that creates and defines the polity/ "culture." On the one hand, in sacrificing the she-camel, the symbol of the whole, and dividing and distributing its flesh among the indigent, the message is that society takes care of its members. On the other hand, in the poet's providing the *jazūr* (slaughter camel) or, as we shall see in later chapters, the avenger's willingness to risk his own life for the sake of his kin group, the message is that the individual in society sacrifices for the common weal. We can therefore expect a convergence of aggregate social values around this image.

Let us note first that the poet is not merely a commensal participant; he boasts of initiating the *maysir* and providing the victim.[62] Above all it is the preeminent cultural virtue of hospitality that is emphasized: for it is hospitality, more than any other quality, that separates man from beast, the law of civilization from the law of the jungle (read "desert").[63] Thus the refugees and clients of the clan, not merely blood kin, partake (verse 74).[64] Through this feast the natural cycle of seasonally alternating abundance and starvation is overcome by culture: the prosperous clan or tribe provides for kin, guests, and refugees a perpetual springtime, the bounty of a valley ever verdant (75). This provides an exact counterpart to the forced seasonal migration and privation expressed in the nature-dominated ruined abodes of the nasīb. Indeed, it is precisely when nature is at its harshest, in the bitter winter when the food stores of lesser tribes run short, when the widow and orphan with no protector are cast out, that the powerful and prosperous tribe is able to provide for its own and succor the weak and defenseless as well (76, 77). Once again the images and diction are carefully selected. The impoverished

61. Douglas, *Implicit Meanings*, 68.
62. See al-Ālūsī, *Bulūgh al-Arab* 3:53–55.
63. See Robertson Smith, *Religion of the Semites*, 76, 265, 269, 284.
64. Note that in women's rithā' this virtue is praised in the deceased: "He didn't consider his cooking pot for his kin alone."

widow is likened (76) to the *baliyyah* (the she-camel tethered as a sort of sacrifice and left to die of starvation at her master's grave) because she, too, is left to starve when she has no kinsman to protect her, the first, as it were, to be "sacrificed" by poor or weak tribes when food stores run low, likewise her orphaned offspring. In verse 77 the deadly privation of the natural cycle is conveyed by attributing to the winter winds the verb *tanāwaḥat*, wailing or howling back and forth, but essential to the root meaning of *n-w-ḥ* is the ritual wailing and mourning of women for the dead. Deadly nature in the first hemistich is countered in the second by the "cultural" bounty of the magnanimous tribe depicted in its streams of gravy into which the orphans plunge in an image of plenty and fertility that recalls the onagers' plunging into the pool of water in the raḥīl (34).

The bountiful tribe of the fakhr section thus constitutes the goal of the poet/passenger's quest for immortality or perpetuity. This is depicted as culture vanquishing nature, as society providing perpetual bounty, thereby overcoming at once the seasonal alternation of plenitude and privation and the transhumant alternation that it produces. The ephemeral abode is here replaced by the permanent one (verse 85), the temporary spring encampment whose herbage and waterways wither and desiccate with the coming of summer by the year-round prosperity of the tribe, now likened to the ever-verdant lowlands of a fertile valley (87).

The subject of verses 78–82 is the power of the poet's clan or tribe in tribal politics. The diction is reminiscent of that of the earlier "political" section (70–72), only now the poet speaks not of his personal authority but of that of his clan or its members. The transition from the first person singular, which dominates verses 55–73 of the fakhr section, to the first person plural somewhere (around verse 74) in the *maysir*/feast scene is of special significance since it expresses the poet/passenger's increasing identification with his kin group. From verse 78 through the end of the poem the poet speaks of "us" and "one of us" or otherwise in the objectivizing rhetoric of the third person plural. The poet's sense of tribal solidarity is made emphatic in verse 78 through the reiteration of the first-person-plural pronoun at the beginning of each hemistich: *innā . . . minnā* (indeed we . . . one of us). What follows is a catalog of aggregate societal virtues: in tribal councils it is always one of us who assumes responsibility in grave affairs (78), who divides the spoils and determines rights (79), who is munificent, generous, and so on (80). The institutions of tribal leadership and law are expressed in verse 81 in diction destined to become distinctly Islamic: *sunnah*, path, road, hence tribal traditions, customs, law, and *imām*, leader. The virtues of mature and effective leadership are celebrated in verse 82.

In the closing of his *Muʿallaqah* (verses 83–88), Labīd apostrophizes rival or enemy tribes. He first admonishes them to be content with their lesser status, for the power and dominance of his clan or tribe has been divinely determined (83–84). The reiteration of the root *q-s-m* (divide, apportion, allot) in verse 83 (*qasama . . . qasama*, he allotted . . . he allotted) and in its emphatic verbal (II) and intensive participial (*faʿʿāl*) forms in verse 84 (*qussimat . . . qassāmuhā*, they were apportioned . . . their apportioner) deserves some comment. The concept of division, distribution, and apportionment is an essential element of the concept of ordering and, in particular here, the ordering of society. In these two verses, moreover, allotment is depicted as a divine attribute, which leads us back to the biblical Genesis, where creation itself is viewed above all as a process of dividing, imposing order where previously chaos had reigned. In terms of our nature/culture dialectic too, the imposing of social order is eminently cultural. Within the poem, the division of the *jazūr* (slaughter camel) by the *maysir* arrows is likewise a form of divine apportionment, distribution, and social ordering. There is as well a moral aspect, that of distinguishing between right and wrong, the worthy and the unworthy. This moral distinction is lauded as a human virtue in verse 72, with its antithesis (*ṭibāq*) between the denial of false claims and recognition of due rights, and more explicitly in verse 79, where the term *muqassim*, divider, distributor, is applied to the apportioner of spoils, who alone has the authority to determine upon whom rights will be conferred and from whom withheld.

The apportioner has also built for them a high-roofed edifice (*baytan rafīʿan samkuhu*). It seems that this edifice might better be taken metaphorically than architecturally. The point in the context of my argument, however, is that such an edifice is a permanent structure, a *dār al-qarār*, if you will, that constitutes the exact counterpart of the effaced and ephemeral *diyār* (abodes) of the opening verse of the nasīb. Verse 85 marks a final shift from the first person plural to the third person plural, from the subjective boast to the objective encomium. The closing verses provide a recapitulation of the paramount aggregate virtues, given weight and momentum by the reiteration at the beginning of each verse of "And they are . . ." (*wa humu . . .*). "They are" those that take the initiative in war and in council (86). In verse 87 the vanquishing of the natural cycle by culture is succinctly stated, they are a (perpetual) springtime offering year-round bounty to the indigent, whose stores the vicissitudes of the seasons have depleted. The supreme virtue of culture/society is reserved for the final verse: the solidarity of the clan/polity which guarantees the loyalty of all its members and fears the treachery of none.

From Pre-Islamic to Proto-Islamic

The Arabic tradition considers Labīd's *Muʿallaqah* a composition of the poet's pre-Islamic period. Yet in many ways it serves as a transitional poem, just as Labīd himself served as a transitional figure from the Jāhiliyyah to Islam. Among Muslims Labīd's *Muʿallaqah* has been read as a virtual allegory of this transition, a "rite of passage" from the ruined abode of paganism to the everlasting abode (*dār al-qarār*) of Islam. Both the values of the fakhr section and the diction through which they are expressed are, from our vantage point, distinctly proto-Islamic, for medieval Muslims perhaps simply Islamic. Although in light of the Qurʾānic proscription of wine and *maysir* those two scenes might appear explicitly pagan, they nevertheless have Islamic facets. From the Qurʾānic admonition of Muḥammad, "They will question thee concerning wine, and arrow-shuffling. Say 'In both is heinous sin, and uses for men, but the sin is more heinous than the usefulness' " (Qurʾān 2:216), we can deduce that the nature of the sin is the same as that of other similar proscriptions: "These things only has He forbidden you: carrion, blood, the flesh of swine, *what has been hallowed to other than God*" (Qurʾān 2:168, emphasis mine). That is, these elements were intimately connected with pagan, "non-Ibrāhīmic," religious or cultic practices, which Islam purged in its effort to reestablish "Ibrāhīmic" purity of religion.[65] If, however, earthly wine consumption has been prohibited, the Qurʾān has nevertheless preserved the old Middle Eastern (including Judaic, Christian, and Persian) sacramental significance of wine in the description of the Islamic garden/paradise:

> Surely the pious shall drink of a cup whose mixture is camphor, a fountain whereat drink the servants of God, making it to gush forth plenteously. They fulfill their vows, and fear a day whose evil is on the wing; they

65. This is essentially what Robertson Smith argues in *Religion of the Semites*.

> give food, for love of Him, to the needy, the orphan, the captive. . . . God has procured them radiancy and gladness, and recompensed them for their patience with a garden and silk; therein they shall recline on couches, therein they shall see neither sun nor bitter cold; near them shall be its shades, and its clusters hung meekly down, and there shall be passed around them vessels of silver, and goblets of crystal. . . . And therein they shall be given to drink a cup whose mixture is ginger, therein a fountain whose name is Salsabil. [Qurʾān 76:5–17]

> Surely the pious shall be in bliss, upon couches gazing; thou knowest in their faces the radiancy of bliss as they are given to drink of a wine sealed whose seal is musk—so after that let the strivers strive—and whose mixture is Tasnim, a fountain at which do drink those brought nigh. [Qurʾān 83:21–29]

Wine is thus depicted in the Qurʾān as the reward of the pious and must therefore be understood as a symbol of life everlasting. The heavenly garden is described in terms much like the "perpetual springtime" of Labīd's tribe, as having "neither sun nor bitter cold." It is of note too that the deeds thus rewarded are those celebrated in the fakhr section: fulfilling the vow, succoring the destitute.

As for *maysir*, although a pagan cultic practice in the Jāhiliyyah and hence condemned by the Qurʾān, its communal aspect of distributing meat to the needy in times of dearth, providing for the widow, orphan, guest, and refugee, as described in Labīd's *Muʿallaqah* is strikingly close to Qurʾānic discourse on the subject:

> True piety is this: to believe in God, and the Last Day, the angels, the Book, and the Prophets, to give of one's substance, however cherished, to kinsmen, and orphans, the needy, the traveller, beggars, and to ransom the slave, to perform the prayer, to pay the alms. And they who fulfill their covenant when they have engaged in a covenant, and endure with fortitude misfortune, hardship and peril, these are they who are true in their faith, these are the truly godfearing. [Qurʾān 2:173]

> Be kind to parents, and the near kinsman, and to orphans, and to the needy, and to the neighbor who is of kin, and to the neighbor who is a stranger, and to the companion at your side, and to the traveller, and to what your right hands own. [Qurʾān 4:40]

It is precisely these elements, the keeping of vows, the sustaining of the destitute, that figure in the akhbār concerning Labīd as the constant factor in his conversion from pagan to Muslim.

More suggestive still to the Muslim reader is the diction of verse 81: *sunnah* (law, custom) and *imām* (leader, chief) were both destined to become terms for fundamental Islamic concepts. The first, *sunnah*, meant initially "a way, course, rule, mode, or manner of acting or conduct of life . . . a way . . . that has been instituted, or pursued, by a former people, and has become one pursued by those after them." In Islamic usage it came to mean a practice or saying or the practices and sayings collectively, of Muḥammad or any other person of authority in matters of religion, a prophet or a Companion of Muḥammad, as handed down by tradition.[66] *Al-Sunnah* then came to mean Islamic law and *Ahl al-Sunnah* to refer to Orthodox Muslims.[67] The second, *imām*, derives from a root ʾ-*m-m* that embraces *amma* (to direct one's course, to aim at, to precede, to lead so as to serve as an example) and *ummah* (a way, religion, nation, people). Hence *imām* signifies a person or learned man whose example is followed, such as a head, chief, leader. The Prophet Muḥammad is thus called *imām al-ummah* or *imām ummatih* (the leader, exemplar of the/his nation), and *imām al-Muslimīn* (guide of the Muslims), the latter also an epithet of the Qurʾān. The leaders of the four Orthodox sects were termed *aʾimmah* (imams); the leader in prayer is likewise called *imām*; the caliph is *imām al-raʿiyyah*, the leader of his subjects.[68] The imamate (*imāmah*) came to mean "the supreme leadership" of the Muslim community after Muḥammad's death and assumed far-ranging theological, judicial, and institutional implications. Among the Twelver (Imāmiyyah) Shiʿites, for example, we find the institutionalization of a hereditary imamate to provide mankind with a divinely guided and infallible leader and authoritative teacher in religion.[69]

Verses 83–85 are, or have always been read as, explicitly theistic, with *al-mālik*, owner, possessor, in verse 83, taken to refer to the supreme Sovereign. The concept of the deity as divider and apportioner, as mentioned in the discussion of *maysir*, also in the Qurʾān, where in

66. Lane, *s-n-n*.

67. See A. J. Wensinck, "Sunnah," *The Encyclopaedia of Islam*, 1st ed., ed. M. Th. Houtsma et al. (Leiden: E J. Brill, 1913–36), hereafter EI_1.

68. Lane, ʾ-*m-m*.

69. See W. Madelung, "Imāmah," *The Encyclopaedia of Islam*, 2d ed., ed. H. A.R. Gibb et al. (Leiden: E. J. Brill, 1960–), hereafter EI_2.

Sūrat al-Zukhruf (The Ornaments) those that are not contented with Allāh's choice of Prophet are admonished in much the same way as those who question His/his allotment of power among the clans or tribes in Labīd's poem:

> They say, "Why was this Koran not sent down upon some man of moment in the two cities?" What, is it they who divide the mercy of the Lord? We have divided between them their livelihood in the present life, and raised some of them above others in ranks, that some of them may take others in servitude; and the mercy of thy Lord is better than what they amass. And were it not that mankind would be one nation, we would have appointed for those who disbelieve in the All-merciful roofs of silver to their houses, and stairs whereon to mount, and doors to their houses, and couches whereon to recline, and ornaments; surely all this is but the enjoyment of the present life, and the world to come with thy Lord is for the godfearing. [Qur'ān 43:30–34]

The silver-roofed houses with stairways that Allāh withholds from the disbelievers bear a striking resemblance to the "high-roofed edifice" that the sovereign has built for Labīd's kinsmen to mount. In the context of the Qur'ānic discourse, distinction and allotment are preeminently moral categories: right from wrong, believer from unbeliever, the saved from the damned.

To return to the argument at hand, there is much in the fakhr section of Labīd's *Muʿallaqah* that sounds distinctly Islamic in tone and diction. It could thus be considered "proto-Islamic," or perhaps, more precisely, to express that part of the Jāhiliyyah that, in the Islamic purgation process, was salvageable or "Ibrāhīmic." In an age that takes its epithet from *jahl*, which means not so much ignorance as impetuousness, lack of restraint, Labīd's *Muʿallaqah* is a model, both in form and content, of forbearance, restraint, balance (*ḥilm*). It is this Islamic reading of Labīd's *Muʿallaqah*, I would argue, that is responsible for the shaping in Islamic times of the biographical accounts of his life. For his biography, too, constitutes a paradigm of transition from the Jāhiliyyah to the Islamic age.

If *nomen est omen* then the name Labīd itself has something to tell us. For if the lexica insist that *labīd* means "a sack," the root *l-b-d* gives us as well the verb *labida* (*a*), to stick, cleave, adhere, and *labida* (*a*) or *labada* (*u*) *bi al-makāni*, to remain, stay, continue, abide in a place, to cleave to it; and *labid*/*lubad*, one who does not travel or quit his abode or place or seek sustenance. Hence, Lubad, the last of Luqmān's eagles, with whose death Luqmān's own life was to terminate, was so named because Luqmān thought it would never depart or die.[70] We are then morphologically justified (taking *labīd* to be a *faʿīl bi maʿnā fāʿil* and noting that *faʿil* is equivalent to *fāʿil* in verbs of the form *faʿila/a*) in considering "Labīd" to be synonymous with *labid* (longevous, dwelling permanently in one abode). The concept of *labad* (verbal noun) (to remain continuously in one abode without having to depart to seek sustenance) is then precisely the concept of the permanent abode of the powerful tribe that is able to provide for both kin and non-kin in a "perpetual springtime" and to the Islamic epithet of Paradise as *dār al-qarār*.[71]

It is the concept of longevity/salvation, too, that dominates the akhbār of Labīd in the classical Arab-Islamic sources, in literary-critical works such as Ibn Qutaybah's (d. 276/889) *Al-Shiʿr wa al-Shuʿarāʾ*, and in the compendia of poetry and biographical lore, chief among them Abū al-Faraj al-Iṣbahānī's (d. 356/967) *Kitāb al-Aghānī*.[72] It is curious that although all his major poetry is attributed to the period before his conversion to Islam, this period is given little attention in the akhbār. That is, as an individual it is Labīd the pious Muslim more than the pre-Islamic poet who is celebrated. Nevertheless, his eminently "Islamic" virtues were already apparent in his Jāhilī days.

The poet's father, Rabīʿah, bore the sobriquet Rabīʿ al-Muqtirīn, "Springtime of the Destitute," on account of his generosity toward the poor. As for Labīd himself, al-Iṣbahānī and Ibn Qutaybah summarize his biography, saying that he was one of the poets of the Jāhiliyyah and is also counted among the Mukhaḍramūn, that is, those who survived into the Islamic period. He was one of the most illustrious poets, munificent hosts, and longevous Methuselans, surviving until the age of 145 or 157. He is said to have converted to Islam at the age of ninety and to have settled in the Muslim garrison town of Kufa, where he died late in the reign of Muʿāwiyah.[73]

Of Labīd's pre-Islamic exploits, al-Iṣbahānī treats extensively his first

70. Lane, *l-b-d*. For the story of Luqmān, see al-Nuwayrī, *Nihāyat al-Arab* 13:60–61.

71. One could speculate that the root *l-b-d* is related to *ʾ-b-d* and more clearly still to *r-b-d*.

72. Ibn Qutaybah, *Al-Shiʿr wa al-Shuʿarāʾ*, 148–56, passim; Abū al-Faraj al-Iṣbahānī, *Kitāb al-Aghānī*, ed. Ibrāhīm al-Abyārī, 32 vols. (Cairo: Dār al-Shaʿb, 1970), 16:5718–41, passim.

73. Al-Iṣbahānī, *Kitāb al-Aghānī* 16:5718–21; Ibn Qutaybah, *Al-Shiʿr wa al-Shuʿarāʾ*, 148–49.

poetic conquest, a sort of poetic rite of initiation or passage from boyhood to manhood. As a youth Labīd accompanied a delegation of the Banū Jaʿfar led by his paternal uncle ʿĀmir ibn Mālik, known as Mulāʿib al-Asinnah, "the Player with Spear-heads," to the court of the Lakhmid king al-Nuʿmān at al-Ḥīrah. There they found in the company of the king his drinking companion and confidant, a certain al-Rabīʿ ibn Ziyād al-ʿAbsī, who was an enemy of the Banū Jaʿfar. In the course of their interview, the delegation discovered that this man had defamed them to the king, poisoning his mind against them. Now the young Labīd had not accompanied the delegates to their royal audience but had remained behind guarding their mounts and gear and pasturing their camels. When the delegation returned, Labīd asked why they were angry. They replied that his "maternal uncle" (Labīd's mother was an ʿAbsiyyah) had spoken against them and blocked their way to al-Nuʿmān's favor. Labīd then offered, if they could arrange a confrontation between al-Rabīʿ and himself, to assail him with verses of invective so powerful that al-Nuʿmān would never look at him again. Labīd's clansmen first tested his poetic abilities by having him extemporize some invective against a scrawny tuft of herbage. They told him they would give him their decision in the morning. Meanwhile his uncle instructed his men to watch the youth: if he slept through the night, then he was not a real poet but merely recited the verses of others; but if he remained awake, his verses were of his own composition. They observed him and found him mounting his saddled camel and riding through the night until morning. Then they shaved his head, leaving the forelock intact, dressed him in a *ḥullah*, a set of ceremonial vestments, and took him before al-Nuʿmān. There they found the king taking his breakfast with no companion but al-Rabīʿ, whereupon Labīd recited the following lines of fakhr for his clan combined with scatological hijāʾ (invective) against al-Rabīʿ:

Is my head to be shaved for battle every day?
  Many a battle day is better
    Than a day of ease.
We, the four sons of Umm al-Banīn,
  Are cutting swords
    And dishes deep and full.
We are the best of the ʿĀmir ibn Ṣaʿṣaʿah,
  The strikers of skulls
    Right through their helmets,

The feeders[74] with the brimming bowl.
Go easy!—May you avert all evil!—
Don't eat with him!
His ass is blotched with leprosy,
And he sticks
His finger up it
All the way to the knuckle,
As if he's trying to find
Something he lost.[75] [4]

Upon hearing these lines, "al-Nuʿmān remove[d] his hand from his food," writes al-Iṣbahānī with masterful understatement, and accused Labīd of ruining his breakfast. In fact, the poet had spoiled the king's appetite for al-Rabīʿ as well. The latter tried to counterattack by claiming to have committed unspecified outrages with Labīd's mother. Labīd neatly rebutted these accusations, declaring that his mother was above such things; that it msut have been the women of al-Rabīʿ's own house with whom he committed such acts. Al-Rabīʿ was sent away in disgrace; al-Nuʿmān granted the requests of the Banū Jaʿfar.[76]

This anecdote should not be read merely for its entertainment value and certainly not for its historical value, if indeed it has any. Rather, it serves to mark Labīd's initiation into full manhood and membership in the Banū Jaʿfar and it does so by following in its narrative the established ritual pattern for such passages. At the beginning Labīd is a youth accompanying the tribal delegation but given none of the responsibilities of adulthood. He does not attend the royal audience but remains behind, assigned the traditional, indeed archetypal, boyhood chores of tending the gear, livestock, and mounts. He has already undergone separation in that he has not been left home like a little child, but he is still not one of the men. The liminal phase is expressed here by the youthful Labīd's mounting his she-camel and riding through the night, an image that has the effect of equating the traditional raḥīl section of the qaṣīdah with poetic inspiration, the outer journey with the inner journey. This episode should give us some insight into the significance of the Night Journey (*al-isrāʾ wa al-miʿrāj*) of the Prophet Muḥammad

74. Following the *Dīwān* reading *al-muṭʿimūna*. See Labīd ibn Rabīʿah al-ʿĀmirī, *Dīwān* (Beirut: Dār Ṣādir, n.d.), 93.
75. Al-Iṣbahānī, *Kitāb al-Aghānī* 16:5723–24.
76. Ibid., 16:5721–24.

as well. The poet's aggregation is marked, on the one hand, by his assuming the signs and accouterments of "culture"—the shaving of the head except for the forelock, as if for battle, and donning the sacerdotal *ḥullah*—and, on the other, by his going to face the foe before al-Nuʿmān, to battle not with sword and spear but with his verse, combining fakhr for his kin with hijāʾ for the enemy—the poetic equivalent of defending the tribe and slaying the enemy on the field of battle. Aggregation is further marked by the resolution of the formerly ambiguous status of the young Labīd—boy or man, ʿAbsite (his paternal kin refer to their enemy as "your maternal uncle") or Jaʿfarite—in favor of Jaʿfarite manhood.

Male potency is likewise the dominant theme of aggregation/fakhr, and is evidenced in this anecdote in Labīd's hijāʾ. Its potency is demonstrated first by the ineffectuality of his victim's riposte and, subsequently, of his importuning al-Nuʿmān to reinstate him. It is of note that the reason for al-Nuʿmān's intransigence is not that he believes that Labīd's accusations are true but rather that his verses have impressed themselves so indelibly on his mind and on the tongues of the people that al-Rabīʿ will never be disassociated from them. Al-Iṣbahānī relates further that al-Rabīʿ wrote to al-Nuʿmān from exile saying, "I know that you have taken Labīd's words to heart, but I will not stop beseeching you until you send me someone who will clear my name, so that those who attend your court will know that I am not as Labīd said." To which al-Nuʿmān sent the reply, "You can do nothing to cleanse your name of what Labīd has said, nor can you revoke what has slipped from the tongues of men."[77] In a poetic exchange between the two which al-Iṣbahānī records, al-Nuʿmān replies:

Turn your camel saddle from me
  to any place you want;
 Talk to me no more,
  don't waste your words!
Things were said of you
  I'll never forget
 As long as Egypt borders on
  the Land of Shām and River Nile.
. . . . .

77. Ibid., 16:5724.

This has been said,
  whether true or false,
And no excuse can help you
  once it's been said.[78] [5]

A further anecdote concerning Labīd's coming of age as a poet (which exists with several variations) relates the story of his encounter with the master poet of the earlier generation, al-Nābighah al-Dhubyānī, at the gate of al-Nuʿmān ibn Mundhir's palace. The older poet asks the youth to recite, whereupon Labīd recites the poem that opens "Have you not drawn near the camp traces of Khawlā?" (*A-lam tulmim ʿalā dimani al-Khawlā/*). Al-Nābighah proclaims him the best poet of the Banū ʿĀmir and bids him recite more. Labīd then recites the poem that opens "An ancient ruin at al-Rusays where Khawlah once dwelt" (*Ṭalalun li-Khawlata bi al-Rusaysi qadīmū/*), whereupon al-Nābighah declares him the best poet of all the Banū Hawāzin and again bids him recite. Labīd then recites his *Muʿallaqah*: "Effaced are the abodes" (*ʿAfat al-diyāru*) and al-Nābighah declares, "Go, for you are the best poet of all the Arabs."[79]

As for Labīd's knightly or martial accomplishments, al-Iṣbahānī mentions none of them, and Ibn Qutaybah gives brief notice to only one of Labīd's military exploits when he led an expedition of one hundred horsemen for the Ghassanid king al-Ḥārith ibn Shamir against the Lakhmid al-Mundhir ibn Māʾ al-Samāʾ. Labīd and his men entered al-Mundhir's camp on pretense of obedience and then treacherously slew the king. In the ensuing fray, most of Labīd's men were killed, only he and a handful of others escaping. Al-Ḥārith's reply was his successful and renowned Battle Day of Ḥalīmah.[80]

The bulk of Labīd's akhbār, then, concerns his conversion and subsequent piety, along with the citation of a number of short poetic pieces on his longevity. After living ninety years in the Jāhiliyyah, Labīd is said to have presented himself to the Prophet Muḥammad in a delegation of the Banū Kalb after the death of his brother Arbad ibn Qays and the renowned warrior-poet ʿĀmir ibn al-Ṭufayl, to have converted to Islam, and accompanied the Hijrah to Medina. In the time of the Caliph ʿUmar ibn al-Khaṭṭāb he settled in the Muslim garrison town of Kufa, where he lived a life of exemplary piety until his death in the latter part

78. Ibid., 16:5725.
79. Ibid., 16:5739.
80. Ibn Qutaybah, *Al-Shiʿr wa al-Shuʿarāʾ*, 148.

of the caliphate of Muʿāwiyah at the age of (variously) 145 or 157.[81] It is above all stressed that Labīd ceased composing poetry after his conversion, although the sources cite a number of different lines and brief fragments of verse said to be "the only line" or "the only fakhr" he wrote after he converted.[82] The significance of his silence is obvious from the often-repeated anecdote of the Caliph ʿUmar ibn al-Khaṭṭāb, who asked the governor of Kufa, al-Mughīrah ibn Shuʿbah, to hear some poetry of the Islamic period. When Labīd was asked to recite he inquired, "Of what has been forgiven?"—meaning, from the Jāhiliyyah? "No, of what you have composed since the coming of Islam." Labīd departed, then wrote down Sūrat al-Baqarah (and Sūrat Āl ʿImrān) on a sheet of parchment (*ṣaḥīfah*) and brought it saying, "God has given me this in place of poetry." Upon hearing of this episode from al-Mughīrah, ʿUmar raised Labīd's stipend by five hundred dirhams.[83] What this "substitution" makes clear is that the role of the Qurʾān in Islamic times was perceived as equatable with that of poetry in the Jāhiliyyah, and that the Qurʾān played, as it were, the "New Testament" to the pre-Islamic poetic "Old Testament," at once abrogating and fulfilling it.[84]

Another anecdote reveals that while Islam purged some aspects of the Jāhiliyyah, other elements were retained and Islamicized. Here too Labīd serves as an exemplar. He was one of the munificent Arabs renowned for their generosity. In the Jāhiliyyah he had vowed that whenever the east wind blew he would provide food for the people, and even after his conversion to Islam he held himself to this vow. He had two large bowls that he would take to the mosque of his people to feed them. One day, when al-Walīd ibn ʿUqbah was governor of Kufa, the east wind blew. So al-Walīd mounted the *minbar* of the mosque, delivered his sermon, and then said, "Your kinsman Labīd ibn Rabīʿah swore an oath in the Jāhiliyyah to feed the people whenever the east wind blows, and today is one of those days when the east wind has blown, so help him! I will be the first to do so. Then he descended from the *minbar* and sent Labīd one hundred young camels.[85]

81. Al-Iṣbahānī, *Kitāb al-Aghānī* 16:5719–20; Ibn Qutaybah, *Al-Shiʿr wa al-Shuʿarāʾ*, 148–49.

82. E.g, al-Iṣbahānī, *Kitāb al-Aghānī* 16:5727, 5729; Ibn Qutaybah, *Al-Shiʿr wa al-Shuʿarāʾ*, 149.

83. Al-Iṣbahānī, *Kitāb al-Aghānī* 16:5729; Ibn Qutaybah, *Al-Shiʿr wa al-Shuʿarāʾ*, 149.

84. See S. Stetkevych, "Intoxication and Immortality," 35 and passim.

85. Al-Iṣbahānī, *Kitāb al-Aghānī* 16:5730; Ibn Qutaybah, *Al-Shiʿr wa al-Shuʿarāʾ*, 149.

Labīd's conversion to Islam must, in light of the akhbār, be seen as yet another passage. His abandoning paganism for Islam, poetry for the Qur'ān, the bedouin desert for the garrison settlement of Kufa are all metaphorical expressions of his having taken up habitation in a *dār al-qarār*. So too must his longevity be understood. It is unlikely here that we are dealing with a historical fact; it is, moreover, irrelevant. For the meaning of the Arabic term *muʿammar* is not merely "longevous" but, as a passive participle, "having been granted long life." Moreover, if we examine the root meanings of *ʿ-m-r*,[86] we find that it embraces precisely those concepts that we have associated with aggregation in the ritual sphere, fakhr in the poetic: prosperity, cultivation, habitation, longevity. *Muʿammar* is thus, in one respect, virtually synonymous with the name Labīd. But what is essential here is that we understand that the granting of long life is intended not merely in the historical or biographical sense but in the moral and spiritual sense, as a synecdochic expression of the granting of life everlasting, of salvation. Ultimately the akhbār of Labīd convey the message that longevity is salvation, and this in two ways. First, it was granted to him to live until the coming of the Prophet Muḥammad and Islam. Indeed, one of the lines said to be the only line of poetry he composed after his conversion to Islam is:

> Praise be to God that my doom did not overtake me
> before He had clothed me in the shirt of Islam.[87] [6]

Second, Islam confers longevity, that is, immortality. Labīd's munificence in the Jāhiliyyah must be understood as the reason for Allāh's blessing, for his extension of Labīd's life beyond the usual mortal span until the appearance of Islam, for his continued prosperity thereafter, and finally, in the Islamic salvific sense, for his immortality. The message is thus ultimately one of sacrifice and redemption—that Labīd's sacrifice of his possessions or livestock to feed the needy was the reason for his longevity, his Islam, his salvation.

If we still entertain any doubts as to the metaphorical expression of salvation in Labīd's longevity, we can find confirmation in the negative example of Labīd's half brother, Arbad ibn Qays. Here too the vagaries of etymology have something to tell us, for Arbad is suspiciously close to Labīd. The l → r shift is common enough in Arabic, and indeed the

86. Lane, *ʿ-m-r*.
87. Ibn Qutaybah, *Al-Shiʿr wa al-Shuʿarāʾ*, 149.

first meaning of *rabada (u) rubūdan (bi makānin)* is synonymous with *labada*—to remain, dwell, abide, in a place.[88] Thus, in one sense, Arbad is the elative of Labīd, "more abiding" and we thus have another case of the familiar phenomenon of brothers having similar or related names: Ḥasan and Ḥusayn, Shadīd and Shaddād. We should keep in mind too that fraternity and near synonymity in myth and fairy tale often express conflicting sides or stages of the same personality—ego and alter ego.[89] This too the Arabic etymology provides, for *arbad*, f. *rabdā*ʾ, means dark or dust-colored, speckled with black, having a dusty hue of lips, but also a species of poisonous serpent; *dāhiyah rabdā*ʾ means a terrible calamity; *ʿām arbad*, a year of drought. In this last meaning the exact opposite of Labīd as permanent settlement and perpetual spring is achieved and Arbad becomes *min al-aḍdād* (a word having two opposite meanings).[90]

As al-Iṣbahānī tells the story, Arbad it was who, along with the formidable poet-warrior of the Jāhiliyyah, ʿĀmir ibn al-Ṭufayl, and Jabbār ibn Salmā—all three chieftains of their clans—went with a delegation of the Banū ʿĀmir ibn Ṣaʿṣaʿah before the Prophet Muḥammad. ʿĀmir ibn al-Ṭufayl intended an act of treachery against the Prophet. His kinsmen had said to him: "O ʿĀmir, the people have submitted to Islam, so you submit too." To which he replied, "By God, I swore that I would not quit fighting until all the Arabs followed at my heels. Should I now follow at the heels of this young upstart from the Quraysh?" So he said to Arbad, "When we approach Muḥammad, I will distract him. When I've done so, you strike him with your sword." When they approached the Prophet, ʿĀmir said to him, "O Muḥammad, befriend me!" "No, by God," he replied, "Not until you believe in God alone." "O Muḥammad, befriend me!" ʿĀmir repeated, and began talking with him and waiting for Arbad to do as he had ordered him. Meanwhile Arbad was doing nothing, and when ʿĀmir saw this he repeated his request to Muḥammad once more, and once again received the same reply. After Muḥammad's refusal, ʿĀmir said, "By God I will help them [the Arabs] against you with red horses and brown men!" The Prophet said as he turned away, "O God, protect me from ʿĀmir ibn al-Ṭufayl!" When the delegation had departed, ʿĀmir upbraided Arbad, "Woe to you, Arbad! Why didn't you do what I ordered you? By God,

88. Lane, *r-b-d*.
89. See Bettelheim, *Uses of Enchantment*, 95–96.
90. On the Arabic etymological generation of paradox, see J. Stetkevych, "Arabic Hermeneutical Terminology," 81–96 and passim.

there was no man on the face of the earth I feared more than you, but, God's oath, I will never fear you again after today!" "Don't be so hasty, you bastard!" replied Arbad, "By God, every time I was about to carry out your order you came between the man and me. Should I have struck you with my sword?" When the delegates were on their way back to their country, God struck ʿĀmir with the plague and he died and was buried along the way. When the rest arrived home, their kinsmen asked Arbad what had happened. He replied, "Muḥammad called us to the worship of such a thing that I wish he were here so that I could shoot him with my arrow and kill him on the spot." A day or two after this, when Arbad went out with a camel that he was going to sell, God struck him and his camel with a lightning bolt that consumed them both in flame.[91]

A neat series of diametrical oppositions is easily extracted: Labīd/Arbad → Islam/Shirk (polytheism) → longevity/calamity → salvation/damnation. My point here, however, is not to impose a structuralist argument but rather to demonstrate that the value and the intention of the Labīd and Arbad stories is not historical and biographical but essentially literary and moral. Furthermore, the univocity of the message conveyed by both his *Muʿallaqah* and the notices concerning Labīd suggests that the primary function of akhbār is to serve as a *sharḥ*, commentary or explication, of the poetic text. The need in the period of primary orality for such a commentary to be in memorable narrative form is obvious, although, as I shall argue further on, it is above all the intertextuality or interreferentiality among qaṣīdahs that performs the exegetical function. In literary times, moreover, I suggest that it was the existence of this extensive body of essentially explanatory or exegetical anecdotes, whether or not they were expressly designated as such, that led the classical commentarists to limit their work almost exclusively to matters philological and grammatical, and classical critics largely to matters rhetorical. Perhaps, after all, the frustration of modern critics at the apparent lack of discussion of the "meaning" of the qaṣīdah results largely from "barking up the wrong tree."

91. Al-Iṣbahānī, *Kitāb al-Aghānī* 18:6328–31, and see 18:6333–35 for a fascinating variant of this story, in which, however, Arbad does not appear.

CHAPTER 2

Eating the Dead / The Dead Eating: Blood Vengeance as Sacrifice

It is my intention in this chapter to expand upon the findings of Chapter 1 through the examination of a particular poetic genre, as I think it may be called, that is, the poetry that takes as its major theme blood vengeance (*tha'r*). Two parallel, if not indeed identical, ritual patterns shed light on its structure and its distinctive imagery: first, as with *The Muʿallaqah of Labīd*, the rite of passage as formulated by Arnold van Gennep and elucidated by, among others, Mary Douglas, Victor Turner, and (adding here) Edmund Leach;[1] and second, the rite of sacrifice according to the schema described by Henri Hubert and Marcel Mauss in their classic work *Sacrifice*, keeping in mind Mauss's later findings on the forms and functions of exchange in archaic societies as propounded in *The Gift*.[2] I also take into account a number of major works, both Orientalist and anthropological, that treat the subjects of blood vengeance and sacrifice, including those of Otto Procksch, Henri Lammens, W. Robertson Smith, Joseph Chelhod, René Girard, and Walter Burkert.[3]

1. Edmund Leach, "Against Genres: Are Parables Lights Set in Candlesticks or Put under a Bushel?" in Leach and D. Alan Aycock, *Structuralist Interpretations of Biblical Myth* (Cambridge: Cambridge University Press, 1983), 89–112.

2. Henri Hubert and Marcel Mauss, *Sacrifice: Its Nature and Function*, trans. W. D. Halls (Chicago: University of Chicago Press, 1981) [*Essai sur la nature et la fonction du sacrifice*, 1898]; Marcel Mauss, *The Gift: The Forms and Functions of Exchange in Archaic Societies*, trans. Ian Cunnison (New York: Norton, 1967) [*Essai sur le don, forme archaïque de l'échange*, 1925].

3. Otto Procksch, *Über die Blutrache bei den vorislamischen Arabern und Mohammeds Stellung zu ihr* (Leipzig: B. G. Teubner, 1899); Henri Lammens, "Le caractère religieux du ṯār; ou, Vendetta chez les Arabes préislamistes," *Bulletin de l'Institut Français d'Archéologie Orientale* 26

Let us begin with a brief presentation of these ritual formulas. Leach's summary, which pinpoints the aspects of the rite of passage pattern most appropriate to the discussion at hand, provides a useful review:

> According to Van Gennep . . . rituals which result in a change of ritual status of an initiate (and these of course include "sacrifices" in the sense I have specified above) always have a tripartite structure: (i) "a rite of separation," in which the initiate is separated from his/her original social role (ritual condition), is followed by (ii) a marginal state in which, temporarily, the initiate is outside society in a "tabooed" condition which is ambivalently treated as dangerous-polluting or dangerous-holy. This is followed by (iii) "a rite of aggregation" in which the initiate is brought back into society in his/her new social role (ritual condition). The logic of the exercise plainly implies that the symbolism involved in (i) should be more or less identical to that of (iii) but presented in reverse. For example if, as frequently happens, (i) the rite of separation includes a symbolic death and burial it is likely that (iii) the rite of aggregation will include a symbolic rebirth from the tomb (which has now become a womb symbol).[4]

Turning to the specific case of sacrifice, we find that in both formulation and definition, it constitutes a category of the rite of passage. Hubert and Mauss define sacrifice as "a religious act which, through the consecration of a victim, modifies the condition of the moral person who accomplishes it or that of certain objects with which he is concerned." That is, it is a ritual that results in a change of ritual status. Their scheme of sacrifice is tripartite, consisting of the rites of entry into the sacrifice; the sacrifice itself; and the rites of exit. Of particular note here is their remark, "The rites by which this exit from the sacrifices is effected are the exact counterparts of those we observed at the entry."[5] That is, the chiastic (abba) pattern that Leach noted in the rite of passage in general is likewise discernible in the rites of sacrifice: the transition from the profane to the sacred and from the sacred back to the profane.

Robertson Smith suspected the ritual and sacrificial aspects of blood

---

(1926): 83–127; Robertson Smith, *Kinship and Marriage* and *Religion of the Semites*; Chelhod, *Le sacrifice chez les Arabes*; René Girard, *Violence and the Sacred*, trans. Patrick Gregory (Baltimore: Johns Hopkins University Press, 1979) [*La violence et le sacré*, 1972]; Walter Burkert, *Homo Necans: The Anthropology of Ancient Greek Ritual and Myth*, trans. Peter Bing (Berkeley: University of California Press, 1983) [*Homo Necans*, 1972].

4. Leach, "Against Genres," 99.

5. Hubert and Mauss, *Sacrifice*, 13, 20–49, 46.

vengeance, and Lammens took up the fuller study and specific discussion of these aspects.[6] He states explicitly that blood vengeance was like a type of sacrifice or ritual act ("comme une façon de sacrifice, d'acte rituel").[7] Chelhod confirms Lammens's conclusions, remarking that blood vengeance seems to be a veiled form of human sacrifice ("une forme voilée du sacrifice humain").[8] Moreover, on a further point that warrants emphasis here Lammens and Chelhod concur, that is, that the taking of blood vengeance was "one of the duties of filial piety, a manifestation of the funerary cult. . . . This obligation impelled the Arab to procure for the manes of the dead this last satisfaction, to give him to drink the blood of his enemy. . . . One cannot help but see in the victim put to death to satisfy the dictates of blood vengeance a true human sacrifice due the manes of the deceased."[9]

In turning to the early Arabic materials concerned with blood vengeance, both in poetry (*ashʿār*) and prose (akhbār), I propose to demonstrate, first, that the taking of blood vengeance as presented in these materials performs the function of a rite of passage or of sacrifice, that is, the transition of the avenger from one ritual state to another, and, second, that the taking of blood vengeance as portrayed in these materials exhibits the same tripartite form and chiastic progression that characterize or inform the rites of passage and sacrifice. Further, it will become apparent that the taking of blood vengeance often constitutes a rite of initiation, that is, the rite of passage that marks the transition from boyhood to manhood. Finally, inasmuch as my primary concern in this book is poetry, not cultural anthropology, I demonstrate that the structure and imagery of the poem of blood vengeance is ritually determined.

The most famous Arabic poem of blood vengeance and, in terms of provenance, the most problematic is the so-called *Rithāʾ of Taʾabbaṭa Sharran*, the premier poem in the premier anthology of Arabic poetry, Abū Tammām's (d. 231/845) *Ḥamāsah*. Abū Tammām attributes it to the pre-Islamic *ṣuʿlūk* (brigand) poet Taʾabbaṭa Sharran, but his is not the final word. Among the diverse opinions on the subject are that Taʾabbaṭa Sharran wrote it as an elegy for himself when he knew he was about to die; that it was composed as an elegy for him by his ṣuʿlūk companion al-Shanfarā (the claim sometimes made that Taʾabbaṭa Sharran was al-Shanfarā's maternal uncle would appear to spring from a conflation of

6. Robertson Smith, *Religion of the Semites*, 462.
7. Lammens, "Le caractère religieux du *ṯār*," 115.
8. Chelhod, *Le sacrifice chez les Arabes*, 100–104, 116–20.
9. Ibid., 101, 102, 104.

these two attributions); and finally, the opinion to which the two major commentators on the *Ḥamāsah*, al-Marzūqī (d. 421/1030) and al-Tibrīzī (d. 502/1109), both give credence, that it is the work of the notorious second-century Basran transmitter and forger, Khalaf al-Aḥmar.[10] Given, however, the striking stylistic similarities between *The Rithāʾ of Taʾabbataa Sharran* and *Mufaḍḍaliyyah no. 1* (the opening poem of the Mufaḍḍaliyyāt, the anthology compiled by the renowned philologist al-Mufaḍḍal al-Ḍabbī [d. ca. 170/786]), also attributed to Taʾabbata Sharran, and *Mufaḍḍaliyyah no. 20*, attributed to al-Shanfarā, I think it is fair to assume that all three are products of the same literary milieu.

The Rithāʾ of Taʾabbaṭa Sharran [7]

1. On the mountain path that lies below Salʿ
   lies a slain man whose blood
   will not go unavenged.
2. He left the burden to me and departed;
   I have assumed that burden
   for him.
3. Bent on vengeance am I, his sister's son,
   a steadfast warrior,
   his knot not to be loosed.
4. Eyes downcast, he oozes poison death,
   like a glowering adder,
   ejecting venom, deadly.
5. Harsh was the news that reached us,
   so grave it made the weightiest affair
   seem mean.
6. Fate, tyrannical, plundered me
   of a disdainful man whose client
   none dared disdain.
7. He was sunshine on a cold day,
   but when the Dog Star blazed,
   cool and shade.

10. Abū ʿAlī Aḥmad ibn Muḥammad b. al-Ḥasan al-Marzūqī, *Sharḥ Dīwān al-Ḥamāsah*, ed. Aḥmad Amīn and ʿAbd al-Salām Hārūn, 4 vols., 2d ed. (Cairo: Maṭbaʿat Lajnat al-Taʾlīf wa al-Tarjamah wa al-Nashr, 1967), 2:827; Abū Zakariyyā Yaḥyā ibn ʿAlī al-Shaybānī al-Tibrīzī, *Sharḥ al-Tibrīzī ʿalā Dīwān Ashʿār al-Ḥamāsah*, 2 vols. (Cairo: Būlāq, 1879), 2:160–61. The authenticity and attribution of this poem are discussed at length by Yūsuf Khulayyif, in *Al-Shuʿarāʾ al-Ṣaʿālīk fī al-ʿAṣr al-Jāhilī* (Cairo: Dār al-Maʿārif, 1966), 169–81.

8. Lean-flanked, but not from hardship,
open-handed he was,
sharp-witted, self-reliant,
9. Departing with such resolve
that wherever he alighted
his resolve alighted too,
10. O'erspreading rain of white clouds giving gifts;
when he assaulted,
a lawless lion,
11. Ungirded among his clan, trailing his robe,
dark-lipped; in battle, a wolf-hyena whelp,
thin-hipped.
12. He has two tastes: colocynth and honey,
and each of these tastes
every man has tried.
13. He rode forth alone against dread,
the notched Yemeni
his sole comrade.
14. Many a band of youths set out in the midday heat,
then journeyed through the night, till at daybreak,
they alighted.
15. Each keen youth was girded with a keen blade
like a flash of lightning
when it was drawn.
16. Then we wreaked vengeance upon them,
and of the two clans
but few escaped.
17. They drank sleep sip by sip
till drowsy-drunk; then you startled them
and they scattered.
18. Then, if Hudhayl have notched his blade,
it was because he had notched
the blades of Hudhayl,
19. And brought them to kneel upon
rough ground that bruised
their camels' feet,
20. And gave them in their shelters, after killing,
a morning draught of plundering
and driving off their herds.
21. In me Hudhayl have been burned by a bountiful man
who does not weary of evil
till they weary,

22. Who gives his lance a first draught,
then, when it has drunk,
a second.
23. Lawful is wine now that once was forbidden;
by great effort it came
to be lawful.
24. So give me a drink, O Sawād ibn ʿAmr,
for my body, after my uncle's death,
has wasted away.
25. The hyena laughs over the slain of Hudhayl;
you see the wolf grinning
above them.
26. At morn the ancient vultures flap about, bloat-bellied,
unable to take flight, they tread
upon the dead.[11]

Before proceeding to the discussion and analysis of this poem, the outline of action—a source of confusion to Arab and Orientalist commentators alike until finally put straight by Charles James Lyall—should be related. The poem opens with the poet's slain uncle lying dead on a mountain trail and the poet's acceptance of the obligation of vengeance (verses 1–2); verses 3 and 4 describe the avenger-poet; verse 5, the news or announcement of the uncle's death; verses 6–13 comprise an elegy to the deceased. Both al-Marzūqī and al-Tibrīzī took verses 14–17 as a description of the band of warriors the uncle had led (taking *ishmaʿallū* to mean "hasten" rather than "scatter"), but they should instead be understood, as Lyall suggests, as the (many) bands of Hudhalī warriors that the deceased uncle had attacked and devastated in his day (this in keeping with verses 13 and 18).[12] In verses 18–20 the poet describes the death of his uncle at the hands of the Banū Hudhayl as vengeance for his previous attacks on them (14–17). Next, the poet calls for a drink, thereby affirming that he has avenged his uncle and, having thus fulfilled

11. I have given the poem as it appears in al-Tibrīzī, *Ḥamāsah* 2:160–64. Al-Marzūqī's recension (*Ḥamāsah* 2:827–39) lacks verses 16 and 20; verses 23 and 24 follow al-Tibrīzī's verse 26; the following variants are to be noted: verse 4, *mawtan* (death) for *sammam* (poison); verse 10, *ḥīna* for *ḥaythu*; verse 17, *thamilū* (they got drunk, intoxicated) for *hawwamū* (they became drowsy, dozed off); verse 26, *tahfū* (flutter, stumble) for *taghdū* (go, come early in the morning). The reader may want to consult Lyall's translation and notes in Charles James Lyall, *Translations of Ancient Arabian Poetry, Chiefly Prae-Islamic, with Introduction and Notes* (New York: Columbia University Press, 1930), 48–51.

12. Lyall, *Ancient Arabian Poetry*, 50–51; al-Tibrīzī, *Ḥamāsah* 2:62; al-Marzūqī, *Ḥamāsah* 2:833–35.

his vow to forgo wine until vengeance was taken, is now free to drink once more (23–24). The poem closes with the description of the vultures, hyenas, and wolves feasting on the corpses of the Hudhalī slain.

The basic action of the poem having been established, we can proceed to a more analytic and interpretative reading. The poem opens with the announcement of the death and the declaration that a man lies slain and that his blood will not go unavenged; the cause, purpose, and conclusion of the poem are thus succinctly stated as being bloodshed and blood vengeance. Furthermore, as is apparent from the comparison of this poem with other poems of blood vengeance, the opening verse constitutes, in effect, the poet's vow to avenge his uncle. Verses 2 and 3 carry the weight of a legal or ritual transfer not of goods but of obligation. The blood tie that forms the basis of the poem inheres in the metaphor of inheritance in the terms *khallafa* (to appoint as a successor, leave behind) and *wallā* (to entrust, assign). It should be noted here that accepting the obligation of vengeance and carrying it out are the equivalent of being the heir. Indeed, the avenger often inherits the weapons and position of the relative (most often the father or elder brother) whom he avenges.[13] The taking of vengeance thus reaffirms the blood tie and determines inheritance; in other words, it marks the accession of the avenger to the possessions and position of the man he has avenged.

The transactional nature of this ritual pact is given rhetorical emphasis in the balancing of the uncle's appointment of his heir and avenger in the first hemistich with the poet's avowed assumption of that burden in the second (verse 2). The equation of vengeance and the blood tie is stated explicitly in verse 3 with the juxtaposition of *thaʾr* to *ibn ukht* (sister's son). Further, it should be noted that the nephew's avenging and taking the place of his maternal uncle marks the passing of the older generation and the accession to power of the younger. In verse 4 the avenging nephew describes himself as a deadly adder by means of a powerful simile in which the subject and object appear in the end to merge. This the poet does by the *tajnīs* (paronomasia) of *muṭriq* (eyes downcast) and *aṭraqa* (to glower), one for the poet and one for the snake, and then concluding the line with *ṣillū* (deadly), ambiguously applying to both. The effect of this line is to contrast the life-giving liquids, blood and semen, which form a bond within the kin group, to

13. Procksch, *Über die Blutrache*, 25–26. See also Lammens's remarks on *waṣiyyah* (testament) and *walī* (heir, avenger) in "Le caractère religieux du *ṯār*," 83 n. 2, 98–100, 105, 110.

the blood and venom that represent the poet's relationship to the non-kin, his uncle's slayers.

Thus the opening section of the poem with its declaration of defilement—that is, the slaying of a kinsman, the vow to vengeance, and claim to inheritance—performs a function similar to that of separation in the rite of passage or entry in the rite of sacrifice. The poet leaves the profane state and enters a sacred one with his vow to avenge/sacrifice.

The more routine subjects of *rithā*ʾ (elegy) follow: the *na*ʿ*y* (the announcement of the death) that traditionally opens a rithāʾ comes in verse 5. As Lyall has noted, this verse, with its rhymed hemistichs, may have originally been an opening verse.[14] It is followed by the eulogy of the deceased (6–13). Note that the descriptions employed here are largely expressed in terms of *ṭibāq* (antithesis); it is my contention that this rhetorical device has a semantic foundation, that is, that the two sides of the antithesis represent the two opposing ritual states of tribal society: *ḥalāl* and *ḥarām*, that is, purity (having no unavenged blood) and pollution (having blood awaiting vengeance), the profane and the sacred (or consecrated), or otherwise put, at peace and at war. Thus, in verse 10, the uncle's bounty within the kin is likened to a rain cloud, a symbol of fertility and abundance (social), whereas to the enemy he is a lawless lion, a dangerous, antisocial, liminal entity. In verse 11, too, the *marthī* (subject of the elegy) is first described among his kin as loosening his *izār* (loincloth), the garment in which one girds oneself as part of the *iḥrām* for the taking of blood vengeance and for sacrifice.[15] His robe is trailing as opposed to the common image of tucking up one's tunic for battle. Then, as if custom-made to fit Turner's description of the liminal entity as "betwixt and between,"[16] comes the comparison of the uncle in battle to the *sim*ʿ, a cross between wolf and hyena—precisely those animals associated with antihuman and liminal behavior (11). It can be argued too that the familiar *ṭibāq* between honey and colocynth (12) likewise ultimately refers to these two antithetical ritual states: honey with its connotations of sweetness and fertility/immortality refers to the profane social *ḥalāl* state (the relation of man to kin), whereas colocynth in its associations with bitterness, departure, and abortion represents the sacred/anathema *ḥarām* state (the relation

14. Lyall, *Ancient Arabian Poetry*, 48–51.

15. Lammens, "Le caractère religieux du *ṯār*," 85–86; Chelhod, *Le sacrifice chez les Arabes*, 101.

16. Turner, *Ritual Process*, 95.

of man to non-kin).[17] That is, it is the equivalent of the semen/venom antithesis already discussed.

That the pre-Islamic Arab perceived his life as alternating between two antithetical states is perhaps best expressed in *Ḥamāsiyyah no. 272* by Durayd ibn al-Ṣimmah which concludes:

Then we, no doubt, are meat for the sword
  and, doubtless, sometimes
    we feed it meat.
By a foe bent on vengeance, we are attacked,
  our fall his cure; or we, vengeance-bent,
    attack the foe.
Thus have we divided time in two,
  between us and our foe,
    till not a day goes by but we're
      in one half or the other.[18] [8]

The next section of the poem (verses 14–17) is the description of the enemy warriors. In literary terms, this should fall under the heading of *inṣāf* (the verbal noun of *anṣafa*, to treat equitably, with justice), that is, the praise of the enemy in order to magnify, by indirection, oneself. This rhetorical device has a particular function in the poetry of blood vengeance, with which it is often associated.[19] For the basis of blood vengeance among the Arabs of the Jāhiliyyah is not necessarily the slaying of the slayer of one's kinsman but rather the slaying of that kinsman's equal or counterpart (*naẓīr, qirn*).[20] By establishing this necessary precondition of equality, *inṣāf* thus performs a crucial ritual function, that of guaranteeing the suitability of the "sacrificial victim." The heavy losses on both sides (16) thus testify to the equal status of the

17. See Haydar, "*The Muʿallaqa of Imruʾ al-Qays*, I," 239; S. Stetkevych, "Structuralist Analyses," 96.

18. Al-Marzūqī, *Ḥamāsah* 2:825–27. A full translation and discussion of this poem appears in Suzanne Pinckney Stetkevych, *Abū Tammām and the Poetics of the ʿAbbāssid Age* (Leiden: E. J. Brill, 1991), 317–18.

19. It is significant that the first use of *inṣāf* is said to be that of Muhalhil ibn Rabīʿah in a poem of blood vengeance which I discuss later; see *Aṣmaʿiyyah no. 53* in Abū Saʿīd ʿAbd al-Malik ibn Qurayb al-Aṣmaʿī, *Al-Aṣmaʿiyyāt*, ed. Aḥmad Muḥammad Shākir and ʿAbd al-Salām Hārūn, 3d ed. (Cairo: Dār al-Maʿārif, 1967), 155 n. 8. For further examples, see nos. 151 and 152, in al-Marzūqī, *Ḥamāsah* 1:440–50; Luwīs Shaykhū, *Riyāḍ al-Adab fī Marāthī Shawāʿir al-ʿArab: al-juzʾ al-awwal fī Shawāʿir al-Jāhiliyyah* (Beirut: al-Maṭbaʿah al-Kāthūlīkiyyah lil-Ābāʾ al-Yasūʿiyyah, 1897), 56ff.

20. Lammens, "Le caractère religieux du *ṯār*," 115–18.

warring parties (taking "the two clans" to refer to the clan of the poet and that of the enemy, the Banū Hudhayl, not, as Lyall suggests, two clans of the Banū Hudhayl).[21]

The chiastic structure that characterizes rites of passage and sacrifice in general and the institution of blood vengeance in particular receives succinct rhetorical expression in verse 18 through a richly alliterative chiasmus: *fallat Hudhaylun . . . Hudhaylan yafullū* (Hudhayl have notched his blade . . . he had notched the blades of Hudhayl). As the *wāw rubba* ("and many a") of line 14 and the progression of the poem itself suggest, we are not dealing here with an isolated incident of violence; rather, as in Durayd ibn al-Ṣimmah's poem, the two tribes, that of the poet and the Banū Hudhayl, are engaged in an inexorable sequence of vengeance and countervengeance, a self-perpetuating state of tension in which no equilibrium is ever possible and any victory by either side is inevitably short-lived. The death of the poet's uncle is merely another step in the contrapuntal progression of vengeance.

In this light, it is possible to consider the institution of blood vengeance as a form of ritual exchange. Like the institutionalized exchange of gifts, as analyzed by Mauss, this mutual exchange of violence involves the obligation both to give and to receive, what amounts to a sort of "contractual sacrifice." Likewise, it establishes a perpetual give and take that both binds tribes or clans together and keeps them separate.[22] Further, we can suggest that what is exchanged through blood vengeance is oedipal violence. The succession of son to father (or, analogously, nephew to uncle, younger brother to older brother) is not achieved in direct oedipal terms by killing the father; it is achieved by avenging him, that is, by killing his counterpart in a non-kin clan. This amounts to a ritual exchange through which the threat of oedipal violence is defused by displacing it from kin to non-kin. Such an interpretation of the function of blood vengeance appears to bear some relation to Girard's speculations concerning the nature of sacrifice.[23]

Not to be overlooked is the use of the verb *ṣabbaḥa* (verse 20). This verb originally refers to giving a morning draught of wine—a sort of commensal meal (recall *The Muʿallaqah of Labīd*, line 60). But it is just as often used tropically for a morning attack upon the enemy from whom vengeance is sought. This conflation should already begin to

21. Lyall, *Ancient Arabian Poetry*, 51.

22. Mauss, *The Gift*, passim. Of particular note is the German use of *revanchieren*, to repay a gift, p. 5.

23. Girard, *Violence and the Sacred*, 68–88.

hint at what will be one of the primary conclusions of this book—that the taking of blood vengeance is a sort of inverted commensal meal, serving as a definition of kinship by negation. Kin are those whom one is obligated to avenge; non-kin are those upon whom vengeance is wreaked.[24] Kin participate in the commensal meal of renewed life; non-kin in the commensal meal of death.[25] This image, too, would appear to be related to the semen/venom dialectic of verse 4.

When the poet then turns to the next step in the progression of vengeance, that is, his slaying of the Banū Hudhayl to avenge his uncle (verses 21–22), it is precisely in terms of sacrifice and the commensal meal or drink. The verb *ṣaliya* (verse 21) means to warm oneself at a fire or endure the heat of a fire, but in this context it seems to take on the meaning of *ṣalā* (to roast). That is, the poet has roasted them in the (metaphorical) fire of blood vengeance, just as a generous man slaughters and roasts a camel for his kin and clients during times of hardship (keeping in mind Robertson Smith's contention that in the Jāhiliyyah "every slaughter was a clan sacrifice," a commensal meal), or as a human victim is roasted and offered as a sacrifice to a deity.[26] The image of plenty and magnanimity is continued in verse 22 when the poet uses the verb *anhala* (to give a first drink) and the noun *ʿall* (a second draught), originally of wine or water, to his lance.[27] The persistence of this imagery should alert us that, like sacrifice, the killing of the enemy in blood vengeance is perceived as revitalizing the kin.

If we now proceed to verses 25 and 26, which in al-Marzūqī's recension follow verse 22 directly, we find that those who gorge themselves at this sacrificial feast provided by the avenger are the eaters of carrion. Their glee is reminiscent of that of the poor kinsmen, clients, and refugees when a magnanimous man has provided a feast. Thus we can say that, whereas the flesh and blood of the sacrificial animal at the commensal meal, or the wine that stands as a metaphor for blood, serve to nourish, revitalize, or even immortalize the kin (that is, the life forces of the victim, particularly as embodied in the blood,[28] are absorbed by the kin group), here it would seem that the flesh and blood, the life-

24. Robertson Smith, *Kinship and Marriage*, 25–27.

25. For examples of the poetic image of giving the enemy a draught of death, see *Ḥamāsiyyāt nos. 229* and *236* in al-Marzūqī, *Ḥamāsah* 2:682, 691.

26. Robertson Smith, *Religion of the Semites*, 281, 371; Chelhod, *Le sacrifice chez les Arabes*, 178–79.

27. See, for example, *Ḥamāsiyyah no. 81*, in al-Marzūqī, *Ḥamāsah* 1:276–77.

28. Chelhod, *Le sacrifice chez les Arabes*, 174–75.

force of the enemy non-kin, is wrested from them and transferred either to these unclean animals or, through the drinking lances (22), to the kin group.[29] Further, the imagery of roasting meat in verse 21 and giving drink reinforces the message that the warrior in taking blood vengeance is serving the kin in a manner analogous to the provision of *jazūr* (slaughter camel) and wine that we saw in *The Muʿallaqah of Labīd*. In the poetry of blood vengeance, the purification of the kin is thus achieved through the pollution of the non-kin.

This underlying message is intensified by a second reading, for *taḍḥaku al-ḍabʿu* (the hyena [f.] laughs or grins) can also mean "the hyena menstruates." The usage of *ḍaḥikat* in the meaning "to menstruate" is curious because, although attested in the lexica,[30] we find that in both Qurʾānic and poetic commentary it is denied almost as soon as it is affirmed (or vice versa). Both al-Marzūqī and al-Tibrīzī, in their commentaries on this line, insist that "there is nothing to the claim of those who say that *taḍḥaku* means 'she menstruates' (*taḥīḍu*)."[31] Nevertheless, the connection between menstruation and unavenged blood or defeat on the battlefield is too well established to leave any doubt that there is a pun at work here, however much the commentarists try to deny it. The female hyena was believed to menstruate[32] and also to couple with the corpses of fallen warriors, even to impregnate itself on them. Certainly the connection between menstruation and impregnation is suggestive.

Perhaps even more convincing is the *locus classicus* for the controversy over the laughing versus menstruating reading of *ḍaḥikat*, Qurʾān 11:71: "Our messengers came to Abraham [Ibrāhīm] with the good tidings. . . . And his wife was standing by; then she laughed [*ḍaḥikat*], therefore we gave her the glad tidings of Isaac, and, after Isaac, of Jacob. She said, 'Woe is me! Shall I bear [a child], being an old woman, and this my husband is an old man? This assuredly is a strange thing.' " In this case, likewise, the Qurʾānic commentarists, on the whole, reject the meaning "she menstruated."[33] And yet in both cases it seems that

29. This image may be a metaphorical expression of the custom, of which there is evidence in the Jāhiliyyah, of drinking the blood of the slain enemy; see Robertson Smith, *Religion of the Semites*, 313, and *Kinship and Marriage*, 296.

30. Lane and *Lisān*, *ḍ-ḥ-k*. [*Lisān* = Muḥammad ibn Mukarram ibn Manẓūr, *Lisān al-ʿArab*, 15 vols. (Beirut: Dār Ṣādir, 1955–56)].

31. Al-Marzūqī, *Ḥamāsah* 2:837; al-Tibrīzī, *Ḥamāsah* 2:163.

32. Robertson Smith, *Kinship and Marriage*, 231.

33. See Abū Jaʿfar Muḥammad ibn Jarīr al-Ṭabarī, *Jāmiʿ al-Bayān ʿan Āy al-Qurʾān*, 30 vols., 3d ed. (Cairo: Muṣṭafā al-Bābī al-Ḥalabī, 1968), 11:71–76 (commentary on Qurʾān 11:71).

the scholiasts protest too much, for just as saying "no pun intended" functions precisely to call the listener's attention to a pun that might otherwise escape his notice, while at the same time protesting false innocence, the denials of the commentarists—both poetic and Qur'ānic—alert the modern reader to a recognized, perhaps even inevitable, reading of "menstruate" in both cases. Any modern reading must insist on the intentionality of the double entendre. In the case of Ibrāhīm's wife, the point of her remarks is precisely that she is well beyond menopause. She may well laugh at the absurd announcement, but she must also menstruate before she can conceive. *Ḍaḥikat* clearly bears two equally intended meanings: first, on the narrative level, upon hearing the announcement that in her old age she would bear a child, "she laughed"; but equally, at the level of the semantic core of the story, "she menstruated."[34]

As for the hyena, in light of its many bizarre and peculiarly human characteristics, among them, according to the Arabs, menstruation, an intertextual reading of the qaṣīdah at hand would inevitably take *taḍḥaku* as a double entendre. It conveys first, in the surface context of the grinning wolf, the grinning or laughing of the hyena as it curls back its lips and bares it teeth to eat the corpse. And I might add, this particular verb serves to create the sense of jubilation or celebration that we otherwise associate in the qaṣīdah with the commensal feast. Second, given the customary beliefs concerning the hyena and their frequent poetic expression and the common comparison of unavenged blood to menstrual blood, menstruation forms a natural complement to the idea of the sexual pollution of the corpse.

Of particular interest, furthermore, is the description of the "ancient birds" (*ʿitāqū al-ṭayri*), the vultures (or eagles) that stumble or flap their wings about the corpses of the slain, too glutted to fly (verse 26). Let us first note that the vulture (*nasr*, pl. *nusūr*) in early Arabian lore is noted for its longevity, as in the story of Luqmān,[35] and, further, that the regular occurrence of this image in the poetry of blood vengeance often employs an epithet referring to this quality.[36] Here, *ʿitāq* (sing.

34. I pursue this matter further, taking into account the Genesis version of the story, in "Sarah and the Hyena: Laughter, Menstruation, and the Genesis of a Double Entendre," presented at the annual meeting of the American Oriental Society, Berkeley, Calif., 1991.

35. Al-Nuwayrī, *Nihāyat al-Arab* 13:60–61; al-Jāḥiẓ, *Al-Ḥayawān* 6:325–28.

36. For example, *Aṣmaʿiyyah no. 53*, by Muhalhil ibn Rabīʿah, line 6, *qashʿamayn* (two old vultures), in al-Aṣmaʿī, *Al-Aṣmaʿiyyāt*, 154–55; and *The Muʿallaqah of ʿAntarah*, line 7, *nasr qashʿam* (old vulture), in al-Anbārī, *Sharḥ al-Qaṣāʾid al-Sabʿ*, 365. It is of note, too, that among the deities of the Jāhiliyyah was the Himyarite vulture-god, Nasr; see Robertson Smith, *Religion of the Semites*, 226.

ʿ*atīq*), of which al-Marzūqī and al-Tibrīzī remark merely that it refers to eaters of flesh and carrion,[37] has as its root meaning "old" or "ancient" and hence is best read epithetically as "long-lived birds." The use of this same epithet, ʿ*atīq*, to mean an aged wine should alert us to the intimations of longevity, even of immortality, suggested by its use here. Keeping in mind that the blood of the sacrificial animal is the source of life, or even, as in Christian doctrine, of immortal life, we can deduce that the source of the proverbial longevity of the vulture is precisely the flesh and blood of the carrion it devours.

This assumption both elucidates and is in turn elucidated by the heretofore elusive biblical passage (Matthew 24:28 and Luke 17:37): "Wheresoever the carcase is, there will the eagles be gathered together" (Matthew 24:28, King James Version).[38] More recent biblical scholarship has—quite correctly I believe —preferred "vulture" over "eagle" to translate the Greek *aetos*, but this technical improvement has not resulted in improved understanding. John Fenton compares this passage to Job 29:30 and remarks, "This saying is probably proverbial; it means here that just as the vultures gather immediately the corpse appears, so the Son of Man will come to earth suddenly."[39] Edmund Leach at least discerns what the main elements stand for: "Surely the body is the body of Christ and the eagles are the elect gathered at the Eucharist?" Unable to overcome the sense of opprobrium attached to the eating of carrion, he concludes that, despite the greater ornithological accuracy of "vultures," the traditional translation of "eagles" is nevertheless closer to the original sense, the majestic raptor being a more appropriate allegory of the Elect than the disgusting scavenger.[40] He fails to grasp the crux of the allegory and is left with merely a metaphor for speed: the Elect will be the first to arrive, as in the "early bird gets the worm," the bird being the Elect and the worm being the Christ. The correct interpretation would seem rather to be that the Elect will know Christ immedi-

37. Al-Marzūqī, *Ḥamāsah* 2:837; al-Tibrīzī, *Ḥamāsah* 2:164.

38. I am following Leach's discussion in "Against Genres," 100.

39. Quoted ibid.

40. Ibid. The Arabs distinguished ornithologically between the raptor and the scavenger, as in al-Jāḥiẓ's remark that the vulture (*nasr*) has a beak (*minsar*) but no talons (*mikhlab*). He states, too, that the *nasr* is not counted "among the free and noble birds" (*min aḥrār al-ṭayr wa ʿitāqihā*), taking ʿ*itāq* in its more standard meaning. See al-Jāḥiẓ, *Al-Ḥayawān* 6:334. Others however, do consider the *nasr* to be of the ʿ*itāq al-ṭayr*, see Lane, *n-s-r*. Lexically, *nasr* is said to mean vulture, but also eagle; ʿ*uqāb*, pl. ʿ*uqbān*, to mean eagle. See Lane, *n-s-r*, ʿ*-q-b*. In blood-vengeance and battle poetry the two appear to be used almost interchangeably, or rather, the type of bird is not specified.

ately and instinctively, as vultures know carrion; but this parable is above all an allegory of the Eucharist. For just as the vultures acquire long life through the flesh and blood of the carrion, so will the Elect achieve life everlasting through the flesh and blood of Christ.

I would like to carry the meaning of this vulture-carrion image one step further. We read in the *Mufaḍḍaliyyāt* and elsewhere that the Arabs of the Jāhiliyyah believed that "if a slain man went unavenged, an owl would emerge from his grave and cry 'Give me drink! Give me drink!' until the slain man's killer was slain."[41] In more general terms, the depiction of the soul in the form of a bird is commonplace in Semitic and Ancient Mediterranean cultures.[42] Familiar too is the thirst of the souls of the dead for blood (*Odyssey* 11). Keeping in mind the relation of blood vengeance to ancestor cult, we can surmise that the vultures that feed on the carcasses of those slain in vengeance may be an expression—mythic or metaphoric—for the souls of those slain kinsmen who are thereby avenged, or perhaps even the souls of the ancestors of the clan in general. That is, they are in effect equivalent to the *hāmah* (owl). Such an assumption would complete the logical structure of the poem of blood vengeance; the vital forces of the slain enemy would serve in a direct way to nourish the souls of the dead kin, and the repeated occurrence of the image of the vulture in the poetry of blood-vengeance would thus be explained by its requisite role in this ritual code. Moreover, the ritual of vengeance would begin to reveal a more precise and more neatly "structuralist" relationship to sacrifices in the form of a commensal meal: whereas in the commensal meal the consecrated animal is slaughtered to nourish the living of the clan, in the taking of blood vengeance the human victim is slain to nourish (reincarnate) its dead.[43] This reading of the role of the vulture/eagle serves further to explain the joint presence of the two constant elements Theodor Gaster has identified at seasonal festivals, the return of the dead and the commu-

41. Lyall, *The Mufaḍḍalīyāt* 1:322. See Chelhod, *Le sacrifice chez les Arabes*, 102. For an extensive discussion of the motif of the owl in Arabic poetry, see Th. E. Homerin, "Echoes of a Thirsty Owl," *Journal of Near Eastern Studies* 44, no. 3 (1985): 165–84.

42. Ignaz Goldziher, "Der Seelenvogel im islamischen Volksglauben," in J. Desomogyi, ed., *Gesammelte Schriften* (Hildesheim: G. Olms, 1970), 4:403–6; Delcourt, *Oedipe*, 108–14.

43. For those disturbed by the absence of a deity in this sacrificial formulation, see Robertson Smith's comment concerning Arabia: "As Wellhausen has justly remarked, religious feeling was quite put in the shade by the feeling for the sanctity of kindred blood. . . . in Arabia the rules and customs of the kin retained the sanctity which they originally derived from their connection with the religion of the kin, long after the kindred god had been forgotten or had sunk to a subordinate place." Robertson Smith, *Religion of the Semites*, 283.

nal meal. Adapting his words to the present context, we can say of the taking of blood vengeance, as Gaster says of the seasonal festivals, that "these occasions are of concern not only to the actual and present but equally to the ideal and durative community."[44]

If we then apply these findings to the image at hand (verse 26), the meaning is further enriched: the etherial vultures now glutted, too heavy to take flight, become the image of the disembodied souls of the dead recorporealized and reincarnate. There is then an analogy to the events in *Odyssey* 11, where the souls of the dead form an amorphous swarm, resuming their human, rational identities only after Odysseus performs the proper funerary sacrifices for them and they have drunk a draught of black blood. By thus interpreting the slaying of the enemy and the feasting of the wolves, hyenas, and vultures on their corpses in the poetry of blood vengeance as a form of sacrifice and commensal meal, we can begin to understand this motif and its imagery as a variation (or symmetrical inversion) of the hunting and feasting motifs of the classical Arabic qaṣīdah.

Turning now to verses 23 and 24, which form the conclusion of the poem in al-Marzūqī's recension, we discover the clue that unlocks the full ritual pattern of the code of blood vengeance and the scheme of interlocking signs and symbols through which that ritual message is encoded. The tripartite profane-sacred-profane pattern of the rites of passage is expressed with utter lucidity: *ḥallat . . . ḥarāman . . . taḥillū* (permitted . . . forbidden . . . permitted) (23). The verb *ḥalla-yaḥillu* encompasses within its semantic field all those qualities associated with the profane, that is, to be lawful, permitted, pure.[45] The noun *ḥarām*, with its range of meanings extending from the inviolable sacred/taboo to the polluted/dangerous, encompasses precisely that ambivalence that characterizes the marginal, liminal (sacred) middle phase of the rites of passage and sacrifice.[46] That this ritual pattern of pollution and purification makes up the basic metaphorical and structural unit, the semantic underpinning of the poem, is revealed rhetorically through the *radd al-ʿajuz ʿalā al-ṣadr* (repetition in the rhyme word of an earlier word in the line, or epanadiplosis) combined with the *ṭibāq* (antithesis) of *ḥalāl* and *ḥarām*.

The word *ḥalla* should by this time sound suspiciously familiar,

44. Theodor H. Gaster, *Thespis: Ritual, Myth, and Drama in the Ancient Near East* (New York: W. W. Norton, 1977), 44.

45. Lane, *ḥ-l-l*.

46. Ibid., *ḥ-r-m*.

and indeed, the poem is structured both semantically and rhetorically around the concept of *ḥalla*. Forms of this verb provide the rhyme word in verses 3, 9, and 14, as well as 23, creating a pun or *jinās* (paronomasia) that extends throughout the poem. When considered together, these verses reveal what is ultimately a single message: the fulfillment of the obligation to vengeance. In verse 3, the "knot" (*ʿuqdah*) also means moral obligation, bond, thus in the context of this poem, it refers to the obligation to exact vengeance for the slain uncle. Verse 9 is marked by extensive *jinās* of the words *ḥalla* and *ḥazm* (resolution) compounded with a *ṭibāq* between *ẓāʿin* (departing) and *ḥalla*, here meaning alighted. Given the ritual context I have established, it might also be possible to read the verse: "departing with resolve [separation and liminality] until when he becomes *ḥalāl*," that is, pure once more. Once he has achieved his vengeance (reaggregation), his resolve also becomes pure; that is, he maintains his resolute nature in both of the ritual states. Surely so urgent a rhetorical insistence on *ḥalla* in this verse demands that we read the word as what classical rhetoric termed *al-mumāthalah min al-jinās*, in which the reiterated root takes on a different meaning each time,[47] that is, as a pun and not merely repetition or alliteration. If we then take *ḥalla* first as alighted, with the understanding that it is the alighting of the avenger after having exacted his vengeance (what amounts to the aggregation phase of the rite of passage, in which, as Turner puts it, the passenger enters a relatively stable state once more),[48] the obvious second meaning is to be *ḥalāl*, to be legally and ritually pure. If we then turn to verse 14, we can further surmise that *ḥallū*, applied to the band of Hudhalīs upon whom the deceased uncle in his day wreaked *his* vengeance, might carry the secondary meaning of permitted. That is, their blood, inasmuch as they are non-kin that have slain the poet's kinsman, is permitted, lawful to him.

Returning at last to verse 23, we find the *ḥalāl/ḥarām* dialectic expressed in terms of wine. This, as can be deduced from Semitic symbolism in general, as well as from the juxtaposition of this particular verse to the image of the blood-imbibing lance (22), is a metaphor for blood. To say that wine is *ḥarām* and then *ḥalāl* (forbidden and then permitted) is equivalent to saying that the blood of the poet (and his kin) was *ḥarām* and then *ḥalal*, that is, polluted and then purified. This metaphorical

47. Ibn Rashīq, *Al-ʿUmdah* 1:321–23. The repetition of the same rhyme word here does not qualify as *īṭāʾ*, since here the meaning as well as the form of the repeated rhyme word varies. See ibid., 1:169–70.

48. Turner, *Ritual Process*, 94.

form of expression goes far in explaining an aspect of the ritual of blood vengeance which figures prominently in the poetry of blood vengeance and the akhbār that accompany it, and one that did not go unnoticed by the Arab commentators of this poem.[49] The avenger forswore wine, women, meat, ointment, shaving, and washing until he had taken his vengeance, whereupon these things became permitted to him once more.[50] This practice constitutes a clear expression of the sacrificial pattern of entry into the sacrifice, the sacrificial state, and exit from the sacrifice (the separation, liminality, aggregation of the rite of passage). The pattern takes on an added significance if we note that all things forsworn are symbols or expressions of the community, the communal life, or attributes of culture as opposed to nature. Wine and meat are associated with commensal eating; washing, shaving, ointment, and perfume with the accouterments of culture; women with fertility, reproduction, and its associated institutions (marriage, sacred prostitution).[51] Thus to forswear these particular things amounts to an excommunication or anathema and the entry into the liminal or sacrificial phase. The slaying of the victim in both blood vengeance and in animal sacrifice marks the end of the *iḥrām*,[52] the reentry into society, that is, the transition from the sacred/liminal to the aggregate/profane.

Nor does the poet abandon the complex polysemy of his imagery in verse 24. The drink for which he calls is at once the blood of vengeance and wine; his body, emaciated after the death of his uncle, needs nourishment. Another reading is to take the more common meaning of *khall*, vinegar, thereby adding a *ṭibāq* between wine—a metaphor for blood that is wholesome, pure, *ḥalāl*—and vinegar—standing by analogy for blood that is spoiled, polluted, *ḥarām*.

This analysis leads us to several conclusions concerning the early Arabic poetry of blood vengeance as exemplified in *The Rithāʾ of Taʾabbaṭa Sharran*. Foremost among them is that blood vengeance is not merely a theme; it is a patterned ritual that informs and determines the structure of that poetry and the complex network of images and metaphors that characterize it. Blood vengeance, perceived as a social code and encoded in poetry, is expressed in a tripartite pattern that

49. Al-Marzūqī, *Ḥamasah* 2:838–39.

50. The various forms of oath among the Arabs are most extensively discussed in Johannes Pedersen, *Der Eid bei den Semiten in seinem Verhältnis zu verwandten Erscheinungen sowie die Stellung des Eides im Islam* (Strassburg: Karl J. Trübner, 1914).

51. Chelhod, *Le sacrifice chez les Arabes*, 160–67.

52. Lammens, "Le caractère religieux du *ṯār*," 85–86, 121.

corresponds to the analogous paradigms of the rite of passage (separation/liminality/aggregation) and of sacrifice (entry/sacrifice/exit) and, furthermore, displays the chiastic progression characteristic of such rites. The poetry of blood vengeance takes as its metaphorical matter images of blood and its tropical equivalents, especially wine, and operates extensively with imagery appropriate to the commensal meal or the symmetrical inversion thereof. That is, the taking of blood vengeance is perceived and poetically expressed as an act of nourishing and revitalizing the kin. The poem of blood vengeance can thus be considered a subclass of the dominant classical qaṣīdah-form in which the underlying sacrificial pattern more commonly finds expression in terms of the battle, the hunt, and the commensal feast.

I would like to apply these initial findings to the analysis of another poem that takes blood vengeance as its theme, *Maᶜshar Has Been Deserted of Its People,* attributed to the last great warrior-poet of the Jāhiliyyah, Durayd ibn al-Ṣimmah.[53] In doing so, I hope to substantiate the theoretical conclusions presented thus far and to demonstrate the poet's power to draw upon an extensive store of images from the classical Arabic poetic tradition in such a way as to situate the poem of blood vengeance both semantically and formally within the boundaries of the classical qaṣīdah form.

Undoubtedly the semianonymous *Rithāʾ of Taʾabbaṭa Sharran* is the most famous poem of blood vengeance in the pre-Islamic poetic legacy. Obscure as to attribution and provenance and devoid of proper names (except for the place-name Salᶜ) and of the intimate aura of akhbār, its renown derives from the power of its abstracted and impersonal expression of the Jāhilī ethos. Durayd's rithāʾ, by contrast, is replete with proper names and, in the medieval compendia of Arabic poetry and lore, firmly ascribed and situated in what purports to be its historical setting. Thus the akhbār among which the poem is set serve both to explicate and to complement it. The anecdotes in the *Kitāb al-Aghānī* concerning Durayd ibn al-Ṣimmah's avenging of his brothers and accession to the chieftainship of the Banū Jusham demonstrate the function of the institution of blood vengeance as a rite of initiation or passage from boyhood to manhood and reveal the oedipal tensions for which the taking of blood vengeance provides both expression and outlet.[54]

Durayd's elder brother ᶜAbd Allāh had inherited the chieftainship of

53. Sezgin, *Poesie*, 267–68.
54. Al-Iṣbahānī, *Kitāb al-Aghānī* 10:3467–504.

the Banū Jusham from his father. Thus, the oedipal tensions involved here are in the form of sibling rivalry, for it is only through succession to his elder brother that Durayd can accede to the chieftainship. The frustrated ambitions of the younger brother and his resentment of the elder brother form the crux of an anecdote about the battle of the Banū ʿĀmir ibn Ṣaʿṣaʿah and the Banū Jusham against the Banū Asad and the Banū Ghaṭafān. ʿAbd Allāh, having made a pact with his ally Sharāḥīl to share the booty, refused to appoint Durayd as a leader, lest he have to share with him, and appointed him instead as an auxiliary. When it appeared that ʿAbd Allāh had been slain, Durayd persuaded Sharāḥīl to swear a similar pact with him. No sooner was this oath sworn at the idol Dhū al-Khalaṣah than ʿAbd Allāh returned with herds of plundered livestock. Durayd demanded his share, but Sharāḥīl considered that since ʿAbd Allāh was not dead after all, his pact with Durayd was not binding.[55] Thus all that stood between Durayd and manhood (full participation in battle, chieftainship, and booty) was his elder brother. At the Day of al-Liwā, a cattle raid undertaken by ʿAbd Allāh against Durayd's advice, but with which he nevertheless went along, ʿAbd Allāh was finally slain. As the akhbār themselves make clear, however, it was not merely his elder brother's death that marked Durayd's accession to the chieftainship of the Banū Jusham but his avenging that death.

An anecdote related in the *Kitāb al-Aghānī* on the authority of Ibn al-Kalbī shows Durayd somewhat dilatory, even reluctant, in avenging his brother and asserting his manhood:

> Rayḥānah bint Maʿdī Karib [Durayd's mother] said to Durayd, "My son, if you are unable to seek vengeance for your brother, then seek help from your maternal uncle and his band of Zubayd." This made him ashamed, so he swore not to put on kohl, anoint himself, eat meat, or drink wine until he had taken his vengeance. Then he carried out the raid [of the Day of Ghadīr], brought her [the captive] Dhuʾāb ibn Asmāʾ, and slew him in her courtyard, saying, "Have I brought you what you wanted?" "Yes," she replied, "and I am pleased with you."[56]

Durayd is ashamed because his mother's suggestion impugns his manhood. Rayḥānah is telling Durayd that he must either accept the obligations and prerogatives of manhood or else relinquish them to the older

55. Ibid., 10:3479.
56. Ibid., 10:3477.

generation (her brother) and remain a child. The youth then takes up the challenge of proving his manhood by avenging his brother according to the prescribed (ritual) pattern. He swears to forgo those things that are a sign of membership in society (*ḥalāl*) and, upon achieving his vengeance, reenters society once more, now with the status of adult and chief.

In both form and function the taking of blood vengeance fits the ritual paradigm. It exhibits the tripartite structure of the rite of passage and results in a change of social status: the separation of the youth from society is marked by the oath, whereby the poet enters the marginal taboo state until, with the slaying of the captive, he signals his reentry (aggregation) into society, now with the status of an adult. The manner in which the victim is slain is, more than other stories of blood vengeance, quite explicitly a sacrifice. The three phases defined by Hubert and Mauss—entry into the sacrifice, sacrifice, and exit from the sacrifice[57]—are marked by the oath of renunciation of society (that is, of its symbols), the slaying of the victim, and the resumption of social participation. Furthermore, inasmuch as the act of avenging his brother fulfills an obligation that the poet has been shirking, this example admirably fits the definition of Hubert and Mauss: "Sacrifice is a religious act which, through the consecration of a victim, modifies the condition of the moral person who accomplishes it."[58]

The poem I have proposed to discuss is itself associated with the Day of Ghadīr on which Durayd avenged his brother. In the *Kitāb al-Aghānī* it is introduced as follows:

> After his brother ʿAbd Allāh had been slain, Durayd ibn al-Ṣimmah set out on a raid against the Ghaṭafān seeking to avenge his blood. He visited them clan by clan, killing Sāʿidah ibn Murr of the Banū ʿAbs and capturing Dhuʾāb ibn Asmāʾ ibn Zayd ibn Qārib (it was actually Murrah ibn ʿAwf al-Jushamī who captured him). Then the Banū Jusham said, "Why don't we ransom him?" But Durayd would not stand for this and instead slew him for his brother ʿAbd Allāh. Then of the Banū Fazārah, he slew a man named Ḥizām and some of his brothers, as well as a number of the Banū Murrah, the Banū Thaʿlabah ibn Saʿd, and the clans of Ghaṭafān; and that was on the Day of Ghadīr. Concerning the battle day and those slain on it he recited:

57. Hubert and Mauss, *Sacrifice*, 19–49.
58. Ibid., 13.

Maᶜshar Has Been Deserted of Its People [9]

1. Maᶜshar has been deserted of its people,
   then Jaww Suwayqah,
   and then al-Aṣfar,
2. From the wadi's bend at al-Ḥulayf until al-Wāsiṭ,
   one was a bedouin camp,
   one a fixed abode.
3. So tell the Banū Sulaym and those gathered round them,
   and perhaps the greatest lineage
   will incline [an ear],
4. That I have avenged my brothers,
   when before it was as though
   I had betrayed them.
5. We gave the brown spears a morning draught
   of the Banū Fazārah. Go easy, Fazārah,
   don't grumble (when you're milked).
6. And say to the Banū Māzin, in person,
   "What good is a threat
   if you don't enforce it?
7. "For if you slay a lone band of young warriors,
   marked for death, or if
   you vanquish them,
8. "[Know] that Ḥizām lies fallen on the field,
   and over his brothers
   buzzards hover,
9. "[That] on the day Yazīd of the Banū Nāshib [fell]
   and before him your Yazīd
   the Elder,
10. "We stirred up the cry for help
    among the Banū Nāshib and the kin of Laqīṭ.
    So do not boast.
11. "The hyenas drag off their limbs
    and get pregnant on them;
    they lie, even now,
    unburied."[59]

This short poem is striking for its opening image, that most traditional of the opening motifs of the classical qaṣīdah, the abandoned campsite (*aṭlāl*). What is remarkable in this case is that this otherwise lyric, nostalgic, or melancholic motif (as we see it, for example, in *The*

59. Al-Iṣbahānī, *Kitāb al-Aghānī* 10:3475–76.

Muᶜallaqah of Labīd or *The Muᶜallaqah of Imruʾ al-Qays*) assumes an eerie polysemy in the poem of blood vengeance. We read it first as the melancholy musings of the poet-lover over the ruins of the abandoned dwelling of a long-lost mistress. We must keep in mind, too, that the classical *aṭlāl* motif has a tragic as well as nostalgic or lyric element and further, when taken together with the Qurʾānic lore of ᶜĀd and Thamūd, a moral one. Perhaps the devastation in Durayd's poem is the devastation of treachery (as suggested by verse 4), of the social dissolution that would inevitably result from the failure to avenge kindred blood. Such a reading would associate the image of abandonment and desertion with the common metaphor for unavenged blood, that is, thirst or drought. When we read the two opening verses in the more specific context of the khabar (itself apparently drawn from the poem), the anecdote that accompanies it in the *Kitāb al-Aghānī*, and of the boastful declaration of vengeance achieved that makes up the remainder of the poem, however, the image takes on a curious bivalency: it seems to allude not only to the devastation of the Banū Jusham, the death of ᶜAbd Allāh, but also to the counterdevastation the poet has wreaked on the Banū Ghaṭafān.

An examination of the toponyms in this poem reveals an etymological, that is, semantic rather than geographical, significance. Maᶜshar (literally a party or band of men) is the noun of place or *maṣdar mīmī* of a root whose meanings encompass friendship, intimacy, social intercourse, kinship (specifically cognation), and tribe. The concept of desertion and abandonment thus receives a rhetorical emphasis in the first verse through the *ṭibāq* (antithesis) between *maᶜshar*, which suggests human society and habitation, and *taʾabbada*, which means to become wild and deserted (this is then merely another expression of the *ṭibāq* that commonly occurs in the *aṭlāl* motif, between *anisa*, to be sociable, familiar, intimate, and *taʾabbada*). The place-names of the second hemistich are likewise suggestive: Jaww Suwayqah, the hollow of the little market, and al-Aṣfar, empty. Verse 2 refers in a similar way to the breakdown of the social order, the outbreak of war: the riverbed of alliance (Ḥulayf, little ally or covenant) and mediation (al-Wāsiṭ, mediator) has dried up and been abandoned.[60] Let us recall at this point that the image of the deserted encampment, the disintegration of tribal alliances and of the social order are signs of separation, of entry into

60. Gaster's seasonal pattern of kenosis (emptying) and plerosis (filling), which I discuss later, is equally applicable here.

the marginal state, the dangerous, polluted, and taboo medial phase of the rite of passage or sacrifice. It is not surprising then that they form the introduction to the theme of blood vengeance.

The remainder of the poem is divided into two parts, each in the form of an announcement or declaration, a message to be delivered. In the first part, verses 3–5, the poet instructs a messenger to announce to the kin group that their blood has been avenged. The pollution/purification aspect of the blood-vengeance ritual finds expression here. The poet had been treacherous, as though an enemy rather than kin, until, by avenging his slain kinsman, he has reestablished the bonds of fidelity and kinship. The verb *ṣabaḥa* (give a morning draught) in verse 5 is bivalent because of the ambiguity of the two accusatives (indirect object and direct object). One can read, "We gave Fazārah a morning draught of the brown spears (that is, death)," but also, "We gave the brown spears a morning draught (of the blood) of the Banū Fazārah." Both metaphors are widely used in such poetry.[61] In this case I have preferred the second reading, since the verb that might have been translated simply as to grieve (*ḍajira*) also means to grumble at being milked (said of a she-camel).[62] Expression is thus given to the idea that blood vengeance depletes the vital forces of the enemy while it nourishes and revitalizes the kin.

The announcement to be made to the kin is then complemented by the message to the enemy, thereby presenting the two complementary sides of the blood-vengeance dialectic: the purification, revitalization of the kin (verses 3–5) and the concomitant pollution, devitalization of the enemy (6–11). The argument of verses 7–9 is familiar in the poetry of blood vengeance: if you (have) shed our blood, we (have) shed yours.[63] The enemy dead are enumerated and the pollution of their corpses expressed in images that are familiar, if not indeed obligatory, in Arabic poetry of blood vengeance.[64] As I have already discussed, the vultures that glut themselves on the flesh and blood of those fallen in battle express both the defilement of the corpses of the enemy and their devitalization. In poetry longevity is the most common attribute of

61. Recall *The Rithā᾽ of Ta᾽abbaṭa Sharran*, verse 20, and cf. *Aṣmaʿiyyah no. 53*, by Muhalhil ibn Rabīʿah, verse 7, which is discussed later.

62. Lane, *ḍ-j-r*.

63. Its converse is also found: see *The Rithā᾽ of Ta᾽abbaṭa Sharran*, verse 17.

64. For a discussion of excarnation of predators in the ancient Mediterranean tradition generally and of dogs and birds "feasting" on humiliated corpses in Homeric epics, see Emily Vermeule, *Aspects of Death in Early Greek Art and Poetry* (Berkeley: University of California Press, 1979), 46–48.

the vulture, and it would appear that the blood, the liquid life-force upon which it feeds, is the source of its long life. The image of the vultures, then, expresses the diverting of this life stream from the enemy lineage to these scavengers, or perhaps—if the vulture is, like the owl, an image of the soul of the deceased kinsman or of the ancestral souls of the clan—the diversion of this life-force from the enemy to the kin group.

The closing line of the poem adds, for most of us, a new dimension to the expression "to violate a corpse." The hyenas in this poem do not merely feast on the corpses of the dead but couple with them. This rather unfair advantage that the female hyenas take of the bloated corpses of fallen warriors is described in detail by al-Jāḥiẓ in *Kitāb al-Ḥayawān*:

> It used to be claimed that, when a man's head was cut off, he would fall on his face. Then, when his corpse bloated, his penis would swell and become erect and enlarged so that it would roll him over on his back. Then, when the female hyena came to eat him and saw him in this state and saw his penis in this condition, she would try to have intercourse with him and satisfy her need in this manner. Then she would eat the man after this had gratified her more than coupling with a male hyena. One of the desert Arabs said that he had witnessed [a female hyena] doing this and also coupling with her mate and discovered that in the former state she thrashed about and cried out, whereas with the male hyena she did not.[65]

In a similar vein al-Nuwayrī writes in *Nihāyat al-Arab* that: "the female hyena has a passion for digging up graves, and this is solely because of her craving for human flesh. It is her habit, when a slain man is left in a deserted place and the corpse has swollen and the penis is engorged to come up to it, then mount it and gratify her needs on it. Then she eats it."[66] This image of the hyenas impregnating them-

65. Al-Jāḥiẓ, *Al-Ḥayawān* 6:50–51.

66. Al-Nuwayrī, *Nihāyat al-Arab* 9:274. The ruthless, wanton, and what we would term liminal nature of the hyena is further described; of particular interest is the claim that the hyena is at one time male, at another female (9:274–76). Of note in this regard too is the female domination of the hyena pack and, in the spotted hyena, the enlarged clitoris and sham scrotum that make the female appear almost identical to the male. For modern zoological sources on the hyena and an intriguing interpretation of the role of the hyena in ancient Indian myth and ritual, see Stephanie W. Jamison, *The Ravenous Hyenas and the Wounded Sun: Myth and Ritual in Ancient India* (Ithaca, N.Y.: Cornell University Press, 1991), 73–74 and 45–130 passim. I thank Gregory Nagy for this reference. See also *Aṣmaʿiyyah no. 70*, verse 22, for a description of hyenas as brides in al-Aṣmaʿī, *Al-Aṣmaʿiyyāt*, 206.

selves on the corpses should surely be seen as analogous to that of the vultures devouring the corpses of the slain. It expresses the diversion of yet another life-giving liquid, semen, from the enemy to propagate, instead of enemy progeny, this polluted and polluting species. It should be noted, too, that the image of the hyena in the poetry of blood vengeance forms a diametrical opposition to the *nawāʾiḥ* (wailing women) in rithāʾ: female feasting and revitalization in celebration of the death of the enemy as opposed to female mourning and devitalization following the death of a kinsman.

At this point, we can begin to perceive how the poem of blood vengeance fits into the nasīb-raḥīl-fakhr pattern of the classical qaṣīdah. The use of the *aṭlāl* motif in Durayd's poem already establishes a metaphorical link between this poem and the standard qaṣīdah form. I suggest that whereas the standard qaṣīdah most often exhibits the marginal phase in the form of the desert journey and the aggregation phase in the form of the feast (as in *The Muʿallaqah of Labīd*) or of the hunt (for example, *The Muʿallaqah of Imruʾ al-Qays*), the celebration of the bounty and fertility of the tribe and its life-sustaining and life-propagating forces, the poem of blood vengeance expresses marginality in the anathema, antisocial state (*iḥrām*)[67] of the avenger and signals his reaggregation or reentry through the slaying (sacrifice) of his victim. The feasting and copulation of the vultures and hyenas, then, perhaps describe not the abundance and propagation of the poet's tribe but its obverse, the deprivation and diversion of the life-forces of the enemy. There is thus a symmetrically inverse relationship between the rite of sacrifice or commensal meal (the slaying of an animal victim to revitalize the kin group) and the rite of blood vengeance (the slaying of a human victim to devitalize the enemy): they are two sides of the same coin. Furthermore, just as blood vengeance is a subclass of sacrifice,[68] so too, the poem of blood vengeance is a subcategory of the classical qaṣīdah. In both we find the progression from an image of loss, drought, and desertion by way of separation and sacrifice (the hunt, the commensal meal, the enemy slain) to a final image of congregation, feasting, and fertility (in one by the revitalized kin, in the other by scavenger beasts). The juxtaposition or interweaving of these two diametrically opposed images in the same poem is possible because they are complementary

67. Lammens, "Le caractère religieux du *ṯār*," 85–86; Chelhod, *Le sacrifice chez les Arabes*, 101.

68. Lammens, "Le caractère religieux du *ṯār*," 115; Chelhod, *Le sacrifice chez les Arabes*, 100–104, 116–20.

and ultimately convey the same message: the necessity of the survival and propagation of the kin group. What is celebrated, above all, is life itself. The association between blood vengeance and animal sacrifice is drawn explicitly in a tribal battle poem from the Islamic period in which Zayd ibn Bishr al-Taghlibī boasts over his kinsmen's slaying of ʿUmayr ibn al-Ḥubāb:

Let no Muḍarī cross our land,
  neither with an escort nor without one,
For the Banū Taghlib have ground the Hawāzin [like flour]
  and hard pressed the Banū Manṣūr
On the day the ironclad warriors leapt round ʿUmayr,
  like vultures hopping round the slaughter camel.[69]

The epistolary formula of Durayd's and other poems, the apostrophic *abligh* (tell, inform) (verse 4), should remind us of the function of poetry in the Jāhiliyyah. It was indeed "the *dīwān* of the Arabs," their archive or register. Thus we find in this poem and in others a certification documenting the accomplishment of blood vengeance and, with the careful enumeration of names, a balancing of the books. As Lammens's remarks on the relation of the poem of blood vengeance to the act of taking vengeance would suggest, the act becomes "official" or "officially recognized" only through the poem.[70] We can begin to understand that poetry was above all mnemonic both in its purpose and its composition. Such an understanding would go far to explain the features that characterize, indeed define, poetry as opposed to prose: they are mnemonic devices to assure the stability of the text and the preservation of the underlying message in a society in which such messages or documents were not preserved in writing. Rhyme, meter, the sequential, and archetypal patterning of well-known images, rhetorical devices, especially antithesis (*ṭibāq*) and paronomasia (*jinās*), the condensation of expression, and the reiteration of the same message using a variety of metaphors—all these are mnemonic in origin and function. They are means to ensure that the underlying message is not lost.[71]

The juxtaposition of medieval literary to modern anthropological theory will perhaps shed some light on the character of poetry in tribal

69. Al-Jāḥiẓ, *Al-Ḥayawān* 6:331. See also, al-Iṣbahānī, *Kitāb al-Aghānī* 12:1371.
70. Lammens, "Le caractère religieux du *ṯār*," 108–10.
71. See Havelock, *The Muse*, passim; and Ong, *Orality and Literacy*, passim.

society and its ritual function. Of the sociopolitical role of poetry in the Jāhiliyyah, Ibn Rashīq states:

> The Arabs needed to sing about the nobility of their character, the purity of their blood, and to recall their good battle days and faraway abodes, their brave horsemen and compliant steeds, in order to incite themselves to nobility and direct their sons toward good character . . . , to perpetuate memorable deeds, strengthen their honor, guard the tribe and inspire the awe of it in other tribes, since others would not advance against them for fear of their poet.[72]

Burkert gives the definition and function of ritual as follows:

> Since the work of Sir Julian Huxley and Konrad Lorenz, biology has defined *ritual* as a behavioural pattern that has lost its primary function—present in its unritualized model—but which persists in a new function, that of communication. . . . This communicating function reveals the two basic characteristics of ritual behaviour, namely, repetition and theatrical exaggeration. For the essentially immutable patterns do not transmit differentiated and complex information but, rather, just one piece of information each. This single piece of information is considered so important that it is reinforced by constant repetition so as to avoid misunderstanding or misuse. The fact of understanding is thus more important than what is understood. Above all, then, ritual creates and affirms social interaction.[73]

Applying these remarks to poems I am discussing, I suggest that whereas the original function of the poem may have been merely to inform kin and enemy alike that vengeance had been taken, the literary or ritual function of the poem, that is, the reason that it is preserved and reiterated, is to communicate information vital to the survival of the kin group.[74] The message of the poetry of blood vengeance, so

72. Ibn Rashīq, *Al-ʿUmdah* 1:22, 82.

73. Burkert, *Homo Necans*, 23.

74. It should be added at this point that in the case of early Arabic poetry we need not always posit an original epistolary function for each poem. The *abligh* (Inform!) and *yā rākiban* (O, rider!) may often be no more than a literary conceit, albeit hearkening back to the actual earlier function of poetry. On the early Arabic poem as announcement and missive, see Alfred Bloch, "Qaṣīda," *Etudes Asiatiques: Revue de la Société Suisse d'Etudes Asiatiques* 2 (1948): 117–22. On the epistolary aspect of the classical qaṣīdah form, see J. Stetkevych, *Zephyrs of Najd*, chap. 1. A striking example of this type of poem is *Aṣmaʿiyyah no. 29*, by Durayd ibn al-Ṣimmah in al-Aṣmaʿī, *Al-Aṣmaʿiyyāt*, 111–13.

precisely stated in theme, structure, and a variety of images and metaphors, is that kindred blood must be avenged in order to revitalize the kin and devitalize the enemy. If we accept the application of Burkert's definition of ritual to this body of poetry, it will point out to us what we should have already known, that the genius of poetry lies not in the ultimate message that it conveys but rather in the striking and indelible manner in which that message is conveyed—the concision of meaning, the power of the metaphor.

PART TWO

THE PARADIGM OF PASSAGE MANQUÉ

CHAPTER 3

Taʾabbaṭa Sharran and Oedipus: A Paradigm of Passage Manqué

The poetry of the pre-Islamic "brigand poets" (*ṣaʿālīk*, s. ṣuʿlūk), though it does not on the whole exhibit the tripartite structure of the classical qaṣīdah form, can nevertheless be interpreted in terms of the rite of passage. In this case, however, it is a failed or aborted rite in which the passenger does not achieve reintegration into the community or tribe. Instead, the hardships and perils of the liminal state are realized and become a permanent way of life instead of a temporary transitional stage.

The traditional definition of the word ṣuʿlūk—poor, needy, having no property, no reliance on anything; a thief, robber[1]—lends support to the interpretation of the ṣuʿlūk as a liminal, antisocial character. Even more suggestive is the etymology put forth by Aḥmad Harīdī in the course of his research on Arabic quadriliterals. He proposes, quite correctly I believe, that ṣuʿlūk is an intensified adjectival form of the verb *salaka*—to travel, to go along a road (*salaka al-ṭarīqa*)—and hence equivalent to *sallāk**, that is, the *faʿʿāl*-form.[2] This etymology produces precisely what I have proposed as the archetypal character of the ṣuʿlūk: one who journeys repeatedly and habitually, never arriving at a destination, a perpetual passenger in a transitional state. In psychological terms we might view the ṣuʿlūk, then, as one whose course of development is arrested, perverted, or diverted. In ritual terms, the ṣuʿlūk is a permanent liminal entity.

1. Lane, *ṣ-ʿ-l-k*.
2. Verbal communication from Aḥmad Harīdī, University of Minya, Egypt.

According to the definition here put forth, we should expect ṣuᶜlūk poetry to exhibit in its form and imagery the phases of separation and liminality to the exclusion of reaggregation into society; or in the terms of the classical Arabic qaṣīdah form, we should expect to see elements of the nasīb and raḥīl without the culminating fakhr and its images of the hunt and commensal meal in which the poet/passenger's newly acquired adult status in the tribe and the life-sustaining and propagating functions of the tribe are praised. Rather fakhr, when it occurs in ṣuᶜlūk poetry, should consist exclusively of the poet's boasting of himself or his ṣaᶜālīk companions and praising the antisocial individualism that characṭerizes the brigand-poet.

In addition to the characteristics of liminality described by the anthropologists van Gennep, Douglas, Turner, and Leach, Pierre Vidal-Naquet has pointed out some key features in two articles in which he has applied van Gennep's formulation of the rite of passage to the classical Greek institutions of "military apprenticeship," the Athenian *ephebeia* and the Spartan *krypteia*. Several of Vidal-Naquet's points are of particular interest to the present argument: first, in comparing the *krypteia* to the life and ethos of the mature, "reaggregate" hoplite (warrior), he notes that the two ways of life are by no means unrelated; rather, they are symmetrical opposites. "In sum," he concludes his comparison of the two,

> with the hoplite, order (*taxis*) reigns; in the *krypteia* there is nothing but cunning, deception, disorder, irrationality. To borrow Lévi-Strauss's terms, one might say that the hoplite is on the side of Culture, of what is "cooked," while the *krypteia* is on the side of Nature, of the "raw," bearing in mind of course that this "Nature," the side of non-culture, is itself to some degree socially organized. . . . I think we may generalize and extend what I have already said in discussing the Spartan *krypteia*: for we must recognize that in Athens, and in many other parts of the Greek world . . . the transition between childhood and adulthood (the period of marriage and fighting) is dramatized in both ritual and in myth by what we might call the "law of symmetrical inversion."[3]

Second, he observes that ruse or cunning (*apate*) is characteristic of the liminal mode of combat, as opposed to the straightforward and

3. Pierre Vidal-Naquet, "The Black Hunter and the Origin of the Athenian Ephebeia," in R. L. Gordon, ed., *Myth, Religion, and Society: Structuralist Essays by M. Detienne, L. Gernet, J.-P. Vernant, and P. Vidal-Naquet* (Cambridge: Cambridge University Press, 1981), 154–55. I am particularly grateful to Pierre Vidal-Naquet for some emendations of the Greek materials in this chapter.

honest combat of the manly hoplite. Thus, Melanthos, "the Black One," defeats Xanthos "the Fair One" by crying out as they are engaged in duel, "Xanthos, you do not play according to the rules . . .—there is someone at your side!" When Xanthos turns to look, Melanthos seizes the opportunity and slays him.[4] Third, as Vidal-Naquet demonstrates in the case of Sophocles' *Philoctetes*, in which the mature warrior Odysseus persuades Achilles' youthful son Neoptolemus to trick the liminal Philoctetes out of the bow of Hercules, only a liminal entity can successfully fight another—a case of fighting fire with fire.[5] Finally, we should note that in his definition of the perpetual liminal figure, the solitary and misogynistic Melanion, the Black Hunter, as an "ephebe manqué," Vidal-Naquet has arrived at a formulation that is analogous to my definition of the ṣuʿlūk, or brigand-poet, as a "passenger manqué."[6]

In sum, according to this scheme, the burden of ṣuʿlūk poetry should consist of those images of night, violence, danger, hunger and thirst, wild beasts, and loneliness that characterize or symbolize ritual liminality. We should note too that these bear an antithetical relation to the values espoused in tribal fakhr: ease, abundance, satiety, communal eating and drinking, the protection and propagation of the tribe. Furthermore, it is precisely the ṣuʿlūk's acceptance of this permanent contact with danger and what Mary Douglas terms "the source of power" that confers upon him a "heroic" dimension, but this is not to be confused with the heroism of the aggregate tribal male.

Thus, in terms of form and content, the relation of the ṣuʿlūk poem to the classical qaṣīdah is synecdochic—that of the part to the whole—but also, inasmuch as the liminal phase is diametrically opposed to reaggregation, dialectical. Furthermore, with respect to imagery, those motifs or images of the nasīb or raḥīl which function as metaphors or prefigurations of reaggregation or tribal fakhr—images of fertility, safety, abundance and domesticity—must in ṣuʿlūk poetry be either altered or omitted.

In this chapter I will limit myself to examples from the poetry and akhbār of one of the two most notorious ṣaʿālīk, Taʾabbaṭa Sharran, turning my attention to the other, al-Shanfarā, in the next chapter.

A short poem attributed to Taʾabbaṭa Sharran demonstrates the

4. Ibid., 150–51.

5. Pierre Vidal-Naquet, "Sophocles' *Philoctetes* and the Ephebeia," in Jean-Pierre Vernant and Vidal-Naquet, *Tragedy and Myth in Ancient Greece*, trans. Janet Lloyd (Sussex: Harvester Press, 1981), 171–84.

6. Vidal-Naquet, "The Black Hunter," 160–62.

permanent liminality or marginality of the ṣuʿlūk. It is related in the *Kitāb al-Aghānī* that Taʾabbaṭa Sharran proposed marriage to a Hudhalī woman of the Banū Sahm. But one of her clansmen warned her, "Do not marry him, for he will be the first arrowhead to be lost." Upon the rejection of his proposal Taʾabbaṭa Sharran recited:

Do Not Marry Him [11]

1. They said to her, "Do not marry him, for he
will be the first arrowhead
to meet its mark."
2. This advice she thought not trifling.
She guarded her maidenhood, wary of widowhood,
from a formidable man who dons the night,
3. Meager his sip of sleep, his greatest care
the blood of vengeance or the encounter with
a foe fully armed and iron-helmeted;
4. Meager his provision store,
but one drink more remaining;
his ribs jut out, his gut sucked in.
5. Each youth who strives for brave repute combats him;
but when *he* strikes, it is not
for brave repute.
6. He would spend the night in wild herds' coverts,
till they were tame; at morn he would not keep them
from their pasture ground.
7. They saw a youth who cared not to hunt wild game;
were they to greet a human, they would greet him
one and all.
8. But the lords of the pregnant camel he emaciates,
whether they trace his lone track or spot him
with his band.
9. However long I live, indeed I know
that I will meet death's spearhead,
glistening, bare,
10. Taken unawares or openly, outnumbered by a foe
who prolongs the death match
till the end.
11. What do I think of death among my tribe?
Either I think it the sweeter death, and sleep,
or else I die still in my helmet.

12. A night does not go by but that I
  plunder a brave youth or terrify
   the whole herd of gazelles.
13. He who strikes heroes will without fail
  face his last encounter on
   death's battleground.[7]

The warning to the prospective bride in the first verse already situates the ṣuʿlūk in a liminal state: "He will be the first arrowhead to meet its mark." The primary meaning, that he will fall to the first arrow that is shot, is really an inversion (*qalb*) of this. At the same time, it seems to mean that he is a troublemaker, the first arrow shot is always his. Both interpretations give the same result, namely, that his prospects for survival are slim. Thus marriage, which is the prerogative of the aggregate tribal member who can protect, provide, and propagate, is denied to Ta'abbaṭa Sharran. What Mary Douglas says of the passenger in the marginal state is eminently true of the ṣuʿlūk: he is both endangered and dangerous, emanating danger to those around him. Whereas the tribal bridegroom offers life, perpetuated and propagated, the ṣuʿlūk is, as it were, marked for death and promises widowhood (*ta'ayyum* means widowhood as well as chastity) rather than motherhood. The ṣuʿlūk is sly and nocturnal, epithets that identify him with beasts of prey rather than tribal hunters and warriors (verse 2). Whereas tribal values, or in literary terms tribal fakhr, center on abundance and plenty, the ṣuʿlūk prides himself on the paucity and privation of his liminal condition, as the repetition (*al-takrār lil-ta'kīd*) of *qalīl* (meager, little) at the beginning of verses 3 and 4 emphasizes. He prefers battle and blood vengeance to ease and sleep. It should be noted too that the liminal ṣuʿlūk, light-armed and emaciated—admirably expressed in the *ṭibāq* (antithesis) between his protruding ribs and hollow belly (4)—is diametrically opposed to the tribal warrior, who is fully armed and helmeted (3).[8] Again in verse 5 the "aggregate" concern of his opponent, who strives for tribal reputation, is in direct contrast to the instinctive pouncing by night of the ṣuʿlūk (*ṭaraqa* means both to strike and to come at night) like a beast of prey.

In verses 6 and 7 the poet sets up a dialectic of nature versus culture.

7. Al-Iṣbahānī, *Kitāb al-Aghānī* 24:8348–50. For another version of this poem, see al-Marzūqī, *Ḥamāsah* 2:491–98. For a translation and discussion of the *Ḥamāsah* version, see S. Stetkevych, *Abū Tammām*, 304–7.

8. See Vidal-Naquet's "law of symmetrical inversion," "The Black Hunter," 155.

The ṣuʿlūk's rejection of culture is expressed in his lack of concern for the hunt, a key motif of the reaggregation theme. He seeks instead the company of wild beasts in an inversion neatly summed up in the antithesis between *waḥsh* (wild, untamed animals; a desert, a place deserted by its inhabitants), and *alifnahu* (they have become familiar, sociable, tame to him). The second hemistich reinforces the nature/culture dialectic: unlike the civilized man, Taʾabbaṭa Sharran does not hunt these wild herds of gazelle or oryx but, to the contrary, leaves them to graze unmolested.

Those that embody the fecundity and abundance of tribal society, the lords of the pregnant camels, he emaciates (verse 8). Again, the semantic dialectic is reinforced in the rhetorical antithesis between the bulk and plenitude of the camels about to bring forth young (*makhāḍ*) and the form IV verb *ashaffa* (to make thin, transparent; to emaciate). The tribe produces fat and plenty, the ṣuʿlūk dissolves it.

The concluding section of the poem (verses 9–13) is the ṣuʿlūk's proclamation of his inevitable violent death. However long he lives, he knows that in the end he will die in battle (9), be it an ambush or an unequal fight (10). The ṣuʿlūk is portrayed not as the tribal warrior in a match between equals, according to the tribal ideal of a manly battle, but as outnumbered by an enemy that will fight to the death. Verse 11 is notable for the *ṭibāq* between *mawt* (death) and *ḥayy* (tribe, but here suggesting life), for the two are really antithetical. The tribe fosters life; hence to reject it or to be rejected by it is tantamount to death. Here the poet states his heroic preference to die in combat, not in bed, but also, the poem suggests, to die at war with his kin, not at peace with them. The ṣuʿlūk's negative relation to society is reiterated in verse 12. He is nocturnal, preying on the youths of the tribe and frightening the gazelles—a traditional metaphor for women—as he has frightened off his prospective bride.

Death is portrayed in martial terms: *sināna al-mawti*, the spearhead of death (verse 9); *nizāla al-mawti*, the battle of death, mortal combat (10); and finally *maṣraʿi al-mawti*, the battleground or wrestling place of death (13). These images of violent death conclude the poem in a manner that is the symmetrical opposite of tribal fakhr. The prosperity, protection, and propagation of the social group are here replaced by danger and the ineluctability of death. The poet realizes all too well that the advice proffered his prospective bride in verse 1 was sound.

Returning to the paradigm of the rite of passage and the classical tripartite (nasīb-raḥīl-fakhr) qaṣīdah, this poem is generally in accord with our expectations for a ṣuʿlūk qaṣīdah. The first two verses approximate, in the prospective bride's rejection of the poet, the traditional nasīb motif of broken-off love and the ritual theme of separation. Only here there is no hint of a well-directed journey by she-camel to a higher goal; rather, the poet's imminent and ineluctable death, with which the poem concludes, is already predicted in the opening verse. The poem's progression is not linear but circular. Although verse 2 suggests the departure of the poet by night, it appears to be a habitual practice, not an individual instance. His end is perpetual liminality. Night, danger, hardship, exclusion, wild beasts—all the elements of the poetic raḥīl and ritual liminality—are found here; the only aggregation is the poet's assimilation into the society of wild animals, diametrically opposed to reincorporation into the tribe. The poem concludes not with the reaffirmation of the life-giving and life-sustaining institutions of the tribe but rather with an obsessive reiteration of its opposite: death.

Taʾabbaṭa Sharran and Oedipus

The *Kitāb al-Aghānī* presents several etiological anecdotes that profess to explain the origin of Thābit ibn Jābir ibn Sufyān's *laqab* (surname) Taʾabbaṭa Sharran ("he carried evil under his arm"). An analysis of these anecdotes reveals that Taʾabbaṭa Sharran's name is as indicative of his true nature as Oedipus's ("swollen foot") was to his. Furthermore, just as the Sphinx is Oedipus's monstrous other, so is the ghūl Taʾabbaṭa Sharran's. The legends of both Oedipus and Taʾabbaṭa Sharran can be interpreted as myths of perversion of the normal developmental process or deviation from the proper path of passage.

The *Kitāb al-Aghānī* akhbār, or biographical materials, on the early Arab poets have generally been either misused—that is, taken to be factual history in the modern sense—or else discarded because of their questionable historicity or obvious folkloric nature. But however unreliable they may be as a basis for factual literary biography, they nevertheless offer a rich vein of largely unmined mythic/folkloric gold. For however far back the association of the akhbār with the poetry goes and whatever its nature, this association, I would argue, is not arbitrary but semantic. That is, the anecdotes somehow reflect, reinforce, or complement the meaning of the poems or the archetypal image of the poet. Furthermore, the explication of the structure and symbolism of the many variant stories and anecdotes juxtaposed in the *Kitāb al-*

Aghānī narrative reveals that even apparently divergent or contradictory versions often yield what might be called the same mythic message.

The first of the etiological anecdotes in the *Kitāb al-Aghānī* concerning Thābit ibn Jābir's *laqab* runs thus: Ta'abbaṭa Sharran saw a ram in the desert; so he picked it up and carried it under his arm, and it urinated on him all the way home. As he approached his clan, the ram became so heavy that he could no longer bear it. So he flung it down, and lo and behold, it was the ghūl! When his clansmen asked what he had been carrying under his arm, he replied, "The ghūl." So they said, "*Ta'abbaṭa sharran* (he carried evil, an evil thing under his arm)," and this became his sobriquet.[9]

This story points to the Protean character of the ghūl, expressed in the phrase *tataghawwalu taghawwulan*. Ibn Manẓūr writes, "*Ghūl* is the singular of *ghīlān*, and is a species of *shayṭān* or *jinn*. The Arabs claim that it appears before people in the desert and then changes form, that is, takes on various appearances (*fa tataghawwalu taghawwulan ay tatalawwanu talawwunan fī ṣuwarin shattā*)."[10] The ghūl is thus an especially appropriate embodiment of the ambiguity and indeterminacy of the liminal phase; indeed, it is a liminal entity par excellence.

Another story has it that Ta'abbaṭa Sharran's mother said to him during the truffle (*kam'ah*) season, "Do you not see that the boys of the tribe are gathering truffles for their families and bringing them home?" He replied, "Give me your leather bag so I can gather some for you." So she gave it to him and he went out and caught a lot of vipers, the biggest he could find. When he returned home he brought them in the leather bag which he carried under his arm. He threw it before her and when she opened it, the snakes wriggled out into the tent. She jumped up and ran out. The women of the tribe asked her, "What did Thābit bring you?" She replied, "He brought me vipers in a leather bag." They asked, "How did he carry them?" She replied, "Under his arm (*ta'abbaṭahā*)." So they said, "He certainly brought an evil thing! (*la-qad ta'abbaṭa sharran*)" And the name stuck.[11]

Although the particulars of the two stories differ, on closer inspection they exhibit a structural and semantic similarity and ultimately explain Ta'abbaṭa Sharran's true nature, not merely his name. In both stories, he is to bring back to his family or clan something that is phallic (or

9. Al-Iṣbahānī, *Kitāb al-Aghānī* 24:8323.
10. *Lisān*, *gh-w-l*.
11. Al-Iṣbahānī, *Kitāb al-Aghānī* 24:8324, 8323. I have conflated two versions.

chthonic) and productive, what is expected of a son, that he provide for and propagate his line. But what Taʾabbaṭa Sharran brings back turns out to be destructive or deadly. In the first story he brings a ram, a male emblem, a sacrificial (and hence sacred) animal, something that should sire more flocks or provide sustenance. Instead, it urinates on him (giving waste rather than semen/seed) and finally reveals itself to be the ghūl, something evil and destructive. Likewise, Taʾabbaṭa Sharran will prove to be not a youth who will provide and propagate but a brigand and a murderer. This al-Tibrīzī confirms in his commentary to the *Mufaḍḍaliyyāt*: "The reasons given for his surname differ. They say that his mother gave it to him, for every time that she saw him looking wary and anxious, having girt his sword as though wrapped in a cloak, she said, 'He has put evil under his arm!' [*qad taʾabbaṭa sharran*]; that is, he bore a burden of enmity and blood vengeance."[12]

An oedipal aspect begins to emerge in the second story. The other boys of the tribe are gathering truffles, a tuber embodying chthonic fertility, self-productive and life-sustaining. Taʾabbaṭa Sharran, however, takes his mother's leather pouch, a female emblem, and brings her vipers, something phallic but deadly, producing venom, not semen. The episode is oedipal not so much in the elements that Freud emphasized—the male infant's desire to kill his father and sleep with his mother—but in the perversion or confusion of the natural order which leads to the extinction rather than the propagation of the line. Oedipus's abomination began with parricide but led too to his mother's/wife's suicide and the curse on his sons Polyneices and Eteocles that they should die at each other's hands, thereby extinguishing the Labdacid line of the royal house of Thebes.

The description of the ṣuʿlūk in *Do Not Marry Him* as bringing death and widowhood instead of life and motherhood is complemented in these stories by a similar message, now expressed on a mythic/symbolic level. He brings his mother or tribe that which is deadly; he brings them death. More elements of the same mythic configuration that informs Sophocles' Oedipus cycle and the many popular versions of that myth appear in Taʾabbaṭa Sharran's poems about the ghūl.[13]

The *Kitāb al-Aghānī* relates that Taʾabbaṭa Sharran met the ghūl one dark night in a place named Raḥā Biṭān in Hudhalī territory (that is,

12. Abū Zakariyyā Yaḥyā ibn ʿAlī al-Shaybānī al-Tibrīzī, *Sharḥ al-Mufaḍḍaliyyāt*, ed. ʿAlī Muḥammad al-Bijāwī, 3 vols. (Cairo: Dār Nahḍat Miṣr lil-Ṭabʿ wa al-Nashr, 1977), 1:5.

13. The fullest study of the motifs of the Oedipus legend is Delcourt's *Oedipe*.

enemy territory, since Ta'abbaṭa Sharran was one of the Banū Fahm and constantly at war with the Banū Hudhayl). The ghūl cut off his path and he struggled with her until he had killed her. Then he spent the night on top of her (*bāta ʿalayhā*—in Arabic, as in English, ambiguous) and in the morning carried her under his arm and brought her to his friends. Upon seeing this they remarked, "*la-qad ta'abbaṭa sharran*!" Of this he recited:

How I Met the Ghūl [12]

1. O who will bear my news to the young men of Fahm
   of what I met at Raḥā Biṭān?
2. Of how I met the ghūl swooping down
   on the desert bare and flat as a sheet.
3. I said to her, "We are both worn with exhaustion,
   brothers of travel, so leave my place to me!"
4. She sprang at me; then my hand raised
   against her a polished Yemeni blade.
5. Then undismayed I struck her: she fell flat
   prostrated on her two hands and on her throatlatch.
6. She said, "Strike again!" I replied to her, "Calm down,
   mind your place! For I am indeed stouthearted."
7. I lay upon her through the night
   that in the morning I might see what had come to me.
8. Behold! Two eyes set in a hideous head,
   like the head of a cat, split-tongued,
9. Legs like a deformed fetus, the back of a dog,
   clothes of haircloth or worn-out skins![14]

The setting of this poem is characteristically liminal. The ṣuʿlūk is abroad in enemy territory on a dark night. The place-name, Raḥā Biṭān, is itself suggestive of the struggle that ensues there, for *raḥan* (literally, hand mill) is used to mean the heat of battle but apparently has sexual overtones as well. *Biṭān* (literally, girth), from the root *b-ṭ-n,* intimates concealment and interiority, suggesting that this struggle is above all a spiritual one. The poem as a whole functions as a parody or perversion of the Arabic poetic convention of the amorous encounter. The setting is similar: the lover meets his mistress by night outside the tribal confines.

14. Al-Iṣbahānī, *Kitāb al-Aghānī* 24:8333–34.

Typical of love poetry too is the use of the dialogue format "She said . . . then I said . . ."(*qālat . . . fa qultu . . .*). The ṣuʿlūk's demand that the ghūl leave represents an inversion of the traditional protest of the mistress against the amorous advances of her poet-lover. The "symmetrical inversion" of the love poem replaces the passive and beautiful mistress with the aggressive (*tahwī* in verse 2 is to dart or swoop as a predatory bird on its prey) and hideous ghūl. The sexual act is replaced by a lethal lancing; the result of the night's "erotic" activity is a deformed and fetuslike corpse. If the erotic episodes of the classical qaṣīdah or of the *ghazal* represent normal—however illicit and liminal—passion between male and female, this inversion represents that passion in its deviant form. The ode and the love poem deal with what might be called adolescent antecedents to marriage, but the ṣuʿlūk poem presages no such wholesome developments. The hate and revulsion toward the female expressed in this poem recall the perverted attitude that Ta'abbaṭa Sharran displayed toward his mother in the etiological anecdote.

The poet's depiction of the ghūl waylaying the night traveler is typical of the function of mythical seductresses: they lure the traveler from his path and kill him. The lexicographers, too, are aware of this characteristic of the ghūl. Ibn Manẓūr writes: "The Arabs claim that the ghūl manifests itself to people in the desert; then it transforms itself, that is, changes into all sorts of different shapes; then it takes them away (*taghūluhum*), that is, leads them astray and kills them."[15] At this point, we should take account of the less mythic meanings of the root *gh-w-l*. In Form I, it means to destroy, seize or take away unexpectedly, unawares or from an unknown quarter. *Ghālathum tilka al-arḍu* means "that land caused them to perish." In Form II, *falātun tughawwilu* is a desert whose roads or paths are unclear, causing travelers to go astray. Of Form V Ibn Manẓūr writes, *taghawwalat al-arḍu bi fulānin ay ahlakathu wa ḍallalathu*, "the land made him perish and led him astray" (in the *ʿalla fa nahila* order).[16]

The relevance of the ghūl to the rite of passage paradigm should by this time be quite apparent, for as the etymology of the word reveals, the ghūl is finally nothing other than the personification of the terror of one lost and perishing in the desert. The traveler lost in the wayless desert by night imagines now this way, now that, is the right path; and

15. *Lisān*, *gh-w-l*.
16. Lane and *Lisān*, *gh-w-l*.

the more frantic and distraught he becomes, the more quickly the desert appears to shift and change, until, drawn far from the path, the traveler perishes of exhaustion, thirst, and exposure. This perpetual shifting and changing of the unmarked desert is thus personified in the constantly changing ghūl that waylays and kills the night traveler.

In terms of the passage paradigm, then, and the structure of the classical qaṣīdah, the liminal phase corresponds to the crossing of the desert, the raḥīl of the qaṣīdah, and the rite of passage requires the right passage or path through the liminal desert to the arrival at the tribe and reintegration into it. Therefore, to be lost, wandering, wayless, or waylaid in the desert—precisely that state which the encounter with the ghūl embodies—represents the failure to complete the ritual passage that the rite demands and the failure to complete the *riḥlah* (journey) that the qaṣīdah form demands.

The ghūl that Taʾabbaṭa Sharran describes perfectly embodies the primary characteristics of liminality and of *taṣaʿluk*. Verse 6 supports Vidal-Naquet's claim that the use of ruse and cunning is characteristic of liminal combat, and hence, that it takes one liminal entity to defeat another. For it was believed that if the ghūl were struck one lethal blow, it would die, but if it were then struck a second time, it would come back to life.[17] Here the ghūl tries to trick Taʾabbaṭa Sharran into reviving her with a second blow, but the liminal ṣuʿlūk sees through her ruse and stays his hand. She is, as depicted in verses 8 and 9, betwixt and between genera, ambiguous and indeterminate. Her withered fetuslike legs suggest abortion, distortion, and arrested development, that is, the inability to develop or walk properly and complete the required passage. She wears, like the ṣuʿlūk himself, the worn-out rags and skins that indicate a marginal relation to society and its accouterments.

The most obvious association that we have with such a creature is the Sphinx, which suggests once again that we compare the stories about Taʾabbaṭa Sharran with the myth or legend of Oedipus. The Sphinx, that is, "Strangler" or "Throttler," was a winged lioness or bitch with the head of a virgin which carried off young men and strangled them. Marie Delcourt remarks on the hybrid and erotic aspects of the Sphinx: "The mythic being that the Greeks ended up calling Sphinx was born in their minds of two superimposed species. One is a physiological reality, the suffocating nightmare [*cauchemar opprimant*];

17. Al-Ālūsī, *Bulūgh al-Arab* 3:341–42. Michael Sells has termed this the "toggle-switch effect" of the ghūl (verbal communication).

the other is of a religious nature, that is, the belief in the souls of the dead represented with wings. These two conceptions were able to produce a unique creation because they had quite a number of points in common, notably their erotic character."[18] Both the Sphinx and the ghūl are hybrids, horrible confusions of nature. In the Oedipus myth, this female abomination of the animal/mythical world is the reflection of the confusion and abomination in the social world, especially of the female element as represented by Iocasta, at once mother and wife of Oedipus. The Sphinx, born of the union of the serpent goddess Echidna with her own son, the dog Orthos, is the perfect embodiment of the oedipal abomination.[19] Furthermore, the social and genealogical confusion proves as barren and deadly as the natural freak. The parallel of the two female monstrosities, the Sphinx and Iocasta, goes yet further. Just as the Sphinx, the smotherer of young men, throws herself off a cliff to her death when Oedipus solves her riddle, so too Iocasta kills herself (by hanging, that is, strangulation) when Oedipus discovers his and her true identity. The two female abominations in turn reflect two male ones: Oedipus, the husband/son who blinds himself for having seen what is forbidden (his mother's nakedness) and ends up a blind seer at Colonus, and Teiresias, a strangely hermaphroditic figure who likewise was blinded for having seen what he should not (Athena bathing) and given, in return for his lost sight, the gift of prophecy. What all the interlocking and interreflecting abominations and confusions finally reveal is the core of the Oedipus myth, which can thus be understood in terms of an aborted or perverted (in the etymological sense of the word) rite of passage.

Just as Ta'abbaṭa Sharran slew the ghūl, so Oedipus killed the Sphinx. But Ta'abbaṭa Sharran did not then return to the right path, nor did Oedipus free Thebes of the plague. Indeed, Oedipus's and Thebes's problems were just beginning. The key to passage is the riddle of the Sphinx: What walks on four legs in the morning, two at noon and three in the evening? The answer that Oedipus gave, man, was true enough; but the problem was that it did not apply to Oedipus himself. For his father Laios, warned by the Delphic Oracle that his son would slay him, exposed the infant to die and pierced his ankle with a stake, leaving him permanently crippled. Paul Diel discusses the importance of the

18. Delcourt, *Oedipe*, 108–9.

19. See Hesiod, *Theogony*, lines 305–29, in *Hesiod, the Homeric Hymns, Fragments of the Epic Cycle, and Homerica,* trans. Hugh G. Evelyn-White, Loeb Classical Library, 57 (Cambridge: Harvard University Press, 1982), 100–103.

swollen foot and Oedipus's inability to walk in the gaits indicated by the Sphinx's riddle, but he takes the swollen foot to indicate excessive pride, one swollen with vanity. His remarks on the symbolism of the foot are most astute, however, and particularly appropriate to the discussion of certain ṣuʿlūk characteristics.

> [Laios] has the tendons of the infant's feet cut before exposing him. This theme has already been explained. Typhus cuts the tendons of Zeus' feet. A typical symbol, the foot represents the state and destiny of the soul. In this way, the myth compares man's gait with his psychic behaviour. The attributes wounded, ill-shod, washed (in the Christian myth) add particular qualities to the symbol "foot," and define the orientation of the translation. (Witness also Achilles' vulnerable foot, which symbolizes the vulnerability of his soul, his inclination towards anger, the cause of his downfall.) The cut tendons of the child Oedipus symbolize a diminishing of the soul's resources, a psychic deformation which is to characterize the hero throughout his life.[20]

In symbolic terms, then, the crippled son cannot perform the normal passage. Forced to rely on a crutch or cane, Oedipus walks on three legs too soon. Indeed, Diel suggests that the staff or club with which Oedipus slew his father was the stick he used to walk—that is, the father dies by the symbol of the crippling he inflicted on his son.[21] Jean-Pierre Vernant's structuralist approach to this same subject, which he terms "the lame tyrant," arrives at a formulation quite consonant with Diel's Jungian reading of Oedipus's lameness, "Among the Greeks themselves, the category of 'lameness' should not be limited strictly to defects of the foot, leg, or gait, but should symbolically extend to take in more than just the domain of spatial locomotion, and metaphorically express any form of behavior that may be seen as unbalanced, deviant, impeded, or blocked."[22] Vernant's reading of the riddle, too, is of interest here:

> Oedipus, *Oidipous*, guesses the riddle; he himself is the *dipous*, the man with two feet. But his error, or rather the effect of the curse that affects

20. Paul Diel, *Symbolism in Greek Mythology: Human Desire and Its Transformations* (Boulder, Colo.: Shambhala, 1980), 125.

21. Ibid., 129–30.

22. Jean-Pierre Vernant, "The Lame Tyrant: From Oedipus to Periander," in Vernant and Pierre Vidal-Naquet, *Myth and Tragedy in Ancient Greece*, trans. Janet Lloyd (New York: Zone Books, 1988), 209. My thanks to Gregory Nagy for this reference.

> his lame lineage, is that, through solving the riddle . . . he also returns to his place of origin, his father's throne and his mother's bed. Instead of rendering him like a man who walks straight in life, following on directly in his lineage, his success identifies him with the monster evoked by the Sphinx's words: the being who at one and the same time has two feet, three feet, and four feet, the man who, in his progression through life, does not respect the social and cosmic order of the generations but instead blurs and confuses them. Oedipus, the adult with two feet, is the same as his father, the old man who walks with a stick, the "three-footed" one whose place he has taken as the leader of Thebes and even in Iocasta's bed; he is also the same as his children who crawl on all fours and who are not only his sons but also his brothers.[23]

Lacking the proper gait, Oedipus is unable, following the paradigm of the present discussion, to follow the correct path of passage; the deviant *turns back* to his mother, and the Labdacid line, rather than being propagated by its heir, is extinguished.[24]

To return to Taʾabbaṭa Sharran and the ghūl, Oedipus's example makes it clear that killing the ghūl will not solve the problem. For in the end, the ghūl is no more than a reflection or doubling of the poet himself.[25] In *How I Met the Ghūl,* Taʾabbaṭa Sharran notes his affinity to the ghūl (verse 3), but the description of verse 9 is even more telling if we consider it a reflection of the ṣuʿlūk. For the legs of a deformed miscarried fetus are like Oedipus's swollen foot, unable to walk properly, to perform the prescribed passage—a perfect image for the passenger manqué.

Another example from the poetry of Taʾabbaṭa Sharran is remarkable in several respects. First of all, it draws the primarily folkloric ghūl fully into the poetic world of early Arabic literary motifs and conventions. Second, by a series of verbal identifications, the poet exploits the image of the ghūl to describe the ambiguous character of the female species and to expose his own double-edged and Protean character.

Sulaymā Says to Her Neighbor Women [13]

1. Sulaymā says to her neighbor women, "I see that Thābit
   is worn out and impotent."

23. Ibid., 215.
24. See Vernant's summary and analysis, ibid., 212–13 and passim.
25. Diel, *Symbolism in Greek Mythology*, 129–31. See also Hubert and Mauss on the theomachy and the battle of the hero and monster, *Sacrifice*, 85–88.

2. Woe upon her! She never found Thābit
   clumsy nor cowardly,
3. Nor shaky-kneed in the race
   in a sudden attack on an armed warrior band.
4. He outstrips coursers with his gallop
   and coats their necks with dust.
5. Many a moonless night, its cloak I donned
   as a nubile maid slips on her chemise,
6. Till morning followed behind its folds
   and tore to shreds its night-black cloak.
7. I spied a far-off fire and hoped to find it,
   then spent the night retreating and approaching.
8. The next morning I found that the ghūl was my neighboress;
   "O neighboress, you, how hideous!"
9. I tried to couple with her, but she writhed
   exposing a face that was horrible, ghūlish.
10. Then I said to her, "Look, so you may see!"
   She turned, and I turned more ghūlish than she!
11. Then there let fly the jinn daughter's skull
   a streaked blade that had worn out its sword belt.
12. When it is blunt, I whet it on a rock
   till it is sharp; I never show it to a sharpener.
13. Like a large lizard of the wasteland that has
   two suits of acacia leaves, not of spun thread.
14. To whomever asks where my neighboress has alighted
   say, "On the twisting sand dune lies her abode."
15. My aspiration always met with fixed resolve.
   How fit I was to match my words
   with deeds![26]

The power of this poem lies in the various levels of verbal and motival play by means of which the poet establishes a series of double identities. The poem opens with Sulaymā, the poet's neighbor (*jārah*) or mistress (*maḥbūbah*), in the role of the reproacher (*ʿādhilah*). Most often the *ʿādhilah* upbraids the poet for being a good-for-nothing profligate, but here the accusation is more biting: old age and impotence.[27] The poet first counters her by boasting of his prowess in battle. He takes the initiative in the attack and outruns fleet coursers on foot (the ṣaʿālīk, especially Taʾabbaṭa Sharran, al-Shanfarā, and ʿAmr ibn Barrāq, were renowned for their fleet-footedness).

26. Ibn Qutaybah, *Al-Shiʿr wa al-Shuʿarāʾ*, 176–77.
27. The accusation is not entirely groundless; see al-Iṣbahānī, *Kitāb al-Aghānī* 24:8329.

He turns next (verses 5–6) to the essential ṣuʿlūk undertaking, the many moonless nights of travel. He describes himself as the worn-out night traveler who searches the darkness for the flicker of a campfire where he might be accorded food and warmth or, as often happens in the traditional nasīb, a campfire that the poet imagines to be that of his departed mistress. But he is seduced instead by the elusive flicker of the ghūl's fire (7–8). This represents the diametrical opposite of the poetic and "aggregate" expectation of hospitality. We find in this poem too, as in *How I Met the Ghūl,* the symmetrical inversion of the traditional amorous/erotic motifs. The mythic monster takes the place of the usual nightly vision that comes to the poet, the *ṭayf al-khayāl*, the wandering phantom of the poet's beloved, the dreamlike vision that stirs his passion.[28] The ghūl is rather a Lileth-like creature or, as Marie Delcourt terms the Sphinx, a "suffocating nightmare." In verse 8, by referring to the ghūl as his female neighbor (*jārah*), the poet implicitly identifies her with Sulaymā in verse 1. Just as his mistress Sulaymā has turned on him, so too the ghūl, when he tries to couple with her, twists, revealing a hideous, Protean face (9). Thus the association between verses 1 and 8 initiates a series of identifications by which the poet reveals on the literary level the same insights into the relation between man and monster which modern critics have extracted from the Greek myth.

Taʾabbaṭa Sharran recognizes only too well the emotional fickleness of his mistress in the physical mutability of the ghūl. Rather than defeat and slay what Diel terms "the monstrous deformation of the psyche,"[29] as Perseus does Medusa, however, Taʾabbaṭa Sharran first appropriates the ghūl's characteristics, thus identifying them as preeminently his own. This he does by attributing to the ghūl's face the middle-voice form X verb *istaghwala* (be, become ghūlish, mutable) in verse 9, and then rhyming it in the following verse with a more powerful, elative description of himself as *aghwal*, more ghūlish still. With this he transforms himself from a lover trying to "lance" her erotically (*baḍaʿa* I, to lance, to cut, to slit, but also to have sexual intercourse with a woman)[30] in verse 9 to the killer who slices off the top of her head with his sword in verse 11. Taʾabbaṭa Sharran's changing response to the monster, from coupling to killing, reveals that the ghūl, like similar female

28. On this topic see Ḥasan al-Bannā ʿIzz al-Dīn, *Al-Ṭayf wa al-Khayāl fī al-Shiʿr al-ʿArabī al-Qadīm* (Cairo: Dār al-Nadīm, 1988).

29. Diel, *Symbolism in Greek Mythology*, 71.

30. Hava and Lane, *b-ḍ-ʿ*.

monsters in Greek mythology—the Chimera, the Sirens, Medusa, and the Sphinx—is at once both seductive and repulsive. Taʾabbaṭa Sharran and Oedipus are again comparable because they slay the monsters and at the same time appropriate their attributes. Both cases in this respect support Vidal-Naquet's statement that a liminal entity can be defeated only by liminal means (ruse or trickery). But whereas Oedipus remains blind to his monstrosities, the ṣuʿlūk revels in his subhuman or marginally human status "betwixt and between" man and animal.

In verse 12 the poet describes his sword, with its phallic association, which he identifies with himself. It is streaked or scratched, held on with a worn-out belt and sharpened on a rock, never taken to a sword polisher. It is as wild and uncivilized as the ṣuʿlūk. He appears in verse 13 to compare his sword to a desert lizard, the pattern of whose scales resembles the leaves of an acacia tree, a product of nature, not the fruit of the civilized loom. But the verse, as it stands,[31] is ambiguous: is Taʾabbaṭa Sharran describing his sword, the ghūl, or himself? His substitution of sword for phallus, of slaying for copulation, in the end only confirms Sulaymā's accusation. For the ṣuʿlūk proves incapable of propagation; he offers women not sex but death.

Verse 14, through a series of ambiguities or double meanings, binds the poem together. In its diction, down to the word, and in its *topoi*, it is a conventional nasīb line, referring to the poet's departed mistress. In a typical qaṣīdah the poet's companions ask him where his beloved has alighted now and he replies that her abode is in al-Liwā (a twisted sand dune), the archetypal locus of the abandoned abode of the beloved and trysting place of desert lovers. In the present context, however, the line becomes a double entendre, for *jārah* (neighboress) can refer equally to Sulaymā and the ghūl—and al-Liwā becomes the shifting sand dune where Taʾabbaṭa Sharran has left the monstrous corpse. Thus in this poem, the poet and his beloved and even the line of poetry itself, show themselves capable of undergoing ghūlish transformations.

The Ṣuʿlūk Qaṣīdah as a Rite of Passage Manqué

An analysis of the diction, imagery, and structure of the *qāfiyyah* (poem rhymed in the letter *qāf*) of Taʾabbaṭa Sharran, the opening

31. M. J. de Goeje notes that this line appears to be out of place. See Ibn Qutaybah, *Al-Shiʿr wa-al-Shuʿarāʾ*, 176 n. o.

of the *Mufaḍḍaliyyāt*, reveals how the poet, by selection and inversion, transforms the conventions of the classical qaṣīdah to express the ideal of perpetual marginality in what might be called the ṣuᶜlūk qaṣīdah.

Mufaḍḍaliyyah no. 1. O Ever-Returning Memory [14]

1. O ever-returning memory,[32]
   what longing and wakefulness you bring,
   And the passing phantom that, despite the terrors,
   comes by night,
2. Who makes his way by night,
   despite weariness and snakes, unshod,
   May my soul be your ransom, night wayfarer,
   on foot.
3. When a stingy love withholds
   its favor from me,
   And clutches with a frayed
   and worn-out rope,
4. I escape as once from Bajīlah I escaped,
   the night I ran
   On al-Rahṭ's smooth ground
   with all my might.
5. The night they yelled and sent
   their swift hounds after me,
   At al-ᶜAykatayn
   where Ibn Barrāq had run.
6. As if they had stirred up the ostrich,
   his wings' forefeathers scant,
   Or a fawn's mother, lean and swift from grazing
   where *shathth* and *ṭubbāq* grow.
7. None is swifter than I—
   not the forelocked horse[33]
   Or the eagle soaring by the mountain peak,
   beating broad wings.
8. Then I escaped, too fast for them
   to snatch my weapons,
   Racing like a madman,
   running all out.

32. Reading *ᶜīdu*.

33. I have followed al-Tibrīzī and Lyall in reading *laysa* as *lā* rather than *illā*. See al-Tibrīzī, *Sharḥ al-Mufaḍḍaliyyāt* 1:24–26; and Lyall, *The Mufaḍḍalīyāt* 2:3, 5.

9. I do not say, when friendship's
bond is broken,
"O woe is me!" from passion
and self-pity.
10. Rather would I weep,
were I to weep,
For one who knows how glory's won
and wins it,
11. The frontrunner in his band
to glory's goals,
Whose resoundng voice commands
his company,
12. Shank fleshless, arm sinewy,
setting forth at dusk
On a night of cloudbursts,
cold and dark,
13. Bearer of standards,
attender of councils,
Pronouncer of verdicts,
horizon-traverser.
14. This man is my goal and purpose
whose help I seek, when I seek help,
Long and full his hair, his voice
hoarse as the crow's,[34]
15. Hard-packed like a trampled sand dune,[35]
I called him
"Owner of two flocks, of lambs
and nooses to wean them!"
16. Many a peak, like a spearhead,
protruding, bared to the sun,
In the summer months
burning,
17. I raced to its summit before my companions,
though they were not lazy,
Until after sunrise
I mounted it—

34. The translation of this line and the next differs substantially from that in my earlier published version, where, among other things, I followed Shākir and Hārūn's reading, *idhā istaghathta* (when *you* ask help). See Abū al-ʿAbbās al-Mufaḍḍal al-Ḍabbī, *Al-Mufaḍḍaliyyāt*, ed. Aḥmad Muḥammad Shākir and ʿAbd al-Salām Muḥammad Hārūn, 5th ed. (Cairo: Dār al-Maʿārif, 1976), 29.

35. According to al-Tibrīzī this opening simile may mean either that the ṣuʿlūk's body is as hard as a trampled sand dune or that his hair is matted down like one. See al-Tibrīzī, *Sharḥ al-Mufaḍḍaliyyāt* 1:35–36. Al-Anbārī gives the former interpretation. See Lyall, *The Mufaḍḍalīyāt* 1:15–16.

18. Its ridge bare but for a lean-to,
    of which some sticks lie broken,
  While others
    still stand firm—
19. With worn-out sandals,
    protecting just the toes,
  To which I bound new soles
    by leathern thongs.
20. O who will save me from a censurer,
    treacherous, unrelenting,
  Who has scorched my skin
    with burning blame?[36]
21. Saying, "You have destroyed your wealth—
    Would you had been content to keep it!—
  A fine cloak, arms,
    and rich apparel."
22. O Censurer! some blame is too harsh:
    Are there goods that,
  Though I saved them,
    would remain?
23. I declare that if you
    cease not reproaching me,
  The tribe will ask the far horizons' folk
    about me,
24. My clan will ask the wise men
    where I've gone—
  But no man they meet will bear them
    news of Thābit.
25. Then plug the gap of need
    with goods you gather,
  Until you meet what every
    mortal meets.
26. Over me you'll gnash your teeth
    remorsefully,
  When some day you recall
    some of my qualities.[37]

With *Yā ʿīdu . . .* ! (O return!) as its opening phrase the poem establishes the fundamental difference between the ṣuʿlūk qaṣīdah and the

36. Following al-Tibrīzī's reading *yā* and the variant *nashib*. See al-Tibrīzī, *Sharḥ al-Mufaḍḍaliyyāt* 1:41–42.

37. I have relied on the recensions and commentaries of al-Anbārī in Lyall, *The Mufaḍḍalīyāt* 1:1–20; and al-Tibrīzī, *Sharḥ al-Mufaḍḍaliyyāt* 1:3–51; with further reference to Lyall's translation, commentary and notes in *The Mufaḍḍalīyāt* 2:1–8.

classical heroic one. The ṣuʿlūk in his poem, as in life, is reiterative and thus circular, whereas the full heroic poet exhibits a linear progression from one part of the qaṣīdah to the next. Thus the use of *ʿāda/yaʿūdu*, a verb that refers to cyclical repetition and return (compare the use of *ʿīd* for holidays that recur annually), for anything done repeatedly or habitually, is a succinct expression of the perpetually liminal existence of the ṣuʿlūk. More precisely in this poem, as al-Anbārī notes, *ʿīd* refers to recurrent malady or sorrow.[38] The temporary passion and sleeplessness that afflict the tribal poet have become in this poem an ever-recurring state. What at first appears to the reader to be the phantom of the beloved (*ṭayf al-khayāl*), coming to her lover *despite* (*ʿalā*) the terrors of the night, is soon transformed. For by the time we read verse 2 it is clear that the *ṭayf* is a ṣuʿlūk treading *upon* (*ʿalā*) the terrors of the night.[39] The *faʿʿāl*-form (intensive, reiterative) of *ṭarrāq* (coming at night) once more indicates habituality, that this word too embodies the permanent or repeated liminality that is the essence of *taṣaʿluk*. The normal liminal passenger, *ṭāriq*, is thus morphologically transformed into the perpetual night wanderer, *ṭarrāq*, who is destined to repeat rather than complete the liminal stage of the rite of passage.

In verse 2 the meaning of verse 1 is clarified and intensified. Through the use of both the imperfect and that active participle (*yasrī, sārin*) night travel is reiterated. The terrors of verse 1 are specified—snakes and vipers (*ayn* means both weariness and viper). To make the danger all the more immanent or imminent, the ṣuʿlūk is barefoot (*muḥtafin*) and, as *ʿalā sāqī* suggests, without a mount, on "shank's mare." By this time we should have suspected that the physical descriptions of the ṣuʿlūk have more to do with ritual concepts of purity and impurity than they do with realism. To be unshod and unshorn is to be in a state of ritual consecration, that is, to have left society and its constraints behind but also to be exposed, to be without the protection of society. The second verse ends with the poet identifying or equating himself with this *ṭayf al-ṣuʿlūk*, "May my soul be your ransom."

Thus, in the first two verses, the poem has committed itself to *al-taṣaʿluk* in its diction and imagery and has precluded the poetic possibility of completing the pattern of passage with its linear separation-liminality-reincorporation progression. The traditional nasīb sleep-

38. Lyall, *The Mufaḍḍalīyāt* 1:2.

39. For a discussion of this poem in light of the motif of the *ṭayf al-khayāl* (nightly phantom) see ʿIzz al-Dīn, *Al-Ṭayf wa al-Khayāl*, 134–41.

lessness and passion of the lover are introduced only to have what appears to be the phantom of the mistress give way to a more persistent night visitor—the ṣuʿlūk. One senses in this transformation the ghūlishness of Taʾabbaṭa Sharran's other night encounter.

Verse 3 consists of the typical classical qaṣīdah image of transition from the nasīb to the raḥīl. It is only in verse 4 that we once again find a radical variation on the heroic departure. That the ṣuʿlūk normally has no mount is of great import for the rite of passage paradigm, for in the traditional qaṣīdah, the poet departs on a she-camel, which is thus, in a symbolic sense, responsible for the successful completion of the raḥīl or passage. If the she-camel—the totemic, sacred, or sacrificial animal and hence symbol of the tribe or polity—is the vehicle of the raḥīl, it follows that the passenger mounted on the she-camel will complete the passage, whereas the pedestrian passenger will fail. To be without this symbol of the tribal polity is to be without hope of reincorporation, to be without tribal support and direction. Thus, the she-camel, the vehicle of passage, is lacking in ṣuʿlūk poetry, as is the horse, the mount of the tribal hunter and of the warrior who defends the tribe and the symbol of aggregate manhood.[40]

Verses 4–8 describe the poet's flight from broken-off love or friendship not as the purposeful departure of the tribal qaṣīdah but as though he were fleeing for his life. The significance of Taʾabbaṭa Sharran's flight by night from Bajīlah becomes clear when we realize that it consists precisely of a "symmetrical inversion" of the heroic *ghazwah*, or raid by day.[41] Taʾabbaṭa Sharran had to flee in the first place because the raid that he planned had failed, and he, or one of his companions, was taken captive. Thus the relation of the ṣuʿlūk to the tribal hero is analogous to their respective exploits. The ṣuʿlūk is both a failed hero and a perverted one; the ṣuʿlūk's exploit is both a failed *ghazwah* and an inverted one.

The *Kitāb al-Aghānī* offers three versions of Taʾabbaṭa Sharran's escape from the Banū Bajīlah, effected in all of them by a ruse. A rather lengthy digression from the poem itself to analyze one of these will elucidate the peculiar ethos of the ṣuʿlūk. Al-Ashjaʿī's version is the fullest and most illuminating:

40. This argument applies as well, mutatis mutandis, to the madīḥ (panegyric) qaṣīdah.

41. I.e., precisely the relationship that Vidal-Naquet has established between the exploits of the hoplite phalanx, on the one hand, and those of the *ephebeia* or *krypteia*, on the other. His formulation of the "ephebe manqué" and his remarks concerning the appropriateness of ruse and trickery to ephebe exploits are especially to be noted here.

Taʾabbaṭa Sharran, that is, Thābit ibn al-ʿAmaythal al-Fahmī, made a raid, along with Ibn Barrāq al-Fahmī, against Bajīlah, and drove off some of their livestock. But Bajīlah were on their guard for them; so the two of them fled into the mountains of al-Sarāh and mounted the roughlands. Bajīlah then left their trail, taking a shortcut through the lowlands, and reached al-Waht, a spring belonging to ʿAmr ibn al-ʿĀṣ in al-Ṭāʾif, before them, and lay in ambush for them in the reeds of the spring. The two, who were by this time very thirsty, then arrived at the spring. When they reached it, Taʾabbaṭa Sharran said to Ibn Barrāq, "Drink only a little, for tonight will be a hunting night." "How do you know?" he asked. "By Him because of whose bad omen I run,"[42] he replied, "I hear men's hearts beating beneath my feet!"—for he was one of the sharpest-eared Arabs and one of the slyest. "That is your own heart beating," said Ibn Barrāq. Taʾabbaṭa Sharran replied, "By God, [my heart] did not beat at all; it is not one to beat [from fear]." He struck it with his fist, put his ear to the ground to listen and said, "By Him by whose ill omen I run, I do hear the beating of men's hearts!" "Then I will go before you," said Ibn Barrāq and he went down, knelt and drank. Now Bajīlah considered [Ibn Barrāq] the most furious of fighting men; so they let him go. They were [hiding] in the darkness when Thābit descended. When he had reached the middle of the spring, they leapt upon him and seized him and took him handcuffed from the spring. Ibn Barrāq was close by, but they did not even try to catch him, for they knew what a swift runner he was. So Thābit said to them, "He is the most boastful of men about his running and the most vain about it. I will say to him, 'Surrender with me!' and his vanity will force him to run in front of you. He has three gaits: the first is like the wind blowing; the second is like a fleet mare; but in the third, he stumbles and falls. So, when you see him do that, seize him! For I would like to see him fall into your hands as I have, since he disobeyed me." "Do it!" they said. So Taʾabbaṭa Sharran called out to [Ibn Barrāq], "You are my brother through thick and thin and the men [of Bajīlah] have promised that they will be generous to us both. So give yourself up and comfort me with your company in hardship as you were my brother in ease!" When Ibn Barrāq [heard this], he laughed, for he knew that Taʾabbaṭa Sharran had tricked them. Then he said, "Take it easy, Thābit. Would someone who could run like this give himself up?" Then he ran. He ran his first gait like the wind, as [Taʾabbaṭa Sharran] had described to them; and the second like a fleet mare; then with the third he began to trip and stumble and fall on his face. Then Thābit cried, "Seize him!" and they all ran after him. When they

42. I take *ṭayr* to mean what it does in the expression *ṭayru Allāhi wa lā ṭayruka,* God's ill omen not yours. *Ṭayr* here thus means ill omen, an indication of the inherent inauspiciousness of the ṣuʿlūk. See Lane, *ṭ-y-r*.

were thus distracted, Ta'abbaṭa Sharran fled in his handcuffs. Ibn Barrāq met up with him, cut his handcuffs, and together they escaped.[43]

This anecdote is a veritable exposition of the peculiar characteristics of the ṣuᶜlūk which define him as a liminal entity and distinguish him from the tribal hero. First, although the story begins with a raid against the Banū Bajīlah, no sooner do the *ṣuᶜlūkān* (the two brigand-poets) attempt to drive off the cattle than we find them in the role of the hunted, the prey, with the Banū Bajīlah lying in ambush for them. "Drink only a little," Ta'abbaṭa Sharran tells his companion, "for to-night will be a hunting night!" The first phrase is an expression of the paucity, even stinginess that characterizes liminal ṣuᶜlūk existence, as opposed to the abundance and magnanimity that are among the primary attributes of tribal life. In the second phrase Ta'abbaṭa Sharran foresees their fate—to be prey by night, not hunters during the day. Quite clearly, the structuralist nature/culture dialectic can be applied here, and is in fact the basis of the symmetrical opposition of the ṣuᶜlūk and the tribal hero. Again, whereas the tribe depends upon cultural appurtenances, weapons and mounts, the tribal organization itself and its institutions, the ṣuᶜlūk is characterized, as compared to the faint-hearted tribesmen, by his reliance upon his animal attributes, his sharp sense of hearing and his cunning, which al-Ashjaᶜī expresses with admirable succinctness: *Kāna min asmaᶜi al-ᶜArabi wa akyadihim* (He was one of the sharpest-eared Arabs and one of the slyest). The nature/culture dialectic as expressed in the ṣuᶜlūk's reliance on inhumanly keen senses, animal attributes, rather than the appurtenances of tribal culture thus explains the significance of the many references, both poetic and anecdotal, to the fleet-footedness, keen-sightedness and sharp hearing of the ṣaᶜālīk.[44] The relation of the Banū Bajīlah to Ta'abbaṭa Sharran is not that of man to man; rather, they take the ṣuᶜlūk as carnivorous beasts take their prey, as he goes to water. Ta'abbaṭa Sharran's fear and foresight at the water hole amount to nothing more than animal instinct.

His deliverance from the Banū Bajīlah is not through the traditional tribal institution of ransom but by ruse, accomplished at night. He makes what appears to the Banū Bajīlah a legitimate deal: they will go

43. Al-Iṣbahānī, *Kitāb al-Aghānī* 24:8330–33. A translation of Abū ᶜAmr al-Shaybānī's version of this anecdote which appears in the commentaries of al-Tibrīzī and al-Anbārī is given by Lyall. See al-Tibrīzī, *Sharḥ al-Mufaḍḍaliyyāt* 1:16–18; Lyall, *The Mufaḍḍalīyāt* 1:6–7, 2:2.

44. Al-Iṣbahānī, *Kitāb al-Aghānī* 24:8334, 8352, 8376.

easy on him if he can deliver Ibn Barrāq into their hands. That he would want revenge for Ibn Barrāq's disobedience is, in their tribal perception, valid and justified. Similarly, Taʾabbaṭa Sharran's appeal to Ibn Barrāq's loyalty as a friend is perceived by the Banū Bajīlah as a clever ruse against Ibn Barrāq. But the whole double cross is founded upon a marvelous ambiguity. The ruse succeeds precisely because of the "symmetrical opposition" of the tribal ethos and the liminal one. The Banū Bajīlah fall for it because Taʾabbaṭa Sharran frames his plea in terms of the tribal values of loyalty, the obligation never to abandon a clansman on the field of battle. But by the same token, Ibn Barrāq recognizes that a ṣuʿlūk would never make so patently "tribal" a claim. It serves rather as a code word between the two. It is the bivalency of Taʾabbaṭa Sharran's plea to Ibn Barrāq that makes the ruse succeed and serves as the semantic crux of the anecdote: the dialectal opposition between liminal and tribal values. It should be noted too that, although effected here through verbal means, this ruse is basically a natural, animal ruse—the mother bird that feigns a broken wing to lure predators away from her nestlings. In fact, in a variant version, Taʾabbaṭa Sharran tells the Banū Bajīlah that Ibn Barrāq has injured his foot.[45]

The elements of ruse or trickery, nighttime, fleeing on foot, and the failure to obtain sustenance—the goal of the cattle raid in the first place—are all in diametrical opposition to the characteristics of the heroic *ghazwah*, a straightforward attack during daylight, mounted and successful. The ṣuʿlūk exploit is a strictly liminal one, marked by those characteristics of deviation, deviousness, and darkness that are appropriate to the marginal state. Other exploits of Taʾabbaṭa Sharran—the story of his escape through honey; his flight from a raid in which two of his companions were killed; and his flight from a raid in which his wife's nephew, who could not run fast enough, was killed—confirm these initial findings.[46]

The story of Taʾabbaṭa Sharran's last exploit demonstrates once again how the ṣuʿlūk both lived and died, not according to the heroic virtues of the aggregate tribal warrior but according to the rule of deviation that governs the liminal state—ruse, stratagem, the veil of darkness, and the inversion of the most sacred rules of tribal society, in this case, the prohibition against killing in the sacred month and the law of hospitality:

45. Ibid., 24:8330–31.
46. Ibid., 24:8341, 8337, 8334; and al-Marzūqī, *Ḥamāsah* 1:74–84.

Ta'abbaṭa Sharran's last victim was Sāʿidah ibn Sufyān. He spent the last night of the sacred month standing guard against Ta'abbaṭa Sharran and his companions, who, for their part, hoped to catch him off guard. When this failed, they went to him, and deceiving him into believing that they would not kill during the sacred month, gave him assurances and complained of hunger, asking for his hospitality. When he was assured of their sincerity, they leapt upon him and slew him and one of his young sons. Then Ta'abbaṭa Sharran passed by another of Sāʿidah ibn Sufyān's sons, named Sufyān ibn Sāʿidah, whom his father had ordered to keep watch over the herds. Ta'abbaṭa Sharran approached him, guarding himself with his shield. The youth, who was armed with only bow and arrow, was afraid that Ta'abbaṭa Sharran would attack him with his sword, so he put his arrow to his bow, but threw a stone at Ta'abbaṭa Sharran's shield, instead of shooting. He in turn, thinking the youth had shot his arrow, lowered his shield, whereupon the youth did shoot, and slew him.[47]

The inversion of names and roles from the first half of the story to the second points up an important aspect of the liminal/reaggregate dialectic. The tribal ethos of the father proves fatal when dealing with a ṣuʿlūk. Only the son, a youth and thus appropriately and temporarily liminal, can kill the ṣuʿlūk, and then only by precisely those marginal means that Ta'abbaṭa Sharran had employed against his father: the youth slays the ṣuʿlūk at night, by a ruse, and during the sacred month. The weapon employed, the bow and arrow, is as characteristically liminal among the Arabs as Vidal-Naquet has demonstrated it to be among the Greeks. For the aggregate tribal warrior, among both Greeks and Arabs, the manly weapons are those used in direct combat—the lance and sword—not those, like the bow and arrow, or spear, used from hiding or from a distance.[48] The distinction should be made here between the ṣuʿlūk—the permanently liminal entity, the passenger manqué—and the youth who avenges his father. The ruse of the latter is appropriate liminal behavior for the youth in this stage. That he has performed the "aggregate" duty of avenging his father indicates his approach to manhood and reincorporation, at which stage such a ruse would be inappropriate. Just as, with reference to Vidal-Naquet's work, the ṣuʿlūk might be compared to the permanently liminal Philoctetes—wild, exposed, civically dead—so too might the ṣuʿlūk's youthful slayer

47. Al-Iṣbahānī, *Kitāb al-Aghānī* 24:8383.
48. See Vidal-Naquet, "Sophocles' *Philoctetes*," 180–81.

be compared to the youthful Neoptolemus who tricks Philoctetes out of his bow.

Returning at last to the poem itself, we find the ṣuʿlūk portrayed as pursued and hunted, not the pursuing hunter, as emphasized in verse 5 not only by the Banū Bajīlah's pursuit of Taʾabbaṭa Sharran but in the *ṭibāq* between the two place-names: *al-ʿAykatān* (the two proud gaits) from *ʿāka/yaʿīku*, to walk with a proud gait as a warrior walks among his tribe, and *maʿdā Ibn Barrāq*, the running place of the ṣuʿlūk.

In verse 6 the poet compares himself to the swiftest of the hunter's prey: the ostrich, full grown and without heavy plumage to hinder it,[49] and the doe with fawn, thus doubly vulnerable, that grazes on *shathth* and *ṭubbāq*, two plants that, according to al-Tibrīzī, render the grazer slender and muscular.[50] "Nothing is swifter than I," the poet declares in verse 7, "not even" the horse, the mount for the tribal hunt or *ghazwah*, and the bird of prey, the eagle. Thus there is an antithesis between passive and aggressive quadrupeds, the doe and the hunting horse, and between passive and aggressive birds, the ostrich and the eagle. The ṣuʿlūk here identifies himself with the prey and boasts of his ability to outrun the predators. The flight scene in the poem ends with the ṣuʿlūk running blindly, crazed, like a madman. Once again, we should note that the insane and mindless running of the ṣuʿlūk is diametrically opposed to the purposeful and teleological *riḥlah* of the tribal hero, however fraught with difficulty and danger that desert journey may be.

In verse 9, the poet recapitulates, reverting to the diction of the nasīb and separation—the yearning and the pity of the spurned lover—only to reject it explicitly. The ṣuʿlūk does not weep from self-pity but cries for help from one like himself. The fakhr of verses 12–14 of the model ṣuʿlūk (as opposed to the lords of the tribe), although presented in the third person, would seem to be a self-portrait couched in terms of an idealized other. One might also want to consider it a description of al-Shanfarā, a counterpart to the latter's description of Taʾabbaṭa Sharran as *ummu ʿiyālin* (mater familias) of his band of ṣaʿālīk in *Mufaḍḍaliyyah no. 20,* which is discussed later.[51] The two descriptions are, in any case, companion pieces.

The vehemence of the ṣuʿlūk, his relentless striving, is reinforced

49. Lyall, *The Mufaḍḍalīyāt* 2:5.

50. Al-Tibrīzī, *Sharḥ al-Mufaḍḍaliyyāt* 1:22.

51. Lyall, too, has noted the relationship between these two poems in *The Mufaḍḍalīyāt* 2:5.

in this section of the poem by the dominance of the *faᶜᶜāl*-form noun of hyperbole (*ism al-mubālaghah*) which indicates action that is intensive, reiterative, or habitual.[52] Thus *sabbāq* (winner, front-runner) from *sabaqa* (to precede, outstrip) concludes verse 10 and is repeated for further emphasis at the beginning of verse 11. The series of *faᶜᶜāl*-forms is thus initiated by reiterating the determination and fleet-footedness of the ṣuᶜlūk. Even the night through which he travels is not merely dark, but *ghassāq*, pitch-black or bitter cold. The unrelenting tension of the ṣuᶜlūk in his perpetually marginal state is expressed not only in the morphology of this passage (the repeated use of the *faᶜᶜāl*-form) but also in the physiognomy of the ṣuᶜlūk: his shanks are bare and thin, his arm veins tense, distended (12). Once more, this is the description not of a narrative incident but of a permanent state, as the word *midlāj* (setting forth at nightfall) indicates. With this word, the *ism al-ālah* (noun of tool) of *adlaja* IV (to go forth at night) used metaphorically as an intensive or reiterative adjective,[53] the poet gives us a virtual synonym of ṣuᶜlūk, one who habitually and invariably goes forth at night. The progressive intensification of this passage culminates in the *tarṣīᶜ* (internal rhyme) of verse 13 in a formulaic list of epithets, all of the *faᶜᶜāl*-form: *ḥammāl* (bearing); *shahhād* (witnessing, attending); *qawwāl* (speaking); and finally the archetypal definition of the ṣuᶜlūk as *jawwābi āfāqī* (traveling or rambling to the horizons).

The epithets of verse 14, too, are tellingly ṣuᶜlūk. For *ḍāfī al-ra'si* (having abundant or long hair) refers in this context to the liminal quality to which the epithet *ashᶜath* (unkempt) is usually applied—that is, the votive obligation of the warrior, avenger, or sacrificer not to comb, cut, or anoint his head until he has fulfilled his vow or completed his sacrifice.[54] This is the ritual context behind al-Tibrīzī's remark that "[the poet] makes him long-haired because he is so often engaged in raiding that he does not tie back or groom his hair."[55] *Naghghāq* (cawing like a crow) likewise contributes to the repertoire of animal-like ṣuᶜlūk

52. William Wright, *A Grammar of the Arabic Language*, 2 vols., 3d ed. (Cambridge: Cambridge University Press, 1955), 1:137.

53. Ibid., 1:138.

54. Here Lyall's footnote, rather than his initial remarks, seems to contain the correct interpretation: "Another suggestion that has been made to explain the abundance of hair of the man described is that he was perpetually engaged in the prosecution of blood-feuds: a person seeking vengeance for blood shed bound himself by a vow not to cut or dress his hair until he attained his end. So ash-Shanfarā describes himself in the *Lāmīyah*, vv. 63–4." Lyall, *The Mufaḍḍalīyāt* 2:5.

55. Al-Tibrīzī, *Sharḥ al-Mufaḍḍaliyyāt* 1:34.

epithetic qualities. The simile that opens verse 15 *ka al-ḥiqfi damlakahu al-nāmūna* (literally, like the sand dune that climbers trample), whether we take it as a description of the hardened body of the ṣuʿlūk or of his matted hair, is in the same vein. The best reading of "owner of two flocks" would seem to be as an epithet referring to livestock that the ṣuʿlūk has plundered.[56]

The ascent to the mountain peak in verses 16–19 is surely an expression of Mary Douglas's statement: "To enter the margins is to be exposed to power that is enough to kill them or make their manhood."[57] The elements of danger, death, sacrifice, and epiphany are all explicitly or implicitly present. They are first of all implicit in the Semitic connotations of the mountaintop. It is the place of sacrifice[58] (Abraham and Isaac), and the locus of epiphany (Moses), where the natural and the supernatural converge and commune. Thus, it is precisely the farthest margin, the place of utmost danger. The poet's diction speaks first on a literal geographical level and at the same time alludes to the mythic and ritual associations of the mountaintop.

The peak is first described as a spearpoint, recalling the *sināna al-mawti* (spearpoint of death) of *Do Not Marry Him* (verse 11), that is, of lethal sharpness. *Bārizah* describes the peak as protruding, prominent, but likewise hints at epiphany, for *baraza* also means to appear or become apparent after concealment.[59] Similarly *ḍaḥyānah* means exposed to the sun, from *ḍuḥan* (bright sun of the late forenoon). But the root *ḍ-ḥ-y* also has sacrificial connotations: *yawm al-aḍḥā* is the Islamic day of sacrifice (the tenth day of Dhū al-Ḥijjah) and *uḍḥiyyah* is the term for the victim sacrificed on that day. The vehement burning of the sun on this peak the poet terms *miḥrāq*, again, as in verse 12, employing the *ism al-ālah* form to convey intensity. The root *ḥ-r-q* too has ritual associations, that of the burnt offering or holocaust, *muḥraqah*, and

56. See Lyall, *The Mufaḍḍalīyāt* 2:5. The meaning of the verse is not, however, as obvious as Lyall suggests.

57. Douglas, *Purity and Danger,* 97.

58. Robertson Smith gives evidence from the Hebrews and the Arabs. He remarks: "If the explanation of the origin of burnt-offering given above is correct, it is obvious that the barren and unfrequented hill-top above a town would be one of the most natural places to choose for burning the holocaust. . . . That the high places, or hill sanctuaries, of the Semites were primarily places of burnt sacrifice cannot be proved by direct evidence, but may, I think, be made probable. . . . In Arabia we read of only one sanctuary that had a 'place of burning,' and this is the hill of Cozah at Mozdalifa. Among the Hebrews the sacrifice of Isaac takes place on a mountain (Gen. xxii 2), and so does the burnt-sacrifice of Gideon." Robertson Smith, *Religion of the Semites*, 489–90.

59. Lane, *b-r-z*.

martyr by fire, *ḥarīq*. The line is thus replete with subliminal images of prophecy, martyrdom, and sacrifice, all of which take as their locus the margins of the social world, the boundary between the natural and the supernatural, between life and death.

It is to this pinnacle of dread and glory that the ṣuʿlūk precedes his companions. The use of *namaytu* (I mounted, ascended) hearkens back to verse 15, where the same verb is used to describe the tramplers of the sand dune. The ṣuʿlūk is here associated not with what is trampled, hardened, or matted (by the ill treatment of his tribe?) but with the phallic, spearlike protrusion of the mountain peak that he now mounts. He is now the one who ascends, not the one who is trampled. Likewise, the description of the boards or branches that form the lean-to in verse 18 is a metaphor for those who strive for glory: some lie fallen, while others remain upright (for *hazīm* also means routed, put to flight, and *qāʾim* also means standing firm in battle).

Verse 19 concludes the scene of ascent to the peak of danger and the locus of sacrifice and epiphany with the description of the ṣuʿlūk's worn-out and resoled shoes. The image has a double significance. First, it takes the place in the ṣuʿlūk qaṣīdah of the description of the poet's she-camel in the classical qaṣīdah. The tribal poet concludes his *riḥlah* mounted on a she-camel, and signals his reaggregation by exchanging her for the horse and taking part in the hunt, that is, providing for the tribe. The ṣuʿlūk, however, has rejected both of these tribal vehicles; he has ascended to the locus of danger and death, but for him there is no descent into a green valley, no heroic hunt, no commensal feast. The ṣuʿlūk's journey lacks any revitalizing, reaggregating conclusion. The resoling of the shoes is then the second sign. It signals repetition, the perpetual and nondirectional *riḥlah* of the ṣuʿlūk. His journey wears out the soles of his shoes, only for him to resole them and repeat the *riḥlah*.

The final section of the poem, verses 20–26, occurs where, in the structure of the classical qaṣīdah, we would expect to find the tribal fakhr or, in the rite of passage paradigm, the reaggregation or reincorporation of the passenger into the tribe. What we find instead is the symmetrical inversion of this, the mutual rejection and reproach of the ṣuʿlūk and his clan.

Unlike the praiseworthy tribal poet, the ṣuʿlūk portrays himself as the object of constant blame and abuse, the vehemence of which is again morphologically expressed through the intensive *faʿʿālah*-form: *ʿadhdhālah* (censurer) and *khadhdhālah* (treacherous, forsaking). The blame of the reproacher, the spokesman for the tribal order, scorches Ta'abbaṭa Sharran's flesh as harshly as the summer sun; *miḥrāq* (burning), the rhyme word of verse 16 is recalled in verse 20 by the rhyme word *taḥrāq*, the verbal noun of the intensive form II, to scorch. The censurer's reprimand (21) is precisely that the ṣuʿlūk has negated the basic principle of tribal life. Whereas the lords of the pregnant camels of *Do Not Marry Him* embody the tribal ideal, prosperity and propagation, the ṣuʿlūk has destroyed wealth and livestock and has rejected the paramount symbols of culture, weapons and clothing.

The poem is sealed with the poet's rebuttal and threat. Whereas the tribal poet concludes the classical qaṣīdah with the celebration of the perpetuation of life through tribal institutions, the ṣuʿlūk poem ends with an expression of the futility of accumulating herds and goods and of the inevitability of death (verses 22, 25). He threatens now that if his clansmen persist in their reproach of him he will depart altogether, beyond the horizons and the boundaries of their known world (23, 24). The direction of his life is thus finally centrifugal. It proceeds in an ever-expanding orbit that ultimately takes him entirely beyond the sphere of tribal life. He will survive only in the remorse and regret that his clansmen feel when they recall his obdurate fortitude.

With remarkable consistency the ṣuʿlūk thus appears, in both the akhbār concerning him and the poetry attributed to him, to be the perfect model of the passenger manqué. He is both deviant and devious, and just as he deviates from the tribal social norm, so too does his poetry from the full classical qaṣīdah form.

CHAPTER 4

Archetype and Attribution: Al-Shanfarā and the *Lāmiyyat al-ᶜArab*

The premier position of the *Lāmiyyat al-ᶜArab* among the poetry of *al-shuᶜarāʾ al-ṣaᶜālīk* (the brigand-poets) of the Jāhiliyyah is undeniable. Among scholars and philologists, both Arab and Orientalist, it has remained over the centuries the object of the most minute philological commentaries. Its Arab commentators number more than twenty, among them the foremost names in classical Arabic literary scholarship: al-Mubarrad (d. 285/898), the doyen of the Basran school, whose commentary is said actually to have been taken from his Kufan archrival, Thaᶜlab (d. 291/904); the renowned poetic commentarist al-Tibrīzī (d. 502/1109); and the famed grammarian and Qurʾānic commentator al-Zamakhsharī (d. 538/1143).[1] Its European popularity—a phenomenon that Régis Blachère attributes to its appeal to the sensibilities of nineteenth-century Romanticism—dates to Sylvestre de Sacy's study and translation of 1826, followed by Friedrich Rückert's German translation in his *Ḥamāsah* of 1846.[2] In philological studies, of note are the more than twenty pages of his *Beiträge* that Theodor Nöldeke devotes to the lexical aspects of this poem and Georg Jacob's extensive two-part *Schanfarà-Studien*.[3]

1. Sezgin, *Poesie*, 133–37.

2. Régis Blachère, *Histoire de la littérature arabe des origines à la fin du XV*ᵉ siècle de J.-C., 3 vols. (Paris: Maisonneuve, 1952, 1964, 1966), 2:285; Sylvestre de Sacy, *Chrestomathie arabe*, 3 vols. (Paris: Imprimerie royale, 1826), 2:337–403; Friedrich Rückert, *Hamasa; oder, Die ältesten arabischen Volkslieder, gesammelt von Abu Temmâm*, 2 vols. (Stuttgart: S. G. Liesching, 1846), 2:181–85.

3. Theodor Nöldeke, *Beiträge zur Kenntnis der Poesie der alten Araber* (Hildesheim: Georg Olms, 1967) [photorepr. of Hanover, 1864], 200–222; Georg Jacob, *Schanfarà-Studien*, parts

Despite its prominence, the *Lāmiyyah* has been singled out, in a tradition going back to the philologist Ibn Durayd (d. 321/933), as an Umayyad forgery composed by the notorious Basran poet-transmitter Khalaf al-Aḥmar (d. 180/796). The source of this information is al-Qālī's *Al-Amālī* (and al-Suyūṭī's *Al-Muzhir*): "Abū ʿAlī said: Abū Muhriz [Khalaf al-Aḥmar] was the most knowledgeable of men concerning poetry and language, and the most poetic of men in the styles [*madhāhib*] of the Arabs. Abū Bakr ibn Durayd told me that the qaṣīdah attributed to al-Shanfarā that begins: '*aqīmū*. . . .' is his. It is one of the foremost poems in beauty, purity of language, and length, for he was the ablest of men in verse."[4] Yūsuf Khulayyif, whose study of the sources in this matter is most exhaustive, opts for giving credence to Ibn Durayd. He adduces the unusual length of the *Lāmiyyah* (twice that of any other ṣuʿlūk poem), the paucity of variants, and the absence of any mention of it in two definitive works—the *Kitāb al-Aghānī* and the *Lisān al-ʿArab*—as further support for his decision.[5] We should consider, however, that Ibn ʿAbd Rabbih in *Al-ʿIqd al-Farīd*, Ibn Qutaybah in *Al-Shiʿr wa al-Shuʿarāʾ*, and al-Jāḥiẓ in *Al-Ḥayawān* all mention the attribution of another ṣuʿlūk poem rhymed in the letter *lām*, the so-called *Rithāʾ of Taʾabbaṭa Sharran* discussed in Chapter 2, or certain lines from it, to Khalaf al-Aḥmar, but no mention is made of the *Lāmiyyat al-ʿArab*.[6] Furthermore, as Khulayyif points out, except for the tradition of Ibn Durayd cited by al-Qālī and al-Ṣuyūṭī that the *Lāmiyyat al-ʿArab* is a forgery, and al-Zabīdī's attribution of it in *Tāj al-ʿArūs* to al-Shanfarā's ṣuʿlūk companion Taʾabbaṭa Sharran, all the classical sources that mention the *Lāmiyyat al-ʿArab* attribute it to al-Shanfarā.[7] This, especially when we note that *The Rithāʾ of Taʾabbaṭa Sharran* was sometimes attributed to al-Shanfarā,[8] arouses the suspicion that the Ibn Durayd

1 and 2, in *Abhandlungen der Königlich bayerischen Akademie der Wissenschaften, philosophisch-philologische und historische Klasse*, 1914, no. 8, and 1915, no. 4 (Munich, 1914, 1915).

4. Abū ʿAlī Ismāʿīl ibn al-Qāsim al-Qālī, *Kitāb al-Amālī wa yalīh al-Dhayl wa al-Nawādir lil-Muʾallif wa Kitāb al-Tanbīh li Abī ʿUbayd al-Bakrī*, 4 vols. in 2 (Beirut: al-Maktab al-Tijārī, 1965), 1:157; ʿAbd al-Raḥmān Jalāl al-Dīn al-Suyūṭī, *Al-Muzhir fī ʿUlūm al-Lughah wa Anwāʿihā*, ed. Muḥammad Aḥmad Jād al-Mawlā Bek, 2 vols. (Cairo: ʿIsā al-Bābī al-Ḥalabī, 1945), 1:176.

5. Khulayyif, *Al-Shuʿarāʾ al-Ṣaʿālīk*, 179–80.

6. Abū ʿUmar Aḥmad ibn Muḥammad Ibn ʿAbd Rabbih, *Kitāb al-ʿIqd al-Farīd*, ed. Aḥmad Amīn, Aḥmad al-Zayn, and Ibrāhīm al-Abyārī, 7 vols., 3d ed. (Cairo: Maṭbaʿat Lajnat al-Taʾlīf wa al-Tarjamah wa al-Nashr, 1969), 5:307; Ibn Qutaybah, *Al-Shiʿr wa al-Shuʿarāʾ*, 497; al-Jāḥiẓ, *Al-Ḥayawān* 1:182.

7. Khulayyif, *Al-Shuʿarāʾ al-Ṣaʿālīk*, 177.

8. Ibid., 176.

tradition may stem from a confusion of these two ṣuʿlūk poems in *lām*.[9] Thus, it could be argued that within the limits of the classical Arab tradition, the balance weighs in favor of the attribution of the *Lāmiyyat al-ʿArab* to al-Shanfarā, particularly given the reputations of its commentators, the uniqueness of the tradition that attributes it to Khalaf al-Aḥmar, and the possibility of guilt by association through its confusion with the other ṣuʿlūk poem in *lām*, *The Rithāʾ of Taʾabbaṭa Sharran*.

In the Orientalist realm, opinions have varied. Perhaps most telling is Nöldeke's remark that he would never have questioned the poem's authenticity if it were not that the heading in the authoritative manuscripts claimed that it was forged. Once his suspicion is aroused, however, he finds confirmation in the fact that none of the earliest Arab philologists seem to have known of the poem.[10]

The most ardent supporter of the authenticity of the *Lāmiyyat al-ʿArab* was Georg Jacob, who, taking exception to Ibn Durayd's accusation, set out to establish that al-Shanfarā's poem is a typical representative of the Yemenite poetic art. His method for determining the authenticity of the poem, as he presented it in his two-part *Schanfarà-Studien*, consists primarily of citing textual parallels—lexical, syntactic, and metric—from other pre-Islamic sources. Although this study thus demonstrates the authenticity or historicity of diction, subject, and style, it nevertheless does not counter the argument of those who consider the *Lāmiyyah* a pastiche composed by the most philologically knowledgeable and poetically gifted of the Iraqi transmitters.[11]

Fritz Krenkow, on the other hand, insists that the diction of the *Lāmiyyah* includes phrases and terms not easily discoverable in other poems of al-Shanfarā's period. He takes it rather to be a pastiche directly inspired by al-Shanfarā's powerful *lā taqbirūnī (Do Not Bury Me)* poem in the *Ḥamāsah*.[12]

Francesco Gabrieli considers Jacob's diligent word-by-word lexical analysis an anticipated refutation of Krenkow's position. Of interest too is Gabrieli's assessment of Khalaf al-Aḥmar's poem in the bedouin style, *Mufaḍḍaliyyah no. 20* of al-Shanfarā, and the *Lāmiyyah*. He con-

9. Al-ʿUtbī's claim (in an anecdote related in *Ḥamāsat al-Khālidiyyayn*) that Khalaf al-Aḥmar composed a poem in *lām* on the Ahl al-Bayt that is the source of the accusation of his having forged the *Lāmiyyah* refers, according to Khulayyif, to *The Rithāʾ of Taʾabbaṭa Sharran* and not, as Sezgin seems to think, to the *Lāmiyyat al-ʿArab*. Khulayyif, *Al-Shuʿarāʾ al-Ṣaʿālīk*, 175–76; Sezgin, *Poesie*, 460–61.

10. Nöldeke, *Beiträge*, 201.

11. Jacob, *Schanfarà-Studien*, passim.

12. Fritz Krenkow, "Al-Shanfarā," EI_1.

cludes that the first, although bearing a superficial resemblance to the other two, is upon analysis a purely conventionalized and descriptive poem, lacking the element of psychological unity ("unita psicologica fortissima") that is, in his estimation, the basis for the naturalistic descriptions of the other two and of which the *Lāmiyyah* is the example par excellence.[13]

Blachère, who in his critical and analytical history of the transmission, compilation, and recension of early Arabic poetry and akhbār acknowledges the inapplicability of the traditional concept of individual propriety/authorship to early Arabic poetry, nevertheless sees fit to label al-Shanfarā's previously uncontested *Mufaḍḍaliyyah no. 20* a Kufan pastiche and to brand the *Lāmiyyat al-ʿArab* an outright forgery by the hand of Khalaf al-Aḥmar.[14] The more recent studies of J.T. Monroe and Michael Zwettler concerning the oral composition and transmission of early Arabic poetry, particularly when taken together with works such as Eric Havelock's and Walter Ong's on the transition from orality to literacy, render traditional concepts of authorship and forgery as regards pre-Islamic poetry nearly obsolete.[15]

In light of the futility of the traditional arguments for the authenticity or spuriousness of what we term Jāhilī poetry in general and of the *Lāmiyyat al-ʿArab* in particular, I suggest that we reexamine our approach to the problem and rephrase our critical questions. The first step in this reassessment is to reiterate the simple historical fact that is at the base of our scholarly frustration: we have no pre-Islamic sources for pre-Islamic poetry. What we possess is the Islamic reconstruction of a disrupted and largely lost "pagan" tradition. Thus, primary to our considerations must be the fact that virtually all the materials we possess are compilations and recensions by Muslims, the products of Islamic science and Islamic sensibility.

At this point I suggest that we might best understand the nature of the authorship and attribution of early Arabic poetry (with its accompanying akhbār and *ansāb* [genealogies]) by comparing the two great

13. Francesco Gabrieli, "Sull'autenticità della *Lāmiyyat al-ʿarab*," *Revista degli Studi Orientali* 15 (1935): 361; Wilhelm Ahlwardt, *Chalef elahmar's Qasside* (Greifswald: C. A. Koch, 1859). See also Francesco Gabrieli, "Ta'abbaṭa Šarran, Šanfarà, Ḫalaf al-Aḥmar," *Atti della Academia Nazionale dei Lincei*, ser. 8 (1946), 40–69. Note too that the authorship of "Khalaf al-Aḥmar's qaṣīdah" is by no means certain; see Sezgin, *Poesie*, 460.

14. Blachère, *Histoire* 2:285, 1:86–102, 115, 182.

15. Monroe, "Oral Composition in Pre-Islamic Poetry," 1–53; Zwettler, *Oral Tradition*, see especially chap. 4, "Variation and Attribution in the Tradition of Classical Arabic Poetry"; Havelock, *The Muse Learns to Write*; Ong, *Orality and Literacy*.

compilation processes of the early Islamic (second to fourth) centuries: poetry and *ḥadīth* (prophetic tradition).[16] As Blachère has astutely noted, the methodological shift in the theological sciences from *isnād* (chain of transmission) to *ijmāʿ* (consensus) appears to have been paralleled in literary matters:

> The more one advances in time, the more one works on third- and fourthhand material, and the more one becomes dependent upon those from whom the materials are taken. One finds oneself in the same situation as the traditionists who, like al-Bukhārī or Muslim, strove to compile in a corpus juridical, theological, and other data relating to Muḥammad or the first generation of Muslims. . . . The learned man of the third/ninth century is faced with a solution of despair: a certain poem or a certain narrative is admissable because a certain scholar or a certain group of scholars, being authorities, considered it authentic. Certain others are, on the contrary, doubtful or inadmissible because the same authorities considered them suspect. The criticism of "transmitters" thus imposes itself upon the scholars just as it did upon the traditionists who served as their models. Moreover, always according to the tendency that triumphed in law and theology, one would strive to introduce into one's method the principles of *consensus doctorum (ijmāʿ)*.[17]

What remains is to expand upon Blachère's remarks by applying Ignaz Goldziher's conclusions as to the authenticity of the orthodox ḥadīth collections (*al-Kutub al-Sittah*) to the recensions and compilations of poetry. It can thus be said, as in the case of ḥadīth collections, that a compendium such as al-Iṣbahānī's *Kitāb al-Aghānī* derives its authority not so much from the soundness of the chains of transmitters that have related the poetry and akhbār as to the fact that it reflects currently accepted material. Goldziher has concluded with regard to ḥadīth:

> It would be wrong to think that the canonical authority of the two *ṣaḥīḥs* (of al-Bukhārī and Muslim) is due to the undisputed correctness of their contents and is the result of scholarly investigations. The authority of these books has a popular basis and holds good in spite of free scrutiny of individual paragraphs. Nor does it refer to an undisputable correctness of the contents (the details of which may always be and have

16. The relationship between ḥadīth collection and poetry collection has been treated by Blachère, *Histoire* 1:124–27; Nāṣir al-Dīn al-Asad, *Maṣādir al-Shiʿr al-Jāhilī wa Qīmatuhā al-Tārīkhiyyah* (Cairo: Dār al-Maʿārif, 1962); Zwettler, *Oral Tradition*, 203–4; and S. Stetkevych, *Abū Tammām*, chap. 10.

17. Blachère, *Histoire* 1:124.

> been, the subject of criticism), but to the obligation to consider the contents of the *ṣaḥīḥ*s as authoritative in religious practice (*ᶜamal*). The popular basis for this authority is the *ijmāᶜ al-umma*, the unanimous collective consciousness of the Islamic community (*talaqqī al-umma bi'l-qubūl*), which elevated these works to the heights which they attained.[18]

Goldziher's remarks concerning the usefulness of the ḥadīth collections then emerge as particularly appropriate for the literary-historical treatment of the poetic compendia: "The ḥadīth will serve not as a document for the history of the infancy of Islam, but rather as a reflection of the tendencies which appeared in the community during the maturer stages of its development."[19] Therefore, just as the blatant and provable "spuriousness" of some of the ḥadīth (or of their presumptive validation through *isnād*) does not invalidate the collections as expressions of contemporary Muslim belief, so too, even the demonstrable "inauthenticity" or "misattribution" (in strictly historicist terms) of a considerable amount of Jāhilī poetry, akhbār, and genealogies does not invalidate the literary tradition qua literary tradition.

In this regard, the Arabic literary biography, as we have it, is a largely Islamic literary form that began with the collection, by scholars such as Abū ᶜUbaydah in the second half of the second century, of akhbār and genealogies and culminated with the definitive work of Arabic literary biography, al-Iṣbahānī's *Kitāb al-Aghānī*, in the fourth century.[20] Even the individual biographical data or anecdotes out of which the literary biographies of such works as the *Kitāb al-Aghānī* are constructed have little historical validity, or at least verifiability.[21]

As the discussion in previous chapters has suggested, the association of various poems and biographical incidents/anecdotes with a particular poet is neither historical nor arbitrary. Rather, there is a semantic underpinning that binds the disparate elements of the literary biography together into what constitutes a coherent persona. These personae constructs are of a mythic, folkloric, and archetypal nature, with the result that there is a degree of correlation between the archetype reflected in

18. Ignaz Goldziher, *Muslim Studies*, ed. S. M. Stern, trans. C. M. Barber and Stern, 2 vols., vol. 1 (Albany, N.Y.: State University of New York Press, 1967), vol. 2 (Chicago: Aldine, 1970), 2:236. See also Snouck Hurgronje, "Le droit Musulman," trans. Arnold van Gennep, in G. H. Bousquet and Joseph Schacht, eds., *Selected Works of C. Snouck Hurgronje*, (Leiden: E. J. Brill, 1957), 223; Th. W. Juynboll, "Ḥadīth," EI_1.

19. Goldziher, *Muslim Studies* 2:19.

20. Blachère, *Histoire* 1:112–17.

21. Ibid.

the poet's akhbār and the dominant genre of the poetry that has come to be attributed to him.[22]

In this chapter I therefore propose that the traditional question "Is the *Lāmiyyat al-ʿArab* the work of al-Shanfarā?" be discarded altogether and that a new one be posed: "Why was the *Lāmiyyah* attributed to al-Shanfarā?" I will try to show that al-Shanfarā, as portrayed in such classical literary collections as the *Kitāb al-Aghānī*, the *Mufaḍḍaliyyāt*, and the *Ḥamāsah*,[23] can be classified in archetypal terms as a perpetually liminal entity and, further, that the *Lāmiyyat al-ʿArab* in its form and imagery is dominated by the signs and symbols associated with the liminal phase of the rite of passage or, in literary terms, the raḥīl section of the qaṣīdah. It is my contention that this shared archetypal structure is the basis for the attribution of the *Lāmiyyah* to al-Shanfarā and the reason why, despite evidence to the contrary, the *Lāmiyyah* remains—if not in historical judgment, in the popular and literary imagination—the inalienable property of that fierce ṣuʿlūk. Perhaps the analysis of this openly disputed case of authenticity and attribution will serve as a paradigm for the study of the relation of other early Arabic poems to their putative poets.

I begin with the akhbār of al-Shanfarā. In the *Kitāb al-Aghānī* al-Iṣbahānī relates an anecdote on the authority of al-Namarī:

> Al-Shanfarā was of the Azdite clan of al-Awās ibn al-Ḥajr. He was taken captive by the Fahmite clan of Banū Shabābah. He remained among them until another Azdite clan, the Banū Salāmān ibn Mufrij, captured a Fahmite from the clan of Banū Shabābah, and then ransomed him with al-Shanfarā. Thus it was that al-Shanfarā came to stay among the Azdite Banū Salāmān ibn Mufrij, who always treated him as one of them, until one day when he had a quarrel with the daughter of the man who had taken him in. This Salāmī had taken him as a son and treated him with kindness and generosity. So al-Shanfarā said to [this man's daughter], "Wash my head, dear sister,"for he had no doubt that she was his sister. She declared that he was not her brother and slapped him. He went away

22. I first presented these conclusions in two unpublished papers: "The Nature of Narrative in the *Kitāb al-Aghānī*," presented at the annual meeting of Middle East Studies Association, Philadelphia, 1982, and "Durayd ibn al-Ṣimmah and the Passing of the Heroic Age," American Oriental Society, Baltimore, 1983.

23. For the full bibliography of the akhbār and poetry attributed to al-Shanfarā, see Sezgin, *Poesie*, 133–37. The major portion of his poetry, excluding the *Lāmiyyat al-ʿArab* and *Mufaḍḍaliyyah no. 20*, has been edited by ʿAbd al-ʿAzīz al-Maymanī in *Al-Ṭarāʾif al-Adabiyyah* (Cairo: Maṭbaʿat Lajnat al-Taʾlīf wa al-Tarjamah wa al-Nashr, 1937), 31–42.

> angry, until he came to the man who had bought him from the Banū Fahm. Then al-Shanfarā said to him, "Tell me the truth, who am I?" He said, "You are of the Azdite al-Awās ibn al-Ḥajr." Then al-Shanfarā replied: "I will not stop until I have killed a hundred of you, because you have treated me as a slave!" And he kept on killing them until he had slain ninety-nine men. . . . Then al-Shanfarā attached himself to the Banū Fahm, and he used to attack the Banū al-Azd on foot, sometimes in the company of his companions of the Banū Fahm, but more often alone.[24]

This anecdote amounts to an etiological myth explaining the exaggerated animosity of al-Shanfarā for his natal tribe, the Banū al-Azd, and his allying himself with their enemy, the Banū Fahm. It thereby serves to define him in dialectical opposition to the social role of the aggregate warrior who should rather perpetuate his own bloodline and shed the blood of the enemy. Born to one Azdite clan, captured by the Banū Fahm, then turned over to another Azdite clan as ransom for a Fahmite, al-Shanfarā was then kept as a slave and foreigner—however affectionately treated—rather than being returned to his natal clan. This amounts, in effect, to his Azdite kinsmen's denial of his true identity, treating him instead as a Fahmite. It is thus with a certain semiotic logic that al-Shanfarā allies himself with the Banū Fahm and swears to spill rather than perpetuate the blood of the Banū al-Azd. His position vis-à-vis the normal tribal convention is thus betwixt and between, ambiguous and anomalous.

Two other versions of al-Shanfarā's alienation from his natal tribe, the Banū al-Azd, and his alliance with their blood enemy, the Banū Fahm, likewise revolve around the abrogation of kinship obligation by his tribe. Al-Anbārī relates in his commentary on the *Mufaḍḍaliyyāt*:

> It is also said that the reason for al-Shanfarā's attacks against the [Azdite clan of the Banū Salāmān] and killing them was that one of them had leapt on his father and slain him while al-Shanfarā was still small. When al-Shanfarā's mother saw that no one was going to avenge [her husband's] blood, she took al-Shanfarā and a younger brother of his and went to live under the protection of the Banū Fahm. She remained with them until al-Shanfarā grew up. Then his impetuousness began to show itself and he came to be disliked. However, he made an impression on Taʾabbaṭa Sharran, whom he regarded highly, and became attached to him. So

24. Al-Iṣbahānī, *Kitāb al-Aghānī* 24:8391–93; I have simplified the tribal names for the nonspecialist. For al-Anbārī's version of this anecdote, see Lyall, *The Mufaḍḍalīyāt* 1:195.

> he carried out raids with Ta'abbaṭa Sharran until no one dared cross his path.[25]

The law of blood vengeance, which virtually amounts to the definition of the distinction between kin and non-kin, is that a man kills only non-kin and avenges only kin. The behavior of the Banū al-Azd toward al-Shanfarā's father is thus just the opposite of what is required by tribal custom. It is both treacherous and anomalous. To al-Shanfarā's mother the message is clear: the kin status of her husband and children having been denied, she packs up her two small children and seeks refuge with their non-kin (that is, kin have become like non-kin and non-kin have become like kin). Al-Shanfarā grows up in a highly ambiguous situation. In order to become his father's heir, to assume adult status in the tribe, the youth must avenge his father. Yet in al-Shanfarā's case, to do so would mean slaying his natal kin, thus defining himself as non-kin. The marginality and ambiguity that characterize transitional liminality are thus both permanent and essential aspects of al-Shanfarā's identity.

Yet another version, given here as it appears in al-Anbārī's account, attempts to resolve al-Shanfarā's ambiguous status by projecting the ambiguity onto another figure:

> Al-Shanfarā and his mother ended up among the Banū Fahm because the Banū al-Azd had killed one of the Banū Fahm who was under the protection of al-Ḥārith ibn al-Sā'ib al-Fahmī. So the Banū al-Azd gave al-Shanfarā and his mother and brother as a pledge [for the bloodwite] and surrendered them to the Banū Fahm. They never redeemed the pledge, so al-Shanfarā grew up among the Banū Fahm. He was intrepid and stouthearted and was the fiercest of the Banū Fahm in killing and plundering the Banū al-Azd. *And prior to this some of his people had killed his father*, who had been a man of rank among his people, but of meager means. . . . Then when the Banū al-Azd slew al-Ḥārith ibn al-Sā'ib al-Fahmī, they refused at first to pay the bloodwite for him, until finally it was paid by a man called Ḥarām ibn Jābir. . . . When al-Shanfarā grew up he began to carry out raids against the Banū al-Azd and he killed whomever he caught. Then he came to Minā when Ḥarām ibn Jābir was there. Someone said to al-Shanfarā, "That is the man who killed your father." So he attacked him and slew him and escaped on foot. Then he recited:

25. Lyall, *The Mufaḍḍalīyāt* 1:196.

I slew Ḥarām bringing a sacrifice
for a pilgrim with matted hair
In the valley of Minā,
amid the chanting pilgrim
throng.[26] [15]

This story, which appears to be a conflation of two or more others, is striking for its ambiguity. If someone from the Banū al-Azd slew al-Shanfarā's biological father and if al-Shanfarā was reared in the household of al-Ḥārith ibn al-Sā'ib al-Fahmī, who was subsequently slain by the Banū al-Azd, it is not clear whose death al-Shanfarā is avenging. Lyall tries to clarify: "He seems to have looked upon al-Ḥārith as his father."[27] The killer of al-Shanfarā's father would thus be Ḥarām ibn Jābir, who, by paying the bloodwite for al-Ḥārith, accepted the blame for the murder. On the other hand, the statement in al-Anbārī's text that "prior to this some of his people [that is, the Banū al-Azd] had killed his father" seems to be an interpolation aimed at explaining "the man who killed your father" as the Azdite who had killed al-Shanfarā's father—which explanation is in keeping with the previous anecdote.

It would seem that what we have here is a narrative confusion that reveals an underlying semantic confusion of the identities of al-Shanfarā's biological Azdite and adoptive Fahmite fathers. On one level it demonstrates that even to the narrators the issue of al-Shanfarā's paternity—and hence identity—was far from clear. On a deeper level, it shows an attempt to resolve this ambiguity by attributing a dual identity to Ḥarām ibn Jābir as the killer of both al-Shanfarā's biological and adoptive fathers. In any case, as further akhbār will show, this act served to reaffirm al-Shanfarā's hostility toward his natal tribe.

The final episode of al-Shanfarā's life centers on the retaliation of Ḥarām ibn Jābir's kinsmen for his death at the hands of the ṣuʿlūk:

> Then a man from the Banū al-Azd came to Usayd ibn Jābir (the brother of the slain Ḥarām) and said, "I left al-Shanfarā in the market of Ḥubāshā." Usayd ibn Jābir replied, "By God, if you are telling the truth, we shall not return until we have eaten familiar fruit at Ubaydah." Then Usayd lay in wait for him along the road, together with Ḥarām's two sons. They heard him coming in the middle of the night; he had taken off one shoe and was wearing the other to disguise his gait. When the

26. Lyall, *The Mufaḍḍalīyāt* 1:197–98, my emphasis.
27. Ibid., 2:72–73.

two youths heard his footsteps, they said, "It's a hyena!" But Usayd said, "It's not a hyena, it's al-Shanfarā! So each of you put his shoe over his heart [*maqtal*]." When al-Shanfarā saw their outline in the darkness he withdrew for a while to see whether anyone would follow him, then he returned until he was close to them. The two youths said, "He saw us!" but their uncle replied, "No, by God, he did not see you. He merely used a diversionary tactic so you would not follow him. So each of you put a shoe over your heart!" Then al-Shanfarā shot and hit one of the shoes, and the one who was hit did not make a move [so al-Shanfarā thought him dead]. Then he shot again and transfixed Usayd's calves. When he saw this, he drew near until he was in their midst. Then they leapt on him and took him and bound him firmly. They took him to their tribe then and flung him down in their midst. They disagreed upon whether or not to kill him, for some of them said, "He is your brother and your son." When one of Ḥarām's sons heard this, he smote him and cut off his hand at the wrist.[28]

Then they said to him when they wanted to kill him, "Where shall we bury you?" and he replied:

Ḥamāsiyyah no. 164. Do Not Bury Me! [16]

Do not bury me, for my burial
  is forbidden to you,
 But rejoice, hyena,
  at these glad tidings!
When they carry off my head
  —and in my head is most of me—
 And the rest of me lies abandoned
  there on the battlefield,
Then I will have no desire
  for a life to cheer me through
 Stagnating nights, anathematized
  by my crimes.[29]

Al-Shanfarā died falling short by but one of his quota of one hundred Azdites. According to the akhbār, however, he was not one to let death stand in the way of his resolve: "And when al-Shanfarā had been killed and his head flung away, one [of the Banū Salāmān ibn al-Azd] passed

28. Al-Iṣbahānī, *Kitāb al-Aghānī* 24:8399–401.

29. Ibid., 24:8397; and al-Marzūqī, *Ḥamāsah* 2:487–91. I have followed the latter reading of the poem.

by him and kicked his skull, and in so doing injured his foot. He died from this injury, thereby completing the hundred."[30]

The story of al-Shanfarā's capture by Usayd ibn Jābir and the sons of the slain Ḥarām is replete with indications of al-Shanfarā's liminal status and his inverted relationship to his natal tribe, the Banū al-Azd. Usayd refers to his anticipated slaying of the ṣuʿlūk as eating "familiar fruit" (*janan alīf*), apparently a metaphorical expression for the slaying of a kinsman. The attack is an ambush by night during the sacred months, a typical liminal mode of fighting and in symmetrical opposition to aggregate heroic combat in the open, by day, in the permitted months. The weapon is the liminal bow and arrow, not the mature tribal sword or lance, thus reflecting the principle established by Vidal-Naquet that the marginal entity, the ṣuʿlūk in our case, can be defeated only on his own terms.

Al-Shanfarā enacts a ruse that functions on several semantic levels to convey a most concise and striking image of his marginal and ambiguous condition. The very fact of employing a ruse or trick, as Vidal-Naquet has shown, is an indication of liminality. The symbolic significance, as well as the practical effect, of al-Shanfarā's ruse (walking with one shoe off and one shoe on) is to be half man and half animal. The two youths think that he is a hyena, an appropriate liminal symbol because of its nocturnal habits and its peculiarly antisocial function (particularly in the poetry of blood vengeance) of devouring the corpses of those slain on the battlefield. In more precise terms the symmetrical inversion between human and hyena can be expressed in the formula: humans eat slain animals, whereas hyenas eat slain humans. Furthermore, as Diel and Vernant have discussed in the case of Oedipus, and I in the case of Taʾabbaṭa Sharran, to have an improper gait or to be poorly shod or unshod is a symbol of "psychic deformity," of deviation from the proper path or the inability to complete the prescribed passage. It is thus an especially fitting attribute of the passenger manqué. In more general terms, we should note, as Joseph Chelhod has, that the shoe is the paramount symbol of culture, that which in literal as well as symbolic sense separates man from nature, man from animal.[31] Thus, walking with one shoe off and one shoe on places al-Shanfarā in a typically liminal position betwixt and between culture and nature, man and beast.

A ruse demands a counterruse: Usayd ibn Jābir, Ḥarām's brother,

30. Al-Iṣbahānī, *Kitāb al-Aghānī* 24:8401–2.
31. Chelhod, *Le sacrifice chez les Arabes*, 75–79.

orders his two nephews to put one of their shoes over their hearts. Once more, the shoe functions in a richly symbolic manner. Their counterruse has the effect of putting them in the same liminal state as the ṣuʿlūk—one shoe off and one shoe on—in accordance with Vidal-Naquet's rule that only a liminal youth can defeat a perpetually liminal entity. At the same time, it is the shoe, the symbol of culture, that is struck by the ṣuʿlūk's arrow and thus saves the youth's life. When al-Shanfarā shoots and hears the arrow hit but no movement afterwards, he assumes his victim is dead. He then wounds the uncle who, as a mature (reaggregate) man, has suggested the ruse to the youths but has not adopted it himself. When al-Shanfarā approaches his victim, the two youths spring on him and take him captive.

The confusion over al-Shanfarā's identity surfaces once more when the sons of Ḥarām bring him back to Banū al-Azd. There are still those among the tribe who consider him kin: "He is your brother and your son." But the will to vengeance, the determination that he is ultimately non-kin, wins out.

When his captors/kinsmen ask him about his choice of burial place, al-Shanfarā replies, affirming his non-kin status, with his famous poem from the *Ḥamāsah* of Abū Tammām, *Do not bury me*. To leave a corpse naked and unburied for the vultures and hyenas to consume is precisely the treatment prescribed for the enemy dead; the kinsman, by contrast, is buried and avenged. Al-Shanfarā's claim that his burial is *muḥarram* (forbidden, unlawful, taboo) to them is a declaration of his non-kin, enemy status; hence, they are obligated to let his corpse be violated. In so doing, they will have vindicated his life's goal. The ṣuʿlūk's dying words then amount to an ironic inversion of the usual poetic conceit, the plea of the dying kinsman for burial and vengeance.

It is my contention that the analysis of these akhbār of al-Shanfarā, even in cases where the versions appear on the surface to be at odds with one another, reveals a dominant theme that can serve to define al-Shanfarā according to the archetypal pattern of the passenger manqué. His relation to his natal tribe, the Banū al-Azd, constitutes a symmetrical inversion of the normal reaggregate tribal member. He brings death rather than life; he is animallike rather than human. Instead of being temporary behavior, abandoned when the youth reenters the tribe as a fully responsible adult, these characteristics are perpetuated in the case of the ṣuʿlūk until (or even after) his death. Indeed, his death reaffirms them.

Having established this archetypal substratum as the basis for the accumulation of these akhbār around the figure of al-Shanfarā, I would now like to employ it to analyze two of his most famous poems: his *Mufaḍḍaliyyah* rhymed in *tāʾ*, the attribution of which has never (with the single exception of Blachère)[32] been specifically questioned, and the *Lāmiyyat al-ʿArab*, which, conversely, has been the subject of controversy for more than a millennium.

Mufaḍḍaliyyah no. 20. Umm ʿAmr Gathered Her Resolve [17]

1. Alas, Umm ʿAmr gathered her resolve
and departed;
She bade no farewell to her neighbors
when she turned and went away.
2. Umm ʿAmr left before us,
without warning,
And cast over us the shadows of
her camels' necks.
3. Before my two eyes she spent the evening,
then nighttime, then morn preparing,
Then she finished her affairs,
departed and was gone.
4. O how my heart aches for Umaymah!
after my desire—
Consider her, my life's delight,
now slipped away![33]
5. Oh neighbor! you are not a woman who
arouses blame when mentioned,
Nor are you a woman who
elicits hatred.
6. She stirred my delight,
her veil never falling
When she walked forth,
her glance never veering.
7. At night, after a short sleep,
she takes to her neighbor
Milk drawn at evening,
when gifts are scarce.

32. Blachère, *Histoire* 2:285.

33. Following al-Tibrīzī's *sharḥ*—without commas, following his suggestion that *wa zallati* might be read as a *ḥāl* with the *wa qad* omitted (and hence *niʿmata al-ʿayshi* as the second accusative after *hab*), or with commas, in accordance with his preferred reading of *niʿmata al-ʿayshi* as an appositive of *-hā* and *zallati* then as the second accusative. See al-Tibrīzī, *Sharḥ al-Mufaḍḍaliyyāt* 1:380–81.

8. She dwells in a tent pitched on a height
secured from blame,
While others dwell in tents
pitched in rebuke.
9. [She walks] as though looking on the ground
for some lost thing;
If she speaks to you
she's curt.
10. Umaymah's mate is not disgraced
by scandal;
When womenfolk are mentioned,
she is chaste, of high esteem.
11. When he goes out at evening, he comes home
to his eye's delight,
As a happy man returns,
not asking where she's been.
12. She was delicate and dignified,
full-statured, in full bloom;
If beauty could change people into jinn,
a jinni she would be.
13. Then we spent the night,
the tent above us as if ringed
In basil, wind-wafted
in the evening, dew-moistened,
14. Basil from the lowland of Ḥalyah,
abloom and redolent;
From a clime untouched
by drought.
15. Many a troop, their bows wear-reddened,
did I urge on;
He who raids returns at times with plunder,
at times the gloater's butt.
16. We went out of the riverbed [that lies]
between Mishʿal and al-Jabā,
How far off
I led my flock!
17. I trek on and on over ground
that will never harm me
To strike a foe or meet up
with my doom.
18. I trek on, however wearying the raid
and far,

My morn and evening bring me
ever closer to it.
19. A mother of a big brood
have I seen feeding them;
She doles out food
in stingy bits.
[19a. She is not stingy with the goods
in the provision bag,
But it is for fear of hunger
that she holds back.][34]
20. She fears, though we're still hungry,
that if she gives more
We'll soon run out.
How she manages her brood![35]
21. The ṣaʿālīk's companion,
no veil conceals her;
No one expects her home before
her night raid is complete.
22. A quiver she has
of thirty broad-tipped arrows;
When she spies the first of the foe,
frenzied she quivers.
23. She rushes on the battle-ready foe,
her leg bared to the knee;
Roving like the onager herd's lead stallion
warding off his rivals from his mares.
24. When terror strikes them she lets fly
a white and cutting sword;
She shoots her store of arrows,
then draws her blade.
25. A keen blade, salt-colored,
of unsullied steel,
Cutting and aglitter like the ripples
of the oft-described pond.[36]
26. You see the blades after watering,
when they have drunk

34. This verse is not found in al-Anbārī's recension. It figures as verse 20 in al-Tibrīzī's and seems to be reiterative or redundant. See al-Tibrīzī, *Sharḥ al-Mufaḍḍaliyyāt* 1:389.

35. *Taʾallat* is a metathesis for *taʾawwalat* (root *ʾ-w-l*), to manage a family. See al-Tibrīzī, *Sharḥ al-Mufaḍḍaliyyāt* 1:390.

36. Lyall omits this verse from his translation, remarking, with good reason, that "it does not seem probable that the verse is genuine." See Lyall, *The Mufaḍḍalīyāt* 2:72.

One draught of blood, and then a second,[37]
flick like calves' tails.
27. We slew a pilgrim for a pilgrim slain—
one leading a sacrificial beast
for one with matted hair—
At Minā where the stones are thrown,
amid the chanting pilgrim throng.[38]
28. We repaid the Salāmān ibn Mufrij
what we owed them;
For the crimes their hands had committed
and their past sins.
29. A tribe received best wishes at my [birth],
but I brought them no benefit;
For I have come to live among a tribe
that are not my native stock.[39]
30. We quenched by [slaying] ʿAbd Allāh
part of our burning thirst,
and by [slaying] ʿAwf before the battleground
when the battle cry rose shrill.[40]
31. When my death comes,
I shall not mind;
My mother's sisters will not weep for me,
nor my paternal aunt.
32. Let no friend come to tend me,
if illness ails me,
My cure will be to race
up Dhū al-Burayqayn's peak.
33. I am sweet if my sweetness
is desired,

37. The *ṣāḥib al-ḥāl* of *ṣawādiran* (returning from water) is actually the pronoun *hā* (referring, according to the commentarists, to swords), but the nature of the simile requires that swords returning from drinking the blood of battle are like calves/cattle returning from water. The commentarists' claim that the calves are meant to be flicking their tails with joy upon seeing their mothers seems to miss the point. More to the point is Lyall's translation. See al-Tibrīzī, *Sharḥ al-Mufaḍḍaliyyāt* 1:393; Lyall, *The Mufaḍḍalīyāt* 1:205 and 2:70.

38. Note that the *Kitāb al-Aghānī* redaction reads *Ḥarāman* for *qatīlan*. Al-Tibrīzī gives the variant *muḥriman* (consecrated for pilgrimage) for *muhdiyan*. See al-Tibrīzī, *Sharḥ al-Mufaḍḍaliyyāt* 3:393.

39. I have preferred, as has Lyall, al-Tibrīzī's *bi manbitī* (of my origin, birthplace) over al-Anbārī's *bi munyatī* (of my wish, desire). See Lyall, *The Mufaḍḍalīyāt* 2:71, 73; al-Tibrīzī, *Sharḥ al-Mufaḍḍaliyyāt* 1:394.

40. According to al-Anbārī, ʿAbd Allāh and ʿAwf were members of the Banū Salāmān ibn Mufrij. See Lyall, *The Mufaḍḍalīyāt* 1:206.

Bitter when a soul that spurns me
  finds me bitter.
34. Disdainful of what I disdain,
  quick to respond
To every soul that is inclined
  to make me happy.
[34a. For had I never stirred
  from sitting home amid my kin,
Yet between the tent's two poles
  my death would come.][41]

The striking beauty of the nasīb of this poem has long been admired by Orientalists. I cannot, however, agree with Lyall's remark that "the beautiful prelude . . . needs no elucidation."[42] Below the pellucid surface are subtle but forceful suggestions. In the first 14 verses the poet has exploited certain rhetorical features to produce a nasīb that is extraordinary for its intensification of two aspects: the first, femininity; the second, departure, rejection, and loss. These are expressed simultaneously—indeed, are identified with each other—through the persistent repetition of the perfective third-person feminine singular. This is, of course, not an unexpected morphological feature in a poem rhymed in the letter *tāʾ*. But let us observe that in the nasīb eleven of fourteen verses rhyme with this verbal form, whereas it forms the rhyme word in only eight of the remaining twenty-two verses. This insistence is further intensified by what amounts to a secondary rhyme in the letter *lām*, a sort of *luzūm mā lā yalzam* running throughout the nasīb. Thus the *taṣrīʿ* (rhymed hemistichs of the opening verse) is *fa istaqallatī . . . tawallatī*. Ten of the remaining thirteen verses of the nasīb likewise include the secondary *lām* rhyme, all but one of them with *tashdīd*. Of the three, verse 6 has the rhyme word *talaffatī*, the *lām* one syllable removed; and two (12 and 14) have in its place another liquid consonant, *nūn*. This reiterative morphological insistence is then further intensified by the repeated use of the same verbal form (perfect 3fs) within the verse, particularly in verse 1 (four times), verse 3 (six times), and verse 12 (five times). The resonances and reverberations are further enhanced

41. This verse, which does not occur in al-Anbārī's recension, is the closing verse in al-Tibrīzī's. See al-Tibrīzī, *Sharḥ al-Mufaḍḍaliyyāt* 1:396. I have followed Al-Anbārī's recension and commentary in Lyall, *The Mufaḍḍalīyāt* 1:194–207, except where otherwise noted. Also consulted were al-Tibrīzī, *Sharḥ al-Mufaḍḍaliyyāt* 1:379–97; and Shākir and Hārūn, *Al-Mufaḍḍaliyyāt*, 108–12. See also Lyall's translation and notes in Lyall, *The Mufaḍḍalīyāt* 2:68–73.

42. Lyall, *The Mufaḍḍalīyāt* 2:69.

by the repetition of several verbs, in particular the two that establish the semantic burden of the nasīb: *istaqallatī* (she went away from the tents), in verses 1 and 3; and *tawallatī* and *wallatī* (she turned her back, departed), in verses 1 and 3. In addition we find *taqallatī* (to elicit hatred, root *q-l-w*) in verse 5, *qallatī* (to be few, root *q-l-l*) in verse 7, and *jallat*(*ī*) (she was imposing, majestic) in verses 10 and 12.

The effect of this morphological *takrār lil-tawkīd* (repetition for the sake of emphasis) in this lovely description of chaste and modest womanhood, coupled with determination, departure, and the finality of the perfective aspect of the verb, is to create an intense sensation of irretrievable loss and absolute separation. If we then look back to the opening verse, we find already established there (she gathered her resolve, she departed, she did not say farewell, she went away) the psychological setting of loss and departure within which the delicate description takes place. It is perhaps worth mentioning in this context Ibn Rashīq's remark that the use of repetition is particularly appropriate to elegy.[43] Certainly in this nasīb it functions likewise to evoke a sense of obsessive sorrow. By the time we reach the lyrical erotic night scene of the two lovers (verses 13–14), it is quite clear that it is at most an irretrievable memory, more likely an idyllic fantasy.

It is the element of loss and irrevocability of this idealized and then idyllic feminine scene that establishes its analogy to the separation phase of the rite of passage, as Turner puts it, "symbolic behavior signifying the detachment of the individual . . . either from an earlier fixed point in the social structure, from a set of cultural conditions . . . , or from both."[44]

With verse 15 we are abruptly expelled from the feminine modesty, domesticity, and basil-decked bower of the nasīb and thrust into the world of a marauding band of brigands. The liminal identity of this band is established in the imagery and diction of verses 15–18. The band is termed *bāḍiʿah*, a flock, herd of sheep, but also, a portion separated from the rest of the herd.[45] Their bows of *nabʿ* wood have become reddened from constant use and exposure to the sun and rain.[46] Their life is one of perpetual raiding, alternating between failure and success. In verse 16 the ṣuʿlūk continues to speak of his band in terms of a flock (*surbah*). The marginality of liminal life in general and in

43. Ibn Rashīq, *Al-ʿUmdah* 1:248.
44. Turner, *Ritual Process,* 94.
45. Lane, *b-ḍ-ʿ*.
46. See al-Tibrīzī, *Sharḥ al-Mufaḍḍaliyyāt* 1:387; Lyall, *The Mufaḍḍalīyāt* 2:73.

particular the centrifugality of the perpetually liminal ṣaʿālīk are expressed in geographical terms: they depart from the valley or riverbed (where an at-least-seasonal supply of water provides a source of life and civilization) whose place-names connote culture—Mishʿal (strainer), and al-Jabā (reservoir tank). *Hayhāt!* (How far I have led my flock!) suggests how far astray, how far afield. The ṣuʿlūk leading his human flock away from the life- and culture-sustaining riverbed and into the wastelands constitutes a symmetrical inversion of the good shepherd leading his flocks to herbage and water. The ṣuʿlūk is now on the margins or outskirts of the hospitable and habitable world.

Verses 17 and 18 then employ a rhetorical process of morphological intensification similar to that of the nasīb to emphasize the perpetual liminality of the ṣuʿlūk. Whereas the classical qaṣīdah commonly employs a verb such as *qaṭaʿa* (to cut, to cross) to say, "On such a she-camel I *crossed* the desert"—that is, a clean and direct passage through the liminal waste with a she-camel as his mount—the ṣuʿlūk, on foot, treks on and on, seemingly without direction, from one raid to another. The reiterative intensity is expressed through the use of the imperfective aspect of the form II verb *umashshī . . . umashshī* (I keep walking and walking) at the beginning of verses 17 and 18. Again it is significant that the ṣuʿlūk lacks the she-camel, the traditional tribal mount and vehicle of passage, whose presence seems invariably to guarantee the completion of the raḥīl/passage, the incorporation of the passenger into the tribe and the arrival of the poet at the fakhr or madīḥ.

The inversion of status appropriate to the liminal entity is found too in verse 17: the earth, the wilderness, poses no threat to the ṣuʿlūk; but when it comes to human contact, he is, in Mary Douglas's words, "himself in danger and emanates danger to others."[47] The hardship characteristic of the liminal phase, "the physical and psychological weakening" of the passenger, to use van Gennep's phrase,[48] is the subject of verse 18, in which the ṣuʿlūk tramps on night and day, despite distance and exhaustion, to the site of his next raid. The *ṭibāq* (antithesis) between *buʿd* (distance) and *yuqarribu* (bring near) suggests the anomalous nature of the ṣuʿlūk's perpetual liminality: As time passes he is led farther and farther afield, to more deadly attacks against human society rather than back to reincorporation into it.

There follows (verses 19–26) the celebrated description of the *ummu*

47. Douglas, *Purity and Danger,* 96.
48. Van Gennep, *Rites of Passage*, 14.

ʿ*iyālin* (mater familias), traditionally said to be a description of al-Shanfarā's companion, Taʾabbaṭa Sharran, the infamous ṣuʿlūk of the Banū Fahm.[49] The commentaries offer several explanations for the gender inversion in this passage. *Ummu ʿiyālin* is commonly said to be the sobriquet of Taʾabbaṭa Sharran, in which case the retention of the feminine gender falls somewhere between normal grammatical concordance and extended simile "(He) is like a mother with many children who. . . ." The commentaries remark further that the Banū al-Azd call the chief of their *qawm* (fighting men of the tribe) a mother (*umm*), and that the *Lisān al-ʿArab* states that the Arabs call the man who is in charge of feeding and serving the *qawm* their mother. As proof, al-Shāfiʿī adduces this verse.[50] Inasmuch as these explanations appear to be rather circular, having been deduced from the poem at hand, further speculation as to the significance of this gender inversion is in order.

To begin with, in light of the insistence upon delicate, domestic, and modest femininity in the nasīb, the rendering of this ṣuʿlūk description in the feminine sets it up in contrast to the previous section. Umm ʿAmr/Umaymah was veiled, confined herself largely to her tent, adhered strictly to societal demands and expectations (what is intended by the statement that she was never the subject of gossip or a source of shame), and gave generously to the needy even in times of hardship. The "feminine" of the ṣuʿlūk raḥīl, as if by Vidal-Naquet's "law of symmetrical inversion," is stingy, afraid of poverty (verses 19a–20), the unveiled companion of impoverished brigands, who, far from remaining confined to her tent, is rather to be found abroad at night carrying out a raid (21). Further, the image of the indigent mother trying to feed her large brood suggests a widow and her orphaned offspring, who, like the ṣaʿālīk, are cut off from tribal sustenance and protection. Finally, "she" is not even female, as becomes increasingly clear from the battle description in the ensuing verses (22–26). The feminine gender of the ṣuʿlūk chieftain, together with the emphasis on stinginess, destitution, and hunger, constitutes a symmetrical inversion too of the traditional motifs of tribal fakhr—the bounty and liberality of the lords of the tribe, who heap up platters to feed the poor. Indeed, the hunger/satiety or hardship/ease opposition is one of the major subcategories of the nature/culture dialectic as exhibited in the raḥīl/fakhr division of the classical Arabic qaṣīdah.

49. Lyall, *The Mufaḍḍalīyāt* 1:203; 2:72.
50. Shākir and Hārūn, *Al-Mufaḍḍaliyyāt*, 110.

Thus the description of Ta'abbaṭa Sharran (?) as *ummu ʿiyālin*, the destitute mother of a numerous brood, serves a double dialectical function. It establishes at once a symmetrical opposition between the feminine domesticity of the tribal Umm ʿAmr and the liminal ṣuʿlūk, on the one hand, and between the ṣuʿlūk and the aggregate tribal chieftain of the traditional fakhr section, on the other. Further, we should note that among the common symbols or attributes of the liminal phase are transvestism, bisexuality, and androgyny.[51] In this context, the gender inversion serves to suggest sexual confusion. The ṣuʿlūk becomes in terms of sex or gender ambiguous, betwixt and between the domestic femininity of Umm ʿAmr and the "straight" masculinity of the tribal chieftain. Thus the description of the ṣuʿlūk as *ummu ʿiyālin* functions on several semantic levels to depict what Turner calls "a cultural realm that has few or none of the attributes of the past or coming state."[52]

This passage concludes in verse 26 with a striking simile that compares the lively flicking of calves' tails as they return from a water hole to the slashing of swords that have sated their thirst for vengeance with blood. Although the apparent objective correlative is the flicking motion of the tails and swords, the real message is that as cattle are sustained and revived by water, so are ṣaʿālīk by blood.

The poem reaches its climax in verse 27 with the slaying of a pilgrim in retaliation for another pilgrim slain. A dialectic is thus set up between sanctity and sacrilege. The victim is performing a sacred religious duty (the sacrifice at Minā), whereas the avenger is perpetrating the worst abomination—killing a pilgrim within the confines of the *ḥaram* during the sacred month of Dhū al-Ḥijjah.[53] This abomination is obligatory upon the ṣuʿlūk, however, because it is in retaliation for another slain pilgrim (*mulabbad*, a pilgrim whose hair is matted down with *ṣamgh*), or as the commentary paraphrases it, *qatalnā rajulan muḥriman bi rajulin muḥrimin* (we killed a man consecrated for pilgrimage for a man consecrated for pilgrimage.)[54] The khabar that has been handed down concerning this poem claims that the pilgrim leading the beast of sacrifice (*muhdī*) is Ḥarām ibn Jābir, the purported slayer of al-Shanfarā's father,

51. Vidal-Naquet, "Black Hunter," passim; Victor Turner, *The Forest of Symbols: Aspects of Ndembu Ritual* (Ithaca, N.Y.: Cornell University Press, 1967), 98.

52. Turner, *Ritual Process*, 94.

53. So binding was the prohibition against killing during the sacred months that if a man saw the killer of his father or brother, he would not so much as speak to him, let alone kill him. See al-Ālūsī, *Bulūgh al-Arab* 3:79.

54. Lyall, *The Mufaḍḍalīyāt* 1:205.

who would thus be identified with the pilgrim with matted hair. The ṣuʿlūk is therefore face to face with a fierce contradiction when he comes upon his father's killer among the pilgrims at Minā: the obligation to avenge his father (whose death was the same abomination) and the abomination of killing a pilgrim. If we accept Mary Douglas's definition of pollution or abomination as contradiction or anomaly,[55] we will see that verse 28 is carefully constructed to bring out precisely this concept. The ṣuʿlūk has no choice but to complete the circle of sacrilege. That his victim is himself leading a victim to slaughter sets up a further dialectic between sanctity and sacrilege, between sacrifice and its symmetrically inverted form, blood vengeance. In sacrifice an animal is slaughtered to feed to humans, whereas in blood vengeance a human being is killed and left as carrion for animals. It bears repeating that the sacrilege here stems from the confusion of sacrifice and blood vengeance occasioned by Shanfarā's father's murder at the hands of a kinsman.

The blunt juxtaposition of sacrifice and blood vengeance in the first hemistich is followed in the second by the intensification of or insistence upon the sanctity of the scene of the sacrilege at Minā, where the assembled pilgrims chant, *Labbayk, yā Rabb, labbayk!* (At your service, O Lord, at your service!).[56] The equation of blood vengeance with the double abomination involved in this particular case is rhetorically implicit in the double antithesis of verse 27 *Qatalnā qatīlan muhdiyan bi mulabbidin* (We *slew* a *pilgrim to be slain* for a *pilgrim*). It is important here to recognize that *qatīl* is *faʿīl* not in the simple passive participial sense, but rather in the gerundive sense, "one who is to be killed" or even "ought to be killed." The insistence on "the proper victim" emphasizes once again that in the taking of blood vengeance, as in the sacrifice at Minā, the consecrated victim must conform to ritual specifications. Here, ironically and tellingly, the pilgrim is consecrated for the ḥajj as the sacrificer, but through the ṣuʿlūk's liminal inversion of societal values he becomes the consecrated victim. The blood vengeance equation implied in verse 27 is then explicitly stated in the next verse: the avenger is merely requiting the crimes of his enemies against him (28).

The remaining verses of the poem (29–34a) comprise what appear to be several variant endings.[57] In his translation, Lyall has transposed

55. Douglas, *Purity and Danger*, 53 and passim.
56. Lyall, *The Mufaḍḍalīyāt* 1:205.
57. See al-Bijāwī's remark in al-Tibrīzī, *Sharḥ al-Mufaḍḍaliyyāt* 1:397 n. 4; Shākir and Hārūn, *Al-Mufaḍḍaliyyāt*, 110 and 112; Lyall, *The Mufaḍḍalīyāt* 1:207 n. 1., 2:73.

verses 29 and 30 to felicitous effect.[58] A truly convincing ending would require choosing from among the available verses. Rather than take so great a liberty, I will limit myself to the discussion of several verses deserving of comment in the context of the present argument.

The inverted and outcast status of the ṣuʿlūk is aptly expressed in the couplet formed by verses 29 and 30: he did not fulfill the expectations of, or his obligations to, his natal clan but went instead to live among a clan that was not his stock. Those he has slain in blood vengeance, ʿAbd Allāh and ʿAwf, are, we are told in the commentary,[59] members of the Salāmān ibn Mufrij clan—the branch of al-Shanfarā's natal Banū al-Azd tribe that had kept him as a slave. The poem thus precisely conveys the ṣuʿlūk's contradiction or inversion of the basic tribal formula: that those with whom one fights are kin and those against whom one fights are non-kin. The first hemistich of verse 31 is likewise considered to allude to blood vengeance, for in the Arabic poetic-heroic context such nonchalance in the face of death is taken as a boast that vengeance has been achieved.[60] Having thus defined himself as non-kin to his natal tribe, one who takes vengeance from them not for them, it follows that his natal womenfolk will not mourn his death.

The centrifugal thrust of the perpetually liminal entity who seeks refuge not in the tribe but in the wilderness is the theme of verse 32. The ṣuʿlūk wants no friend to tend him in his illness; rather, his cure is the flight to the summit of Dhū al-Burayqayn, which we might translate as "the mountain of the two small lightning bolts." The theophanous nature of the mountain peak and the lightning flash once again evokes Mary Douglas's statement, "To have been in the margins is to have been in contact with danger, to have been at the source of power."[61] The flight to the mountaintop, to the farthest margin, which also forms one of the concluding images of *Mufaḍḍaliyyah no. 1,* attributed to Taʾabbaṭa Sharran, can thus be interpreted as a symmetrical inversion of reincorporation, of the fakhr of the nourishing and protecting tribe, a theme sometimes expressed, as we saw in *The Muʿallaqah of Labīd*, as a descent into a green valley. Thus, the return to safety and society (aggregation) is replaced in the ṣuʿlūk poem by the flight into the wilderness, to exposure and isolation on the mountain peak.

The Lāmiyyat al-ʿArab, too, exhibits in its symbols and imagery

58. Lyall, *The Mufaḍḍalīyāt* 2:71.
59. Ibid., 1:206.
60. See al-Anbārī's remarks in Lyall, *The Mufaḍḍalīyāt* 1:206.
61. Douglas, *Purity and Danger*, 97.

precisely those liminal, antisocial characteristics that informed the diverse akhbār and poetry of al-Shanfarā in the biographical notices and commentaries of the *Kitāb al-Aghānī*, the *Mufaḍḍaliyyāt*, and the *Ḥamāsah*, and served to create a coherent archetypal persona, what I have termed the passenger manqué. I hope to determine to what extent the *Lāmiyyah* satisfies the formal expectations I have established for the typical ṣuʿlūk poem, that is, that it exhibits elements that express separation/nasīb and liminality/raḥīl to the exclusion of those that would signify reincorporation/tribal fakhr. It is my intention to refute Yūsuf Khulayyif's claim that ṣuʿlūk poetry bears no relation to the classical "tribal" qaṣīdah and Gabrieli's remark that the *Lāmiyyat al-ʿArab* does not constitute a proper poem.[62]

Lāmiyyat al-ʿArab [18]

1. Raise, my brothers, the chests of your mounts,
   set them straight;
   As for me, I incline
   toward another tribe.
2. The provisions have been readied,
   the night is moonlit,
   The mounts strapped and saddled
   for your journeys' ends.
3. In the land there is for the noble-hearted
   a place remote from harm;
   For him who fears hatred,
   a refuge.
4. By your life, the earth does not constrain
   a man who travels by night,
   Whether by free will or by force,
   if he has his wits about him.
5. I have closer kin than you,
   a wolf, swift and sleek,
   A smooth and spotted leopard (smooth speckled snake),
   and a long-maned one—a hyena.
6. They are kin among whom a secret, once confided,
   is not revealed;
   Nor is the criminal forsaken
   for his crimes.

62. Khulayyif, *Al-Shuʿarāʾ al-Ṣaʿālīk*, 262–71. Gabrieli contends that the 60-odd verses of the *Lāmiyyah* do not constitute a proper poem, rather, they form an anthology of the ancient poetic patrimony held together by a single motif: the bitter soul (*nafs murrah*) of the Azdite brigand-poet. See Gabrieli, "Taʾabbaṭa Šarran," 56.

7. Each one is haughty-proud and reckless-brave,
   except that I,
When the first of the prey appear,
   am braver.
8. But when hands stretch into the provision bags,
   I am not the quickest;
For then the greediest clansman
   is quicker.
9. This is nothing but my
   more expansive magnanimity,
For the magnanimous man is
   the most virtuous.
10. To recompense the loss of those
   who do not requite my kindness,
From whom no satisfaction can be sought,
   I have
11. Three companions—
   an emboldened heart,
A white and polished sword,
   a slender yellow bow,
12. Its smooth back resonant,
   adorned with ornaments
Suspended from it
   and with a shoulder strap.
13. When an arrow slips from it,
   it resounds like a she-camel
Afflicted and bereft,
   moaning and wailing.
14. I am not one quick to thirst,
   pasturing his herds by night,
Whose young camels get no milk,
   though their mothers' udders are not bound,[63]
15. Nor am I a coward, foul-breathed,
   clinging to his wife,
Consulting her on his affairs,
   how should he go about them?
16. Nor a startled ostrich,
   his heart aflutter

63. This line could also be translated: "I am not one who takes his herds afar until they thirst, / who pastures them by night, / the little ones cut off from milk, / though their mothers' udders are not bound."

As though a sparrow
flitted in it.
17. Nor am I a good-for-nothing stay-at-home,
flirtatious,
Who comes and goes, night and day,
perfume-daubed, kohl-painted.
18. Nor an old man like a camel tick,
more harm than good, bewildered;
Who starts when frightened,
in defenseless frenzy.
19. I am not a man confused by darkness,
when the wayless waste
Confronts the guidance
of the confounded fool.
20. When the ground, hard and flint-strewn,
strikes my hoofs,
Sparks and splinters
fly!
21. I prolong the length of hunger
till I have killed it;
I turn my mind from it
and forget it.
22. I eat the earth's dust dry,
lest any benefactor
Think me indebted
to his favor.
23. Except that I shun blame, there would be
no drink, life giving,
That was not mine
nor any food.
24. But a bitter soul does not let me
remain in blame;
It prods me
to move on.
25. I writhe around the hollow
of my gut,
Like a rope maker twisting his strands,
firm and tight.
26. Early morning I go out on scanty food,
like the thin-hipped wolf,
Led on from waste to waste,
dust-colored.

27. He goes out in the morning famished,
nose to the wind, light-footed,
Swooping down the ends of mountain paths,
or loping.
28. When his sought-out prey evades him,
he calls out,
And others like him, emaciated,
return his call.
29. Fleshless, white-faced,
they are like bare arrows
In a *maysir* player's hands,
clattering,
30. Or like the agitated queen bee,
her swarm astir
From sticks a honey gatherer
has flung down from above.
31. Wide-mouthed, as if their jaws
were splints of branches,
They bare their teeth,
ferocious.
32. Then he clamored and they clamored
on the broad and barren plain,
As if they and he were wailing women,
on the heights, bereaved.
33. He refrained, and they refrained;
he comforted them, and they him;
In their destitution he consoled them and
they consoled him, destitute.
34. He whined and they whined, then afterwards
he desisted and they desisted;
For endurance, when complaining is of no avail,
is better.
35. He returned and they returned,
hastening ahead of him,
Each despite his hunger,
has the kindness to hide it.
36. The dark, dust-colored sandgrouse
drink my dregs;
After traveling all night in search of water,
their brittle ribs rattle.
37. I strove and they strove as we raced;
then they slackened

And I went ahead, at leisure,
rolling up my sleeves.
38. Then I turned away from them,
and they collapsed at the water hole,
Their chins and crops
resting right on it.
39. As if the clamor that arose
on its two sides and all around
Were from bands of tribal travelers
alighting there.
40. From all sides they converged on it;
it gathered them
As a wayside water hole draws
the scattered bunches of the camel herds.
41. They gulped down the water hurriedly,
and then departed,
As if they were riders with the morning
hastening from Uḥāẓah in alarm.
42. I am familiar with the earth's face
when I take it as my bed
On a firm back raised
by desiccated vertebrae.
43. For a cushion I take an arm, fleshless,
its joints like gambler's bones
When he casts them forth,
so they stand out.
44. Then if war, the Mother of Dust,
is grieved at al-Shanfarā,
Yet her delight in him before
was longer.
45. I am an outcast hunted by crimes
that draw lots for his flesh;
The winner gets the first choice
from his carcass.
46. Whenever he sleeps,
they sleep, wide-eyed,
Quick to harm him,
piercing.
47. One accustomed to cares
that ever return to tend him,
Like quartan fever,
or even graver.

48. When they come to drink,
  I disperse them;
But then they regroup
  coming from above and from below.
49. So if you see me, like the snake,
  the sand's daughter,
Exposed to the sun, weakened,
  barefoot and shoeless,
50. Know that I am the master of endurance;
  I don its cloth
Like a shirt on a heart like a young wolf's;
  I am shod with determination.
51. I am at times in want,
  at others, not in need;
He who attains riches is the ambitious man,
  heedless of his honor.
52. I am not impatient over poverty,
  exposing it,
Nor, overweening,
  do I exult in riches.
53. Intemperance does not scorn
  my forbearance,
Nor am I to be seen begging,
  rumormongering.
54. Many a cold, ill-omened night
  when the bow's owner warms himself
By burning it and the arrows
  of his skill,
55. I tramped in the dark and drizzle,
  my companions
Hunger and cold,
  fear and trembling.
56. I widowed women
  and orphaned children,
Then returned as I set out,
  the black night blacker still.
57. In the morning, there sat at Ghumayṣāʾ
  two bands,
One questioned about me,
  the other questioning.[64]

64. Al-Zamakhsharī offers several options for reading this line. I have chosen to take *jālisan* as the *khabar* of *aṣbaḥa*, and *ʿannī* as going with *mas'ūl* and *yas'alu*. See Muḥammad ibn ʿUmar al-Zamakhsharī, *Aʿjab al-ʿAjab fī Sharḥ Lāmiyyat al-ʿArab*, in al-Shanfarā, *Qaṣīdat*

58. They said, "Our dogs
were whimpering in the night."
We said, "Was it a wolf on the prowl
or a prowling hyena whelp?"
59. "It was but a faint noise,
then they went back to sleep."
We replied, "Was it a sandgrouse startled,
or a startled hawk?"
60. "If it was one of the jinn,
then he is a more sinister night visitor;
And if it was a man—
men do not act like that!"
61. Many a day of the Dog Star,
when the heat waves melt,
And the vipers writhe restlessly
on the scorching earth,
62. I faced straight on,
no covering to shield me
Nor any veil, except
a tattered cloak,
63. And full long hair;
when the wind blows
Its matted dreadlocks fly up on all sides,
uncombed.
64. Long since the touch
of balm or delousing,
It is full and caked with filth;
for a full year unwashed.
65. Many a windswept plain, like the back of a shield,
a barren waste,
Its back not to be crossed,
on my two legs I crossed.
66. I joined its end to its beginning,
looking out from a summit,
Now sitting, knees drawn up;
Now standing.
67. The dust-hued does of mountain goats
roamed around me,
As if they were maidens
trailing long-trained gowns.

Lāmiyyat al-ʿArab wa yalīhā. . . . (Istanbul: Maṭbaʿat al-Jawāʾib, 1300 H.), 61–62. Wright opts for another possibility, "and there were the next morning two parties, (one) asked and the other asking about me, (whilst I was) sitting at el-Ghomeiṣā." See Wright, *Grammar* 2:113.

68. Toward sunset motionless they stood about me,
as if among the white-footed goats I were
A long-horned buck, heading for the mountain peak,
unassailable.[65]

Before proceeding to a more detailed analysis, let us observe that the imagery throughout the *Lāmiyyah* is of behavior diametrically and dialectically opposed to the tribal values of protection, propagation, satiety, and ease (that is, aggregation); the poem is fraught instead with images of danger, hardship, poverty and privation, wildness and wilderness. Of particular note is the absence here, as in most ṣuʿlūk poetry, of the she-camel, the mount on which the tribal poet completes the crossing of the liminal desert (raḥīl) and arrives at the safety and satiety of the tribe and its institutions (tribal fakhr). So too, the themes that commonly comprise the fakhr section—the battle and hunt scenes with the horse as the mount, the drinking scene, and the commensal feast—are to be neither expected nor found in the typical ṣuʿlūk poem.[66]

The poem opens with a succinct declaration of the ṣuʿlūk's separation and deviation from his kinsmen and their intended course. This is given rhetorical emphasis through the *ṭibāq* between the first and last words of the verse: *aqīmū*, whose first meaning here is raise, but also straighten, point aright, direct; further, it is related to *qawm*, the aggregate fighting men of the tribe, and *mustaqīm*, following the right course; "Raise the chests of your mounts, set them straight ahead!" he exhorts his kinsmen, for himself, however he concludes the verse with the elative *amyalū* (of *māʾil*)[67] to declare his "inclining more" in a different direction, that is his obliquity vis-à-vis the tribal straight path, his deviation. Thus, both the poet and his kinsmen are setting out on a night journey—a liminal passage—but the kinsmen are mounted and following the straight path (verse 1), and they are provisioned and pointed toward their destination (2). In verse 2 the poet, by means of *jinās* (paronomasia), establishes a semantic identity through false etymology: that is, by a pun on *ṭiyyāt* (destinations) from the root *ṭ-w-y*, and *maṭāyā* (mounts), from the root *m-ṭ-w*. The rhetorical effect of this *jinās* is to establish a causal link

65. Al-Zamakhsharī, *Aʿjab al-ʿAjab*, 10–70 [includes the al-Mubarrad/Thaʿlab commentary]. For another translation see Sells, *Desert Tracings*, 24–31.

66. See Khulayyif's remarks in *Al-Shuʿarāʾ al-Ṣaʿālīk*, 172–73. For a review of the motifs that commonly occur in the final section of the qaṣīdah see Jacobi, *Studien zur Poetik*, 65–99.

67. Al-Zamakhsharī, *Aʿjab al-ʿAjab*, 14.

between the camel mounts and the arrival at the intended destination. The completion of the passage by the ṣuʿlūk's mounted brethren is thus semiotically secured. By contrast, the poet is destined to go far afield (3), for *al-arḍ*, the earth, really means the wilderness, the desert. The two *nomina loci* of this verse, *man'an* and *mutaʿazzal*, indicative of remoteness and isolation, are in symmetrical opposition to his kinsmen's destination—society and aggregation.

Having rejected his human kin, the poet substitutes for them, almost, it would seem, by way of compensation, affinities and associations with wild beasts which recur throughout the poem. In verse 5 the poet names precisely those beasts that are characteristically antihuman, enemies of civilization (as opposed to merely nonhuman): the wolf that preys on humans and their herds; the leopard (or snake), likewise a predator; and the female hyena, notorious for molesting and devouring the unburied corpses of those slain in battle. Further, if we examine the rather obscure diction of this verse, we will notice that these animals are denoted not by name but by epithets that suggest liminality and ambiguity: *ʿamallas* (swift or sleek, but also black and white); *arqaṭ* (black and white spotted snake or leopard, anything of two different colors); *ʿarfāʾ* (long-maned [hyena]).[68] These antihumans the ṣuʿlūk then terms his "people" (*ahl*). This metaphorical substitution entails not merely analogy but also a complex poetic process of antithesis and negation. Indeed, the reader will observe that throughout the poem two metaphorical processes function that are particularly appropriate to express the ambiguous status of the liminal entity betwixt and between the human and the animal: the feralization of the human and the anthropomorphization of the animal. A similar process is at work in verses 11–13, where the poet's weapons are personified as *aṣḥāb* (friends, companions) in lieu of his lost human ones.

Verses 14–19 contain what might be called the ṣuʿlūk's self-definition by negation, or by double negation (litotes). The point of this passage is, I believe, to distinguish the ṣuʿlūk from other types of men who have failed to join the *qawm* (the men who stand up and fight for the tribe). The ṣuʿlūk is not, he states emphatically, to be confused with the effete and effeminate, the old and impotent, the cowardly and incompetent. He then proceeds to describe himself as exceeding, not falling short of, the reaggregate tribal male in endurance, fortitude, and resolve.

68. Ibid., 17.

Verse 20 initiates a series of images that depict the physical hardships of the liminal desert, largely through descriptions of its fauna. In a revealing metaphor, the poet describes "my hoofs," or, more precisely, "my camel-pads" (*manāsimī*), referring, as the al-Mubarrad/Thaʿlab commentary points out, not to any she-camel on which he is mounted but to his own feet, which send sparks flying as they strike against the flinty ground.[69] In one word he thus alludes to the traditional tribal vehicle (the she-camel) while affirming her absence—he is, as it were, his own mount—and indicating the battering his feet are taking.

Verse 21 introduces the theme of an ever-intensifying hunger, which by verse 25 has become almost a cultivated art or acquired skill, like rope making, an intentional, obsessive, and the poet would have us believe, freely chosen occupation (22–24). With an ironic twist the image of the rope maker produces an antithesis curiously appropriate to the ṣuʿlūk's liminal status: the goal of society is to produce satiety, whereas the ṣuʿlūk cultivates the art of starvation. Verse 23 amounts to a rejection of the communal institutions for food and drink, of participation in commensal rituals and the obligations that they entail. The *ṭibāq* of verse 24 yields a similar meaning: the rejection of the stable and stationary (*tuqīmu*, to remain) for the perpetually moving (*ataḥawwalu*, to move from one place to another, be devious, shifting, mutable).

The hunger motif of the preceding passages leads us to the extended wolf simile (verses 26–35), which performs the same function as the *ummu ʿiyālin* (mater familias) passage of *Mufaḍḍaliyyah no. 20*, that is, to establish the image of the ṣuʿlūk antisociety based on hunger in symmetrical opposition to the tribal society based on satiety. The wolf, since he lives in a pack, displays a characteristically liminal ambiguity: he is a *social animal*, and at the same time a symmetrical inversion of the ṣuʿlūk himself, the *antisocial human*. The perpetual wandering in the wilderness of both the wolf and the ṣuʿlūk is succinctly phrased in verse 26: *tahādāhu al-tanāʾifu* (literally, the wastelands led him on), or as al-Zamakhsharī puts it in his commentary, every time he leaves one wasteland he enters another.[70] Thus the usual meaning of the root *h-d-y*, to go or be directed in the right way, is subverted here in the VI-form reciprocity of first one desert leading him on and then another. The passage as a whole depicts animal privation—hunger, emaciation,

69. Ibid., 31.
70. Ibid., 37.

exhaustion—enhanced by similes of human privation—*maysir* arrows in the hands of a gambler who trembles in desperate anticipation (29),[71] bereaved and wailing women (32). This passage, then, with its similes comparing man to wolf and wolf to man, is thus constructed on the metaphorical principle of the feralization of the human and the anthropomorphization (or socialization) of the feral.

The wolf scene is followed by that of the sandgrouse (36–41), in which once again the social animal, the flock of sandgrouse, is compared to human society, the deprived and desperate bedouin migrating in search of water. Here the poet contrasts his own forbearance and dignity in the face of privation to the uninhibited frenzy of the sandgrouse. The poet reiterates here the disdain he expressed in verse 8 for the greedy man quick to stretch his hand into the provision bag. As in the wolf scene, there is again a complex network of oppositions at work between the flock of sandgrouse, the impoverished bedouin, and the ṣuʿlūk, who, with appropriately liminal lack of status, belongs with neither.

"I am familiar with the face of the earth," the poet declares in verse 42. The three words *ālafu wajha al-arḍi* provide a definition that succinctly encompasses the liminal dialectic. The root *ʾ-l-f* signifies socialization—familiarity, custom, domestication. But the familiar face for the ṣuʿlūk is not a human, social one but that of its opposite, the wilderness—precisely what is untamed and unsocialized. Just as the ṣuʿlūk has eschewed the tribal vehicle of the she-camel for his own "hoofs/pads," so too he substitutes his own emaciated body for the other furnishings and accouterments of the civilized world: his bed is his own protruding spine, his cushion a fleshless arm. This literal "self"-sufficiency is at the same time a negation: to have one's own spine for a bed is, plainly speaking, to have no bed.

The opening epithet of verse 45, *ṭarīdu jināyātin* (expelled for crimes), is a phrase imbued with a curious bivocality, for *ṭarada* means to expel, drive away, or banish, but also to hunt or pursue. The expression thus means a man expelled because of his crimes, but also one tracked down or hunted for his crimes. The two meanings reveal two complementary liminal qualities: first, that the ṣuʿlūk is a *khalīʿ*[72]—someone who has been expelled from human society because of his criminal, antisocial behavior—and second, that he has as a result become the prey (feraliza-

71. Note once more that *maysir* was not an idle pastime but rather a means of distributing meat, especially in times of hardship or famine.

72. See al-Ālūsī, *Bulūgh al-Arab* 3:27; Lammens, "Le caractère religieux du *ṯār*," 92.

tion again), hunted by mankind, the inverse of the tribal hunter. Thus the two meanings ultimately yield to univocity: to be expelled from society is to become its prey. The ṣuʿlūk's crimes are personified as *maysir* players gambling over his flesh. The crimes are, no doubt, homicides; the gamblers, the would-be avengers. The metaphor thus identifies the ṣuʿlūk qua *khalīʿ* with the *jazūr*, the camel selected for slaughter. His fate is sealed and the only question is which gambler will win, which of the many avengers who seek his blood will shed it. The final effect of this metaphor is to reinforce, once again, the ritual identity of, or analogy between, animal sacrifice and the taking of blood vengeance.

The ṣuʿlūk describes himself in verse 47 as *ilfu humūmin*, accustomed to, familiar with, cares. Once more, the *ʾ-l-f* root suggests family, society, company, but the ṣuʿlūk is familiar only with troubles. The *humūm*, the cares and anxieties of the poet/lover, are a well-known motif of the classical qaṣīdah which often provides the transition point from the nasīb to the raḥīl: the poet resolves to leave these troubles behind and undertake the desert journey. In this ṣuʿlūk poem, by contrast, these cares are not left behind but constantly return to plague their victim. The incessant recurrence and increasing intensity of these attacks is expressed in the verb *ʿāda*, which means both to return and to visit the sick repeatedly (the verbal noun *ʿiyād* refers to the second meaning). These anxieties then return to the ṣuʿlūk again and again, as attentive as a visitor to an ailing friend. Their intent, however, is not to cure him, but the opposite. Hence, in the second hemistich these attendants are likened to quartan fever, an often fatal form of malaria in which the fever returns regularly (every fourth day) and with increasing intensity, leaving the victim each time more exhausted and closer to death—a particularly fitting metaphor for the passenger manqué. In the following verse (48) the antithesis of *warada* and *ṣadara*, to go to water and return from water (originally of cattle and people, and then a common metaphor for the avenger's sword drinking its victim's blood), is used to describe the *humūm* as livestock that come to quench their thirst and are sent away sated only to return again and again.

The dialectic of liminal exposure/tribal protection is the basis for the images of verses 49 and 50. The ṣuʿlūk is not a man protected by the accouterments of civilization and the institutions of the tribe, of which the shoe, "mediating" (to use an old structuralist standby) between the foot and the ground as culture does between man and nature, is perhaps the most basic symbol. The ṣuʿlūk, like the snake writhing on the burning sand, is directly exposed to the sun and to nature, without mediation. His reliance on himself instead of on society and its concomitants is expressed in metaphorical terms: he is clothed in endurance, shod with determination.

The description of the ṣuʿlūk's night raid (verses 54–60) is remarkable for the precision with which it depicts an episode that is quintessentially liminal in all its details. The time is night, a night so ill-fated and desperate that the hunter burns the very bow and arrows to which he owes his livelihood. It is into this night of darkness, cold, rain, hunger, and fear that the ṣuʿlūk sallies forth to procure his "livelihood," which is, as far as tribal society is concerned, death. The antithetical and lethal relation of the ṣuʿlūk to society is then stated with a terrible concision—*fa ayyamtu niswānan wa aytamtu ildatan*, I widowed women and orphaned children—the symmetrical inversion of the reaggregate tribal male who marries women and fathers children.

The following morning a discussion ensues among the men of the smitten tribe. By an ingenious indirection the poet captures the liminal characteristics of the ṣuʿlūk, his ambiguity and invisibility. The men cannot agree on what transpired, or on who or what the unseen night attacker was. It was only the growling of the dogs that alerted them to his presence. Darkness, invisibility, danger, and indeterminateness, the prime abstractions with which the anthropologists characterize the liminal phase of the rite of passage, are all embodied in this shadowy figure: Was it a wolf or a hyena whelp? A sandgrouse or a hawk? A man or a jinni?

The penultimate section of the poem (verses 61–64) consists of a description that, as would appear to be true for the poem generally, is important more for its ritual intent than for its apparent realism. It presents a portrait of the ṣuʿlūk face to face with nature at its most brutal, with nothing but the most worn-out remnants of the accouterments of civilization that might mediate between him and that brutality. No clothing veils him from the scorching sun; his hair, the grooming of which is a symbol of culture, is uncombed, unanointed, and full of lice and filth. We should note here too Mary Douglas's remark that filth is the proper expression of the liminal condition.[73] More specifically, in the matted dreadlocks of the ṣuʿlūk we can detect in extreme form one of the emblems of the state of ritual consecration, *iḥrām* (the prohibition or forswearing of wine, women, meat, ointment, and washing and

73. Douglas, *Purity and Danger,* 97.

combing the hair), that marks the liminal phase of the rituals of the ḥajj and of blood-vengeance.[74] The portrait depicted in the *Lāmiyyah* is thus particularly appropriate to the archetypal character portrayed in the akhbār of al-Shanfarā, the man perpetually in search of blood vengeance and hence perpetually liminal.

The closing section of the *Lāmiyyah* (verses 65–68) exhibits neither the motifs we might have expected on the basis of other ṣuʿlūk poems—the centrifugal flight, the sun-scorched peak, the ineluctability of death—nor those of the celebration of incorporation into the tribe that we might have expected to find in a full classical qaṣīdah. It has instead as its closure a curious metaphorical aggregation. Verse 65 exhibits diction and motifs that would suggest the transition from the raḥīl to the tribal fakhr in the classical qaṣīdah, except that to cross the wilderness the ṣuʿlūk has substituted "my two legs" for "my she-camel." Likewise, "I joined its end to its beginning" (66) might have been a cue for the conclusion of the raḥīl and the opening of the fakhr or madīḥ and all the images of satiety, abundance, protection, and propagation that the aggregation phase entails. Instead, in a powerful image of masculine domination and fertility the poet likens himself to a long-horned buck surrounded on a mountain slope by white-footed she-goats, which in turn he likens to maidens trailing long robes. The ritual underpinning of this image is that of the *ṭawāf*, the circumambulation of idols in certain pre-Islamic fertility rites.[75]

The image is not an entirely unfamiliar one; rather, it is suggestive of one of the motifs that often closes the raḥīl section of the classical qaṣīdah, the poet's comparison of his she-camel to the triumphant wild bull that has escaped the hunter's hounds or, what is perhaps even closer, to the wild ass with his mate or mates which likewise has escaped a human predator.[76]

The closing vision of survival and salvation is created by precisely that method of double inversion which has informed the poem throughout, the feralization of the human—the ṣuʿlūk (again as in verse 65 in the place of the she-camel) likens himself to the long-horned buck, the hunter's prey—and the anthropomorphization (or socialization) of the

74. Al-Marzūqī, *Sharḥ Dīwān al-Ḥamāsah* 2:838–39; G. E. von Grunebaum, *Muhammaden Festivals* (New York: Schuman, 1951), 26–28; Lammens, "Le caractère religieux du *ṯār*," 85–86.

75. Chelhod, *Le sacrifice chez les Arabes*, 161–62.

76. See for example, Lyall, *The Mufaḍḍalīyāt*, no. 9, verses 9–19, 1:66–70; no. 38, verses 8–19, 1:356–58; no. 39, verses 20–31, 1:378–81; no. 40, verses 51–60, 1:397–99.

animal—the she-goats are likened to maidens in ritual procession. The poem thus proceeds and succeeds through a characteristically liminal symmetrical inversion of the nature/culture dialectic. Moreover, the juxtaposition of this image of triumphant deliverance that concludes the *Lāmiyyah* with the image of al-Shanfarā's death as expressed in his *Ḥamāsiyyah* suggests to us the ultimate ritual significance of the ṣuᶜlūk: he is, like Oedipus, the surrogate victim or scapegoat, the anathematized hero who, for the community, says René Girard, "conjures up a baleful, infectious force that his own death—or triumph—transforms into a guarantee of order and tranquility."[77]

What should perhaps have aroused the critics' suspicion, however, is that the result of this complex metaphorical interplay—the substitution of the ṣuᶜlūk himself for the she-camel and subsequently as the subject of the simile of the escaped prey, and the further substitution of this closing motif of the raḥīl for the concluding image of the poem so as to form a metaphorical aggregation—creates an air of lyrical melancholia that is more akin to the pastoral wasteland of the poetry of Majnūn Laylā or Qays Lubnā—that is, the ᶜUdhrī *ghazal* (love lyric) of the Umayyad period—than to the heroic ethos of the Jāhiliyyah.

This analysis has determined that the "undisputed" akhbār and poetry of al-Shanfarā, on the one hand, and the *Lāmiyyat al-ᶜArab*, on the other, are characterized by an archetypal pattern of perpetual liminality, the passenger manqué. It is this common archetypal substructure, I believe, that is responsible for the accumulation of these materials around the name and legend of al-Shanfarā. If we wish to opt for Islamic authorship of the *Lāmiyyat al-ᶜArab*, there is no evidence to preclude this possibility. When we come to the specific question of the authorship of Khalaf al-Aḥmar, however, there is no historical proof or internal evidence, stylistic or otherwise, to support so specific an attribution. What is more certain is that the *Lāmiyyat al-ᶜArab* was composed in such a way as to define a genre—even to encompass it—with the result that to this day, the relation of every other ṣuᶜlūk poem to the *Lāmiyyah* is that of the part to the whole.

77. Girard, *Violence and the Sacred*, 87. The extensive parallels between the ṣuᶜlūk and Girard's interpretation of Oedipus as a surrogate victim (pp. 68–88) warrant detailed elaboration.

PART THREE

ORALITY AND GENDER IN THE ELEGY

CHAPTER 5

The Obligations and Poetics of Gender: Women's Elegy and Blood Vengeance

Women's rithā᾽ (elegy), or the rithā᾽ attributed to women, in the pre-Islamic and early Islamic periods constitutes a discretely defined body of verse that is particularly appropriate for the study of ritual function and pattern, especially as prescribed by gender role, and for establishing an aesthetics suitable to a ritually determined oral poetic form. The tradition, among Arabs and Orientalists alike, has been to see, especially in the elegies of al-Khansā᾽, the Mukhaḍramah (that is, bridging the pre-Islamic and Islamic periods) poetess who is the leading exponent of the genre of women's elegies, the maudlin expression of "feminine sentimentality." In this view, the corpus of women's poetry, dominated as it is by elegies for fallen kinsmen, testifies at once to the delicate sentiments and sensibilities of bedouin womanhood and to women's artistic and intellectual inferiority to men.[1] Although not entirely free from such stereotypical thinking, Henri Lammens's appraisal of women's elegies makes a more useful starting point for our discussion. Lammens recognizes, first of all, that the *marāthī* (elegies) intoned by the mother and sisters, and by the wife if she was not from another tribe, are ritual lamentations and, further, that the call to vengeance *(taḥrīḍ)* is an integral part of the *marthiyah* (elegy). After commenting on the stereotyped and conventional nature of the wom-

1. A quite useful and accurate descriptive overview of women's poetry in the Jāhiliyyah, coupled with the traditional disparaging explanation of the limited scope and quality of women's poetry in the Arabic tradition, is provided in Aḥmad Muḥammad al-Ḥūfī, *Al-Mar᾽ah fī al-Shi῾r al-Jāhilī*, 2d ed. (Cairo: Dār al-Fikr al-῾Arabī, 1963), 603–88, esp. 644, 668, 677–88.

en's marāthī and their repetition ad nauseam of the same clichés, however, he claims that taḥrīḍ alone escapes this criticism, since it comes truly from the heart, raised above the level of clichéd sentimentality by fierce familial loyalty.[2]

In the context of my argument, the crucial point Lammens makes is that of the ritual nature of women's elegy. The "disconcerting uniformity" of rithāʾ such as al-Khansāʾ's can be explained, he notes, by its traditional, quasi-religious character.[3] His shortcoming, as I see it, is that, having identified the *function* of women's elegy as ritual lamentation, he has not made the second step of recognizing that its *form* and *content*, being ritually determined, cannot be judged by Romantic concepts of "originality" and "sincerity." He is thus equally mistaken in his dismissal of women's elegy as unimaginative and conventionalized sentimentality and in his claim for the "authenticity" and "sincerity" of taḥrīḍ.

I propose that women's elegy (including taḥrīḍ) cannot be properly evaluated as failed or mediocre attempts at individual expression but, rather, must be examined as the performance of a ritual obligation. The limitations of the genre reflect not inherent biological limitations of gender but the limited participation allowed or demanded of women in the public life of the tribe. In this respect, we should begin with Goldziher's recognition of the roots of the marthiyah in the *niyāḥah*, that is, the rhythmic *sajʿ* (rhymed-prose) lament.[4] To this I would add that the women's poem instigating her male relatives to avenge a fallen kinsman, normally termed simply taḥrīḍ (incitement, instigation), reflects another public obligation incumbent on women, that of inciting the warriors during battle, also termed taḥrīḍ or *tashjīʿ* (as is the chieftain's exhortation of the fighting men), which often was in the form of *sajʿ* or the archaic *rajaz* meter.[5] In other words, the pre-Islamic Arabic elegy, especially that composed by women, can reveal to us that point

2. Lammens, "Le caractère religieux du ṯār," 103–4.

3. Ibid., 104.

4. Ignaz Goldziher, "Bemerkungen zur arabischen Trauerpoesie," in Goldziher, *Gesammelte Schriften* 4:361–71 and passim. See also J. A. Bellamy, "Some Observations on the Arabic *rithāʾ* in the *Jāhilīyah* and Islam," *Jerusalem Studies in Arabic and Islam* 13 (1990): 44, 54–55.

5. Further functions of women in battle were giving food and drink to the fighting men, tending the wounded, and on some occasions, carrying a stick or club to administer the coup de grace to enemy wounded. On the roles of women in battle, see al-Ḥūfī, *Al-Marʾah*, 430–62 and, for examples of battle taḥrīḍ, 454–55.

at which liturgy and literature intersect.[6] As a basis for this approach, I offer some general observations concerning the social and ritual role and status of women and of their poetry in the pre-Islamic period.

In the corpus of pre-Islamic poetry that has come down to us the verse attributed to women is almost entirely rithāʾ (including both elegy and taḥrīḍ) for kinsmen (father, brother, husband—if, as Lammens points out, he is of the same tribe) and, moreover, exclusively for the warriors (*fursān*) and lords (*sādah*). There appears, furthermore, to be a preponderance of rithāʾ for those who fell in battle over those who died of natural causes. There is virtually no rithāʾ for anyone but the male warrior: mothers, sisters, wives, daughters, sons not yet old enough to fight were not commemorated in pre-Islamic Arabic elegy, or at least not in elegies the tradition has preserved.[7] In this respect, it is worth noting the locus of women's elegies in the literary canon, for with the exception of secondary anthologies, we find them above all near the conclusion of the akhbār (biographical literary notices) on males of the warrior class. That is, the last "chapter" in the warrior's biography comprises the elegies composed for him by male and female kin and the vengeance taken for him by male kin.[8]

6. I should like to make it clear here that although I entirely agree with Goldziher's discussion of the *niyāḥah* (*Todtenklage*, lament) as being a ritual obligation like that of blood vengeance, I do not agree with his, to my mind, arbitrary distinction between the ritually obligatory *niyāḥah* and the poetic marthiyah in which residual *niyāḥah* elements play merely an emotive role. Rather, I would argue that, formal differences aside, there is more of a continuum between the two and, further, that the marthiyah itself is innately ritual in form and function. I am not dealing here with the issue of historical development. See Goldziher, "Trauerpoesie," 361–65.

7. The major anthology of pre-Islamic women's elegy is Shaykhū, *Riyāḍ al-Adab*. Among general collections of women's verse are Aḥmad ibn Abī Ṭāhir Ṭayfūr, *Balāghāt al-Nisāʾ wa Ṭarāʾif Kalāmihinna wa Mulaḥ Nawādirihinna wa Akhbār Dhawāt al-Raʾy minhunna wa Ashʿāruhunna fī al-Jāhiliyyah wa al-Islām*, ed. Aḥmad al-Alfī (Tunis: al-Maktabah al-ʿAtīqah, 1985) [reprint of Cairo, 1326/1908], esp. 168–203, passim; and ʿAbd al-Badīʿ Ṣaqr, *Shāʿirāt al-ʿArab* (N.p.: Manshūrāt al-Maktab al-Islāmī, n.d.), passim. See references in Sezgin, *Poesie,* 65, 102. Exceptions to the marthī's being an adult male of the warrior class are rare in pre-Islamic poetry. They begin to crop up after the coming of Islam, especially in the early Umayyad period. Al-Mubarrad includes, e.g., a man's elegy for his niece (315); a mother's marthiyah for her two slain children (320); a marthiyah of the Umayyad poet al-Farazdaq for a wife who was pregnant when she died (the lines quoted concern the lost child/fetus rather than the wife), etc. See Abū al-ʿAbbās Muḥammad ibn Yazīd al-Mubarrad, *Al-Kāmil fī al-Lughah wa al-Adab*, 2 vols. (Beirut: Muʾassasat al-Maʿārif, n.d.), 2:313–60.

8. A curious case in point that indicates the ritual and obligatory nature of women's elegy is that of the death of the Prophet Muḥammad's grandfather, ʿAbd al-Muṭṭalib. It is recorded that when ʿAbd al-Muṭṭalib knew that his hour was come, he gathered his six daughters to him and demanded, "Weep for me that I might hear what you are going to say before I die"

Not a single woman is to be found among the major poets of the Jāhiliyyah.[9] The earliest poetess of stature is the Mukhaḍramah al-Khansāʾ, followed by Laylā al-Akhyaliyyah, who is already in the Umayyad period.[10] Both are renowned for their rithāʾ, al-Khansāʾ's for her brothers fallen in battle, Laylā's for her slain ʿUdhrī-style lover, Tawbah. In other words, the full tripartite classical qaṣīdah consisting of nostalgic-amorous prelude (nasīb), desert journey (raḥīl), and tribal boast (fakhr) (or panegyric, madīḥ, or invective, hijāʾ) appears to have been a male domain, as does what J. A. Bellamy terms the "long marthiyah," that is, the elegy that in form and length constitutes a subgenre (*gharaḍ*) of the qaṣīdah.[11] This male authorship should bear some relation to my argument that the structure of the qaṣīdah is analogous to that of the rite of passage of the male, which culminates in the hunt (animal sacrifice) and battle/blood vengeance (human sacrifice). The sole female form or genre of poetry preserved in the classical Arabic poetic corpus is, then, not unexpectedly connected with that obligation that throughout the ancient Mediterranean and Middle Eastern world

(*ibkīna ʿalayya ḥattā asmaʿa mā taqulna qabla an amūta*), whereupon they recited their elegies for him. ʿAbd al-Muṭṭalib nodded as if to say, "Lament me thus," then died. Abū Muḥammad ʿAbd al-Malik ibn Hishām, *Al-Sīrah al-Nabawiyyah*, 4 vols. (Cairo: Dār al-Fikr, n.d.), 1:181–89.

9. See, e.g., Sezgin, *Poesie*, 107–315, passim. Al-Ḥūfī, *Al-Marʾah*, 604–6. What al-Ḥūfī suggests here is, in light of the present argument, quite correct, viz., that the classical tradition took as its measure the full or polythematic qaṣīdah, and this is precisely what women did not compose, hence, their nonrepresentation in the early classical anthologies.

10. See Sezgin, *Poesie*, 311–14, 399–400; and ʿUmar Riḍā Kaḥḥālah, *Aʿlām al-Nisāʾ fī ʿĀlamay al-ʿArab wa al-Islām*, 5 vols. (Damascus: Muʾassasat al-Risālah, 1977), 1:360–71, 4:321–34.

11. Bellamy finds: "It is important to distinguish further between the short *marthiyah* and the long *marthiyah*, on the one hand, and, on the other hand, between elegies composed by men and those composed by women. These two categories of length and sex overlap to some extent: the long *marāthī* are almost always composed by men, the short *marthiyah* is the favorite of women, though men composed them as well. However, the short poems ascribed to men may sometimes be fragments of longer ones, but this is not the case with women. Too many short elegies by women have survived for us to assume that they are all mere fragments." See Bellamy, "Some Observations on the Arabic *Rithāʾ*," 54–55. The main exceptions to the rule that marāthī are composed by men would be al-Khansāʾ and Laylā al-Akhyaliyyah, the latter well beyond the scope of this book. A noteworthy exception to the male dominance of the qaṣīdah form is the latter's madīḥ to the Umayyad caliph Marwān ibn al-Ḥakam. See Laylā al-Akhyaliyyah, *Dīwān*, ed. Khalīl Ibrāhīm al-ʿAṭiyyah and Jalīl al-ʿAṭiyyah (Baghdad: Dār al-Jumhūriyyah, 1967), 53–58. My generalizations here concerning the scope of women's poetry in the Jāhiliyyah and early Islamic periods are easily confirmed by a reading of any of the general collections of women's poetry. The very limited participation of women in other genres (madīḥ, hijāʾ, etc.) and the fact that their poetry is almost always monothematic (as opposed to the polythematic full qaṣīdah form) and usually quite short is discussed by al-Ḥūfī, *Al-Marʾah*, 233–63, 225–27.

is preeminently incumbent upon the female—ritual lamentation, and, to a somewhat lesser extent, inciting the menfolk to blood vengeance and in battle.

It appears that for the class of "free" or "freeborn" (s. *ḥurrah*, *ʿātiq*) women, that is, the kinswomen of the lords and warriors (s. *sayyid*, *fāris*), puberty was marked by confinement and veiling (the inverse of the male liminal expulsion) or "protection," which is the dominant sign of their elevated status throughout their lives. The protection or privacy (especially pudical) of free women set them in opposition, above all, to female captives (s. *sabī*) and slaves (s. *amah*),[12] who were not secluded and veiled but rather defiled by every hand and eye. The essentially public nature of early Arabic poetry versus the privacy of the "freeborn" women, explains, too, the outrage with which poetry addressed to or describing such women was met by their kinsmen: it was virtually the equivalent of seduction or rape. Crucial to the argument at hand is that confinement and privacy thus constitute an expression of "purity" or, in ritual terms, aggregation; hence, to be expelled, unveiled, to appear or speak in public, is an expression of "defilement," of liminality. It is therefore only in the liminal (defiled/sacral) states of a kinsman's death or of warfare that the women of the warrior class have a public—and hence poetic—voice.

In poetry we find this pattern exploited in two closely related images. First, the defilement of once-free/confined women taken captive, exposed and unveiled, implying all that the change in status from "free woman" to "slave/captive" entails of sexual degradation. This image appears in poetry both to express the defilement and devitalization of the enemy—their women exposed, degraded, and their source of offspring carried off to bear another kin group's children—and to express the defilement of the poet's own tribe if or when their women are taken captive. Second, the defilement of women bereft of their kinsman who, in their rites of lamentation exhibit behavior that is analogous to that of women taken captive—going out of their dwellings unveiled, tearing their hair and clothes, scratching their faces and wailing.

Woman's mourning must thus be understood, above all, as an obligatory public lamentation that was ritually prescribed and served to express a typically liminal defiled and yet sacral state. In accordance with my argument concerning the ritually structured perception of the taking of blood vengeance for the male, I contend that, theoretically at least,

12. See al-Ḥūfī, *Al-Marʾah*, 464–524, passim; on the terms, see 492–93.

a woman's period of mourning should have come to an end when her male relatives achieved vengeance for their fallen kinsman or, analogously, with the recitation of her elegy, which puts her "on record," as it were, as being in perpetual mourning and thereby relieves her of the obligation to continue actually mourning.

Given the preeminently public and ritual nature of early Arabic poetry, it follows that the women's limited poetic domain should in large part reflect the limited occasions upon which "free" women of the warrior class were allowed public voice or required to speak publicly: the *niyāḥah*, lament for their adult menfolk, and taḥrīḍ, inciting their menfolk in battle or vengeance. Inasmuch as poetry was preeminently the domain of men of the ruling and warrior class, in terms of both composition and preservation, it should not be surprising that the women's poetry the tradition prescribed and preserved should, in general, reflect exclusively male concerns. The major occupations and preoccupations of women were not considered matters of tribal record to be encoded in verse and preserved for the posterity of the tribe. It seems to me reasonable to assume that women had their own traditional poems and songs of various types but that these were quite distinct from the male qaṣīdah tradition and never made their way into the classical Arabic canon. Aḥmad Muḥammad al-Ḥūfī attributes the absence of feminine topics to women's innate lack of truly creative poetic capacities![13] More to the point, I suggest, is women's limited role in the public (= male) ritual life of the tribe, which it was the function of poetry to record. Moreoever, those who collected and wrote down the oral tribal tradition in the early Islamic period appear to have been exclusively men relying on exclusively male transmitters (*ruwāt*). Further, it is quite possible that the attribution of extant poems of rithāʾ and taḥrīd to women may be largely a literary conceit, much of this poetry having in fact been composed by men.

If we recognize the prescribed ritual function of women's rithāʾ, we can no longer talk of the conventional sentimentality of women's elegy or of the bold individuality of taḥrīḍ. This body of verse is concerned more with ritual obligation than personal expression, and therefore both the elegiac and hortatory elements are equally stereotypical—or rather, archetypal. They express not personal sentiment but ritual intent.

13. Ibid., 644, 677–88.

The ritually—and hence literarily—restricted scope of early Arabic women's rithāʾ provides a neatly defined corpus or "control group" through which to study the literary characteristics of oral-formulaic poetry. My intention here is not to prove oral-formulaic theory or apply it to the poems at hand but rather, assuming its oral-formulaic character, to examine the aesthetic aspects of such verse. Of primary importance in this regard is a shift in aesthetic principles away from the preeminently Romantic notion of individual and original expression. In an oral-formulaic poetry in which both the structure and imagery, in the sense of both content and expression, are largely ritually or traditionally prescribed, what we have to look for is not individuality of expression or personal poetic vision but the power, and hence permanence, of the communal expression of a body of verse and of individual poems or voices within that tradition. We must then ask how the individual poem strengthens and reinforces that collective message.

The issue of individuality cannot, however, be simply dismissed. The intent of any particular marthiyah is, after all, to "recall" or "call back" the marthī (elegized deceased), as an individual, to preserve the memory of a particular human being. The marthiyah was not meant to be recited once in liturgical fashion; it is not merely a stereotyped or archetypal funeral oration in that sense. It was intended to be permanent in the communal sense I have described, while perpetuating the memory or name of a particular individual. It is the *permanence* of the individual which is of the essence, however, not his individuality. This requirement calls for a poem that is at once striking (that is, individual) and conventional (that is, permanent); and it is this dynamic or dialectic that is crucial to women's rithāʾ, indeed, to all oral-formulaic poetry. The poem that is too unusual is too easily forgotten or misunderstood; conversely, the poem that is too conventional has no identity so that neither it nor the identity of the marthī will be preserved. The life of the poem, then, depends on this tension.

I propose that women's lamentation/rithāʾ is in perception and expression the inverse parallel of men's blood vengeance/rithāʾ. Thus we can expect to find a shared imagery and, further, interreferentiality between the two corpora of verse. This is reinforced by a further gender distinction: that it is the kinsman who is obligated to avenge the dead and the kinswoman who is obligated to instigate him to do so, particularly should he be dilatory in shouldering his responsibility or tempted to accept the bloodwite. Furthermore, both types of rithāʾ are ultimately concerned with sacrifice and redemption; but whereas the male redeems his slain kinsmen by pouring out the liquid soul (*al-nafs al-sā'ilah*)[14]—the blood of vengeance or his own blood, should he fall while attempting to take vengeance—the kinswoman does so by the shedding of tears, another "expression" of liquid soul and a metaphor for the composing of rithā' itself.

A comprehensive study of women's rithā' in pre-Islamic poetry is beyond the scope of this book. Here, I propose, rather, to examine in detail several specimens that exemplify the production and perpetuation of meaning in a closed oral-formulaic system of ritually determined poetry, thereby to establish an aesthetics appropriate to evaluate and interpret such verse.

The first poem is a short marthiyah by al-Khirniq bint Badr ibn Hiffān, the sister of one of the poets of the *Muʿallaqāt*, Ṭarafah ibn al-ʿAbd.[15] In it she elegizes her kinsmen, among them her husband Bishr ibn ʿAmr ibn Marthad al-Ḍubaʿī, her son ʿAlqamah ibn Bishr, and her two brothers, Ḥassān and Shuraḥbīl, who fell in a battle against the Banū Asad which took place on a mountain road called Qulāb.[16] The poem is exemplary for the lapidary economy of its images, its archaic formulary style, and its epigrammatic concision.

Let my Kinsmen not be Distant! [19]

1. Let my kinsmen not be distant!
 Men who are the enemy's poison,
  The slaughter camels' bane,
2. The attackers on every battleground,
 The perfumers of
  Their loincloths' knots,[17]
3. The sword-strikers in the thick of battle,
 The lance-thrusters
  With hairy forearms,
4. The minglers of their noble-born and baseborn,
 Of those with wealth among them
  And their poor.

14. See Lammens, "Le caractère religieux du *ṯār*," 84.

15. See Kaḥḥālah, *Aʿlām al-Nisā'* 1:348–50; Sezgin, *Poesie*, 310–11.

16. ʿAbd al-Qādir ibn ʿUmar al-Baghdādī, *Khizānat al-Adab wa Lubb Lubāb Lisān al-ʿArab*, ed. ʿAbd al-Salām Muḥammad Hārūn, 13 vols., 2d ed. (Cairo: Maktabat al-Khānjī, 1984), 5:51.

17. Literally, perfumed on, or pure of, the knots of their loincloths. On *maʿāqida al-uzri* as *ism makān*, see Wright, *Grammar* 2:112.

5. When they drink, they give drink;
 When they desist, admonish one another
  Against foul speech.
6. Men from whom when they ride forth
 You hear the clamor
  Of their shouts and calls
7. And no abuse among them
 For the offspring of
  Their colts and fillies.
[8. On the morning of Qulāb they met their death,
 Led forth like livestock
  To the sacrifice.][18]
9. This is my praise for them while I yet live,
 And when I die
  My grave will cover me.[19]

The poem opens with the elegiac formula "Do not be distant/perish," or "Let (the deceased) not be distant/perish," which occurs in both the negative imperative *lā tabʿad* and the negative jussive *lā yabʿad* and in the causative (IV) negative jussive *lā yubʿid Allāh* (Let God not make distant). This formula has been noted by Orientalist scholars. Goldziher and Lammens both remark on it, but with little insight into its significance.[20] Luwīs Shaykhū perhaps shows more insight in his extensive quotation of the generous commentaries of his predecessors, al-Baghdādī in *Khizānat al-Adab* and al-ʿAynī in *Sharḥ Shawāhid Shurūḥ al-Alfiyyah* on al-Khirniq's line,[21] and it is with the first of these, al-Baghdādī's (d. 1093/1682), that we will begin our discussion:

> Her words *lā yabʿadan* mean "Let them not perish!" It is an optative phrase in the negative. . . . One says *baʿida* [*yabʿadu baʿadan*] according to the paradigm of *fariḥa* to mean "he perished." As for the opposite of

18. This verse is lacking in many versions. See Shaykhū, *Riyāḍ al-Adab*, 31; al-Khirniq, *Dīwān al-Khirniq Ukht Ṭarafah*, ed. Luwīs Shaykhū (Beirut: Maṭbaʿat al-Ābāʾ al-Yasūʿiyyīn, 1899), 15–16; and al-Khirniq, *Dīwān Shiʿr al-Khirniq bint Badr ibn Hiffān*, ed. Husayn Naṣṣār ([Cairo], U.A.R.: Maṭbaʿat Dār al-Kutub, 1969), 32.

19. I have followed Shaykhū's version as given in *Riyāḍ al-Adab*, 27–31 and in al-Khirniq, *Dīwan*, ed. Shaykhū, 10–16. See also al-Khirniq, *Dīwān Shiʿr*, ed. Naṣṣār, 28–32, especially for sources. Also consulted were the versions in al-Qālī, *Kitāb al-Amālī* 2:158; and al-Baghdādī, *Khizānat al-Adab* 5:41–55.

20. See Goldziher, "Bemerkungen zur arabischen Trauerpoesie," 365–66; and Lammens, "Le caractère religieux du *ṯār*," 101. Of interest, as Lammens remarks, is the corresponding use of the imperative *fa ibʿad* (perish! go away!) as an imprecation (101).

21. Shaykhū, *Riyāḍ al-Adab*, 27–28; al-Khirniq, *Dīwān*, ed. Shaykhū, 10–11.

proximity, it is *baᶜuda yabᶜudu*, with *ḍammah* in both tenses, and the verbal noun is *buᶜd*, and it may be used to mean perish as well because of the overlapping of the two meanings [*li-tadākhuli maᶜnayayhimā*] as when God the Exalted said: "Let Madyan perish even as Thamūd perished" [*alā buᶜdan li Madyana kamā baᶜidat Thamūdu*] [Qurʾān 11:95]. . . .[22] Ibn al-Sayyid said in *Sharḥ Abyāt al-Jumal*, "If someone asks, 'How could she invoke her tribesmen not to perish when they were already dead?' the answer is that it was the custom among the Arabs to use this expression in their invocations for the dead, and this they did with two goals in mind: the first was to magnify the death of a great man, as if they could not believe that he had died. This sense is clear in Zuhayr ibn Abī Sulmā's verses:

> They say that Ḥiṣn is dead, but their souls deny it.
> How can he be dead when the mountains still stand?
> And the graves have not cast forth their dead,
> The stars still shine on high,
> And the ground is still firm beneath the foot? [20]

He means that they say that Ḥiṣn has died, but then they find it too grievous to speak about. So they say, 'How can this be, when the mountains have not yet been smashed, the stars have not faded, the graves have not expelled their dead, and the earth's mass still stands firm?' The second goal was that they intended through invoking the deceased that his memory [*dhikr*] would survive and not fade: for after a man's death, the survival of his memory takes the place of his life (*li-anna baqāʾa dhikri al-insāni baᶜda mawtihi bi manzilati ḥayātihi*). Have you not heard the poet's [al-Ḥādirah's] words:

> Praise us then—you bastards' sons!—
> For our deeds. For surely praise
> Is immortality. [21]

And the words of another poet elegizing Yazīd ibn Mazyad al-Shaybānī:

> If the passage of the nights has obliterated him,
> Or almost,
> Then his reputation will obliterate the nights. [22]

And al-Mutanabbī said in a brilliant line:

22. See Lane, *b-ᶜ-d*.

The remembrance of a youth is his second life,
His need is just for sustenance
All else in life is mere distraction. [23]

And Mālik ibn al-Rayb al-Māzinī exposed the absurdity of this expression in his qaṣīdah that begins:

As they bury me they say, 'Do not go far!'
But what place could be farther than
The place I lie? [24]

And al-Farrār al-Sulamī said:

What good was it to me when their women said,
When I, and not their husbands, had been killed,
'Do not perish!'[23] [25]

A fuller understanding of the function of this phrase in terms of the semiotic interrelations of formulaic orality requires the extension of the classical discussion. First of all, in Arabic poetic terms the same synecdochic relationship that so intimately connects the ruined abode of the nasīb with the tomb of the rithāʾ (although it is perhaps not entirely clear which is the part and which the whole) connects the *firāq* (the departure of the poet's mistress and her tribe) of the nasīb with death, the ultimate departure. Thus *lā tabʿad* or, as it appears in this poem, *lā yabʿadan* is equi-vocally "do not depart" and "do not perish." It is precisely because of this polysemous condensation into two words that evoke all the shared emotions of loss and departure which inhabit the twin elegiac worlds of the nasīb and rithāʾ that this phrase was selected as part of the elegiac formulary. Further, it serves as a condensed expression of the purpose of rithāʾ: for the Arab poet or poetess to "recall" the dead is to "call back" the dead to life. Indeed, the concept of poetry as conferring immortality has tremendous implication not only for the study of elegy but for the study of Arabic panegyric poetry. In this poem the "presence" of the dead is conjured, as it were, by the tenselessness or atemporality of verses 1–7 of the poem: the jussive and nominal sentences of verse 1, the active participial forms of verses 2–4, the conditional clauses of verses 5–6, the non-tense-signifying imperfect of verse 7.

23. Al-Baghdādī, *Khizānat al-Adab* 5:45–47.

A similar concision of meaning persists throughout the poem. Already in the first verse the fallen are described in terms of the fulfillment of the two fundamental obligations of the warrior: killing the enemy and feeding the kin. Of interest here is the mode of expression: the parallel positioning in the paired epithets of the enemy and the slaughter camel reinforces the symmetrically inverse relation of blood vengeance to animal sacrifice. In rhetorical terms we have parallelism and antithesis, in mnemonic terms a complex concept of sacrifice and redemption memorably summed up in four words. Nor are the two hemistichs of the opening verse unrelated, for it is precisely the fallen warriors' sacrifice and self-sacrifice that qualify them for "recall" or poetic resurrection.

Verse 2 exhibits once again the compounding of metaphors through the choice of semantically laden diction. What is most peculiar is that despite the extensive philological *sharḥ* (commentary) precisely on the terms *muᶜtarak* (place of battle) and *al-ṭayyibūna maᶜāqida al-uzrī* (perfumed on/pure of the knots of their loincloths), both Shaykhū and the classical critics seem to have missed the essential message of the line:

> . . . *Muᶜtarak*, and likewise *maᶜrak*, . . . means a place of battle. It is derived from the expression *ᶜarakat al-raḥā al-ḥabba* (the hand mill ground the grain), when it crushed it. They meant that the place of battle crushes, just as the hand mill crushes whatever is in it, so they called it a hand mill. ᶜAntarah said:
>
> A crushing mill revolved
> around the fighting clansmen. [26]
>
> Zuhayr ibn Abī Sulmā made this clear in his verse:
>
> Then war will grind you like the grinding
> of a hand mill, its skin [spread out beneath],
> Then conceive two years running, then bear young,
> then wean them.[24] [27]

24. Ibid., 5:48–49. The more common version of this verse from Zuhayr's *Muᶜallaqah* is cited by Lane and Ibn Manẓūr: *fa taᶜrukkumū ᶜarka al-raḥā bi thifālihā / wa talqaḥ kishāfan thumma tuntij fa tut'imī*. Lane translates and comments: "meaning *And it*, i.e., war, *will fret* [or *grind* or *crush*] *you, as the mill with its skin put beneath it, upon which the flour falls, frets* [or *grinds*] *the grain; and it*, i.e., war, *will conceive two years, one after the other; then bring forth, and give birth to twins*: he makes war's destruction of them to be like the mill's grinding of the grain, and the various evils that are engendered from war to be like children." See al-Anbārī, *Sharḥ al-Qaṣāʾid al-Sabᶜ*, in which this is verse 31 and the phrase *turḍiᶜ fa tafṭimi* (nurse, then wean) concludes verse 32; and Lane and *Lisān*, *ᶜ-r-k*.

> By her words *wa al-ṭayyibūna* (and the perfumed, pure, sweet) [al-Khirniq] meant that they are sexually chaste [*aʿiffāʾu fī furūjihim*], because the Arabs allude to a thing by way of its container or covering, as when they say "pure of [his garment's] neck-opening [*jayb*]" meaning "heart." Thus they allude to the heart by the *jayb* that lies over it, or close to it. The poetess says, they do not untie their loincloths for something that is not theirs. Al-Lakhmī said that according to Ibn Khalaf when they describe a man by purity of the loincloth and its being perfumed/sweet, this is an indication of and allusion to his sexual chastity [*ʿiffat al-farj*], meaning that he does not tie his loincloth over the pudenda of an adulteress. The same goes for "purity of the skirt-train." And when someone is described as pure of cuff . . . , they mean that he does not steal or cheat. . . .[25]

The shortcoming of the classical commentarists is that they have treated the two hemistichs as discrete statements and thus have ignored the profound semantic bond between the roots of the two key words—*ʿ-r-k* and *ṭ-y-b*. In fact this line, when read in light of the etymological implications of these words and coupled with the consistent imagery of blood-vengeance poetry, concisely and subtly restates the male/female, pure/polluted dialectic by which men's cleansing themselves of the pollution of unavenged blood is equated with women's washing and perfuming themselves after menstruation.[26] "Perfumed on the knots of their loincloths"—literally, *maʿāqid* are the places where their loincloths are knotted—is, in any case, physiologically too close to women's perfuming themselves after menstruation to be semantically or metaphorically unrelated. Moreover, among the meanings of the root *ʿ-r-k* is *ʿarakat* "to menstruate." Thus *muʿtarak* (battleground, passive participle of VIII as noun of place) can also suggest "a place of menstruation" that is, in the metaphorical terms of blood vengeance, a place of polluted—that is, unavenged—blood. It is odd that the commentarists cite Zuhayr's verse without, it appears, making this connection. For clearly, when *taʿruk* (grind, crush) occurs in the same line with the rest of the female reproductive cycle—conception, pregnancy, and weaning—the meaning of menstruation must at some level be intended.

Of note here, however, is the connection of menstruation with fertility. This suggests that menstruation, like other "taboo" states, has

25. Al-Baghdādī, *Khizānat al-Adab* 5:50.

26. On women's cleansing of the pollution caused by menstruation with perfume see Abū ʿAbd Allāh al-Bukhārī, *Ṣaḥīḥ Abī ʿAbd Allāh al-Bukhārī bi Sharḥ al-Kirmānī*, 25 vols. (Cairo: al-Maṭbaʿah al-Bahiyyah al-Miṣriyyah, 1933–62), 3:178–81.

a certain ambiguity. On the one hand, inasmuch as it indicates a failure to conceive, what Mary Douglas has termed "a sort of human being *manqué*,"[27] menstruation is essentially equivalent to a miscarried fetus. On the other hand, inasmuch as menstruation occurs only during a woman's child-bearing years it is perceived as part of the fertility cycle, a prerequisite for conception. Like menstrual blood, the blood of war is both pure and polluting. The compounding of fertility metaphors in Zuhayr's verse embraces the cereal—the grinding of grain to make bread—the sexual, and the martial—revitalizing the kin group through avenging the dead. Once again, the medieval Christian iconography that depicts Mary and the infant Christ with a mill grinding grain, expresses in virtually identical terms the concept of fertility or redemption through sacrifice: the cereal, the sexual (mother and child), and what is assumed in the portrayal of Christ, the blood sacrifice of the crucifixion.[28] In other words, classical Arabic poetry expresses through etymology what medieval Christian painting expresses through iconography.

The ritual concept of pollution and purification as expressed in al-Khirniq's verse is evident too from the range of meanings associated with the root *ṭ-y-b*. *Ṭayyib* means good, pleasant, sweet in taste or odor, but also pure and clean. It is defined as the antonym of *khabīth* (impure, foul, abominable). The lexicographer Muḥammad ibn Manẓūr mentions too that *ṭayyib* and *khabīth* are used to mean, respectively, *ḥalāl* and *ḥarām*. The noun *ṭīb* thus means sweetness, but also perfume; *ṭābah* means the clearest of wine and is also an epithet of the well of Zamzam.[29] This cluster of purifying liquids among the derivatives of *ṭ-y-b* thus indicates with respect to al-Khirniq's verse that *al-ṭayyibūna* are those who wash the disgrace of unavenged blood from the knots of their loincloths with the blood of vengeance—*ghasl al-dam bi al-dam*.[30] It should be kept in mind too that it is not merely etymological speculation

27. Douglas, *Purity and Danger*, 96.

28. On the iconography of the "mystical mill" in medieval Christianity, see Caroline Walker Bynum, *Holy Feast and Holy Fast: The Religious Significance of Food to Medieval Women* (Berkeley: University of California Press, 1987), 68, 81, plate 1.

29. Lane and *Lisān*, *ṭ-y-b*.

30. The ritual identification of blood and perfume is further suggested by their identical use in sealing pacts. See the famous pact sealed in Mecca between the Banū ʿAbd al-Manāf and the Banū ʿAbd al-Dār. The Banū ʿAbd al-Manāf brought a bowl of perfume, dipped their hands in it, and wiped them on the Kaʿbah; the Banu ʿAbd al-Dār did the same thing, only with blood. The ʿAbd al-Manāf were therefore called *al-muṭayyibūn*, the perfumers; the ʿAbd al-Dār, *laʿaqat al-dam*, the blood-lickers. See al-Ālūsī, *Bulūgh al-Arab* 1:238–39.

that confirms the deeper reading of this verse but the common comparison of men disgraced by unavenged blood to women who have not washed after their menses. In Arabic poetry these two kinds of blood pollution are explicitly identified.

Together with the more straightforward thrust of verses 3 and 4, the poetess creates a string of active participial epithets—*al-ḍāribūna* (the strikers), *al-ṭāʿinūna* (the thrusters), *al-khāliṭūna* (the minglers).[31] These are perhaps best understood as lists of titles or honorifics with which we find a parallel in monumental inscriptions. It is at this point that oral and graven archaic memorials seem to overlap. Note that it is the public, "official" biography that is preserved, that is perceived as being permanent and having permanent value. This suggests to us once more why marāthī were composed only for adult males of the ruling warrior class: they were the only class in bedouin society that had a "public" or "official" presence. Finally, it should be remarked that the ritual reviving or conjuring of the dead through a liturgical recitation of epithets is essentially the same process that operates in Ṣūfī *dhikr*, especially that of the ninety-nine names of God, to conjure the divine presence.

Verses 5–7 describe the fallen as generous men, as pure of speech as of action, men whose steeds are, like them, of noble breed and need no chiding but the battle cry.

A blunt shift occurs in verse 8 from the timelessness or tenselessness of the preceding lines. Suddenly we are confronted with the perfect tense in *lāqaw* (they met their death), and a date "the morning of Qulāb" when the timeless, tenseless qualities of the hero were defeated, as it were, by time and tense. We feel the poem, too, coming to an end with the simile of the warriors to livestock (specifically sheep) consecrated for the ʿItr, the pre-Islamic sacrifice in the month of Rajab,[32] an image that recalls the identification of fallen warriors with sacrificial victims in verse 1.

The heroes' death in verse 8 is followed by a resurrection in verse 9, for as the poets al-Baghdādī cites have told us, praise is immortality. It is ironic that the poetess who thus memorializes and immortalizes her fallen kinsmen concedes, indeed declares, her own mortality: "When I die my grave will cover me." The gender dialectic is again at work: the

31. It is of note that, according to al-Qālī, al-Mufaḍḍal al-Ḍabbī attributes a close variant of verses 3 and 4 to Ḥātim al-Ṭāʾī. See al-Qālī, *Al-Amālī* 2:169.

32. Al-Baghdādī, *Khizānat al-Adab* 5:53; al-Ālūsī, *Bulūgh al-Arab* 3:41. See also Robertson Smith, *Religion of the Semites*, 227–28.

slain warrior is celebrated and thus immortalized; the woman, in death as in life, is concealed.

The further irony is that through sacrifice the victim, too, is redeemed, that through her self-negating praise of her fallen kinsmen, al-Khirniq's name and art survive.

The second poem to be discussed is a short marthiyah by al-Fāriʿah bint Shaddād al-Murriyyah for her brother Masʿūd.[33] It has been chosen because it demonstrates clearly and powerfully the poetics of oral formulism and the metaphoric polysemy of expression of the ritual concept of redemption.

O My Eye, Be Generous [28]

1. O my eye, be generous to Masʿūd son of Shaddād
with every teary gland whose grief
is manifest.
2. O whoever sees a lightning-flashing cloud
that I have gazed for through the night
pouring profuse rain upon the riverbed's
black basalt track,
3. With it would I water the grave of him I intend,
him whose grave is dear to me
though he were unredeemed.
4. Attester at councils, erector of edifices,
bracer of banners, burster of dams,
5. Slitter of camel throats, slayer of tyrants,
alighter on hilltops, breaker of bonds,
6. Orator of the eloquent, revoker of the ratified,
obstructor of water holes, dispeller of doubt,[34]
7. Alighter at pasturelands, endurer of hardships,
dispeller of horrors, scaler of heights,
8. Gatherer of all virtues—as all who knew him knew—
his comrades' ornament, the tyrant's scourge.
9. O Abū Zurārah, do not be distant!
For every youth will one day be hostage
to stone slab and wooden bier.
10. O Banū Jarm, did you give your prisoner no drink?
May my soul be your ransom, O Masʿūd,
from a burning thirst!

33. See Kaḥḥālah, *Aʿlām al-Nisāʾ* 4:19.
34. I have changed the word order to preserve the English meter.

11. The thruster of the wide-gashing thrust
 that is followed by a profuse gush
 after a boiling froth.
12. Who leaves his opponent with fingertips jaundiced,
 and his clothes as if
 mulberry-spattered.
13. The buyer of wineskins for guests
 that alight in his courtyard,
 to the destitute,
 abundant morning rain.[35]

The poem begins with *Yā ʿayni jūdī*[36] (O my eye, be generous), which, along with close variants such as the dual *Yā ʿaynayya jūdā* (O my two eyes, be generous!), constitutes one of the most common openings of women's elegies, indeed of Arabic elegy generally. Closely related but less semantically rich are the likewise common opening formulas *Yā ʿayniya ibkī* (O my eye, weep), *Yā ʿaynu fīḍī* (O eye, overflow), and their variants. Indeed, the recensions of this poem, and others, exhibit considerable variation in this formula. According to the poetics of ritual demonstrated in the formula *lā tabʿad* (Do not be distant/perish!) in al-Khirniq's poem, this "convention" ought not to be dismissed as a mere cliché; rather, we should seek to discover why this phrase was singled out for repetition, what is the depth or intensity of meaning that justifies such repetition? I would like to take into account three aspects: first, the semantic range of the individual terms, then, the grammatical structure, and finally, the metaphorical connections to other rithāʾ images, particularly as they occur in this poem.

ʿAyn is a richly multivalent word. Its core significance is neatly summed up by Ibn Manẓūr: "The eye/*ʿayn* is the organ of sight and perception . . . and the *ʿayn* among the Arabs is the essence of a thing, the *ʿayn* of a thing is its self, its entity, its origin." The *ʿayn* is also *ʿaynu*

35. Variants of this poem appear in a number of sources, among them Shaykhū, *Riyāḍ al-Adab*, 98–100, in 17 verses (with references to various versions and sources); al-Iṣbahānī, *Kitāb al-Aghānī* 12:4276–77, 10 verses; al-Qālī, *Al-Amālī* 2:323–26, 15 verses; Ibrāhīm ibn ʿAlī al-Ḥuṣrī, *Zahr al-Ādāb wa Thamar al-Albāb*, ed. ʿAlī Muḥammad al-Bijāwī, 2 vols., 2d ed. (Cairo: ʿĪsā al-Bābī al-Ḥalabī, 1969), 2:941, 14 verses. The present one includes verse 1 from *Kitāb al-Aghānī* and verses 2, 3, 6–12, and 15–17 from *Riyāḍ al-Adab*. See Kaḥḥālah, *Aʿlām al-Nisāʾ* 4:19.

36. This can also be vocalized *ʿaynu*; I have preferred the possessive form *ʿayni* (shortened to fit the *basīṭ* meter), because it predominates in the variants of this formula.

al-mā'i and *yanbū'* "the source and spring of water."[37] Thus the *'ayn* is initially and ultimately the eye, the I, the identity/ego-entity, the source of self, the soul, the source of light, the eye, the source of life, the spring of water. Moreover, as Ibn Manẓūr's further comments demonstrate, the Arabs were quite aware of the semantic connection among these meanings. In other words, we are not dealing lexically with a discernible distinction between denotative and connotative meanings. Rather, in the Arabic poetic metalanguage, the occurrence of a word almost inevitably elicits an interplay of semantic levels. Ibn Manẓūr cites the ḥadīth: "The best of possessions is a wakeful eye/*'ayn* belonging to a sleeping eye/*'ayn*" and explains: "He meant a spring of water that runs perpetually night and day and is not cut off even when the eye of its owner is sleeping." Citing Tha'lab's explanation of the verse—

> Those are the spring of water among them,
> their haven and refuge from fear [29]

—he declares that *'aynu al-mā'i* here means *al-ḥayātu lil-nāsi* (The spring of water is life for the people).[38]

Nor should *'ayn* as letter and sound be forgotten. For, as al-Khalīl ibn Aḥmad (d. 175/791) explains in his introduction to the first Arabic dictionary, his *Kitāb al-'Ayn* (Book of the *'ayn*), the *'ayn* possesses a certain priority and preeminence among sounds or letters. In establishing an alphabetical sequence by which to order his dictionary, he decided to start with the innermost letter or sound to emerge from the throat, and found it to be the *'ayn.*[39] It is thus the initial and essential sound, the voice and hence expression of the self. At this point the identity of the eye as source of the self and of tears, the liquid expression of the soul, the *'ayn* as source of water and hence of life, and the *'ayn* as the vocal expression of the self—that is, the identity of the soul, tears, life, and poetry—reveals itself.

Jūdī (be generous) from *jāda/yajūdu jawdan* likewise grows from a fertile semantic field. It is most often associated with copious rainfall, as in *jāda al-maṭaru jawdan* (It rained widely and copiously), and hence means to bestow generously. For the eye, it means to produce copious tears: "The eye is copious [*Jādat al-'aynu*] means it produces lots of tears.

37. *Lisān*, *'-y-n*.
38. Ibid.
39. Al-Khalīl ibn Aḥmad al-Farāhīdī, *Kitāb al-'Ayn*, ed. 'Abd Allāh Darwīsh (Baghdad: Maṭba'at al-'Ānī, 1968), 52.

. . . it is said to be taken from copious rain."[40] Thus the root meaning is copiousness, fertility, generosity. When that meaning is extended to the weeping eye, it is not merely the liquid likeness to rain that is to be kept in mind but these associated meanings.

In a radical way, then, the opening phrase conveys a copious pouring forth of liquid. Beneath the translucent surface meaning of "O eye, weep copiously" parallel meanings are clearly discernible: "O well-spring, give abundant water," "O soul, give generously of yourself," and ultimately, if less directly, "O voice, sing generous praise," for the life-giving element the poetic voice bestows is likewise its own self-expression.

This gushing forth of liquid should, in the context of the lamentation/vengeance dialectic, suggest other liquids shed for the dead, another "liquid soul," the blood of vengeance. Further, then, we can conclude from the parallelism of images that the women's shedding of tears is perceived in ritual terms as a liquid sacrifice, a libation, through which the dead are redeemed. Moreover, inasmuch as women's rithāʾ is the literary expression through which the dead are redeemed, the lachrymal expression that so often opens such poems must be understood as a metaphor for the composing of rithāʾ. The *ʿayn* is thus both phonologically and semantically the origin of poetry, the verbal expression of the self. The sacrifice involved here is therefore the poet's diversion of his or her poetic powers from the immortalization of the self in the fakhr genre, to the immortalization of another. *Yā ʿayni jūdī* then is the poetess's apostrophizing of her soul, her self, to give of itself in its lachrymal condensation and poetic sublimation, so that by that outpouring the dead might be cleansed and redeemed.

It is, furthermore, the metaphorical dimensions of the phrase *yā ʿayni jūdī* that connect the opening verse of the poem to the following image (verse 2)—that of the poetess watching through the night for a lightning-flashing storm cloud that will pour copiously down on a basalt track, which, according to Shaykhū's commentary, is the place where her brother was slain.[41] The poetess then declares (3) that with this storm cloud she will water her brother's grave. In the second hemistich she introduces the theme of sacrifice and redemption in explicit terms. It seems that her brother has not yet been "redeemed," which, for a fallen warrior, can only mean that he lies unavenged. In the context of

40. *Lisān*, *j-w-d*.
41. Shaykhū, *Riyāḍ al-Adab*, 98.

blood-vengeance poems, verse 3 creates a metaphorical resonance with the previous verse, for what keeps the poet or poetess awake through the night is a kinsman's unavenged blood, and likewise, what waters the grave of the fallen warrior and redeems him is, above all, the blood of vengeance. Let us note at this point that the storm cloud is not denoted explicitly, but is only epithetically indicated by *bāriqan* "a lightning-flasher" and *jawdan* "pouring profusely." The first is well known from the diction of the battlefield, where it describes the warrior brandishing his flashing sword. Equally familiar is the metaphorical association of rainfall and bloodshed, as, for example, in ʿAlqamah's renowned battle description:

> As if there poured down on them a storm cloud
> whose thunderbolts left the vultures
> creeping on the ground.[42] [30]

We thus perceive behind the transparent diction of the storm scene an expression of purification and redemption through blood vengeance. In other words, the storm cloud flashing with lightning for which the poetess is looking through the night is an avenger or battle for vengeance for her fallen brother. This image thus serves to confirm the connection between the woman's lament (tears/rithāʾ) and man's blood vengeance and, further, between the woman's lament and the traditional opening of the qaṣīdah, the nasīb image of the shedding of tears at the campsite ruins and rain upon them.[43] Moreover, the particular phrasing of the image in this poem—the conditional *yā man raʾā*, "O whoever sees" = "if anyone sees/has seen," followed by an imperfect *asqī* "I will/would water"—has the effect of transforming the poem, however subtly, into taḥrīḍ, instigation to blood vengeance. That is, for the poetess to say that she has spent the night looking for a rain cloud flashing with lightning is to say that she is looking for her kinsmen to avenge her brother.

42. Verse 32 of *Mufaḍḍaliyyah no.119,* by ʿAlqamah ibn ʿAbadah, in Lyall, *The Mufaḍḍaliyāt* 1:784.

43. See S. Stetkevych, *Abū Tammām,* 315–32. The metaphorical and ritual connection of the shedding of tears, blood, and rain is further confirmed by Gaster's findings that among some tribal peoples "tears are regarded—as are blood, sweat, semen, and urine elsewhere—as effusions of the 'soul-substance,' so that the shedding of them serves as a means of reinvigorating the earth and even of reviving the dead." Among others, "the shedding of tears is believed to be an homeopathic method of producing rain." Gaster, *Thespis,* 33.

The next four verses (4–7), like verses 2–4 of al-Khirniq's *Let My Kinsmen Not Be Distant,* constitute a list of what might be termed ceremonial or formulary titles such as we know in other ancient civilizations from monumental inscriptions. At this point we can expand further on this comparison between the oral and the graven. Both require concision of expression, a limitation of the size of the text, the first because of the requirement of memorization, the second because of the difficulty of graving stone. Both, too, I would argue, require a multivalent layering of meaning and metaphor that will guarantee that the "message," not simply the vocal or lithic "text" itself, survives. In both types there is a parallelism of phrases, for the reinforcing of meaning, to be most effective, should occur along two axes: first, that of the multivalent meaning, that is, metaphorical polysemy, of the single phrase; and second, that of reiteration of nearly synonymous concepts through a variety of epithets or expressions. What we have therefore is not a series of personal, idiosyncratic descriptions but rather a heroic formulary or iconography—an official biography.

The archetypal completeness of this iconographic depiction likewise functions to preserve the message: for an iconography itself is nothing more than a gathering of a variety of symbolic or metaphoric expressions of a single idea which have been fashioned into a "pictorial" form. In both the oral and the graven, the structural parallelism of these phrases, together with their semantic association, has the effect of preserving the message should part of the "text" become unreadable, be forgotten or physically lost or damaged, or should the meaning of certain words or phrases be forgotten. Further, meter in poetry and spacing in epigraphic texts serve to preserve the place of a word, letter, or syllable that might be lost. As anyone who has tried to read an incomplete or damaged text knows, it is the context that allows one to reconstruct lost portions of text. What we are dealing with, then, in the "conventionalized" oral and graven texts is what I would term an *intensified contextuality*. That is, the text is constructed in such a way—with rhyme, meter, metaphor, parallelism, reiteration, and archetypal iconography—not merely to be, for the oral, memorizable[44] but also to be eminently reconstructible, verbally and/or semantically, if it should become literally or figuratively obscure. Even if the reconstruction is not verbally identical to what has been lost, it can at least be semantically

44. Ong, *Orality and Literacy*, 39–40.

and metrically—in both the physical and poetic sense—identical. Examination of the morphological patterning of these four verses will elucidate this aspect.

Of interest here is the reiterated rhetorical and morphological formula (termed by Arab critics *tarṣīʿ*, internal rhyme)[45] and its relation to the aesthetics of orality. The pattern here is:

verse 4: *faʿʿālu afʿilatin* × 3 + *faʿʿālu afʿālī*
verse 5: *faʿʿālu fāʿilatin* × 3 + *faʿʿālu afʿālī*
verse 6: *faʿʿālu mufʿalatin* × 3 + *faʿʿālu afʿālī*
verse 7: *faʿʿālu mufʿilatin* × 3 + *faʿʿālu afʿālī*

That is (– = long syllable; ᵕ = short syllable):

– – ᵕ / – ᵕ ᵕ – / – – ᵕ / – ᵕ ᵕ – // – – ᵕ / – ᵕ ᵕ – / – – ᵕ / – – –

According to Khalīlian metrics, the meter is *basīṭ*:

mustafʿilun faʿilun × 3 + *mustafʿilun faʿlun*
– – ᵕ – / ᵕ ᵕ – / – – ᵕ – / ᵕ ᵕ – // – – ᵕ – / ᵕ ᵕ – / – – ᵕ – / – –

In addition, there is in each of these lines an internal rhyme of the second terms of the first three *iḍāfah* units. The power of *tarṣīʿ* derives from the alliance of metrical (quantitative) and morphological (qualitative) stress and, further, the semantic content of the morphology. Aurally this passage is particularly striking for the buildup of momentum within the verse, brought to a closure by the solidity of the three long final syllables. A second surge of momentum builds from verse to verse until it reaches a climax in verse 8, which opens with *faʿʿālu* but then departs from the hammering effect of the short parallel phrases that are coterminous with the metrical foot to return to the normal poetic interplay between meter and phrasing, which now produces a sense of expansion and release.[46]

45. See Ibn Rashīq, *Al-ʿUmdah* 2:26–31; and al-Ḥūfī, *Al-Marʾah*, 669–75. Al-Ḥūfī remarks on the prevalence of *tarṣīʿ* in women's poetry and attributes this phenomenon to the feminine love of adornment and ornamentation (!). I propose that this particular type of *tarṣīʿ* involving participial epithets is distinctive of rithāʾ in general, both men's and women's, for reasons my discussion will suggest. It is also used to powerful effect in madīḥ.

46. In this respect the reader might note Goldziher's remarks concerning the *sajʿ* element in elegy and the characteristic use of the *iḍāfah* construction with the *faʿʿāl*-form as the first element in *tasmīṭ*. See Goldziher, "Bemerkungen zur arabischen Trauerpoesie," 366–67.

A more careful examination of the inner workings of the metrical patterning of verses 4–7 is in order. The momentum of the *tarṣīʿ*, as mentioned, derives from the synchronization of meter and morphology to produce metrically and morphologically reiterated phrases. It should be noted here that the morphological units are coterminous not with the single Khalīlian metrical foot but with the two-foot unit that defines the meter. The morphological pattern here breaks as follows: ––⏑/–⏑⏑–//; whereas, if we approach the matter from the Khalīlian point of view the metrical pattern is: ––⏑–/⏑⏑–//. Given that the poem is logically and chronologically prior to al-Khalīl ibn Aḥmad's theoretical systemization of Arabic metrics, it could reasonably be argued that the origin of meter lies precisely in such formulary list of epithets and that the morphological pattern exhibited in this section of the poem is, in fact, the original metrical pattern. Of course this sort of pattern is very tedious if repeated for long—like having a piece of music in ¾ time with three quarter notes in every bar. In poetry, as in music, it is the constant tension between the "phrasing" (= stress) and metrical units that creates the expressive cadence. What therefore makes the *tarṣīʿ* a powerful rhetorical device is the dramatic abandonment of the lively counterpoint of stress and meter, the interplay of phrase and foot, to create an insistent and unrelieved hammering. In the poem at hand this produces a striking change in style and discourse from the intimate and personal tone of the apostrophe and first person of verses 1–3, to the impersonal, high, formal rhetoric of the formulary register. At the same time, the building tension of the repeated epithetic pattern creates a heightened emotive state. The result is a ritual conjuring of the dead through what amounts to a liturgical recitation of epithets which, as mentioned, is suggestively analogous to the process employed in Ṣūfī *dhikr* to conjure the divine presence. With the abandonment of *tarṣīʿ* in verse 8 the heightened rhetorical tone gives way to one that is, once again, more intimate.

The morphological pattern, moreover, speaks, quite apart from the individual lexical items that fill it, for itself. It is a pattern of dominance and submission: *faʿʿālu* (here referring to the marthī) is both morphologically and syntactically the actor, the doer. *Faʿʿāl* is the masculine singular intensive participial form. We should note, too, that the notion of intensity is not arbitrarily assigned to this form but is physically, that is, phonologically, indicated by the intensification of the medial consonant by doubling and the second vowel by lengthening. Furthermore, the nominative case, even in an abstract sense, is that of the *fāʿil*, the grammatical actor or subject of the verb, or otherwise of that which is grammatically unsubordinated—the subject or predicate (*mubtadaʾ bih* or *khabar* of a nominative sentence). The second term in this pattern, although it has four variants, is in all cases grammatically feminine and genitive, subordinate in both gender and case. More particularly, here the genitive is an objective genitive, hence the "victim," as it were, of *faʿʿālu*. Furthermore, *faʿʿālu* (– – ⏑) is metrically full and powerful, whereas *afʿilatin* (– ⏑ ⏑ –) is metrically hollow and weak. This pattern is most morphologically explicit in verse 6, where the second term is *mufʿalatin*, the feminine passive participle (IV) form. In terms of diction, the first hemistich of verse 5 is the most telling: *naḥḥāru rāghiyatin qattālu ṭāghiyatin* (literally, slaughterer of the grumbling [she-camel], slayer of the tyrant) (*ṭāghiyatin* here being the masculine active participle with feminine grammatical termination for intensification). The point is that the actor/victim concept that is made explicit in "slaughterer of the grumbling she-camel" through diction, morphology, and syntax, is implied in the morphology and syntax of the other units and reinforced by the parallelism of phrases. That is, parallel or identical structure indicates that at some level there is a parallel or identical meaning. If we return at this point to the concept of intensified contextuality, it is clear that in a passage such as this, the interchange or substitution of terms can only create an expression that is largely synonymous with the others, as, in fact, the variants of this poem demonstrate. In reading through the verses once more, we find that this formulary register subsumes the qualities or obligations of the dominant aggregate male—"virtues" in the original sense of the word. In short, the morphological formulaic paradigm is also a societal paradigm.

Verse 8, then, sums up the preceding list—*jammāʿu kulli khiṣāli al-khayri* (gatherer of all virtues)—and then subsumes all virtue in the fundamental tribal kin/non-kin dialectic: his comrades' ornament, the tyrant's scourge.

The poem then reverts from the "official," impersonal third person to the more intimate first and second persons. The poetess first (verse 9) apostrophizes her departed brother with the elegiac formula *lā tabʿad* (Do not be distant!/Do not perish!) discussed in al-Khirniq's poem. This formula, too, suggests that to "recall" the dead in poetry is to call them back to life, to revive or immortalize them. Suddenly the potency and energy of the *faʿʿāl* form are no more. It is of note, too, that the poetess refers to her brother, indeed, the fallen warrior generally, as the *rahīn*, hostage (morphologically as well as semantically the "victim"—*faʿīl bi maʿnā mafʿūl*), of the tomb. The implication is, of course, that the dead, like captives, can be ransomed, redeemed.

The following verse (10) seems to address the tribe that took the poetess's brother captive and, refusing him drink, slew him. Close variants of this verse and the next, however, form a couplet attributed in the *Kitāb al-Aghānī* to both Ukht (the sister of) ʿAmr ibn ʿĀṣiyah al-Sulamī and our poetess al-Fāriʿah ukht Masʿūd ibn Shaddād. Al-Iṣbahānī relates that two men of the Banū Sahm, a clan of the Banū Hudhayl, captured ʿAmr ibn ʿĀṣiyah al-Sulamī during a war and when they discovered who he was, slew him. He had been thirsty and had asked them to give him something to drink, but they refused and slew him still thirsting. On this occasion his sister recited:

O Banū Sahm, did you give your prisoner no drink?
May my soul be your ransom
from a burning thirst.
The thruster of the wide-gashing thrust
that is followed by a bleeding wound
after abundant froth.[47] [31]

Two variants of ʿAmr ibn ʿĀṣiyah's thirsty death at the hands of the Banū Sahm and of his sister's elegy for him are found on subsequent pages of the *Kitāb al-Aghānī*, both containing the first verse of this couplet.[48] Shortly thereafter there occurs yet another attribution, now of verses 1 and 9 of my version of al-Fāriʿah's poem, to the man who is otherwise the marthī, Masʿūd ibn Shaddād, reportedly elegizing his brother whom the Banū Jarm had slain while he was thirsty.[49] It is at this point that al-Iṣbahānī's introduces al-Fāriʿah's elegy, with the remark that the first verse, attributed to her brother Masʿūd, is also said to be the opening verse of his sister's elegy for him. His second verse (9 in my version of al-Fāriʿah's poem) is not found in al-Iṣbahānī's recension.

This variation in text and context of verse 9, coupled with the frequency of the motifs of thirsting and giving drink in rithāʾ and blood-vengeance poetry,[50] suggests that it has more to do with the

47. Al-Iṣbahānī, *Kitāb al-Aghānī* 12:4272.

48. Ibid., 12:4273, 4274, the latter with a slight variation. See also Shaykhū, *Riyāḍ al-Adab*, 96–98.

49. Al-Iṣbahānī, *Kitāb al-Aghānī* 12:4276.

50. See, for example, Lammens's remark in "Le caractère Religieux du *ṯār*," 102.

metaphorical language of death and redemption than with the actual circumstances of the demise of any particular marthī. Certainly the second hemistich strengthens this suspicion: in the corpus of poetry I am examining, to ransom the thirsting is above all to give them to drink of the blood of vengeance. For *ghullah* denotes thirst, but connotes the thirst for vengeance; similarly *ṣādin* (thirsty) is the active participle of *ṣadiya/yaṣdā ṣadan*, to thirst; but *ṣadan* is also the owl, that form assumed by the soul of the unavenged warrior, which sits above the tomb and cries *Isqūnī! Isqūnī!* "Give me drink! Give me drink!"[51] The essential significance of the verse, regardless of whether it refers to an actual incident, is "If you have killed my brother, I will redeem him—with my tears, my poetry," or if the poet is a man, "by risking my own life to avenge him."

The poem comes to a close after another shift from the personal to the impersonal (verses 11–13). It is of interest that two of these three verses of formal and formulaic description are attested, with some variation, elsewhere. Perhaps the most famous exponent of the second verse is ʿAbīd ibn al-Abraṣ:

> Oft have I left my opponent, his fingers jaundiced,
> his clothes as if mulberry-spattered. [32]

Other variants cited in *Khizānat al-Adab* are those of al-Mutanakhkhil al-Hudhalī, Zuhayr ibn Masʿūd al-Ḍabbī, Rayṭah al-Hudhaliyyah (in which both verses occur together), Zuhayr ibn Abī Sulmā, and an unnamed poet of the Banū Jarm. The final citation is of the two verses in our poem with the poetess's name given as ʿAmrah bint Shaddād al-Kalbiyyah.[52] This repetition with variation, particularly at the end of the line to meet varying rhyme requirements, serves once more to remind us that the unit of the poetic lexicon is the phrase, the verse, the formula, the motif, and not merely the single word. Again, the issue at hand is not whether such verses or phrases are formulaic, but why this particular phrase and pattern has achieved formulaic and formulary status. Several possibilities suggest themselves. First, although more richly expansive in form, the final three verses nevertheless share the epithetic and titular quality of the *faʿʿāl* section (verses 4–7).

51. Lyall, *The Mufaḍḍalīyāt* 1:322. See again Homerin's "Echoes of a Thirsty Owl," passim.

52. Al-Baghdādī, *Khizānat al-Adab* 11:253–60.

Further, these verses create through their use of the active participial and imperfective forms a monumental description of the marthī which is at once active and present, that is, alive, and yet, through the tabular rigidity of the titular formulas, permanently preserved. The result is the verbal equivalent of the sort of equestrian statue in which the hero is mounted on a rearing steed—the quintessential moment of manly action immobilized and hence immortalized in metal or stone. In the poem, too, the "pose" is an iconographic archetype of male action and potency—the formulaic phrase, the stone.

In verse 11, the hero is the thruster of the spear. Of note is the emphasis on the gushing of blood, an image of the hero bringing forth life-giving liquid—whether blood or semen—for the kin group, but further indicating that the kin group somehow "feeds" on the dead. This sense is strengthened by the description of the blood as *yaghlī bi izbādī* "boiling with froth," a phrase that cannot help but suggest the sacrificial equivalent of blood vengeance, that is, the boiling kettles of the commensal feast that follows the hunt or animal sacrifice as we find in *The Muʿallaqah of Labīd* (verse 77) or in that of Imruʾ al-Qays (verse 68).

The next verse (12) likewise bears beneath the visual image of contrasting color a "graphic" expression of the blood-vengeance dialectic: the slain foe's fingertips are yellow, that is, from the Arab chromatic perspective, pale, from loss of blood (devitalization), whereas the bloodstains on his clothes are at once an image of defilement, for him, and of alimentation or revitalization—the fruit of the mulberry—for the victor. The spilled blood as ambivalent sign of life/sign of death is thus expressed as blood/mulberry or, more often, blood/henna.

These two verses expressing the revitalizing/devitalizing effects of the shedding of enemy blood are followed by a final verse of closure which likewise deals in images of life-giving liquids that are at once the metaphorical equivalents and symmetrical inversion of blood shed on the battlefield: wine that is purchased for the guest and *ghayth* (copious rain, generosity) toward the needy. The final phrase of the poem: *wa ghaythu al-muḥwiji al-ghādī* (to the destitute, abundant morning rain)—is synonymous, both denotatively and connotatively, with the copious rain and generosity (*jūd*) with which the poem opened. The verse has further rhetorical effects indicative of closure. First, by beginning the verse with an active participle form that echoes the other verses of the poem and then ending it with another active particple, the poetess has created a chiasmus that has the effect of rounding off the ending.

Further, in the final hemistich, the active participle as epithet is replaced by the substantive (or *maṣdar*) *ghayth* (abundant rain), giving a sense of permanence and finality to the identity of the marthī. And yet by finally attributing to it/him the closing active particple *al-ghādī* "the one that/who comes in the early morning" we somehow sense that the imminent return of the deceased is as natural and life-giving as the early morning rain.

A fuller sense of the network of liquid images now begins to emerge. Just as the fallen warrior who has given his blood/life for the tribe deserves to be revived/redeemed through the blood of vengeance, so too, for his generosity—the pouring forth of wine, of rain-like bounty—he deserves the copious pouring forth of life-giving tears, the metaphor for immortalizing verse. The message of this poem, indeed of all rithā', would thus seem to be that it is a man's generosity and self-sacrifice—of his life in time of war, of his food and drink in time of peace—which in the end redeems him.

A third marthiyah demonstrates, like al-Fāriʿah's, how subtle the instigation to vengeance can be. The poem is of further interest in that it exhibits variations in its recensions not only in the number and order of verses but in the name and identity of the poetess, here given as Rayṭah Ukht ʿAmr Dhī al-Kalb. In addition, two of its most striking verses (5 and 6) are close variants of verses 11 and 12 of al-Fāriʿah's poem.

Every Man Is Deceived [33]

1. Every man is deceived by the wiles of fate,
 And every man who contends with the days
  Will meet defeat.
2. And every tribe, however mighty and secure it seems,
 Will one day tread the well-trod road
  To war.
3. Inform Hudhayl and inform the man
 Who will inform them of my message
  —And some speech is lies—
4. That Dhū al-Kalb, ʿAmr, the best of them in lineage,
 Lies in Sharyān's hollow and around him
  Howls the wolf.

5. The thruster of the wide-gashing thrust
That is followed by a streaming gush
Of the belly's black blood.
6. The victor who leaves his opponent
With fingertips jaundiced as if he were dyed
With the belly's black blood.
7. The chooser of the well-kept virgin,
Submissive in captivity, from whose silken cuffs
Fine perfumes waft.
8. The vultures walk upon him in delight,
Frolicking like virgins
Clad in smocks.[53]

It is entirely in accord with my earlier discussion of the public status of men versus the private (veiled, secluded) status of women that the identity of this poem is established not by the poetess, who is variously identified as Rayṭah, Janūb, and ʿAmrah,[54] but by the marthī, their brother ʿAmr Dhū al-Ḳalb, whose identity is as distinct as his sisters' is obscure. This confusion over the identity of the poetess reaches its climax, as it were, in al-Baghdādī's *Khizānat al-Adab*, when, after discussing the poetess Janūb, he introduces this poem with the remark, "It is said that Janūb is [actually] ʿAmrah and that they are not two different people. And [ʿAmr Dhū al-Kalb] had another sister named Rayṭah who was also a poetess. Among her poetry to him is . . . [the poem]."[55] In addition, as I shall presently discuss, verse 4 in particular establishes the identity of the marthī and at the same time defines the genre of the poem as taḥrīḍ. I have chosen the *Khizānat al-Adab* recension because the choice and arrangement of lines seems to me to express most accurately and powerfully the semantic core of the poem.[56]

That semantic core, I believe, is to be found in verses 3 and 4,

53. Al-Baghdādī, *Khizānat al-Adab* 10:390–91. See Al-Hudhaliyyūn, *Dīwān al-Hudhaliyyīn* (Cairo: al-Dār al-Qawmiyyah, 1965) [photo-offset of Cairo: Dār al-Kutub, 1945–50], 124–26 (attrib. to Janūb Ukht ʿAmr Dhī al-Kalb); al-Walīd Abū ʿUbādah al-Buḥturī, *Al-Ḥamāsah*, ed. Kamāl Muṣṭafā (Cairo: al-Maṭbaʿah al-Raḥmāniyyah, 1929), 429–30 (attrib. to ʿAmrah Ukht ʿAmr Dhī al-Kalb); al-Iṣbahānī, *Kitāb al-Aghānī* 26:9101–2 (attrib. to Rayṭah Ukht ʿAmr Dhī al-Kalb); Shaykhū, *Riyāḍ al-Adab*, 75–79 (attrib. to Janūb Ukht ʿAmr Dhī al-Kalb).

54. See Kaḥḥālah, *Aʿlām al-Nisāʾ*: Rayṭah bint al-ʿAjlān, 1:481; Janūb bint al-ʿAjlān, 1:218–19; ʿAmrah al-Kalbiyyah al-Hudhaliyyah, 3:358.

55. Al-Baghdādī, *Khizānat al-Adab* 10:390.

56. See, for example, Shaykhū's reconstruction, which, through the ordering of the lines, gives the effect of marthiyah with little suggestion of taḥrīḍ. *Riyāḍ al-Adab*, 75–79.

particularly the latter. Inasmuch as the purpose of rithāʾ is to commemorate the dead, it would appear self-evident that the identification of the deceased is of the essence. Furthermore, in the context of the urgency or necessity of vengeance, the state of the corpse, avenged or unavenged, is likewise crucial information. Verse 3 has the effect of addressing the message to the kin group concerned. Verse 4 has the concision of a telegram giving the name: ʿAmr Dhū al-Kalb; rank: the best of them in lineage; place of death: the hollow of Sharyān; the state of the corpse: unavenged. As was established in my analysis of blood-vengeance poetry in Chapter 2, the primary image of unavenged blood is that of the corpse being eaten or otherwise defiled by the carrion eaters—here, the wolf. In the terse but suggestive metalanguage of early Arabic poetry, simply to inform the Banū Hudhayl that their kinsman lies with wolves howling around him is sufficient taḥrīḍ. The opposite, the declaration that a fallen kinsman has been avenged, consists simply of stating that the enemy lies with wolves, or hyenas, or vultures, about him.

Let us examine the poetic layers that enclose this core. Verses 1 and 2, which at first sound like tired *ḥikam*, or old saws, take on a contextually appropriate meaning. The poetess's suggestion seems to be that if you think that you can save yourself by avoiding battle (that is, avoiding avenging your kinsman), you will ultimately be defeated (1); similarly, no tribe is so secure or powerful that it can indefinitely avoid being drawn into war (2). The point is that for both the individual and the tribe, once the blood of a kinsman has been shed, the battle for vengeance is unavoidable. These two verses of *ḥikmah* thus put the audience in the proper frame of mind to receive the information that is to follow: the death announcement (*naʿy*) and call for vengeance.

The core verses are followed by four more verses (5–8): the first three, of epithetic description, achieve a closure in the fourth. The first two have a familiar ring, being variants of verses 11 and 12 in al-Fāriʿah's poem (or vice versa): *al-ṭāʿinu al-ṭaʿnata al-najlāʾa* (the thruster of the wide-gashing thrust), *wa al-ṭāriku al-qirna misfarran anāmiluhu* (the victor who leaves his opponent with jaundiced fingertips). The verses of the two poems, except for the change from the imperfect to the active participle in the second, remain the same through the first word of the second hemistich, after which both the meaning and rhyme are adjusted or varied. In this case, small changes have resulted in a change in meaning, or at least in emphasis. For in al-Fāriʿah's poem verses 11 and 12 conclude with imagery of alimentation: the boiling, frothing kettle and the mulberry, presumably suggesting the nourishing effect of blood vengeance on the kin group. In Rayṭah's poem, the reiteration of *min najīʿi al-jawfi* (of the belly's black blood), shifts the emphasis to the devitalization of the enemy: his life's blood spills out (5), leaving his fingertips jaundiced, that is pale from loss of blood, while staining, polluting, his corpse. The imagery here thus revolves around an interior/exterior antithesis of blood of life/blood of death expressed as well through the chromatic antithesis of sanguine complexion in white clothes to blanched complexion in bloodied clothes. The bloodstained garment, it must be remembered, is the dominant image of honor defiled.

The third of these verses (7) functions in two ways. First, inasmuch as it opens with *mikhraj* (chooser), the *ism al-ālah* (noun of tool) signifying the intensive active participle, it functions as the third and culminating verse of the epithetic series. As such it presents a complementary form of the victor defiling the enemy with bloodshed, that of raping or deflowering the virgin captive. The details of her description are worth noting. She is *ʿātiq*, a girl who has just reached puberty and has been put in seclusion in her father's house, not yet presented to a husband;[57] she is *ʿadhrāʾ*, a virgin, too tender or innocent, it would seem, to put up any fight, her purity and innocence, as well as the luxury of her class, suggested by the *ṭīb* (perfume) wafting from her cuffs. This image, then, is one of defiling the enemy but also, as we have come to expect by now, of revitalizing the kin group, inasmuch as it is their offspring that the women and girls taken prisoner will bear.

At the same time, verse 7 bears a special relation to the concluding verse expressed in a number of parallel and contrasting images: the meek virgins defiled by the marthī in verse 7 are replaced by virginlike vultures that defile the marthī's corpse as they frolic and feast. Although modern sensibility tempts us to read a certain "poetic justice" into this final couplet, the poetess's intent is, of course, something quite different: she is calling for yet another reversal of the revitalization/ devitalization equation, that is, for the avenging of her brother's blood. A closer look at the imagery and diction of the final verse is warranted. First, the use of *lāhiyah*, delighting, sporting, playing, sets the tone of celebration and feasting that normally accompanies animal sacrifices or the commensal feast that follows the hunt. The further comparison of vultures to virgins in smocks has both a visual and ritual base. First, the vultures,

57. Al-ʿAynī, as cited in Shaykhū, *Riyāḍ al-Adab*, 78.

full feathered but with naked legs and feet, resemble skinny-legged girls clad in short smocks; the well-known hopping of the vultures is likewise suggestive of the skipping and jumping of girls at play.

Further, since the term *ʿadhārā*, virgins, indicates pubescence, we should recall, as verse 7 reminds us, that girls of this age would under normal circumstances be secluded. This allusion, together with the festive and sacrificial imagery, suggests that the line is based on the inversion of a human ritual celebration involving a special gait and dress or costume in which, likewise in accordance with the liminal inversion that characterizes rites of sacrifice, the normally curtained and secluded pubescent girls engage in public celebration. What the actual rite behind this complex image might have been is a matter of speculation. Perhaps it was the virgins of the tribe coming out to greet or celebrate the return of the victorious warrior. Perhaps too there is some relation here to the image of the does of mountain goats of al-Shanfarā's *Lāmiyyah* (verse 67), or of the herd of oryx in Imruʾ al-Qays's *Muʿallaqah* (verse 64). Whatever the case, the festive vultures and virgins express in this verse the gloating of the victorious enemy.

There remains a further level of meaning. As established in Chapter 2, vultures are known in early Arabic poetry and lore for their longevity. Comparing "ancient vultures" to "young virgins" thus expresses once more the revitalizing or rejuvenating effect of blood sacrifice. The comparison of vultures to virgins, especially in light of the preceding line, also suggests the sexual defilement of the corpse, of the sort usually associated with the female hyena, but well known to us from the ancient Egyptian example of the Isis in the form of a vulture conceiving Horus on the fallen corpse of Osiris.[58] In this respect verse 8 represents a horrible perversion of verse 7. The victor deflowering virgins is now the victim defiled by virgins; kindred seed is usurped instead of sown. This complex image of abomination is of itself sufficient taḥrīḍ.

The following poem is said to have been composed by the pre-Islamic poetess Kabshah bint Maʿdī Karib when her half brother, the

58. The concept that the life-forces can somehow be extracted from the corpse of the fallen hero likewise would seem to lie behind the pre-Islamic custom, recorded by al-Ālūsī, of *maqālīt* (s. *miqlāt*), bereft mothers, all of whose children have died, treading upon the corpses of fallen nobles or heroes so that their children would live. The sexual undertone is suggested by the verb *waṭiʾa*, which can mean to have sexual intercourse (with a woman), and further by al-Ālūsī's example from Bishr ibn Abī Khāzim: "The bereft mothers keep on treading on him / Saying, 'Will no loincloth be thrown over this man!' " (*taẓallu maqālītu al-*

renowned warrior-poet ʿAmr ibn Maʿdī Karib, was inclined to accept the bloodwite for his brother, ʿAbd Allāh. According to al-Qālī (d. 356/967) in *Dhayl al-Amālī*, ʿAbd Allāh was the chieftain of his tribe. One day when drinking with the Banū Māzin clan he insulted and struck the slave of his host. A drunken clansman of the Banū Māzin jumped up and slew him. ʿAmr succeeded his brother ʿAbd Allāh as chieftain, and agreed to the petition of the Banū Māzin that he accept the bloodwite and whatever additional livestock he wanted, since the man that slew ʿAbd Allāh had been drunk at the time. So ʿAmr accepted the bloodwite and much else besides from them and was not moved to avenge his brother until his half sister Kabshah recited the following poem of taḥrīḍ:[59]

Ḥamāsiyyah no. 52. Do Not Accept the Bloodwite [34]

1. When his time had come
 ʿAbd Allāh sent word to his clan
"Do not accept the bloodwite
 for my blood.
2. "Do not accept from them
 camels small and young,
While I am left in Ṣaʿdah
 in a black abode.
3. "Don't listen to ʿAmr,
 for he is reconciled.
How much food can ʿAmr's
 belly hold?
4. "If you accept the bloodwite
 and do not avenge me,
Then go with your ears mutilated
 ostrichlike,
5. "And do not come to water
 but in your women's leavings
When their heels are stained
 with blood."[60]

---

nisāʾi yaṭaʾnahū / yaqulna alā yulqā ʿalā al-marʾi miʾzarū). See (for further examples as well) al-Ālūsī, *Bulūgh al-Arab* 2:317–18; Lane, *q-l-t*.

59. Al-Qālī, *Kitab al-Amālī wa yalīh al-Dhayl* 3:190.

60. The version used is that of Abū Tammām's *Ḥamāsah*; see al-Marzūqī, *Ḥamāsah*, no. 52, 1:217–19; al-Tibrīzī, *Ḥamāsah* 1:117–18. This discussion follows that in S. Stetkevych, *Abū Tammām*, 300–303. For further sources, see Kaḥḥālah, *Aʿlām al-Nisāʾ* 4:234.

The dominant conceit of this marthiyah is that of the slain kinsman speaking for himself. In the first three verses the dead or dying ʿAbd Allāh pleads with his tribe not to accept the bloodwite of young camels while he lies in a dark Yemeni grave. What need does his brother ʿAmr (who would be the main recipient) have of so much livestock anyway?

At verse 4 the tone changes from pleading to threatening. What he threatens his kinsmen with is disgrace, and therefore the poetess introduces in verses 4 and 5 images typical of the classical hijāʾ (invective). If they do not avenge him they will bear the stigma of shame, like the criminal whose ears have been cut off so that he looks like an ostrich. This constitutes a reversal of the usual simile in which the earless ostrich is compared to a man without ears. The final verse brings a return to the imagery of blood that opened the poem, sealing the poem with the same rhyme word with which it began: *damī* (blood). There is, as it were, an extended *jinās*, or pun, no longer with one verse, but between the rhyme word *dam* in verses 1 and 5. The first one refers to the blood of the slain kinsman, polluted/polluting because it is unavenged. The last verse compares the more abstract pollution of unavenged blood to a more literal and tangible pollution—menstrual blood that pollutes the water and those using it. The play on *dam* between verses 1 and 5 is compounded by the possible second reading of the last hemistich of the poem—taking *aʿqāb* to mean sons, offspring—women "whose sons are defiled by [unavenged] blood." In other words, the disgrace of accepting bloodwite will be passed on to the coming generations.

In understanding the relationship of the blood and defilement imagery of this poem to tribal customs, social hierarchy, and ritual concepts of purity and pollution, al-Tibrīzī's remarks (parts of which are taken verbatim from al-Marzūqī) are helpful:

> It was their custom when they came to water for the men of the tribe to go first, then the attendants and herdsmen, and after every group had preceded them, the women went. They would wash themselves and their clothes and then bathe at leisure, undisturbed. To come to water after the women, then, was the worst possible degradation. The women [in this poem] are described as stained with menstrual blood to make the image more disgusting. Al-Namarī quotes Abū Riyāsh as saying: [It means that] if you accept blood money, then afterwards do not abstain from what the Arabs abstain from but have intercourse with your women when they are menstruating; and that "the leavings" (*al-fuḍūl*) here are the remains of menstrual blood, for he considers coming to water a

metaphor for sexual intercourse. Abū Muḥammad al-Aʿrābī said it means: you will not come to tribal councils after taking blood money without your honor being defiled by disgrace, as if you were menstruating women; and this is like Jarīr's verse:

Do not mention the estate of kings, for after Zubayr
You are like a menstruating woman
Who has not washed.[61] [35]

These remarks reveal the prevailing attitudes toward menstrual blood: that it is polluting, defiling, even disgusting. The members of the tribe use the water in order of their social position. The social hierarchy is in turn expressed as ritual status from pure to polluted: the men who rule and defend the tribe are at the top; the women at the bottom. We can suggest further that menstrual blood is defiling because it is, as Mary Douglas terms it, "a sort of human being *manqué*," in other words, a palpable sign of failure to conceive, of infertility, the equivalent of an aborted or miscarried fetus or a corpse.[62] Unavenged blood, in a pastoral society where only those that defend their herds and pasturage keep them, constitutes a similar form of barrenness, or as Kabshah would have it, a worse one. The mention of menstrual blood, then, is added not merely for the sake of disgust but as a metaphor or, rather, a tangible example of pollution by blood and of its social-hierarchical significance.

Thus in this terse and powerful poem, Kabshah has revealed the concept of pollution and purification which lies behind the image of bloodstained garments: a man's honor is compared to a woman's clothes—that is, that which covers her shame and preserves her honor. Unavenged blood, which defiles the metaphorical garment of a man's honor, is equated to menstrual blood, which stains real clothing. Finally, purification by blood restores and purifies one's honor just as purification by water removes menstrual stains from women's clothes. More simply put, just as a woman must wash the disgrace of defiling menstrual blood from her clothing, so must a man whose metaphorical robe of honor is stained by the blood of an unavenged kinsman cleanse it with blood.[63]

Of note here is that whereas Rayṭah attempts to stir indignation and

61. Al-Tibrīzī, *Ḥamāsah* 1:118.
62. Douglas, *Purity and Danger*, 96.
63. See the discussion in S. Stetkevych, *Abū Tammām*, 76, 291–303.

thirst for vengeance among her kinsman by closing her poem with the image of the defiled corpse of the marthī, Kabshah and others emphasize rather the pollution of the surviving kinsmen. Further, as the following short *Ḥamāsiyyah* succinctly states, pollution for the male is equivalent to being female. In other words, the ritual or metaphorical stain of unavenged blood is perceived and expressed in terms of the biological or natural bloodstain of menstruation or of rape/deflowering. Thus the defilement of the male is regularly depicted in sex-linked (female) terms.

This poem of taḥrīḍ by Kabshah's mother, Umm ʿAmr bint Waqdāh, was composed for the same occasion and likewise exploits sex-linked imagery to incite ʿAbd Allāh's kinsmen to avenge him.

Ḥamāsiyyah no. 671. Take up the Eye Pencil! [36]

1. If you will not seek vengeance for your brother,
   Take off your weapons
   And fling them on the flinty ground.
2. Take up the eye pencil, don the camisole,
   Dress yourselves in women's bodices!
   What wretched kin you are to a kinsman oppressed!
3. You have been diverted from avenging your brother
   By a bite of minced meat,
   A lick of meager milk.[64]

The gist of this short piece, as in Kabshah's poem, is that men who do not avenge their slain kinsmen are no longer men. Thus Umm ʿAmr calls upon them to fling down their arms, the insignia of manhood, and take up instead the emblems of womanhood—the eye pencil, bodice, and camisole. The poetess concludes the poem by accusing the men of yielding to harsh circumstances and selling their honor for blood money, for even the meagerest sorts of meat and milk. Her contempt for meat and milk must also be understood in its ritual context. The institution of blood vengeance is based on the principle of the revitalization of the kin through the blood of vengeance. Meat and milk, apparent and more palpable sources of nourishment, are ultimately of less value. The immediate gratification of food in the end will not guarantee the

64. Al-Marzūqī, *Ḥamāsah*, no. 671, 3:1546–47; al-Tibrīzī, *Ḥamāsah* 4:55–56. This poem is discussed in S. Stetkevych, *Abū Tammām*, 339–40. According to al-Tibrīzī, *khazīr* is a dish made of minced meat and flour; *ajrad* may mean buttermilk or perhaps treacle. The first meaning is preferable if the line is taken to refer to the cattle accepted as bloodwite. Al-Tibrīzī, *Ḥamāsah* 4:56.

survival of the kin group, which depends, above all else, on its prowess in battle, its ability to establish a reputation for avenging its kin so that its blood will not be shed with impunity. The overt identification of defilement by unavenged blood with defilement by menstrual blood which is found in Kabshah's poem is not explicitly stated in her mother's. Within the broader context of blood-vengeance imagery, however, the poetess's intent is clear.

A short marthiyah, again involving taḥrīḍ, by Hind bint Ḥudhayfah ibn Badr al-Fazārī, demonstrates to what extent immortality was understood as illustrious repute, which had to be defended or upheld with equally illustrious deeds. It exemplifies, too, the relationship between weeping and avenging, between women's obligations and men's. Hind's brother Ḥiṣn, who had succeeded his father Ḥudhayfah in the chieftainship of the Banū Fazārah (a clan of the Banū Dhubyān), was slain at the Battle of al-Ḥājir during the pre-Islamic War of Dāḥis by one Kurz ibn ʿĀmir of the Banū ʿUqayl.[65]

Ever-Attendant Cares [37]

1. My night was prolonged by ever-attendant cares
   And the day of the Battle of Ḥājir
      Turned my hair white.
2. By my life—and I do not hold it light,
   For an honest man's oath is not
      Like the liar's—
3. On the Day of Ḥājir, Kurz achieved
   A victory that will suffice his tribe
      Till the last remaining night of time!
4. May God bless the two eyes of whoever sees
   A young brave like the one Kurz ibn ʿĀmir
      Took with his spear!
5. So weep, O Banū Dhubyān, for your chief
   With every fine-edged, white,
      And cutting blade,
6. With every spear of Rudaynah's make,
   Mute-jointed, weighted by a spearhead bright
      As a lightning bolt,

65. Shaykhū, *Riyāḍ al-Adab*, 46. See also, Kaḥḥālah, *Aʿlām al-Nisāʾ* 5:230.

7. And every long- and smooth-cheeked steed, thin-bellied,
Like an ostrich, and every mare,
Sleek-coated, lean!
8. For if you don't attack those tribesmen
In a morning raid that is the talk
Of all who go to water and return,
9. And deal the Banū ʿUqayl a blow
After which nothing of them remains,
Then be like slave girls defiled
By every hand.[66]

Hind's poem opens with the familiar long and troubled night and hoary head. The poetess's immediate grief, however, is not in a direct way the loss of her brother but the glory accruing to the enemy for having slain so illustrious a youth. Her statement in verse 3 that her brother's slayer Kurz has achieved a victory that will guarantee his illustrious repute until the last remaining night of time should not be read hastily to mean "forever"; rather, knowing what we know "night" to mean in such poetry, it signifies "as long as we are benighted by unavenged blood"—forever, of course, if we never avenge him. The reiteration of the name of her brother's slayer in verse 4 has two effects: it demonstrates the renown the slayer has achieved, and it designates for the kinsmen she is instigating to vengeance an appropriately glorious hero to slay for her brother's blood. The concept of the perpetuation of the glory of the victor and the concomitant obscurity of the defeated is emphasized when the poetess twice names her brother's slayer but does not register his own name at all.

The poetess then enjoins her kinsmen (verses 5–7) to weep for their fallen brother not with effeminate tears but with the weapons and mounts that are the very emblems of manhood: the sword, the spear, the battle steeds and mares. That is, shed blood, not tears. This conceit sets us up, as it were, for the poetess's subsequent threat of emasculation should her kinsmen fail to achieve a victory that would at once guarantee their future fame and obliterate all trace and memory of the Banū ʿUqayl (8–9). The disgrace of the warrior who does not avenge his fallen kinsman is, as in Kabshah's poem, to be relegated to the bottom rung of the social scale—to be like slave girls passed from hand to hand.

In the context of women's status, this closing image should be

66. The version used is Shaykhū's, *Riyāḍ al-Adab*, 46–47. See also Ṭayfūr, *Balāghāt al-Nisāʾ*, 171–72.

recognized as, in the first place, the opposite of the free woman or virgin, the sequestered girl or married woman of the ruling warrior class, who possessed, above all, the pudical privacy of having her virginity preserved until marriage and within marriage having sexual rights to her limited to one man. Second, what is described here is precisely the status of female slaves, whether purchased or captive, and, thus, in the context of my extended argument, the condition that the poetess fears not merely metaphorically for her menfolk but, given the usual prospects for defeated tribes, for herself.

It should be clear by now that equally in the expressions of mourning and taḥrīḍ, the language of women's rithā' is formulaic and ritually determined. Moreover, what have been dismissed as clichés are, upon examination, carefully condensed and encoded expressions of the ritual concept of sacrifice and redemption.

It would appear from the poems I have discussed that in early Arabic women's poetry there is no hard-and-fast distinction between elegy and the call for vengeance, between rithā' and taḥrīḍ. Rather, as in the men's rithā', the issue of blood vengeance, whether it has or has not been achieved, is one of the dominant themes or concerns. Inasmuch as the woman's poem is a sort of literary oblation of tears, the male counterpart and metaphorical equivalent—the oblation of the blood of vengeance—is always metaphorically present. Or to look at the matter from another point of view, the overarching image of the rainstorm at once bringing the destructive torrent and reviving the dead earth is in Arabic poetry simultaneously an expression of the shedding of elegiac tears and the blood of vengeance.

The ritual structure of elegy and blood vengeance in the Jāhiliyyah and the role of gender within that ritual structure are further exposed by the abomination that results from its confusion or inversion. This forms the backdrop to the infamous episode in the *Sīrah* (Biography) of the Prophet, that of Hind bint ʿUtbah.[67] A brief review of this two-part episode reveals a striking contrast between the Muslim victory at the Battle of Badr in the second year of the Hijrah and the Meccan polytheists' victory in the Battle of Uḥud the following year.[68] The first

67. See Kaḥḥālah, *Aʿlām al-Nisā'* 5:239–51.

68. On the Battles of Badr and Uḥud and Hind's role in them I have relied upon Ibn Hishām, *Al-Sīrah al-Nabawiyyah*, 2:643–803 (Badr); 3:837–967 (Uḥud) (for an English translation, see Alfred Guillaume, trans., *The Life of Muhammad: A Translation of Isḥāq's "Sīrat Rasūl Allāh"* [Lahore: Oxford University Press, Pakistan Branch, 1974], 289–360, 370–433); and Abū Jaʿfar Muḥammad ibn Jarīr al-Ṭabarī, *Ta'rīkh al-Rusul wa al-Mulūk* = Abu Djafar

is a paradigm of heroic combat as proper sacrifice; the second of its perversion, improper and, hence, failed and ineffectual sacrifice.

Hind, by birth and by marriage (to Abū Sufyān) a member of the Meccan Qurashī aristocracy that long opposed Islam, lost her father ʿUtbah ibn Rabīʿah, her paternal uncle Shaybah ibn Rabīʿah, her brother al-Walīd ibn ʿUtbah, and her son Ḥanẓalah ibn Abī Sufyān at the Battle of Badr.[69] Ibn Isḥāq reports that ʿUtbah advised the Meccans against engaging the Muslims in battle, but when calls to vengeance stirred the army to action, he joined to fend off accusations of cowardice. ʿUtbah took the field with Shaybah and al-Walīd and issued a challenge to single combat. When a group of Medinese Anṣārīs responded, ʿUtbah refused them, saying, "We have no business with you." "Noble equals! But we only want men of our own tribe!" and demanded opponents of his own rank and tribe. Another version differs slightly: "We do not want these; we want some of our cousins from the sons of ʿAbd al-Muṭṭalib!"[70] Thereupon the Prophet sent forth the three noblest combatants Islam had to offer: the Prophet's uncle Ḥamzah ibn ʿAbd al-Muṭṭalib, and cousins ʿUbaydah ibn al-Ḥārith and ʿAlī ibn Abī Ṭālib. They paired off by age/rank: ʿUbaydah, the oldest of the Muslims, against ʿUtbah; Ḥamzah against Shaybah; and ʿAlī against al-Walīd. Ḥamzah and ʿAlī dispatched their opponents and then helped the wounded ʿUbaydah finish off ʿUtbah. ʿUbaydah died of his wounds shortly thereafter.[71]

The insistence of the reports concerning the Battle of Badr on the proper matching of opponents in man-to-man single combat points to the ritual requirements of sacrifice and vengeance with their prescription of the proper victim. The redemption or salvation that results from sacrifice properly performed is made explicit when at the point of death the wounded ʿUbaydah asks the Prophet, "Am I not a martyr, O Messenger of God?" "Yes indeed," Muḥammad responded. As if to emphasize the element of self-sacrifice that is the essence of martyrdom, the reports credit ʿUbaydah with a final reply to the Prophet: "If Abū

Mohammed ibn Djarir at-Tabari, *Annales*, ed. M. J. de Goeje, 15 vols. (Leiden: E. J. Brill, 1964–65) [photo ed.] 3:1281–1354 (Badr); 3:1383–1427 (Uḥud) (for an English translation, see *The History of al-Ṭabarī (Taʾrīkh al-rusul waʾl-mulūk)*, vol. 7: *The Foundation of the Community*, ed. and trans. W. Montgomery Watt and M. V. McDonald [Albany: State University of New York Press, 1987], 26–80, 105–38).

69. Ibn Hishām, *Al-Sīrah al-Nabawiyyah* 3:873 n. 1.

70. Al-Ṭabarī, *Taʾrīkh* 3:1315–16, 1290.

71. Ibid., 3:1317–18.

Ṭālib [Muḥammad's uncle and loyal guardian] were alive he would know that I am worthier than he of his line":

> We keep him safe until we are struck down around him,
> forgetful of our sons and wives.[72] [38]

The emphasis on ritual propriety in the accounts of the Battle of Badr where men and angels achieved an astounding Muslim victory is countered in the accounts of the Meccan polytheist victory at Uḥud in the following year by an insistence on abomination and sacrilege. In the first place, the accounts state explicitly that the Meccans undertook the Battle of Uḥud to avenge their dead from the Battle of Badr, but from the outset, they broke the rules. The first outrage was a mismatch. Jubayr ibn Muṭʿim offered to free his Abyssinian slave Waḥshī (a name that could be translated as "savage" or "wild"), a skilled javelin thrower, if he would slay Ḥamzah to avenge Jubayr's uncle, Ṭuʿaymah ibn ʿAdī. Hind bint ʿUtbah, whose husband Abū Sufyān was at the head of the Meccan force, had, in the traditional manner, come out with the other Meccan noblewomen to incite and inspire her Qurashī kinsmen, playing the tambourine and reciting taḥrīḍ. But she also called out to this black slave, Waḥshī, "Go to it, Abū Dusmah [= Father of Blackness]! Quench my thirst for vengeance, and quench your own!"[73]

Waḥshī's recounting of his deed is of interest. Having spotted Ḥamzah who was slaying polytheists right and left, he balanced his javelin and hurled it. It struck Ḥamzah in the lower belly with such force that it came out between his legs. Waḥshī waited until Ḥamzah was dead, then retrieved his javelin and returned to camp, having, as he states in his account, no further business on the battlefield.[74] A noble Qurashī Muslim warrior thus ignominiously fell to a black slave hurling a javelin—as Ḥassān ibn Thābit, the Prophet's poet, remarks, not even one of the weapons of the Arabs.[75] The element of self-sacrifice implicit in man-to-man combat is lacking in Waḥshī's hurling his javelin from afar. This is not heroic combat to avenge kindred blood but a "murder for hire."

As we have seen in previous chapters, one abomination tends to generate others. After having incited the wrong match to avenge ʿUt-

72. Ibid., 3:1318.
73. Ibid., 3:1386–87, 1400.
74. Ibid., 3:1405; Ibn Hishām, *Al-Sīrah al-Nabawiyyah* 3:848–49.
75. Al-Ṭabarī, *Taʾrīkh* 3:1416.

bah, Hind, in a transport of vengeance, mutilated the corpses of the fallen Muslims, strung their cut-off ears and noses into anklets and necklaces, which she donned, and gave her own jewelry to Waḥshī, as if in payment for his services. Finally, she slit open Ḥamzah's belly, cut out his liver, and sank her teeth into it.[76] Hind's actions constitute a confusion of human and animal roles. Vultures and hyenas are supposed to defile, desecrate, and devour fallen warriors, whereas animal sacrifice, from the hunt or the camel slaughter, is meant for human consumption. The sacrificial dialectic of animal sacrifice versus blood vengeance—humans eat animals and animals eat humans—is thrown into confusion, producing the abomination of cannibalism. The accounts are careful to point out, however, that Hind was unable to swallow Ḥamzah's liver, and spat it out.[77] If vultures and hyenas when they consume they flesh and drink the blood of the dead acquire their life-force or liquid soul, Hind's inability to swallow Ḥamzah's liver should indicate her failure to acquire such force or power.[78] And Ḥamzah's power must now be understood as the immortality that Islam confers upon believers. This is clearly the thrust of Muḥammad's statement that had Hind swallowed Ḥamzah's liver, hellfire would never touch her. In other words, *improper sacrifice* fails to achieve immortality, whether in the pagan blood-vengeance sense of somehow acquiring the life-force of the fallen enemy or in the Islamic sense of gaining the immortal garden through faith and martyrdom. The proper self-sacrifice of the Muslims brings revitalization, that is, salvation. In terms whose symbolic import is already evident from my discussion of blood and perfume, Muḥammad declares that on the Day of Resurrection the wounds of Muslims slain at Uḥud will bleed red like blood but with the fragrance of musk.[79] It is clear that the perpetual cycle of vengeance has come to an end when to Abū Sufyān's boast, "You have done a great deed, so rise; war goes by turns

76. Ibid., 3:1415.

77. Ibid.; Ibn Hishām, *Al-Sīrah al-Nabawiyyah* 3:872.

78. Hind's response to the deaths of her kinsmen has been recognized as identical to that of Hecuba, who in her grief and anger over Hector's death expresses her desire to eat Achilles' liver (*Iliad* 24:212); see al-Ḥūfī, *Al-Marʾah*, 449. According to R. B. Onians, who discusses this case and others, such as Prometheus, the liver was understood as the organ of desire. See Richard Broxton Onians, *The Origins of European Thought about the Body, the Mind, the Soul, the World, Time, and Fate* (Cambridge: Cambridge University Press, 1951), 85. I am inclined, particularly in light of the evidence of blood-vengeance poetry and ritual, to see the liver rather as the seat of life, the source of blood, which is the liquid soul. See Guillaume's note: "This seems to be a survival of prehistoric animism. By devouring an enemy's liver it was hoped to absorb his strength." Guillaume, *The Life of Muhammad*, 385 n. 1.

79. Ibn Hishām, *Al-Sīrah al-Nabawiyyah* 3:879.

[one day you win, one day you lose]. Today in exchange for the Day of Badr. Show you are mightier, Hubal!" Muḥammad instructs ʿUmar to issue the reply, "Allāh is greater and mightier. They are not equals, our slain in paradise and your slain in hellfire."[80]

In keeping with the characteristic imagery and metaphors of blood vengeance, the abomination of Hind and Waḥshī is described by the Prophet's kinswoman Hind bint Athāthah ibn ʿAbbād ibn al-Muṭṭalib in terms of whoredom, sexual exposure, and defilement or disgrace. In the exchange of *rajaz* poems between the two Hinds, Hind bint ʿUtbah first boasts that she has slaked her thirst for vengeance. Hind bint Athāthah refutes this boast in metaphorical terms that draw an analogy between improper vengeance and fornication—the illicit satisfaction of lust—or prostitution—trafficking for personal gain to satisfy illicit lust.[81] The disgrace of improper sacrifice or vengeance is that it leaves its perpetrator more polluted than ever. In Hind bint ʿUtbah's poem we find the poetess declaring her unflagging devotion not to her fallen kinsmen, as in al-Khirniq's poem, but to a black slave. In Hind bint Athāthah's reply, we find that their victory at Uḥud, "after Badr," has brought the Meccans as much disgrace as the defeat at Badr and that the sexual pollution and defilement normally attributed to those who fail to achieve vengeance, as in Hind bint Ḥudhayfah's poem, is equally attributable to one who has taken improper vengeance:

Hind bint ʿUtbah's Boast [39]

1. Now we have repaid you
 for the Day of Badr,
A war after another war
 blazes all the more.
2. I could not endure
 the death of ʿUtbah,
Or of my brother and his uncle,
 and my firstborn.

80. Ibid., 3:875; see also Ḥassān ibn Thābit's verses, ibid. 3:929.

81. Ḥassān ibn Thābit's reply to Hind's boasts on the Day of Uḥud likewise take as their dominant theme sexual defilement and disgrace, the failure to gain victory and vengeance, and fornication. See al-Ṭabarī, *Taʾrīkh* 3:1416–17. Ibn Hishām refers to these verses but considers them too obscene to repeat, see Ibn Hishām, *Al-Sīrah al-Nabawiyyah* 3:874. On the prevalent use of sexual defilement in hijāʾ, see S. Stetkevych, *Abū Tammām*, 333–50.

3. I cured my soul and
fulfilled my oath,
And you, O Waḥshī, slaked the thirst
that burned within my breast.
4. To Waḥshī will I be grateful
all my days
Until my bones have rotted
in the tomb.[82]

Hind bint Athāthah's Reply [40]

1. You were disgraced at Badr
and after Badr,
O daughter of a slanderer
whose disbelief was great.
2. God sent against you at morning
just before dawn
The men of the Hāshimites,
fair-skinned and tall,
3. And wielding every slashing blade
that cuts
Were Ḥamzah, my lion,
and my falcon, ʿAlī!
4. When Shaybah and your father
wished to betray me,
It was their own necks that
they dyed with blood.
5. What an evil vow yours was,
the most evil of all!
To Waḥshī you revealed
your heart's secret desire.
6. Waḥshī has rent the veil
of modesty,
What have the harlots to boast of
after [Hind]?[83]

82. I have followed the version in Ibn Hishām, *Al-Sīrah al-Nabawiyyah* 3:872–73 (Guillaume, *Life of Muhammad*, 385); see also Ṭayfūr, *Balāghāt al-Nisā'*, 33–34; and Ibn ʿAbd Rabbih, *Al-ʿIqd al-Farīd* 2:120.

83. I have followed the version given by Ibn Hishām, *Al-Sīrah al-Nabawiyyah* 3:873, adding, in light of Ibn Hishām's remark that he omitted three obscene verses, the final three hemistichs from the version in Ṭayfūr, *Balāghāt al-Nisā'*, 34. There, however, the narrator, Arwā bint al-Ḥārith ibn ʿAbd al-Muṭṭalib, claims these verses as her own. Yet again, Arwā attributes them to her cousin (*bint ʿammī*) in the version of Ibn ʿAbd Rabbih, *Al-ʿIqd al-Farīd* 2:120–21. Both of these poems appear in the translation and analysis of Arwā's diatribe against

This episode serves, through the use of purely Jāhilī concepts of ritual and sacrifice, to express the depravity of the Banū Umayyah at the period when the Meccan oligarchy opposed Islam and the righteousness of the Muslims and their Prophet. Yet, in a manner typical of the ambiguity of the sacred and sacrilegious, Hind bint ʿUtbah's show of fortitude transmutes into a source of pride when, as the mother of Muʿāwiyah, she is recognized as the progenitrix of the Umayyad dynasty.

In the end, what is so fascinating about the accounts of the Battles of Badr and Uḥud, indeed the *Sīrah* literature in general, is the simultaneous expression of two levels of discourse, the pagan and the Islamic. When Muḥammad viewed the mutilated corpse of his uncle Ḥamzah, he vowed that if God ever gave him victory over the Quraysh, he would mutilate thirty of their men, and the Muslims, seeing their Prophet's grief, likewise vowed to mutilate the Qurashis as no Arab had ever mutilated anyone before. But then, God sent down verses (Qurʾān 16:127) proscribing excessive (= unequal) vengeance and advocating patience over punishment, and ever after Muḥammad forbade mutilation.[84] When Muḥammad's "day of reckoning" with the Quraysh finally came, it was a day of mercy. With the conquest of Mecca in the year 8 H., Abū Sufyān surrendered to Islam, and Muḥammad gave orders that no one who took refuge in Abū Sufyān's house or locked his door or entered the mosque should be hurt.[85]

Like al-Shanfarā's vengeance of one hundred and Muhalhil's unquenchable thirst for vengeance for Kulayb, Hind's excess seems to represent what Islam perceived as the *jahl* in Jāhiliyyah—a fortitude and impetuousness that stirred both admiration and horror, an abomination that generated a cycle of destruction and self-destruction. So strong was the rule of *jahl* that even God's Prophet was tempted by it, and only Islam could abrogate it.

Muʿāwiyah in Nancy N. Roberts, "Voice and Gender: An Annotated Translation of Three Passages from Aḥmad Ibn Abī Ṭāhir Ṭayfūr's *Balāghāt al-Nisāʾ*," *Al-ʿArabiyya* (forthcoming).

84. Al-Ṭabarī, *Taʾrīkh* 3:1420–21; Ibn Hishām, *Al-Sīrah al-Nabawiyyah* 3:877–78.

85. Ibn Hishām, *Al-Sīrah al-Nabawiyyah* 4:1242–47.

CHAPTER 6

Memory Inflamed: Muhalhil ibn Rabīʿah and the War of al-Basūs

The subject of this chapter is Muhalhil ibn Rabīʿah, the famed warrior-poet of the War of al-Basūs.[1] He is a figure whose roots lie deep in ancient Arab autochthony and whose later branches formed a lush crown of classical literary poetry and akhbār, on the one hand, and the full-fledged popular romance of *Al-Zīr Sālim* on the other. In other words, the figure of Muhalhil embodies an archetype that continued to generate literature for a number of centuries. It is said that his *laqab* Muhalhil derives from the verb *halhala*, which means to weave fine tissue—and hence to compose refined verse—because he was the first to do so, and further that he was the first poet to compose *qaṣīd*, that is, the classical Arabic ode form.[2] There is some confusion as to whether his true name was ʿAdī or Imruʾ al-Qays (not to be confused with the celebrated poet of that name), or whether there were two brothers who bore these names,[3] but for my literary purposes the *figura* of Muhalhil is clear enough. His persona and poetry are embedded in the lore of the great forty-year war or, more precisely, blood feud of the Jāhiliyyah.

The central argument of this chapter is that the lore and poetry of the War of al-Basūs preserved in the literary compendia of the classical

1. Muhalhil's poetry and akhbār have been collected in Luwīs Shaykhū, *Kitāb Shuʿarāʾ al-Naṣrāniyyah*, 2 vols., 2d ed. (Beirut: al-Maṭbaʿah al-Kāthūlīkiyyah, 1967), 1:160–81; and Ḥasan al-Sandūbī, *Akhbār al-Marāqisah wa Ashʿāruhum fī al-Jāhiliyyah wa Ṣadr al-Islām* (Cairo: Maṭbaʿat al-Istiqāmah, 1939), 9–77. On classical sources, see Sezgin, *Poesie*, 148–49.

2. Al-Iṣbahānī, *Kitāb al-Aghānī* 5:1701; Sezgin, *Poesie*, 148.

3. Sezgin, *Poesie*, 148.

Arab-Islamic period are paradigmatic of *jahl*, that obstinate impetuosity for which Muslims coined their term for the Arab pagan age. I focus on those themes, motifs, and patterns that reverberate throughout Arab-Islamic literary culture, particularly those related to blood vengeance as sacrificial ritual and to gender and the aesthetics of orality.

The blaze of the forty-year blood feud of the War of al-Basūs was ignited by the slaying of a she-camel. Before pursuing the details of this episode, we should note the uncanny extent to which the underlying themes and symbols are identical to those of the Qurʾānic lore of the she-camel of Ṣāliḥ. Both at base are myths of the arrogation of power and wealth to one individual and the resultant breakup or dissolution of the polity, which is symbolized by the illicit slaughter/sacrifice of a she-camel. The bivalency of personal accumulation of wealth and power as blessing and curse bifurcates in the Arab-Islamic tradition into two legends. In the one treated in the Qurʾān and hence co-opted by Islam, God's she-camel is sent as a sign of divine favor, a blessing to the Prophet Ṣāliḥ and to his people the Thamūd, if they follow him. The story makes it clear, however, that it is the resentment and jealousy stirred by the magnificent she-camel that leads to its hocking and the destruction of Thamūd. In the "pagan" legend, as we shall see, the disposition of themes and motifs differs, and the scales are ultimately weighted toward condemnation.

Al-Nuwayrī in his account of the War of al-Basūs puts particular emphasis on the political connotations. He opens by noting that on only three occasions was the entire stock of Maʿadd united, the last of these being under the infamous Kulayb Wāʾil, the elder brother of Muhalhil. Kulayb's tale is one of the usurpation and arrogation of power and wealth to a single individual in a manner at odds with the tribal ethos of the chieftain as a *primus inter pares*. Kulayb defeated and scattered the armies of the Yemen until all of Maʿadd united under him and conferred upon him the emblems and privileges of kingship: a king's allotment of spoils, crown, royal greeting, and obedience. From him the adage "mightier than Kulayb Wāʾil" (*aʿazz min Kulayb Wāʾil*) was coined. He then began to oppress his people, taking all the best pasturage and water holes as his private precinct (*ḥimā*) and forbidding the herds of others to graze or water with his.[4] We read in *Kitāb al-Aghānī* that so overweening had Kulayb become that, as the etiological

4. Al-Nuwayrī, *Nihāyat al-Arab* 15:396–97.

myth of his name (Little Dog) tells us, he took a puppy and whenever he came upon good pastureland he threw it down and claimed as his precinct the entire area over which the puppy's howling could be heard.[5]

Now it happened that the related clans of Taghlib, of which Kulayb was chieftain, and Bakr, whose chieftain was Murrah ibn Dhuhl, were encamped together in Tihāmah. Among the children of Murrah were a daughter, Jalīlah, who was married to Kulayb and a son, Jassās. The latter had a maternal aunt, al-Basūs, who lived under the protection of Jassās and the Banū Murrah and owned a fine she-camel. One day this ill-fated she-camel was tethered before the tent of Jassās when Kulayb's herd went by. She pulled at her tether till it broke and joined Kulayb's herd. When they reached the water hole Kulayb spotted the foreign beast and, enraged, took up his bow and arrow and shot her through the udder so that, in the words of the *Kitāb al-Aghānī*, "her blood mixed with her milk."[6] When al-Basūs saw this, she flung off her veil and cried, "O, for shame! O protector/neighbor!"[7]

What is ultimately at issue here is a failure to observe kinship obligation. Inasmuch as Bakr and Taghlib are related clans, Kulayb should by extension have recognized the rights of even the tenuously connected (through maternal kin and bond of clientage) al-Basūs. The mixture of blood and milk suggests a confusion of kinship ties—the blood tie through the male and the ancient Arab milk kinship through the female. One message is clear: that to arrogate power and privilege to oneself is to abrogate one's responsibilities to others. Further, al-Basūs's gesture and cry are the emblems of disgraced womanhood, which the menfolk must either avenge or assume themselves.

The impetuous and heroic Jassās rose to the occasion, jumped on his mount, spear in hand, and accompanied by his cousin ʿAmr, slew Kulayb. Thus originated the expression "more baleful than al-Basūs" (*ash'am min al-Basūs*).[8]

From the inception of the war the rule of the generation of abominations is at work. The confusion of personal privilege and kinship obligation results in the "improper sacrifice" in which the udder that should give milk gives blood. The outrageous slaughter of the she-camel, the source of life and prosperity, the symbol of the polity, signals the demise and disintegration of that polity. With the slaying of Kulayb, a

5. Al-Iṣbahānī, *Kitāb al-Aghānī* 5:1678.
6. Ibid., 5:1680.
7. Al-Nuwayrī, *Nihāyat al-Arab* 15:397.
8. Ibid.

further abomination ensues: for it is standard within the kin group to pay a man's bloodwite in camels, but to invert this and pay a human life—and the tribal chieftain-king's at that—for a camel's is, on the surface of things, horrific. But perhaps on a deeper level the equation is fair: one symbol of the polity for another. And perhaps the intended message is that an outrage to the rights of even the lowliest member—an old female client—of the kin group can topple the entire social edifice.

The response of Muhalhil and the Banū Taghlib is recorded in terms of the ritual and sacrificial concepts with which we are by now familiar:

> So al-Muhalhil prepared for war against the Banū Bakr: he abandoned women and flirtation, forswore gambling and wine, and gathered his fighting men. He then sent a delegation to the Banū Shaybān [i.e., Bakr] to seek expiation for what had happened. They came upon Murrah ibn Dhuhl ibn Shaybān in his tribal council and said: "You have committed a grave act in slaying Kulayb for an old she-camel. You have cut the bond of blood kinship and have violated what is held sacred [*fa qaṭaʿtum al-raḥim wa intahaktum al-ḥurmah*]. But for our part we deplore rushing into war against you without seeking expiation from you. We therefore offer you four actions by which you can escape war and we will be satisfied." "What are they?" replied Murrah. They said: "Revive Kulayb for us, or surrender to us his slayer, Jassās, so that we can kill him for him, or [your son] Hammām, for he is his equal [*kafʾ*], or turn yourself over to us, for in you his blood would be redeemed [*wafāʾ*]." Then Murrah said, "As for my reviving Kulayb, this can never be. And as for Jassās, he is an impetuous youth who quickly thrust his spear, then mounted his horse till I know not to what country he has fled. As for Hammām, he is the father of ten, the brother of ten, and the paternal uncle of ten, all of whom are the horsemen of their tribe. They will never surrender him to me for me to deliver him up to you to be slain for someone else's crime. As for me, another foray of horsemen tomorrow and I may be the first to fall, so why hasten my death? But I will give you two choices: First, there are my other sons. Fasten a camel's girth around the neck of any one of them you wish, take him to your men, and slaughter him like a slaughter camel [*fa idhbaḥūh dhabḥ al-jazūr*]. Otherwise, I will give you, in place of [*kafīl*] [one of] the Bakr ibn Wāʾil, one thousand dark-eyed she-camels." Then the men grew angry and said, "It's no good for you to give us your little sons and offer to sell us milk for the blood of Kulayb!"[9]

9. Ibid., 15:399.

A careful reading of this passage suggests that war was inevitable, for the normal rule is that within the kin group the bloodwite of a hundred she-camels is paid as restitution for murder. That the Banū Taghlib from the beginning offer to accept only blood for blood and, indeed, refuse even a thousand she-camels is an indication that the tribal bond has been broken, and, we can argue, it was the overvaluation of the overweening Kulayb that caused this break. Al-Nuwayrī's further remarks indicate precisely this dissolution of the federated clans or tribes:

> War broke out between them, and Jalīlah, Kulayb's wife, rejoined her father and his clan, and the tribes of Bakr ibn Wāʾil separated. They abhorred joining the Banū Shaybān and helping them fight against their brothers and considered Jassās's slaying Kulayb over an old she-camel a grievous affair. So [the Banū] Lujaym departed, and [the Banū] Yashkur refused to assist them, and al-Ḥārith ibn ʿUbād withdrew to his own people, and he was the father of Bujayr and the horseman of the battle steed al-Naʿāmah.[10]

The dissolution of the polity is further expressed in an anecdote about the boon companionship between Kulayb's brother, Muhalhil, and Jassās's brother, Hammām. The two were like brothers and were sworn never to withhold secrets from each other, until, that is, Jassās slew Kulayb and the two became blood enemies.[11]

An oedipal drama, too, finds its way into the lore of the relationship between Muhalhil and Kulayb, just as it did in the case of Durayd ibn al-Ṣimmah and his elder brother. The chieftain Kulayb finds the young Muhalhil constantly in the company of women and so dubs him *zīr al-nisāʾ* (visitor of women = "sissy") declaring, "By God, if I were killed you would take nothing but milk for my blood!"[12]

In yet another narrative, Muhalhil's niece Umāmah, the twelve-year-old daughter of Kulayb and Jalīlah, searches for her uncle to avenge her father, only to find him drunk, whereupon she recites a poem of taḥrīḍ that opens:

10. Ibid.
11. Al-Iṣbahānī, *Kitāb al-Aghānī* 5:1683–84.
12. Shaykhū, *Shuʿarāʾ al-Naṣrāniyyah* 1:161.

Do you delight in diversions and wine
  Unaware of the course of events?
Do you know that Kulayb lies slain
  In broad daylight by the treacherous Jassās?[13] [41]

A related version tells of Muhalhil drinking with his boon companion Hammām when the news of Kulayb's death reaches him. His response, however, is virtually that of the youthful profligate Imru᾿ al-Qays at the announcement of his father's death at the hands of the treacherous Banū Asad: he continues to carouse for a day, to take up the call to vengeance only on the morrow.[14]

Such stories appear to be the result of the transformation of the ritual pattern of the oath of blood vengeance into narrative pattern. It is perhaps such archetypal links rather than actual blood kinship that led to the claim that Muhalhil was the maternal uncle of the renowned poet Imru᾿ al-Qays ibn Ḥujr.[15] In this particular case, one cannot help but suspect that the better known legend of Imru᾿ al-Qays and the announcement of his father's death might have generated a parallel one for his "uncle." It is within this proliferation of archetypally generated lore that the classical Arabic literary tradition situates the poems of Muhalhil ibn Rabīʿah.

The poem that is said to be Muhalhil's first poetic response to the slaying of Kulayb[16] serves as a fitting riposte to Kulayb's taunts to his younger brother, for it begins with the poet identifying his sorrow with that of the female mourners only to end with a sharp distinction between male and female mourning. The poem is informed by a ritual pattern of passage that moves from the feminine lament of shedding tears to the masculine lament of shedding blood. We find in this and in others like it that the poet first participates in the shedding of tears, perceived as puerile or

13. Shaykhū, *Riyāḍ al-Adab*, 6. The second chapter of this book (pp. 5–20) is devoted to the women's marāthī associated with the War of al-Basūs. Although much of it, like the men's poetry associated with this war, seems to be "second-generation" material engendered by the rich lore of that conflict, it provides a wealth of expressions of the abominations resulting from the intratribal hostilities between Bakr and Taghlib, especially concerning the confusion of enemy and kin, a breakdown of ritual categories. For example, Jalīlah, the sister of Jassās and wife of Kulayb, laments that vengeance for her husband will bring her not renewed life but further bereavement (13).

14. Shaykhū, *Shuʿarā᾿ al-Naṣrāniyyah* 1:161–62.

15. Ibid., 1:160.

16. Ibid., 1:162; ʿIzz al-Dīn Ibn al-Athīr, *Al-Kāmil fī al-Ta᾿rīkh*, 13 vols. (Beirut: Dār Ṣādir/Dār Bayrūt, 1965), 1:529.

effeminate for the male, but then moves beyond weeping to assume the manly obligation of shedding the blood of vengeance.

Once We Used to Guard the Freeborn Maidens [42]

1. Once we used to guard the freeborn maidens
 jealously, that no eye should see them
  leaving their abodes.
2. Then when Kulayb was buried they went forth
 reluctantly, sure that after him
  would come disgrace.
3. You see the maids with rounded breasts, gazellelike,
 stripped, now that Kulayb is fallen,
  of their shrouds.
4. They scratch their faces, bareheaded, sighing
 after him, and promise
  to continue long.
5. Bereft and mourning their harsh lot,
 their bellies burn as if with fire, they gaze
  from red and swollen eyes.[17]
6. They say: "Who will help the indigent
 when they cry out? Who will stain
  the tips of supple spears with blood?
7. "Who will cast lots for the slaughter camel
 when the morning wind cuts through
  the knotted ropes?
8. "Who will come forward first with blood monies
 and gather them? and who will succor us
  when calamities afflict us?"
9. He was my store against adversity to come;
 then he was lost and left
  my storehouse bare.
10. O my soul's sorrow for a grievous time
 like a camel kneeling down upon me
  with ponderous chest and neck,
11. And with a calamity, irresistible, mighty,
 that has overwhelmed the tribesmen
  and their womenfolk.
12. It leveled the strongholds that once had been
 refuges for elders
  and youths alike.

17. Following al-Sandūbī's reading of *nakdahunna* for *nukdahunna* and his *sharḥ*. Al-Sandūbī, *Akhbār al-Marāqisah*, 73.

13. It struck in the forenoon and their wall
  after [Kulayb's death] was demolished,
    base and edifice.
14. Weep for the tribe's lord, women, and bewail him
  about whom shrouds of Coptic linen
    have been bound.
15. Weep for the orphans now struck by drought,
  weep for the protected neighbor
    now betrayed.
16. Weep for him fallen, his neck
  wrapped in his blood,
    for this has made me weep.
17. And for this will I leave the tribes of Wāʾil
  slain in every dwelling
    and abode,
18. Slain, with vultures tearing
  at their hands by turns,
  and hopping crows.[18]

This first selection from the poetry of Muhalhil offers a particularly useful perspective for defining the ritual intent of the elegiac/rithāʾ section of the poem of blood vengeance, especially the gender differentiation that operates in early Arabic rites of mourning. The poem employs the status and obligation of the women of the tribe to state indirectly the obligation of the man. It begins by describing the inversion of status occasioned by blood pollution through the condition of the noble maidens of the tribe. Once their honor was jealously guarded; they were confined so that no eye might see them. With Kulayb's death they are, as it were, expelled from their protected quarters, exposed, unveiled, degraded. The alluring image of pubescent maids, like gazelles with budding breasts (verse 3) is countered in verses 4 and 5 with the repulsive picture of their faces now scratched open, their eyes now red and swollen. The strangely suggestive metonymy of shrouds (*akfān*) for veils (3) is best understood as contributing to the gender-defined symmetrical inversion in operation here: in peacetime, when there is no unavenged blood, women are veiled and men bareheaded; defilement is therefore expressed by the unveiling (= deflowering) of women and

18. Following al-Sandūbī, *ghirbān* for Shaykhū's *ghurbān*. See al-Sandūbī, *Akhbār al-Marāqisah*, 74; Shaykhū, *Shuʿarāʾ al-Naṣrāniyyah* 1:163. I have given Shaykhū's version of the poem, 1:162–63. See also Ibn al-Athīr, *Al-Kāmil* 1:529–30; al-Sandūbi, 72–74.

shrouding (= veiling) of (dead) men (14). Muhalhil then presents a chorus of mourning women intoning their ritual lament or dirge.

It is above all the loss of the living which is here recorded in terms of the obligations of manhood: "Who will" fulfill these obligations now that Kulayb is fallen (verses 6–8)—generosity to the needy, going to battle for vengeance, casting *maysir* lots to distribute food in times of hardship, paying and gathering blood monies, succoring the afflicted. The expression *idhā ghadā rīḥun yuqaṭṭiᶜu maᶜqida al-ashṭānī* (When the morning wind cuts through the knotted ropes) (7) should be noted as an expression both literal and figurative of hard times, for ropes and bonds in Arabic poetry are common expressions of the bonds of obligation to kin, clients, refugees, and it was of course precisely in times of dearth that the destitute client, orphan, or widow was least likely to be succored.

At verse 9 the poet turns from the chorus of wailing women to the expression of his own sorrow. The metaphors for calamity and bereavement here employed are of particular interest because some of them appear in a greatly expanded but less evident manner in *The Muᶜallaqah of Imruʾ al-Qays*. Verse 9 describes the deceased as a storehouse against misfortune, now emptied. The oppressiveness of loss is described in verse 10 as a grievous time or fate, as a camel kneeling down on the bereft poet, nearly suffocating him with its ponderous chest and neck. Time is described as motionless, as standing still, like the never-ending night that opens others of his poems. The calamity of Kulayb's death is metaphorically expressed as a razing or leveling of strongholds and refuges (12), as the demolishing of a fortress wall (13).

At verse 14 the poet turns to the conceit of exhorting the female mourners to lament. It is especially striking as an inversion of the female poetry of taḥrīḍ, of instigating the kin of the fallen warrior to avenge him. The poet here bids the women to weep in a passage that has the same ritual-liturgical flavor as the "Who will" passage of verses 6–8 and serves as a sort of antiphon to it: *Fa/wa ibkīna* . . . (Then/and weep for . . .) (14–16). A parallel is established between the slain Kulayb wrapped in Coptic linen (14) and, after the accelerated pace of the repetition of *wa ibkīna* (and weep!), the fallen Kulayb, his neck wrapped in his blood (16).

The mention of blood triggers a dramatic inversion from the feminine plural imperative form I "Weep!" that has introduced the last four phrases to the form IV causative perfect indicative "This is what made me weep." This entails a rhetorical inversion whereby the poet changes from the active issuer of the imperative to the passive object of a causative verb in the *radd al-ʿajuz ʿalā al-ṣadr* (repetition of an earlier word in the rhyme word) and a grammatical inversion of mood, tense, and person: *wa ibkīna . . . mā abkānī* (Weep! . . . what made me weep). The effect of this line is to identify, through the shared use of the verb *bakā* (weep)/*abkā* (make weep), male and female mourning and, at the same time, through the morphological and grammatical manipulation of the verb, to highlight the distinction. Whereas the women are repeatedly urged to weep, for the man the perfect tense of *fa la-dhāka ma abkānī* (for this is what made me weep) is immediately juxtaposed in verse 17 to the intensive energetic future form, now with the poet as actor, not object, *fa la-atrukanna* (I will leave) thus expressing with utter clarity and concision the poet's dramatic transition from mourner to avenger, from one who had first shared in the mourning of the womenfolk, to the one who has put weeping behind him and will now go forth to slay the foe. The progression from "made me weep" to "I will leave" constitutes, in terms of the ritual model, the transition from separation to liminality. Of note too is the use of emphatic enclitics, *la-*, *-anna*: thus *atruku* "I will leave" becomes *la-atrukanna*. The effect here is clearly not one of *ḥashw* (metrical filler), but rather of giving metrical weight and volume at this dramatic turning point in the poem so that the terse and forceful final two verses are able to counterpoise the extended dirge of the preceding sixteen verses.

The purification of polluted kindred blood is expressed bluntly and boldly: the slaying of the tribes of the Banū Wāʾil wherever they dwell, the abandoning of their corpses to the vultures and the hopping crows. Of rhetorical interest here is the utter simplicity of the diction, especially of verse 17: to "leave the tribes of Wāʾil slain in every dwelling" in this poem has the same effect as "and every trace of them destroyed" in the next poem to be discussed (verse 31)—to recall the abandoned encampments of the nasīb. The force of the final lines is augmented, too, through the alliterative momentum of *qāf*, long *alif*, and *lām*: *qabāʾila Wāʾilin qatlā . . . qatlā* (the tribes of Wāʾil slain . . . slain). As we have come to expect, the death of the enemy is countered by revitalization, here expressed by the feasting vultures and hopping crows that take turns tearing and biting at the hands of the slain warriors.

In terms of the gender dialectic established in Chapter 5, it appears that whereas kinswomen redeem the sacrificial blood of the fallen warrior with tears, the kinsman has a further obligation to redeem it with the blood of vengeance.

The following poem is said to have been recited by Muhalhil the morning after the announcement of Kulayb's death, when the poet had buried his brother and stood over his grave:[19]

Memory Inflamed [43]

1. Memory inflamed the mote in my eye
 in the still watch of the night,
 then tears rolled down.
2. Then came the night,
 enveloping us as if
 it had no day.
3. All night I watched the Gemini
 until the first of them
 began to set,
4. And sent my glance on the trail of a tribe
 that was drawn far off from land to land,
 then disappeared.
5. And weeping till the stars blazed forth
 as if no vast expanses held them
 back from me
6. For him who had he, living, heard the herald
 of my death, would have led forth horsemen
 veiled in dust.

7. I called you, Kulayb,
 and you did not reply.
 But how can the wasteland reply?
8. Answer me, O Kulayb! May no blame touch you!
 To souls that we begrudged the grave
 we owe a visit.
9 Answer me, O Kulayb! May no blame touch you!
 Their knight's death has devastated
 Nizār's sons.
10. May you be watered by abundant rain,
 you who were rain abundant and prosperity
 to every outstretched hand.[20]

19. Shaykhū, *Shuʿarāʾ al-Naṣrāniyyah* 1:163.
20. Literally, "when prosperity was sought."

11. My eyes refused to leave off weeping after you,
swollen, red, as if a thorny *qitād* thicket grew
where lashes grow.
12. To men you were forbearing,
forgiving them;
you wielded power.
13. You let no foul tongue defile them out of fear
for a man who grants refuge but from whose wrath
there is no refuge.
14. When merchants counted up their gains
I counted being close to you
my gain.

15. Do not be distant!
for every man will meet a fate
round which his axis turns.
16. A man lives with his father's sons
and at any time may go
where they have gone.
17. A life-span, once entrusted to a man,
is like a loan to be recalled
at any time.

18. When the herald cried, "Kulayb is slain!"
it was as if between my ribs
sparks flew.
19. Then my head reeled, my eye dimmed from him,
like a drinker whose head the wine
has caused to reel.
20. I asked the tribe, "Where have you buried him?"
"At the foot of the tribal mount," they said,
"is his abode."
21. I sped to him from my land, hastening;
sleep fled
and I refused all rest.
22. My she-camel shied from the shade of a grave
in which nobility and pride
lay buried,
23. Before the dwelling of a man, formidable,
neither tainted by disgrace
nor tainting others.

24. Will you go forth at morn with me, Kulayb,
when the coward of the tribe
is saved by flight?
25. Will you go forth at morn with me, Kulayb,
when the tribesmen's throats are whetted
by the blade?
26. I will say to Taghlib, for glory is theirs,
"Incite a war, for victory today
is ours!"
27. One by one my brothers came, passed on
to what the tribesmen came to, one by one,
with neither helmet, nor chain mail, nor shield.

28. Hold me, by my life, to the firm oath
that I will abandon all
that the abodes enclose:
29. That I will shun women fair and modest,
forsake the drinking cup, forswear
the wearing of unborrowed robe,
30. That I will not cast off my chain mail
or ungird my sword
until the day casts off the night,
31. Until the Banū Bakr's lofty summit
is demolished and no trace of them
remains.[21]

Memory Inflamed is striking for its revealing contrast of elements of elegy and blood vengeance. It should be clear by now that in this type of *thaʾr* rithāʾ these two elements perform a structural and ritual function. What was in the past construed as an elegiac genre that should (and sometimes appears to) stand on its own and what was construed as a theme—blood vengeance—that had no necessary connection to, or place in, elegy are, quite the contrary, the two necessary and contrasting parts of a ritually conceived poetic structure. The elegiac element expresses a state of loss and despair, a passive response to the death of a kinsman which in the pre-Islamic tribal context is perceived as effeminate or puerile. It is an expression of separation and the grief that it evokes and, for the man at least, a sign of immaturity. In this respect

21. Shaykhū, *Shuʿarāʾ al-Naṣrāniyyah* 1:163–64; see also al-Sandūbī, *Akhbār al-Marāqisah*, 47–50 (30 lines).

the elegiac elements of nasīb and rithāʾ are identical. However powerfully and poignantly developed, the elegiac element in pre-Islamic men's poetry does not appear to stand on its own. Its countermovement would seem always to be either explicitly stated or understood.[22] This countermovement—the active and masculine response to the death of the fallen kinsman, the transition from loss to triumph, from death to new life—then provides what is for the pre-Islamic men's rithāʾ a necessary aesthetic and ritual balance. The subject of blood vengeance is not, therefore, merely a theme among other themes that may or may not occur in pre-Islamic elegy; instead, lamentation and blood vengeance, loss and sacrifice, are the necessary contrasting components that determine the literary form. For women the lament, the libation of tears, appears to be the required redemption for the fallen warrior's sacrifice. If, however, the marthī lies unavenged, taḥrīd is likewise incumbent upon her.

The argument for this structural integrity—both ritual and literary—is further supported by the fact established in Chapter 5 that almost all the marāthī of the Jāhiliyyah are for warriors and chiefs, usually those fallen in battle. In other words, we are not dealing with a personal poetry that registers or expresses the full range of human experience: neither Romanticism nor Realism applies here. Rather we are dealing with a public and ritual mode of expression which has selected from the range of human emotions those elements that most powerfully—whether directly or metaphorically—convey or conserve the intended message. That early Arabic elegy is overwhelmingly for the fallen warrior suggests that the survival of the kin group or tribe as a polity depends above all else on avenging the slain. The message is that a tribe without military might soon ceases to be a polity: its men are killed with impunity, its women and children are carried off into captivity, or else they come to live as abject clients or protégées dependent upon the generosity of a powerful tribe—the sorts of wretches described in the last section of the *The Muʿallaqah of Labīd.*

In the poem at hand, the elegiac section is more expansive than the brief or ambiguous descriptions of night in some of Muhalhil's other marāthī. The lapidary has here yielded to the lyrical in the five-verse opening so eminently like nasīb. Whereas in *Once We Used to Guard the Freeborn Maidens* the poet juxtaposes to and thereby identifies women's

22. Correspondingly, *ghazal* (love lyric) is not found as a free-standing genre in Jāhilī poetry either.

mourning with the initial (immature) phase of the men's, in the poem at hand the identification of the immature, effeminate mourning of the youth with that of the women is achieved directly through the employment of imagery and diction that are virtually identical to those of women's marāthī.

Muhalhil's marthiyah opens with the tears evoked by memory, then the enshrouding of an endless night during which the wakeful poet watches the stars (verses 1–3). In verses 4 and 5 the poet seems to imagine that the stars are bedouin tribes. The first is the image of the *ẓaʿn*, the departure of the tribe that is carried off from one land to another and ultimately disappears from view. The second is that of the poet's tears whose blurring effect makes the stars blaze so brightly that it seems as though the poet could reach out and touch them with his hand. On one level these two images convey the idea of forgetfulness and memory, that those who are forgotten disappear forever, whereas those who are remembered, who are watered by the shedding of tears, are "recalled," brought close once more. The suggestion is that the common elegiac expression *lā tabʿad* (Do not go far!) means, above all, do not be forgotten. The images function, further, as an expression of blood vengeance, or the parallel significance of the shedding of tears and blood. For tears "bring back" the dead just as blood vengeance does. In this case, the two verses take on a political dimension: the first is the image of the breakup or dissolution of the polity, the departure and scattering of tribes; the second, of the polity renewed, brought close and together once more.

The effect of this virtual nasīb is to present a deep but unspecified sense of loss. At the outset it is ambiguous not only as to speaker—male or female?—but also as to the object of loss—is it a departed mistress or a fallen kinsman? Once again, the effect of this initial ambiguity is to identify the two emotions of loss.

In verse 6 the elegiac and melancholic nasīb stance of the first five verses—the wakeful poet watching the stars, the *ẓaʿn*, departure of the tribe—is suddenly thrown into perspective and into focus by introducing the marthī and describing him in quite different terms from the poet: had the poet himself been slain and were his slain brother still alive, his brother would not be suffering the genteel and effeminate torments of lyrical insomnia but would have rushed forth with his horsemen to avenge him. The poet condemns himself for his elegiac lingering, which he has thus exposed as, in effect, adolescent procrastination. The verse thus serves to alert us to the differing psychosocial positions of the two brothers: the dead brother is a mature man, a warrior; the survivor still a youth, who thus expresses the bivalent fraternal bond that combines admiration with resentment. Our young hero, however, is not yet ready to take up his quest. The lyric-elegiac tone persists.

We find in verse 7 a telling variant of the traditional nasīb motif of the poet questioning the ruined abode of his departed mistress's tribe. Here it is the deceased rather than the departed who is addressed, and the wasteland (*al-balad al-qifār*) is explicitly the tomb. The following verses continue to evoke the connection between nasīb and rithā᾽ through the fusion of motifs.[23] By an almost metaphorical substitution the visit to the grave reveals its identity to stopping at the abandoned campsite.

In verse 10 the deceased (or his tomb) again holds the place of the ruined abode in the *istisqā᾽* (call for rain), which presents yet another expression of the obligation of the living to the dead. In this case, in what could almost be termed a pun, the word *ghayth*, like the word *jūd*, refers both to the abundant generosity of the marthī and to the abundant rain that should justly fall upon his grave. Once again, there is a ritual or metaphorical equivalence among the rain that revives the thirsty earth, bringing forth carpets of plants and flowers; the tears that revive the memory of the departed or deceased; and the blood of vengeance, which likewise has a revivifying effect. A further extension of this concept is the expression *ṭalla damahu* (to fail to avenge a man's blood), that is, to give a scanty drizzle (*ṭall*) where a copious downpour is due.[24]

The poet's immediate response to the *istisqā᾽* is a downpour not of blood but of tears (verse 11) that lead, for reasons that are clear to us now, into a eulogistic reminiscence. The appearance of the conventional *lā tabʿad* (Do not go far!) in this connection (15) suggests that the shedding of tears brings back the deceased/departed, just as rainfall revives desert wastes and, as I remarked concerning *Odyssey*, book 11, the blood of sacrifice revives, reincarnates the pale shades of the underworld. Perhaps, too, we should begin to understand that this reincarnation or revivification of shades by blood sacrifice is largely, like the shedding of tears, a metaphor for the commemoration of the dead among the living. When we remember or commemorate the dead,

23. On this issue, see S. Stetkevych, *Abū Tammām*, chap. 14.
24. Lane, *ṭ-l-l*.

we bring them, as it were, back to life or into our lives; when we forget them, they depart, cease to exist. "Do not depart!" perhaps means, above all, "Let us not forget you!"

This expression leads to two verses of *ḥikam* (16–17), of aphorisms concerning the inevitability of death. They appear to help the poet objectify his situation in a process that, in terms of the psychosocial ritual pattern, should suggest that he is outgrowing the egoism of adolescence. Nevertheless, when in verse 18 Kulayb's death is announced, the *ḥikam*, with a certain psychological veracity, prove to be of little immediate comfort. The poet, reeling and blinded as though drunk, recounts his visit to his brother's tomb (19–20). It is worth remarking that in verse 20 the tomb or grave is referred to simply as *dār* (house, dwelling), once more blurring the distinction between, or identifying, the ruined abode of the nasīb with the tomb of the rithāʾ.

The motif of sleeplessness returns once more in verse 21, but it is now the active wakefulness of the hastening traveler, not the motionless insomnia of the stargazer in the endless night. In the following verse (22) the horror of death is expressed by the shying of the poet's she-camel at the grave of Kulayb—presumably at the stench of death. Then in verse 23 there occurs a curious substitution of *qabr* (grave, tomb) by *awṭān* (dwellings, homelands), those native pasturelands for which the she-camel of the Arabic poetic tradition perpetually and disconsolately yearns. The effect of this diction is a strange inversion of emotion, perhaps an expression of the poet's still-ambivalent reaction to his brother's death or, more precisely, his inability to accept it.

Verse 24 picks up on the *awṭān* (dwellings) of verse 23 rather than the *qabr* (grave) of verse 21, and the poet addresses Kulayb, calling him to battle. It appears at first that he considers Kulayb still among the living: "Will you go forth at morn with me, Kulayb?" But at verse 27 the poet perceives an inevitable procession toward death and seems to realize that he is next in line. It is the poet's realization of his own mortality that accounts for the change in his behavior, that marks the transition from boyhood to manhood. The conceit is suddenly inverted from the dead Kulayb going to battle with the living to that of the living joining the ranks of the dead. It is at this point, after the elegiac tone of the first twenty-seven verses, that the poet, finally comprehending his own mortality, is able to put his own life on the line. And it is precisely the willingness to sacrifice one's own life for another that constitutes mature manhood.

In the final four verses the ramblingly lyric and aphoristic elegiac tone that has characterized the poem up till now gives way abruptly to the terse concision of the oath. The votive elements are here stated with model precision: the liminal state of "excommunication" is phrased as *bi tarkī kulla mā ḥawat al-diyārū* (to abandon all that the abodes enclose) (verse 28). The poet then elucidates (29): he will abstain from women/ wives, wine, and the trailing the robe that is the sign of peace and leisure. In this last image the change of ritual status is expressed through a change of garb: the full and flowing *jubbah* is abandoned for armor and sword that will not be removed until his vengeance is complete (30). By a further analogy between the avenger's casting off the garb of vengeance and the day's casting off the night, the poet once more indicates to us that the elegiac night of the opening section of the poem is ultimately too an expression of the state of pollution, of unavenged blood, and the return of day is thus an expression of purification through sacrifice—in this case, as verse 31 states, the annihilation of the Banū Bakr.

The final hemistich *fa lā yabqā lahā abadan athārū* (and no trace of them remains) is at first striking for its terse simplicity. But it has an aftershock, for in both diction and image it inevitably evokes the ruined abodes (*aṭlāl*) and the erased traces of the nasīb and its air of elegiac melancholy. We are reminded of verse 4, *fī ithri qawmin . . . ghārū* (on the trail of a tribe . . . that disappeared). The stark simplicity and subtle ambiguity of the final few words thus brings the poem full circle—or almost. For the beginning point of the classical Arabic nasīb is the trace of a ruin, however dim, however worn by time and the elements. Indeed, for the poet, the dimmer the trace, the richer the poem. It is the trace that stirs the memory, from which germinates the poem that preserves the memory of the tribe forever. To be without a trace is to be deprived of any form of perpetuity, whether biological or poetic, to be utterly lost.

At this point we should take note of the element of *jahl* that has made its way so powerfully and poetically into the poem. For however striking and evocative the closing verse, what it expresses is a lust for vengeance far beyond the accepted tribal norm of slaying a *qirn,* or equal counterpart, of one's slain kinsman. We should remember that it was the abomination of the shedding of kindred blood which led al-Shanfarā to vow his vengeance of a hundred, and as we will see in Chapter 7, the abomination of the Banū Asad slaying their own king which likewise produced Imruʾ al-Qays's unquenchable thirst for the blood of vengeance. It is my contention that the Islamic age perceived this particular form of *jahl,* or impetuousness, which led to the dissolution of the polity and the disbanding and scattering of the tribe, as the tragic flaw of its pagan age.

The first two poems discussed culminate with the poet's vow to avenge his slain brother. The next is rather a boast or celebration of vengeance achieved. The battle days and warriors alluded to in this poem are well-established in the body of lore surrounding the War of al-Basūs. One battle of concern to us is the Day of al-Dhanāʾib, which resulted in a great victory for the Banū Taghlib with heavy losses for the Banū Bakr. Another Taghlibite victory was the Day of Wāridāt, where the two Shaʿthams fell, and also Jassās's brother Hammām ibn Murrah. It is said that when Muhalhil saw his former boon companion slain he remarked, "No death after that of Kulayb has been as grievous a loss to me as yours." Yet again, on the Day of ʿUnayzah the Banū Taghlib took the day.[25]

Perhaps the most telling instance of impetuous excess in the classical accounts of the War of al-Basūs, are the events surrounding Muhalhil's slaying of al-Bujayr ibn al-Ḥārith on the Day of Wāridāt. Muhalhil had exceeded all bounds in killing and did not care what tribe of the Banū Bakr he fought. Now most of the tribes of Bakr had refused to aid the Banū Shaybān because of their killing Kulayb, and among those who refused to get involved in the war was al-Ḥārith ibn ʿUbād. When word reach him that his son Bujayr had been slain, he exclaimed, "What a noble slain man is he who made peace between the two sons of Wāʾil!" for he thought that Muhalhil had considered Bujayr Kulayb's equal and thus achieved his vengeance. But when he was told that Muhalhil had exclaimed as he slew Bujayr, "Die in retaliation for Kulayb's sandle thong!" he grew angry, called for his battle steed al-Naʿāmah and led the Banū Bakr to victory on the Day of al-Qiḍah.[26]

Tradition places the following poem by Muhalhil after the Taghlibite victories of al-Dhanāʾib, Wāridāt, and their victory, or draw, at ʿUnayzah:

25. Al-Nuwayrī, *Nihāyat al-Arab* 15:400–402. Elsewhere the Day of ʿUnayzah is said to have ended in a draw. See al-Iṣbahānī, *Kitāb al-Aghānī* 5:1685; Shaykhū, *Shuʿarāʾ al-Naṣrāniyyah* 1:165.

26. Al-Nuwayrī, *Nihāyat al-Arab* 15:402–3.

Aṣmaʿiyyah no. 53. O Night of Ours at Dhū Ḥusum [44]

1. O night of ours at Dhū Ḥusum,
give way to day
When you have ended,
and do not return.
2. For if my night was long
at al-Dhanāʾib,
Sometimes a short night
may make one weep.
3. Would that Kulayb were dug up
from his grave
So that some flirtatious youth might tell him
at al-Dhanāʾib
4. Of the day two Shaʿthams [were cut short],
it would cool his weeping eye—
But how can one meet a man
in the tomb interred?
5. At the water paths
of Wāridāt
I left Bujayr in blood
like compound perfume.
6. And Hammām ibn Murrah
we left
With two ancient vultures
above him.
7. We gave al-Wukhūm a morning draught
on an evil day,
As they warded off the spearheads
with their throats.
8. As if, in the early morning,
we and our father's sons
In ʿUnayzah's hollow were
two millstones grinding.
9. Were it not for the wind,
the people of Ḥajr would have heard
The clanging of casques
struck by steel.[27]

27. Al-Aṣmaʿī, *Al-Aṣmaʿiyyāt*, 154–55. Other recensions are much longer, cf. Shaykhū, *Shuʿarāʾ al-Naṣrāniyyah* 1:168–70 (36 lines); and al-Sandūbī, *Akhbār al-Marāqisah*, 50–53 (30 lines).

This short piece by Muhalhil opens, like the preceding poem, with an image familiar from the classical nasīb: the poet-lover waiting through the seemingly endless night. Here, too, the image is constructed as a rithāʾ: the death of the brother takes the place of the departure of the mistress and evokes the same sense of loss and separation; the slain brother's grave stands in the place of the *aṭlāl*, the ruined encampments of the poet's beloved, and is haunted, as they are, by melancholia over the irrevocable past. The poet in verse 2 alludes to the irony of the lover's night, that the length of the night of separation from his beloved makes him weep, but so too does the shortness of the night of union. Muhalhil's rhetorical query in verse 4 is none other than that of Labīd in his *Muʿallaqah*: how can we question deaf-mute rocks?

Let us note too that this poem alludes to a sibling rivalry with oedipal overtones when, in verse 3, the poet refers to himself as *zīr*, a flirt, "one who mixes with women to talk to them, without evil intent."[28] For Muhalhil's brother Kulayb had once censured him, saying, "You are a visitor of women [*zīr al-nisāʾ*]."[29] It is an expression of the ambivalent oedipal attachment that love and resentment mingle in the younger brother's desire to prove himself, his manhood, to his slain elder brother by avenging his death. Further, if we recall that such innocent womanizing is an adolescent attribute, the rite of passage pattern becomes apparent, the transition from boyhood with its frivolous sport and innocent coquetry to manhood and tribal chieftainship marked by blood vengeance, blood sacrifice, on the field of battle. Thus the taking of blood vengeance serves to transfer oedipal violence outside the kin (although, in the case of Bakr and Taghlib, not far enough), establishing in its place a ritual exchange of violence.

The remainder of the poem exhibits the symmetrical opposition, expressed by rhetorical means as well as through the imagery, between the devitalization of the enemy and the revitalization of the kin. The ear is alerted to the morphological parallelism and the quadriliteral duals *al-shaʿthamān* (verse 4) and *al-qashʿamān* or *-ayn* (6). The two share three of their four radicals, thus forming a *jinās nāqiṣ* (partial paronomasia). Furthermore, the etymology of *shaʿtham* reveals an underlying *ṭibāq* (antithesis) between the two, the meaning of which is the crux of the poem of vengeance: the enemy slain bear the name Shaʿtham,[30] the root

28. Al-Aṣmaʿī, *Al-Aṣmaʿiyyāt*, 154.

29. Ibid.; al-Mubarrad, *Al-Kāmil* 1:360.

30. The commentators take al-Shaʿthamayn either as a place name, denoting where the battle was fought, or as the name of two brothers whom Muhalhil slew on the Day of

of which, *sh-ʿ-th*, means unkempt, unannointed, defiled; it is a typical epithet of the liminal passenger (one in a state of *iḥrām* and thus under oath not to comb or wash his hair) and includes among its meanings "to cut (short)," whereas the vultures, an expression of the now-avenged (and hence reaggregated) souls of dead kin, bear the epithet, *qashʿam* (long-lived, advanced in years).

The semiotics of proper names is apparent too in the place where vengeance is achieved: Wāridāt (verse 5) means paths to water, whereas the place where Kulayb fell or lies buried, al-Dhanāʾib (2–3), means ends, extremities, the dried-up ends of a streambed, where fertility first fails. These place-names are otherwise attested in the commentaries and the accounts of the battle days,[31] but surely this all-too-telling etymological appropriateness is no mere accident. If we return to Durayd's poem *Maʿshar Has Been Deserted of Its People,* we see that Muhalhil's is not unique in this respect. For Durayd's brother ʿAbd Allāh fell on the day of al-Liwā, "the winding sand dune," a traditional locus for liminal events (the trysting place of illicit lovers, of Taʾabbaṭa Sharran and the ghūl, and Imruʾ al-Qays and his inamorata) with its semiotic association with barrenness and instability; he avenged his brother on the day of al-Ghadīr—"a pool left by rain, a pond."[32] This, then, is yet another expression of the metaphor found very commonly in the poetry of blood vengeance, that is, of thirst for vengeance and vengeance quenching thirst.

Nor is the juxtaposition in verse 5 of Wāridāt to blood like perfume without significance, for all three liquids—water, enemy blood, and perfume—perform the same function: purification, *ghasl al-dam bi al-dam*, cleansing the unavenged, polluted blood of the kin with the purifying blood of the slain enemy. The source of this metaphor is connected with several other aspects of blood pollution and purification in early Arab (including Islamic) rituals. I noted that the blood pollution of menstruation is cleansed with water and perfume and, further, that unavenged blood is commonly described in terms of menstrual blood. Thus, it is to be expected on the basis of both ritual and of metaphor that the bloodshed that cleanses this pollution should be compared to

---

Wāridāt, Shaʿtham and Shaʿīth, the two sons of ʿĀmir ibn Dhahl ibn Thaʿlabah. See al-Aṣmaʿī, *Al-Aṣmaʿiyyāt,* 155.

31. See notes in Ibn ʿAbd Rabbih, *Al-ʿIqd al-Farīd* 5:318–20.

32. It is curious that in al-Iṣbahānī's remarks concerning Durayd ibn al-Ṣimmah's *Bāʾiyyah* (*Aṣmaʿiyyah no. 29*), his brother ʿAbd Allāh is said to have died on the Day of al-Dhanāʾib. See al-Iṣbahānī, *Kitāb al-Aghānī* 10:3477.

water and perfume. The blood of the enemy slain in vengeance is one of a group of liquids that are perceived as purifying, life giving, and life sustaining: water, blood, perfume, milk, and wine. It is therefore not surprising that these are precisely the liquids that are poured as libations on the graves of the dead not only among the Arabs but among other Mediterranean peoples as well,[33] or that it is precisely these liquids that stand metaphorically for one another in the poetry of blood-vengeance.

The converse image is that of verse 7, in which the enemy combatants are given a draught of death. As death is their only drink, so too, their only shields are their throats, *naḥr* (throat) being, notably, the place where the sacrificial beast is cut (cf. *manḥar*, place of slaughter, sacrifice). The name of the enemy clan, al-Wukhūm, too, is remarkable, for it is a verbal noun meaning "to be tainted, unwholesome." A *ṭibāq* is thus established that perfectly expresses the bivalency of blood vengeance: for the avengers it is purifying, for the enemy, polluting. Since *ṣabbaḥa* (to give a morning draught) can take two accusatives (indirect object and direct object), the first hemistich has a second reading or pun: "We gave an unwholesome, tainted drink in the morning."

The taking of vengeance in the early morning hours is the sacrifice that marks the end of the liminal night of mourning and separation, of unavenged blood, the transition of ritual states from polluted to pure, from thirsting to quenching, from *ḥarām* to *ḥalāl*, from darkness to light. The use of the same verb (*ṣabbaḥa*) for the (commensal) morning draught of wine and the morning attack (for blood vengeance) is thus an expression of their ultimate ritual or metaphorical equivalence, not merely their temporal concurrence. This equivalence explains, too, the common metaphorical or rhetorical interplay between these two indirect expressions of blood sacrifice. The morning drinking scene and the morning attack are common qaṣīdah features, one or both of which often occur at the point at which the poem makes the transition from the raḥīl/liminal section to the fakhr/aggregation section. It is also of note that when another form of sacrifice and commensal meal—the hunt—marks this transition, it, too, takes place in the early morning hours. Perhaps the most famous and most explicit case in point is *The Muʿallaqah of Imruʾ al-Qays*, in which the description of the seemingly

33. See, for example, *Ḥamāsiyyāt nos. 289, 306, 371* in al-Marzūqī, *Ḥamāsah*; see also *Odyssey*, book 11.

endless night is followed by the hunt scene that opens: "I would ride forth early, the birds still in their nests" (verse 53).[34]

Like the rest of the poem, verse 8 is constructed around a well-known metaphor of early Arabic poetry, that of the thick of the battle as a hand mill.[35] It is an extension of that imagery that describes the taking of blood vengeance as revitalizing and nourishing the kin. Thus, the spilling of blood to avenge slain kinsmen is likened to the milling of grain to feed the clan. In this equation of blood sacrifice with the milling of grain the word *maᶜrakah* (battle) itself is most revealing, for its root meanings are to rub, scrape, knead, but also to menstruate. Hence *maᶜrakah* refers to the heat of the battle as a source of alimentation and blood pollution at once. Muhalhil has added something further to this image: his clan (the Banū Rabīᶜah) and their enemy cousins (the Banū Murrah) (here termed Banū Abīnā [sons of our father], but taken by the commentators to be cousins) are likened to the upper and lower stones of the hand mill. Some early critics have taken this to be the first case of *inṣāf* (the equitable treatment of the enemy),[36] a rhetorical device that is particularly appropriate in the poetry of blood vengeance, since only the blood of an equal of the deceased can avenge his blood.[37] In addition, the image of the two millstones grinding against each other constitutes a perfect expression of the dialectic of blood-vengeance, the revitalization of the kin and the devitalization of the enemy, through the implicit equation of slaying the enemy with nourishing the kin. In the context of the War of al-Basūs the ambiguity of the image takes on an even deeper significance, for kin and enemy here are cousins, and mutual annihilation has taken the place of mutual alimentation.

The poem closes with a verse that is at once martial and sexual; that is, the martial imagery of the casques (*bayḍ*) and swords (*dhukūr*) has a second reading as ova and phalli.[38] Once again in this poem the ambiguity is itself ambiguous, for at one level the double reading expresses the standard blood-vengeance identification of the devitalization of the

34. Al-Zawzanī, *Sharḥ al-Muᶜallaqāt al-Sabᶜ*, 112.

35. See, for example, *Mufaḍḍaliyyah no. 60*, verse 3, Lyall, *The Mufaḍḍalīyāt* 1:510.

36. Al-Aṣmaᶜī, *Al-Aṣmaᶜiyyāt*, 155.

37. See Lammens, "Le caractère religieux du *ṯār*," 115–18.

38. A striking example of the (at least metaphorical) perception of bloodshed in terms of fertility is found by Qabīṣah ibn Jābir in *Ḥamāsiyyah no. 243*, verse 3, in which a war with little killing is likened to a virgin whose breast is cut off (producing neither offspring nor milk), whereas a bloody war is likened to a pregnant woman. See al-Marzūqī, *Ḥamāsah* 2:707–8.

enemy with the revitalization of the kin, but it further suggests the confusion of this principle in a war between blood relatives.

When the Herald Cried [45]

1. When the herald cried, "Kulayb is dead!"
the sun of daylight darkened
and would shine no more.
2. They slew Kulayb and then said, "Graze your steeds!"
They belie themselves, they have forbade
the steeds to graze.
3. No, by the idols of our ancient custom,
worshiped and well graven,
[they will not graze]
4. Until I have annihilated
tribe after tribe after tribe
and two tribes all at once;
5. Until Bakr's people, all of them,
have tasted death; until we have pulled down
their high-raised roof;
6. Until we see their limbs torn from them
and the lame hyenas
fall upon their skulls;
7. Until we see the birds of prey
peck out their eyes,
pull at their limbs and ribs,
8. And the *mashrafī* blade avert not from them
a blow that pierces
hauberk and casque,
9. And the glowering steeds on battle day
plunge into the battle dust
loath to retreat.[39]

By contrast to the previous poem, which announces vengeance achieved, *When the Herald Cried,* like the first two poems, climaxes with a vow to vengeance. The crux of blood-vengeance poetry, at least in psychological terms, is the willingness to risk or sacrifice one's own life in assuming responsibility for the fallen kinsmen as much as it is the

39. Shaykhū, *Shuʿarāʾ al-Naṣrāniyyah* 1:172. See also al-Sandūbī, *Akhbār al-Marāqisah*, 56–57.

shedding of enemy blood. The blood of vengeance can then be understood as a votive offering. This poem has a lapidary terseness that differs distinctly from the expansive lyricism of the first sections of *Once We Used to Guard the Freeborn Maidens* and *Memory Inflamed* and indeed from the extended versions of *O Night of Ours at Dhū Ḥusum*. It shares with them the call for excessive vengeance, for the total annihilation of the Banū Bakr.

The poem opens with the *naʿy* (death announcement) and, following it, the darkening of the sun. The opening verse thus serves as a *sharḥ*, explanation or commentary, on the opening verse of *O Night of Ours at Dhū Ḥusum,* another night of bereavement and blood unavenged. Once again it is apparent that the transition from night to day and vice versa in early Arabic poetry indicates a change in ritual status. Further, we begin to grasp the exegetical function of a body of oral-formulaic and ritual verse: that in the absence of reliably preservable akhbār and *shurūḥ* (commentaries), oral-mnemonic poetry depends on a sort of mutual exegesis by which variations in a motif from poem to poem guarantee that the meaning of the image or metaphorical expression will be preserved. It was thus through maintaining a corpus or group of poems that shared the same images, metaphors, and structures, but expressed them with subtle but crucial variations, that the meaning, the message, was preserved. If a particular poem, a particular statement of the message, was ambiguous or recondite, the other poems in the corpus would clarify or reinforce it. This constant interreferentiality (what in other contexts might be termed intertextuality) between poems, through which each poem in the corpus alludes to all the other poems, is, I believe, a distinctive feature of oral poetry and of the classical Arabic poetic tradition in both its oral phase and later literary stages that preserved, now for "literary" rather than "mnemonic" reasons, many "oral" characteristics. This requirement of interreferentiality explains, too, the preeminently conservative, as well as preservative, nature of the classical Arabic poetic tradition. If a qaṣīdah did not at every point refer or allude to the established corpus, its forms and formulas, then it had no place in that corpus.

The remaining seven verses of the poem take the form of a vow, this time cast in terms of the herds or steeds of the tribe. We must first understand that "grazing" is construed as the equine equivalent of the human *ḥalāl*, profane, state. After Kulayb's death the steeds are not free to graze any more than the poet/avenger is free to trail his robes leisurely about the tribal enclosure. The poet thus swears by the idols of his tribe that the steeds or herds will not graze until the Banū Bakr have been annihilated.

The enemy's "high-raised roof" of verse 5 should be understood metaphorically as their glory and honor, as we saw in *The Muʿallaqah of Labīd* and as will appear from similar expressions in other poems. It should be remarked that another fundamental characteristic of this type of poetry is reiteration through variation within the poem. That is to say, within a single poem the overall message is reinforced by restatement through a series of images and metaphors. This repetition has the effect, on the one hand, of intensifying the message and, on the other, of ensuring that if the meaning of one image or metaphor is obscure or misunderstood, the others will clarify it and preserve the message. Thus, in addition to the exegetical function of interreferentiality between poems, we find at work an intrareferentiality within the poem. So, for example, in the poem at hand, verses 4–7 carry what is ultimately the same meaning—the annihilation of the enemy. In practical oral-mnemonic terms, this restatement guarantees that the loss of a verse or two does not result in the loss of the message of the poem. In terms of the preservations of "texts" this phenomenon further explains much of the variation in number and order of verses in various recensions that have come down to us. For the tendency is for one statement or metaphor of a meaning to generate or attract other equivalent metaphorical statements or restatements—what has otherwise been termed the "redundancy" or "copiousness" of oral literature.[40] In strictly practical terms, this phenomenon results in various versions of a poem exhibiting fewer or more of these reiterative metaphors. In literary terms, this generation of equivalent images can create a great intensity of meaning and, as in the present poem, build a tremendous momentum.

Here that momentum already starts building within verse 4, where the pace of slaughter doubles from "tribe by tribe" to "two tribes at once" (*qabīlatan wa qabīlatan wa qabīlatan wa qabīlatayni jamīʿā*). Verse 5 reiterates in somewhat figurative language the blunt statement of verse 4, "tasted death," "pulled down their high-raised roof." The poet then depicts the desecration and humiliation of the enemy corpses in terms that are by now familiar to us—scavenger beasts and birds dismembering and devouring them.

It is worth remarking that those animals that defile the corpses are

40. Ong, *Orality and Literacy*, 39–40.

often referred to epithetically by their peculiar gaits.[41] Here, for example, the term for hyenas is *al-khāmiᶜāt*, that is, the lame or limping ones. Among the epithets of the female hyena are *al-khāmiᶜah* (the limping one) and *al-ᶜarjāʾ* (the lame one).[42] The wolf is said to be *aqzal* (lame).[43] For the crow or raven, and also the vulture, a common epithet is *ḥājil* "hopping," from the root *ḥ-j-l*—to walk with the legs shackled, for a hocked camel to walk on three legs, for a crow or raven to hop as though shackled,[44] as we have seen in *ḥawājilu al-ghirbāni* (hopping crows) and *ḥajalāna al-nusūri* (like the hopping of vultures).

It seems more than coincidental that those animals to which epithets of impaired or irregular gaits are attributed are the scavengers in a particular poetic motif—the desecration of the dead. It is hard to escape the suggestion that the irregular or impaired gait may be a ritual or poetic requirement rather than merely naturalistic description. In other words, in terms of the argument at hand, the liminal or sacrificial stage is often distinguished by a peculiar gait. Even today, religious, military, and courtly ceremonials still require special gaits, whether the Prussian goose step or the bridal lockstep, which are distinguished from the everyday saunter of the ordinary citizen. The permanently liminal entity, as we saw in the case of the ṣaᶜālīk, is distinguished from the temporary passenger by having a gait that is naturally or permanently impaired.

At this point I can suggest a further connection between the animal sacrifice/commensal ritual and the human sacrifice/blood vengeance—that the hopping or limping or "frolicking like virgins" of the scavengers in these poems is intended to suggest the human hopping associated with rites of revitalization of the polity, what Gaster terms "rites of jubilation" or what Robertson Smith calls "the sacrificial dance."[45] Conversely, it could be argued that the ritual hopping of humans had its origin in the rites of ancestor worship and revitalization in the imitation of precisely those animals that gained longevity through or even procreated by consuming the life-force, primarily blood, of others.

In *When the Herald Cried,* we find once again in verse 6, the usurping of the life-forces of the fallen in terms whose significance exceeds the

41. On the significance of the extensive use of epithetic nomenclature in classical Arabic poetry, see J. Stetkevych, "Name and Epithet," passim.

42. Al-Nuwayrī, *Nihāyat al-Arab* 9:274–76; al-Jāḥiẓ, *Al-Ḥayawān* 5:212–13.

43. Al-Jāḥiẓ, *Al-Ḥayawān* 5:213.

44. Lane, *ḥ-j-l.*

45. See Gaster, *Thespis,* 43–44; Robertson Smith, *Religion of the Semites,* 432.

depiction of nature. The pecking out of eyes is, as it were, going to the heart of the matter, for the eye, as I established in Chapter 5, is perceived as the source of soul or self, the very essence of the individual. The light of the eye is the essential sign of life; the tears, like blood, a liquid expression of the soul. For the scavenger, too, the eye is the source of life, of life-giving liquid. It is in fact *ʿayn al-māʾ*, the source or spring of water. For indeed, zoologists tell us of the vulture, and of the raptor as well, that its only source of water is from the carrion (or, in the raptor's case, the prey) that it eats. The vulture thus incarnates, if you will, the closed system of blood-to-blood, life-to-life, which is the paradigm of the concept of blood sacrifice. It is thus fitting that the early Arabs, among others, should have chosen the vulture or eagle to express the concept of the perpetuation of life through the perpetual passing on of blood, the liquid soul.

In the two-verse closure the battle to come is described through the warrior's metonymy of sword and steed. The final verse in which the steeds plunge headlong into battle, concludes the poem in terms of the equine conceit that shaped the opening and the oath. It thus becomes apparent that the image of the glowering, grim-faced (*ʿawābis*) battle steeds is constructed so as to reinforce the symmetrical inversion between the steed at pasture and at war, what is ultimately a metonymy for the profane and consecrated (oath-bound) states of the poet-warrior himself.

The final poem in my discussion of Muhalhil is of special interest because of the peculiar interplay it exhibits between elements or images that are elegiac, mournful, and melancholy, and therefore traditionally associated with the rithāʾ or the nasīb, and those that are bellicose and bloodthirsty and thus typical of the poem of blood vengeance. The effect of this strange interplay is exegetical, for it reveals the further dimensions of meaning that create semantic bonds between apparently discrete poetic images.

Long Was My Night at Anʿamayn [46]

1. Long was my night at Anʿamayn,
    as I gazed sleepless at the stars,
        unending.
2. How can I know my fate
    when Banū Wāʾil's slain man still cries out
        for another to be slain?

3. I chide my eye for weeping over ruined abodes,
for in my breast Kulayb has left
an unclosed wound.
4. In my breast is a need unsatisfied
as long as a voice calls out
among the branches, cooing.
5. How can I forget you, O Kulayb, when I
have not yet quelled the grief that overwhelms me,
or quenched revenge's thirst?
6. Today, O heart, fulfill your vow
against the Banū Ḥiṣn; when they go forth at morn,
take your revenge!
7. How can a man weep at ruined abodes
who is pledged to combat mankind
generation after generation!
8. They grabbed their bow grips,
we flashed lightning bolts:
like stallions menacing stallions.
9. Steadfast we stood beneath the flashing blades
until the swords had pounded on them
hard and long.
10. Then they could attack no more, but we
kept on attacking; he who can take the field
is war's true kin![46]

The opening verse contains the movingly elegiac motif, associated in Arabic poetry with both the abandoned lover (nasīb) and the bereft kin (rithāʾ) of the sleepless poet gazing at the nightly stars or tending them as a pastor tends his flocks.[47] We have seen this motif already in *Memory Inflamed*. Here, however, the poet does not linger in melancholia but presents in the next verse the slain kinsman, presumably Kulayb, still crying out for the slaying of another to avenge his death. *Qatīlun . . . yunādī qatīlā* (a slain man calling for a man to be slain) is a rhetorically precise and powerful expression of the law of retaliation, especially when we understand the morphological implications of the form *faʿīl bi maʿnā mafʿūl* (with the meaning of the passive participle): the first *qatīl* is to be taken in the past sense—"one who has been killed"—the second in the gerundive sense—"one who ought to be killed." That is, for a *slain* kinsman a non-kinsman *ought to be slain*.

46. Shaykhū, *Shuʿarāʾ al-Naṣrāniyyah* 1:178; al-Sandūbī, *Akhbār al-Marāqisah*, 65–66.

47. On the pastor of the stars, see J. Stetkevych, *Zephyrs of Najd*, chap. 4. On the shared elegiac element in nasīb and rithāʾ, see S. Stetkevych, *Abū Tammām*, chap. 14.

Verse 3 is most curious for its inversion of the poetic commonplace in which the poet's two companions chide him for weeping at ruined abodes, the abandoned encampment of his lost mistress. Here the poet chides himself. The essentially elegiac nature of the *ṭulūl* (ruins) is suggested here by the curious ambiguity of the image: is the poet chiding himself for indulging in longing for a lost mistress when his brother lies slain, or are the ruins the grave of Kulayb over which the younger brother sheds maudlin tears rather than assume the obligations of manhood? Again the ambiguity tends to point to an identity of meaning—that separation and death are one, that the effects of loss are the same, and further, that weeping is not the becoming response for a man.

Whereas the first two verses alternated between elegy and revenge, verse 3 alternates hemistichs: the first is elegiac in its conceit and diction; the second is apparently elegiac until the last word *falīl* (notched). Almost any other word for wound would have fallen solidly within the realm of elegiac diction, but the metaphoric use of "notched" introduces the diction of blood vengeance, for as we read in verse 18 of *The Rithā᾽ of Ta᾽abbaṭa Sharran* to notch someone's blade is to have a "hit" or point against him in the blood-vengeance tally. To be "notched" is thus to have unavenged blood.

Verse 4 presents a beguiling ambiguity. The diction of the first hemistich, centering on the word *ḥājah* (need), can, especially given the ambiguity of the poetic context here, apply equally to the burning need for the lost loved one—either the mistress or the deceased—or the burning thirst for blood vengeance. Given the bivalency (or trivalency) of the first hemistich, when we reach *daʿā* (call out) we don't know whether to expect the elegiac dove cooing on the branch, or the bloodthirsty owl perched on the tomb crying, *Isqūnī, isqūnī*! (Give me drink, give me drink!). It is only when we reach *fī al-ghuṣūni* (among the branches) that we are assured of the dove, as the final word *hadīl*, the cooing of the dove, confirms. Still, there is a disturbing parallel between *yunādī qatīlā* (cries out for a slain man) at the end of verse 2 and *dāʿin hadīlā* (calls out, cooing) at the end of verse 4. This should give us pause for further speculation.

The cooing of the dove on the bough is one of the most sentimental and lyrical, as well as conventional, of elegiac motifs. "I will weep as long as the dove coos on the bough" is normally taken to mean forever. Further, as is evident from the examples, the cooing of the dove is connected with the weeping of the mourning women; indeed, the verb *nāḥa-yanūḥu* is commonly used for both. If we then posit that the dove, like other less fair fowl, is a symbol of the soul, we arrive at a fuller significance of the imagery of both elegy and blood vengeance: the dove cooing on the branch must be the soul of the dead calling out to be watered by the tears of the living, that is, to be given life through memory as expressed through the shedding of tears. This image is then parallel to that of the owl (*ṣadā, hāmah*), the form that the soul of the unavenged takes to sit on top of the tomb and cry for the blood of vengeance. It thus appears that the use of ambiguous or bivalent diction and even imagery has a crucial semantic function: that of alerting the audience to the semantic connection, or even ultimate identity, of two apparently distinct images.

If we then look once more at the weeping over the ruins of verse 3, a fuller meaning seems to emerge. Perhaps the poet is suggesting through his ambiguous use of *ṭulūl* that weeping over a slain kinsman is as useless and self-indulgent as weeping over a lost mistress or the lost past altogether. The poet should rather be avenging, restoring what is lost, than weeping over it. Implicit in this verse is the gender differentiation established in Chapter 5: watering the grave with tears is the appropriate or required response for women; watering it with blood, that of men. The poet is thus chiding himself to eschew the effeminate and puerile in favor of the mature and masculine.

The intimate connection—or even identity?—between mourning and avenging is further revealed in verse 5 in the parallel placement of *ḥuzn* (grief, mourning) and *ghalīl* (thirst for vengeance) as direct objects of *lammā aqḍi* (I have not yet satisfied/fulfilled).

The anxiety built up in verses 4 and 5 through the reiteration of *lan taqaḍḍā* (will not be fulfilled) and *lammā aqḍi* (I have not yet fulfilled) is forcefully released in verse 6 by the imperative *anjiz naḥban . . . wa dhuḥūlā* (fulfill your vow . . . and your revenge!). Weeping at ruins or tombs is suddenly unthinkable (7) now that the vow to vengeance pledges the avenger to unending war. The vacillation between the effeminate elegiac and the vengeful masculine which was expressed in the ambiguously shifting diction and imagery of the first five verses gives way to an imagery that is purely masculine. The interrogative (2, 5) and the various moods of the imperfective give way in verses 8 through 10 to the perfect: *intaḍaw . . . abraqnā . . . Ṣabarnā . . . dakdakat . . . nazalnā* (They grabbed . . . we flashed/threatened . . . We stood firm . . . the swords pounded . . . we attacked). Male violence and potency dominate the imagery and diction: "Like stallions menacing stallions" (8) affirms through the repetition of *fuḥūl* (stallions) the equal strength and status of the opposing sides. As mentioned, *inṣāf* (the equitable treatment of the enemy in poetry), is above all an expression of the ritual requirement of blood vengeance that the slain kinsman's blood be atoned for with blood of equal value. Furthermore, when we keep in mind that what stallions compete for is access to mares for breeding, the element of fertility, of revitalization, once more comes to the fore. Masculinity is further emphasized through the use of diction or images that are archetypally associated with the male: the lightning flash, appearing in verse 8 in the verb *abraqnā*, to lightning, to threaten, and in verse 9 in the epithet *bawāriq*, flashing, for swords. Similarly the pounding (*dakdakat*) of the swords in verse 9 appears to have a sexual connotation. The verb is used in the phrase *yudakdiku al-nāqata,* said of a male camel that "distresses the she-camel by his weight" when he covers her; apparently it is related to the expression *dakka al-jāriyata* (slave girl).[48] The closing line declares that the enemy could not sustain the power to attack, and so the poet's tribe attacked and took the day. The more potent one wins.

48. Lane, *d-k-k*.

PART FOUR

THE MASTER POEM

CHAPTER 7

Regicide and Retribution: *The Muʿallaqah of Imruʾ al-Qays*

In the closing chapter we turn to *The Muʿallaqah of Imruʾ al-Qays*, a poem widely considered to be the finest in the Arabic language, composed by that tradition's most renowned poet.[1] In keeping with the method established in the previous chapters, the poem will be analyzed in light of the akhbār that have accumulated around the name of the poet to whom it is attributed. In the case of Imruʾ al-Qays ibn Ḥujr, those akhbār have generated a persona of tragic and mythic proportions. My reading of the akhbār, following primarily the *Kitāb al-Aghānī* notice on Imruʾ al-Qays, will aim not at correlating (pseudo-)biographical items with the contents of the poem (although such akhbār, whether or not they have been generated by the poetic text, can certainly aid our reading) but at identifying dominant themes and patterns that might help interpret the poem on levels beyond the literal. It is my argument that the akhbār of Imruʾ al-Qays are informed by the now-familiar ritual pattern of blood vengeance and, further, that his *Muʿallaqah* shares the same ritually determined structure.[2]

The *Kitāb al-Aghānī* account can, for the present discussion, be

1. See Sezgin, *Poesie*, 122–26; S. Boustany, "Imruʾ al-Ḳays b. Ḥudjr," *EI*$_2$; Arberry, *The Seven Odes*, 31–66. Major modern studies of the *Muʿallaqah* are Yūsuf al-Yūsuf, "Taḥlīl Muʿallaqat Imriʾ al-Qays," *Al-Maʿrifah* 163 (1975): 62–91; Kamal Abu-Deeb, "Towards a Structural Analysis of pre-Islamic Poetry (II): Haydar, "*The Muʿallaqa of Imruʾ al-Qays* (I and II)"; and S. Stetkevych, "Structuralist Analyses" (in which I have discussed Abu-Deeb's and Haydar's studies) and "Al-Qaṣīdah al-ʿArabiyyah."

2. It is noteworthy that none of the major modern studies of *The Muʿallaqah of Imruʾ al-Qays* has made any attempt to correlate the poem with the akhbār. It is nevertheless of interest

roughly divided into three sections: Imruʾ al-Qays's royal Kindite lineage and its history, culminating in the regicide of the poet's father Ḥujr; the poet's rebellious youth as expressed in his amorous/poetic exploits prior to his father's death; and the poet's vow to vengeance and never-ending quest to avenge his father. These themes are recognizable as the constituent elements of the blood-vengeance ritual as previously established.

Imruʾ al-Qays is said to have been the scion of the royal house of Kindah (the Arab tribe that in the fifth and sixth centuries A.D. spread from southern Arabia to dominate the Arab tribes of central and northern Arabia).[3] Ancestors of note include Ḥujr, the founder of the dynasty, from whose sobriquet, "the eater of bitter herbs," his descendants were known as the Banū Ākil al-Murār, and Imruʾ al-Qays's grandfather al-Ḥārith ibn ʿAmr. It was he who during the reign of the Sasanian king Qubādh displaced the Lakhmid king al-Mundhir ibn Māʾ al-Samāʾ at al-Ḥīrah, whence he was subsequently ousted by its former master. Al-Ḥārith took flight, but forty-eight of the Banū Ākil al-Murār were captured, handed over to al-Mundhir, and beheaded.

It was during al-Ḥārith's reign in al-Ḥīrah that the tribes of Nizār became so torn by dissension that their lords appealed to the Kindite ruler to appoint his sons kings over the various factions to keep them from fighting. Thus to Ḥujr ibn al-Ḥārith, the father of Imruʾ al-Qays, fell the kingship over the Banū Asad and Banū Ghaṭafān.[4] The outstanding event in Ḥujr's rule—at least in literary terms—is his assassination. It is perhaps indicative of the weight of this regicide that the *Kitāb al-Aghānī* notice on Imruʾ al-Qays presents four variant accounts,[5] of which the first and fullest is that of Ibn al-Kalbī.

that the studies of al-Yūsuf, Abu-Deeb, and to some extent Haydar, focus on the erotic aspects of the poem, thus reflecting the association in the classical tradition between the Dārat Juljul passage in the poem and the khabar that purports to describe the "real-life" episode. See al-Yūsuf, "Taḥlīl Muʿallaqat Imriʾ al-Qays;" Abu-Deeb, "Towards a Structural Analysis (II)"; Haydar, "*The Muʿallaqa* of Imruʾ al-Qays (I and II)."

3. On the history of Kindah, see I. Shahîd, "Kinda," EI_2. I give the literary rather than the historical account. It should be noted that there are many divergences between the two and, further, many variant accounts in the *Kitāb al-Aghānī* and other classical literary sources.

4. Al-Iṣbahānī, *Kitāb al-Aghānī* 9:3197–3201.

5. Lyall, who appears to have had some appreciation of the weight of this event, relates all four *Kitāb al-Aghānī* versions in the introduction to his edition and translation of the *Dīwān of ʿAbīd ibn al-Abraṣ*. See also his remarks on the political and poetic relations between ʿAbīd and Imruʾ al-Qays. Charles James Lyall, ed. and trans., *The Dīwāns of ʿAbīd ibn al-Abraṣ, of Asad, and ʿĀmir ibn aṭ-Ṭufail, of ʿĀmir ibn Ṣaʿṣaʿah* (Cambridge: Cambridge University Press, 1980) [reprint of E. J. W. Gibb Memorial Series, vol. 21, 1913], 2–5 and 1–9 passim.

It happened once when Ḥujr was in Tihāmah that the Banū Asad refused to pay their tribute, turned back his tax collector, and beat his messengers. In response he gathered a large army and set out against them. After attacking the Banū Asad and taking their leaders, he began to slay them with a rod—whence their sobriquet ʿAbīd al-ʿAṣā (Slaves of the Rod). He seized their livestock and exiled them to Tihāmah, swearing that they would never dwell in Najd again. Ḥujr kept in custody, however, two of the Banū Asad, ʿAmr ibn Masʿūd, one of their lords, and the renowned poet, ʿAbīd ibn al-Abraṣ, who composed on behalf of his tribe a poem of contrition and submission which Ḥujr accepted.[6] No sooner had word reached the Banū Asad that Ḥujr had relented than they turned back to Najd. They were but one day's journey from Ḥujr's encampment, when their *kāhin* (soothsayer) predicted that Ḥujr would be the first man to be plundered on the morrow. With this omen they mounted their steeds and by sunrise of the next day had arrived at Ḥujr's encampment. The king's loyal guard of the Banū Khaddān (a subtribe of the Banū Asad whose father's life Ḥujr had spared) pitched their tents around his to protect him from the murderous onslaught. But ʿIlbāʾ ibn al-Ḥārith al-Kāhilī, whose father Ḥujr had killed, thrust his spear between them, striking Ḥujr's heel tendon, then slew him. The Banū Asad then appealed to Ḥujr's erstwhile allies against them, the Banū Kinānah and the Banū Qays, saying, "You are our brothers and our uncle's sons, whereas this man is a distant relative from you and from us. You have seen how he and his kinsmen used to treat you!" The Banū Asad proceeded to loot and plunder. Once Kinānah and Qays saw the slain king wrapped in a white sheet and thrown out in the roadway, they too joined in. ʿAmr ibn Masʿūd alone leapt to the defense of Ḥujr's women and children and took them under his protection.[7]

Of the four *Kitāb al-Aghānī* versions of the slaying of Ḥujr, it is worth noting that only in the third, that of al-Haytham ibn ʿAdī, which, according to Lyall, has the strongest claim to authenticity, does ʿIlbāʾ attack and spear Ḥujr on the field of battle.[8] And it is in this version alone that Imruʾ al-Qays is mentioned, fleeing the scene of battle on his sorrel mare. In the second version, al-Shaybānī's, ʿIlbāʾ, having failed to persuade one of the Banū Khaddān to slay Ḥujr, waits until the king

6. A translation can be found in Lyall, *Dīwān of ʿAbīd ibn al-Abraṣ*, no. 29, pp. 60–61.
7. Al-Iṣbahānī, *Kitāb al-Aghānī* 9:3202–4.
8. Ibid., 9:3205; Lyall, *Dīwān of ʿAbīd ibn al-Abraṣ*, 3–4.

is off his guard and slays him with a broken spear.[9] In the fourth, Ibn al-Sikkīt's, the Banū Asad take Ḥujr prisoner, and ʿIlbāʾ, fearing he will escape, persuades his sister's son, whose father Ḥujr has killed, to slay the bound king with a dagger.[10] Apparently, the intent of these nonheroic versions is to magnify the treachery and ignominy of the regicide.

In Frazerian terms, the death or murder of the king signals the failure of fertility on both natural and political levels—the wasteland. The mythic force of the abomination of regicide is somewhat vitiated in the modern age, but its central place in the Western literary tradition—Oedipus, Julius Caesar, Hamlet, Macbeth—should alert us to the primordial horror associated with it. It is of note that in all these literary regicides "treachery" is involved; that is, the regicide is perpetrated by kin or allies—members of the polity—not the enemy. The polity is destroyed from within, not from without. In the War of al-Basūs the polity was likewise destroyed by an internal conflict, one set in motion precisely by the overweening "kinglike" behavior of Kulayb Wāʾil. Here, too, the genealogical connection —Imruʾ al-Qays's mother is said to be Fāṭimah ibn Rabīʿah, the sister of Kulayb Wāʾil and Muhalhil[11]—is telling.

The *Kitāb al-Aghānī* accounts of Imruʾ al-Qays's wayward youth are presented in the context of the poet's receiving news of and vowing to avenge his father's death. Evident in these anecdotes is the ritual pattern of blood vengeance established in the earlier chapters: that of youthful irresponsibility and oedipal antagonism toward the mature male—elder brother or father—followed, upon his death, by the vow to vengeance and assumption of the obligations of manhood.

In Ibn al-Sikkīt's version, before he was given the last stroke, Ḥujr made his testament and sent it with a messenger whom he instructed to go to each of his sons, starting with the eldest, and to give the testament (which contained information about his killer), his weapons, steeds, and cauldrons to whichever of them did not mourn, for this one would be his heir and avenger. The older sons put dust on their heads and wept, but not the youngest, Imruʾ al-Qays. When the messenger found him playing backgammon with one of his boon companions and announced that Ḥujr was dead, Imruʾ al-Qays paid no attention but

9. Al-Iṣbahānī, *Kitāb al-Aghānī* 9:3205.
10. Ibid., 9:3205–6.
11. Ibid., 9:3197.

told his friend to take his turn. When he had, Imruʾ al-Qays said, "I didn't want to spoil your turn," and then asked the messenger about his father. The poet then proclaimed, "Wine and women are forbidden to me until I have killed a hundred of the Banū Asad and cut the forelocks of a hundred more!"[12]

The same pattern finds expression in Ibn al-Kalbī's version. Ḥujr had banished Imruʾ al-Qays out of disdain for his poetry. So Imruʾ al-Qays used to rove among the Arab tribes along with a motley collection of outcasts from the tribes of Ṭayyiʾ, Kalb, and Bakr ibn Wāʾil. Whenever they chanced upon a pool or meadow or a good hunting spot, he would stop and slaughter a beast every day for whoever was with him. Then he would go hunting, shoot game, and return. He would eat, and his companions with him; he would drink wine and give them drink, and his slave girls would delight him with song. He would continue thus until the water in the pool was exhausted, then he would move on to another. Such was his state in Dammūn in the Yemen when the news of Ḥujr's death reached him. He replied, "He neglected me in my youth and has burdened me [with avenging him] now that I am grown. I will neither be sober today, nor drunk tomorrow (*lā ṣaḥwa al-yawma wa lā sukra ghadan*)." And the dictum that became proverbial, "Wine today, business tomorrow (*al-yawma khamrun wa ghadan amrun*)." Imruʾ al-Qays then went on a seven-day drinking binge, and when he sobered up swore not to eat meat or drink wine or anoint himself with oil or touch a woman or wash his head of impurity until he had achieved his vengeance.[13]

Yet another version of Imruʾ al-Qays's wayward youth, one exhibiting *topoi* familiar from Hellenistic romance, is found in Ibn Qutaybah's *Al-Shiʿr wa al-Shuʿarāʾ*. Of interest here is the explicit identification of poetry with eroticism and the function of eroticism as a source of oedipal tension and rivalry between father and son. And of course, it is hard not to see Laius's exposure of Oedipus behind this narrative:

Imruʾ al-Qays had been banished by his father because of the poetry he had composed about [his cousin] Fāṭimah.[14] Imruʾ al-Qays was enamored of her and had pursued her for a long time without success; so he was always trying to catch her off guard. This he finally did in

12. Ibid., 9:3207.
13. Ibid., 9:3207–8.
14. Other, more explicitly oedipal versions of this story claim rather that Imruʾ al-Qays incurred his father's wrath by trying to seduce his wife, a woman named Hirr. See al-Sandūbī, *Akhbār al-Marāqisah*, 8.

the incident at the pool at Dārat Juljul,[15] of which he said: "Halt, two friends, and we will weep for the memory of one beloved and an abode," (*The Muʿallaqah of Imruʾ al-Qays*, verse 1). When news of this episode reached his father, he ordered a servant to take Imruʾ al-Qays, slay him, and bring back his eyes as proof that the deed was done. The servant slew instead a wild calf and brought its eyes. When later Ḥujr repented, the servant returned Imruʾ al-Qays to his father, who forbade him to compose verse. Imruʾ al-Qays, however, persisted in his poetry and when his father discovered this he banished him once more. This was the poet's state when the news of his father's death reached him at Dammūn.[16]

The narratives of Imruʾ al-Qays's poetic and erotic precocity, his father's attempt to have him killed, his expulsion from his father's house, and his initial expressions of resentment over the burden of blood vengeance, suggest to us once more that the taking of vengeance serves to deflect oedipal violence outside the kin group. On one level, then, Imruʾ al-Qays's excessive vengeance reflects his exaggerated (oedipal) hostility toward his father. That is, the poet is not merely avenging his father but avenging himself on his father.

By now it should strike us that there is a direct relation between the motif of treacherous murder within the polity and that of exaggerated vengeance. Imruʾ al-Qays's "vengeance of one hundred" is already familiar to us from al-Shanfarā; Muhalhil's thirst was likewise unquenchable. Such patterns tell us not merely that the price to be paid for abominations such as "murther most foul" and regicide is high but also that it can never be paid except by the destruction of the polity itself. Within the Arabic literary context, then, Imruʾ al-Qays's vow of one hundred signals to us that he will never accede to the kingship of his father, that he marks the end of the royal line of the Banū Ākil al-Murār, and the akhbār indeed fulfill this expectation:

The *Kitāb al-Aghānī* account of Imruʾ al-Qays's battle against the Banū Asad, related by both Ibn al-Kalbī and Ibn al-Sikkīt, states explicitly that Imruʾ al-Qays exceeds the bounds of the Arab tribal ethos in his insatiable pursuit of vengeance (note, too, the "thirst-quenching" symbolic subtext).

Imruʾ al-Qays enlisted the aid of the Banū Bakr and Banū Taghlib

15. A full account of Dārat Juljul is given in the discussion of verses 10–12 of *The Muʿallaqah of Imruʾ al-Qays*. Note that the cousin's name is there given as ʿUnayzah.

16. Ibn Qutaybah, *Al-Shiʿr wa al-Shuʿarāʾ*, 38.

and set out against the Banū Asad. After mistakenly attacking the Banū Kinānah, with whom the Banū Asad had taken refuge but then fled, Imruʾ al-Qays finally reached them the next day at noon. His horsemen were exhausted and dying of thirst, whereas the Banū Asad were gathered at the water. He rushed upon them and fought until many of them fell wounded and slain. When night let down its veil between them, the Banū Asad took flight. In the morning the Banū Taghlib and Banū Bakr refused to follow him further, saying, "You have achieved your vengeance." To which Imruʾ al-Qays replied: "By God, I have not! for I have killed no one from the Banū Kāhil [the clan of Ḥujr's murderer], or from some of the other clans of the Banū Asad!" "No," they replied, "You are inauspicious." They abhorred having fought the Banū Kinānah, and left him.[17]

Much of the remainder of the *Kitāb al-Aghānī* notice details Imruʾ al-Qays's life-long peregrinations, having exhausted his wealth and his allies, to rally support for his cause. Imruʾ al-Qays's transgression of tribal custom in his obsessive pursuit of vengeance is reiterated in the episode of his consulting the idol Dhū al-Khalaṣah at Tabālah, related by Ibn al-Kalbī and others.

Having been abandoned by Bakr and Taghlib, Imruʾ al-Qays acquired a five-hundred-man Ḥimyarite army, some outcasts, and some mercenaries and set out with them against the Banū Asad. Passing by Tabālah, he decided to take an oracle from Dhū al-Khalaṣah with his three arrows: the commanding, the forbidding, and the waiting. He tried three times, and each time the forbidding arrow came out. So he gathered them up, broke them, and flung them in the face of the idol, crying, "Go suck your mother's clitoris! If your father had been killed, you would not have held me back!" Then he went out and vanquished the Banū Asad. It is said that divining arrows were never again used before Dhū al-Khalaṣah until its destruction after the coming of Islam.[18]

Deprived of his kingdom and abandoned by his newfound Ḥimyarite allies, Imruʾ al-Qays retained only a handful of kinsmen of the Banū Ākil al-Murār and the five ancestral suits of armor that had been handed down from king to king. Pursued by al-Mundhir IV of al-Ḥīrah, Imruʾ al-Qays sought refuge and assistance from one tribal overlord and brigand after another. It is from this period that Imruʾ al-Qays's epithet al-Malik al-Ḍillīl, usually translated as "the wandering king," is said to

17. Al-Iṣbahānī, *Kitāb al-Aghānī* 9:3211–12.
18. Ibid., 9:3212–13.

derive. There is a mythopoeically telling irony at work in Imruʾ al-Qays's exaggerated quest for vengeance. For if to avenge is to inherit, then the relentless pursuit of unslakable vengeance can lead only to dispossession. Indeed, Imruʾ al-Qays ultimately abandons his patrimony.

Imruʾ al-Qays was advised to go to al-Samawʾal, the Jewish overlord of Taymāʾ, to seek from him a letter to the Ghassanid al-Ḥārith ibn Abī Shamir to introduce him to Caesar. Entrusting his property and armor to al-Samawʾal, he then proceeded to the Byzantine court where he was honorably received and accorded a position of rank. Caesar gathered a numerous army under Imruʾ al-Qays, who set off forthwith. Meanwhile, al-Ṭammāḥ, an Asadī intriguer whose brother Imruʾ al-Qays had killed, had infiltrated the Byzantine court. No sooner had Imruʾ al-Qays departed than he suggested to Caesar that Imruʾ al-Qays was not to be trusted—according to one version, because he might vanquish the Banū Asad and then turn his royal aspirations back toward Byzantium and attack Caesar with the very army he had given him. Ibn al-Kalbī's version states rather that al-Ṭammāḥ told Caesar that Imruʾ al-Qays was a womanizer and that he had been corresponding with Caesar's daughter, meeting in secret, and—the worst scandal of all—reciting poems about her to the Arabs! Thereupon Caesar sent Imruʾ al-Qays an embroidered robe interwoven with gold and permeated with poison and with it the message, "I have sent my robe, which I myself have worn, in order to honor you. When it reaches you, don it with blessings and good luck, and write me of your news at every stage of your campaign." No sooner did the elated Imruʾ al-Qays don the robe than the poison took effect. His skin sloughed off, for which he was called Dhū al-Qurūḥ (the Man with Sores); he died and lies buried near Anqirah.[19]

The abandonment of ancestral Kindite coats of arms for Caesar's royal robe interwoven with gold and poison succinctly symbolizes Imruʾ al-Qays's loss of patrimony. The very names of the Kindite suits of armor tell of regal power and glory: al-Faḍfāḍah (ample), al-Ḍāfiyah (abundant, overflowing), al-Muḥaṣṣinah (surrounding, fortifying), al-Khirrīq (bountiful), and Umm al-Dhuyūl (Mother of Trailing Robes).[20] Entrusting these to al-Samawʾal and abandoning the Arab homeland for the land of the Byzantines, Imruʾ al-Qays is in symbolic as well as

19. Ibid., 9:3219–21.
20. Ibid., 9:3213, following n. 3, *al-khirrīq* for *al-kharbaq*.

political terms naked and defenseless. Not only is he without the armor itself, he is stripped of all that the ancestral armor represents: his royal lineage and his inherited identity, the tribal allegiances that attend his inherited position, "Arabness" itself. These, Imruʾ al-Qays exchanges for the very embodiment of Byzantine intrigue, a robe of honor whose rich embroideries suggest the labyrinthine dangers of Caesar's court, gold thread and deadly poison interwoven. Thus for the Arab poet-prince who has abandoned the armor and land of his ancestors to make his way unaided through the maze of the Byzantine court, even the honors of the emperor prove lethal. To the loss of kingdom and patrimony is added, as the sloughing of his skin so powerfully expresses, the loss of self. The Kindite prince and poet dies in exile, unavenged. The line of Ākil al-Murār, at least in literary terms, comes to an end.[21]

In Imruʾ al-Qays's *Muʿallaqah* we find a poem that exhibits exquisitely achieved examples of traditional themes and motifs when it conforms to standard qaṣīdah form and conventions, and striking new images when, having built up a formal momentum, it then leaps beyonds the bounds of our poetic expectations. The nasīb opens (verses 1–6) with the poet's asking his companions to stop and weep with him (the *istīqāf* convention) at the ruins, and then begins a series of reminiscences of erotic encounters (7–43) which far exceed in number and length the standard formal contours. Where a raḥīl would be expected we find the description of an unending night filled with motionless stars (44–48) and then a ṣuʿlūk-like description of man and wolf (49–52). The fakhr section opens by formally regrounding the poem through a superb description of the poet's horse (53–70), only to close with the unexpected and majestic storm scene (71–82).

The Muʿallaqah of Imruʾ al-Qays [47]

1. Halt, two friends, and we will weep
   for the memory of one beloved
   And an abode at Siqṭ al-Liwā
   between al-Dakhūl, then Ḥawmal,
2. Then Tūḍiḥ, then al-Miqrāt, whose trace
   was not effaced
   By the two winds weaving over it
   from south and north.

21. This is not so far from the historical facts, for it is this time, the second half of the sixth century, that witnessed the disintegration of Kindite power in central and north Arabia. See Shahîd, "Kinda."

3. You see the droppings
   of white antelope
Scattered on its outer grounds and lowlands
   like peppercorns,
4. As if I, on the morning
   that they loaded up their beasts,
Before the tribe's acacia trees,
   were splitting colocynth.
5. My companions, halting there
   their mounts for me,
Say, Do not perish out of grief,
   control yourself!
6. Surely my cure is tears
   poured forth;
Then, at a worn-out trace is there
   a place for weeping?
7. [Console yourself] As was your wont before her
   with Umm al-Ḥuwayrith
And her neighbor at Mount Maʾsal,
   Umm al-Rabāb!
8. When they arose there wafted from them
   musk as redolent
As the east breeze when it bears
   the scent of clove.
9. Then my eyes, out of ardent love, sent down
   a flood of tears upon my neck
Till my sword belt was soaked
   in tears.
10. Did you not have many a fine day
   from them?
And best of all the day
   at Dārat Juljul?
11. And the day when, for the virgins,
   I hocked my mount,
—What an amazing sight!—they made off
   with her saddle and its gear!
12. Then through the day the virgins
   tossed her meat,
And her fat like twisted fringes
   of white Damascus silk.
13. And the day I entered the howdah,
   ʿUnayzah's howdah,

Then she said, Woe to you! You'll make me
go on foot.
14. She kept saying, when the high-sided saddle
listed with our weight,
You have hocked my camel, O Imruʾ al-Qays,
So get down!
15. Keep going, I said to her,
slacken his reins,
But don't drive me away from your
twice-to-be-tasted fruit!
16. Then many a woman like you, pregnant and nursing,
have I visited by night,
And distracted from her amuleted
one-year-old.
17. When he cried from behind her, she turned
her upper half toward him,
But the half that was beneath me
did not budge.
18. And one day on a sand dune's back
she rebuffed me,
And swore an oath never
to be broken.
19. O Fāṭimah, don't try me
with your teasing,
[Or] if you have resolved to cut me off,
then do it gently.
20. Are you deluded about me because
your love is my slayer
And whatever you command my heart
it does?
21. If something of my character
has hurt you,
Then pull my clothes away from yours,
they will slip off.
22. Your eyes do not shed tears
but to pierce
with your two shafts the pieces of
my slaughtered heart.
23. Many an "egg" of the curtained quarters,
whose tent none dares to seek,
I took my pleasure with her,
unhurried.

24. I stole past guards
  to get to her, past clansmen
Eager, could they conceal it,
  to slay me.
25. When the Pleiades spread out
  across the sky
Like a girdle's spread-out pleats,
  alternating gold and gems,
26. I came when she, before the tent curtain,
  had shed her clothes for sleep,
And was clad in nothing but
  an untied shift.
27. She said, God's oath! There's no way
  to dissuade you,
And I don't see the veil lift
  from your error.
28. I led her forth from her tent,
  walking as she trailed
Over our tracks the train
  of her gown of figured silk.
29. Then, when we had crossed
  the clan's enclosure
And made our way to a sandy hollow
  surrounded by long-winding dunes,
30. I drew her temples toward me, and she
  leaned over me
With hollow waist, but plump the place
  that anklets ring.
31. Slender-waisted, white,
  not flabby,
Her collarbone shone like
  a polished mirror.
32. Now hiding, now baring a cheek
  long and wide,
She guards herself with the glance
  of a wild doe at Wajrah with fawn,
33. And a neck like the neck
  of the white antelope,
Not overly long when she raises it,
  or lacking ornament.
34. A head of hair, jet-black,
  adorns her back,

Luxuriant as a bunch of dates
on a cluster-laden palm.
35. Some of its locks are
secured on top,
While others stray between the plaited
and the loose.
36. A waist delicate, like
a twisted bowstring, trim,
A lower leg like the papyrus reed,
well-watered, tender.
37. In the forenoon crumbs of musk
still deck her bed,
And she, late morning sleeper, still is clad
in sleeping gown, ungirded.
38. She grasps with fingers, soft, uncalloused,
as if they were
The worms of Ẓaby or the supple tooth sticks
of the *isḥil* tree.
39. When night falls she lights up the dark
as if she were
A lamp in the night cell
of an anchorite.
40. At one like her the staid man
gazes with ardor
When she stands in her full stature between
woman's gown and maiden's shift,
41. Like the first inviolate bloom,
white mixed with yellow,
Nurtured on water limpid and unmuddied
by alighting traveler.
42. [Grown] men find consolation from
the follies of their youth,
But my heart refuses solace for
its love for you.
43. How many an enemy,
quarreling over you,
Not neglectful of advice or of rebuke,
did I repel?
44. Many a night like the billowing sea
let down its veils over me
With all kinds of cares
to test me.

45. Then I said to it when
 it stretched out its spine,
Followed with its hindquarters,
 and heaved its ponderous breast,
46. Alas, long night, will you not dispel,
 revealing dawn,
Though the dawn of day will be
 no better for me.
47. Then, oh what a night you are!
 as if its stars
Were all bound by tight-twisted ropes
 to Mount Yadhbul,
48. As if the Pleiades were
 in midcourse suspended
By flaxen cords
 from obdurate rock.
49. And many a waterskin of the clans
 have I borne its leathern strap
Upon my shoulder, submissive
 and much traveled.
50. And many a riverbed, a bare waste like
 the belly of an ass, I crossed,
Where the wolf howled like an outcast profligate
 with many mouths to feed.
51. So when he howled I said to him,
 Our lot is meager sustenance
If you have not gained wealth,
 [for I have none].
52. Each of us when he acquires a thing,
 it soon escapes him,
Whoever tills your tilth and mine,
 it will leave lean.
53. I would ride forth early,
 the birds still in their nests,
On a steed sleek and swift,
 a shackle for wild game, huge.
54. Now wheeling, now charging, advancing, retreating,
 all at once,
Like a mighty boulder the torrent has washed
 down from the heights.
55. A dark bay from whose back
 the saddle pad slips,

Like raindrops
  from hard rock,
56. Despite leanness, spirited
  as if his bursting gallop,
When he seethes with heat,
  were a cauldron's boil,
57. Pouring forth his gallop
  when, despite fatigue, the coursers
On the hard and trampled plain
  stir up the dust.
58. The slender youth he makes slip
  from his back,
The robes of the rugged, bulky rider
  he sends flying out behind,
59. Streaming like a boy's button-on-a-string,
  when he has tightly twisted it
By his hands' successive circling
  the connecting string.
60. He has the flanks of a gazelle fawn,
  the ostrich's two legs,
The wolf's lope,
  the fox cub's canter.
61. Huge-ribbed, when you look from behind,
  a full tail blocks the gap between his legs,
Reaching almost to the ground,
  not crooked.
62. As if when he heads off there were mounted
  on his rump a stone
A bride pounds perfumes with or on which
  colocynth is crushed,
63. As if the blood of the herd's front-runners
  upon his throat
Were henna juice upon an old man's
  combed and hoary head.
64. Then there appeared before us an oryx herd
  as if its cows were virgins
Circling round a sacred stone
  in long-trained gowns.
65. They turned about like alternated onyx beads
  upon the neck
Of a child nobly uncled in the clan
  from dam and sire.

66. Then he let us catch
the herd's lead runners
And outstripped those that lagged
in an unbroken cluster.
67. One after the other, he hit
a bull and cow,
And yet was not awash
with sweat.
68. Then the meat cooks kept on cooking
both meat laid upon the rocks
To roast well-done, and meat
quick boiled in cauldrons.
69. And our glance, in the evening,
almost failed before him,
To whatever spot the eye was raised,
dazzled, it dropped.
70. All night he remained, his saddle and bridle
upon him,
All night he stood beneath my eye, not
loosed to graze.
71. O friend, do you see the lightning?
There is its flash—
Like two hands shining in a high-crowned
cumulus!
72. Its flash illumining the sky, or like
the sudden flare of a monk's lamp,
When, tilting it, he soaks with oil
the tightly twisted wick.
73. Between Dārij and al-ʿUdhayb I sat with my companions
to watch the storm,
How distant was the object
of my gaze!
74. Over Mount Qaṭan, as I read the signs,
the right flank of its downpour falls,
Over Mount al-Sitār, then Mount Yadhbul,
falls the left.
75. Then in the forenoon it was pouring
its water down around Kutayfah,
Overturning the lofty *kanahbal* trees
upon their beards.
76. It passed its fringes over
Mount Qanān,

And drove the white-footed mountain goats
down every path.
77. In Taymāʾ it did not leave
a single palm trunk standing,
Or a single castle but
those built of stone.
78. As if Mount Thabīr in the foremost
of its rains
Were a tribal chieftain wrapped
in a striped cloak,
79. As if the peaks of Mount Mujaymir's crest
at morning
Ringed with the torrent's dross
were the whorl of a spindle,
80. It deposited its load on
the low-lying desert
Like a Yemeni alighting with
his [fabric]-laden bags,
81. As if, early in the morning,
the songbirds of the valley
Had drunk a morning draught
of fine spiced wine,
82. As if the wild beasts drowned at evening
in its remotest stretches
Were wild onions'
plucked-out bulbs.[22]

It would certainly be a mistake to assume a literal historical connection between *The Muʿallaqah of Imruʾ al-Qays* and the akhbār concerning him, but it would be equally wrong to ignore the literary connection between them. In this respect, as I have established in the preceding chapters, there should be some connection between the persona of the poet created by the akhbār and the most renowned qaṣīdah attributed to that poet. The most obvious place to begin is with Ibn Qutaybah's

22. I have followed al-Zawzanī's recension with the following emendations: verses 3 and 4 are lacking in al-Zawzanī and have been taken from al-Tibrīzī and al-Anbārī; verse 41 has been moved from between my 31 and 32, where it occurs in al-Zawzanī, to its position in al-Tibrīzī and al-Anbārī. Verses 47 and 48 are those of al-Tibrīzī and al-Anbārī, replacing a single verse in al-Zawzanī. See al-Zawzanī, *Sharḥ al-Muʿallaqāt al-Sabʿ*, 71–129; al-Anbārī, *Sharḥ al-Qaṣāʾid al-Sabʿ*, 2–112; al-Tibrīzī, *Sharḥ al-Qaṣāʾid al-ʿAshr*, 10–73. For further recensions and commentaries, see Sezgin, *Poesie*, 48–53, 125–26.

explicit placing of the composition of the *Muʿallaqah* in the midst of the poet's wayward youth, directly after his frolic with the virgins at Dārat Juljul. The significance of the disproportionately long and unusually explicit erotic nasīb will become clearer in this light. But perhaps the identification of place names is too facile, and the khabar concerning the day at Dārat Juljul has merely been generated by the poem itself. A further drawback is that, although this association locates the *Muʿallaqah* biographically, it does little to explain the other passages of the poem, or its structure.

Rather than attempt to locate the *Muʿallaqah* historically within the chronology of the akhbār, I propose to read it in light of the ritual pattern of regicide and retribution that informs the akhbār. In other words, the poem is structurally related to poems of blood vengeance such as those of al-Muhalhil, regardless of the differences in apparent subject matter. It is the literary expression of the ritual and mythic pattern of passage to manhood, accession to power, and it bears the added intensity that befits a king, the son of a king.

At this point, I want to add to van Gennep's rite of passage and Hubert and Mauss's rite of sacrifice a further structural paradigm, Theodor Gaster's formulation of the seasonal pattern of rite and myth.[23] Although Gaster conceives of this pattern as primarily agrarian, it is virtually identical to the devitalization → revitalization model I have established for the ritual of blood vengeance. Gaster summarizes the seasonal pattern:

> The activities fall into two main divisions which we may call, respectively, rites of Kenosis, or Emptying, and rites of Plerosis, or Filling. The former portray and symbolize the eclipse of life and vitality at the end of each lease, and are exemplified by lenten periods, fasts, austerities, and other expressions of mortification or suspended animation. The latter, on the other hand, portray and symbolize the revitalization that ensues at the beginning of the new lease, and are exemplified by rites of mass mating, ceremonial purgations of evil and noxiousness (both physical and "moral"), and magical procedures designed to promote fertility, produce rain, relume the sun, and so forth.[24]

23. Gaster, *Thespis*, passim. Hamori has employed Gaster's kenosis/plerosis in discussing the relationship of some elements within the qaṣīdah, but in a manner quite different from the present discussion. See Hamori, *Medieval Arabic Literature*, 11–19, passim. For an extensive analysis of qaṣīdah structure in light of Gaster's paradigm, see S. Stetkevych, "Pre-Islamic Panegyric and the Poetics of Redemption: *Mufaḍḍalīyah 119* of ʿAlqamah and *Bānat Suʿād* of Kaʿb ibn Zuhayr," in S. Stetkevych, ed., *Reorientations.*

24. Gaster, *Thespis*, 23.

These two sections are subdivided to produce four major elements:

> First come rites of *mortification*, symbolizing the state of suspended animation that ensues at the end of the year, when one lease on life has drawn to a close and the next is not yet assured. Second come rites of *purgation*, whereby the community seeks to rid itself of all noxiousness and contagion, both physical and moral, and of all evil influences which might impair the prosperity of the coming year and thereby threaten the desired renewal of vitality. Third come rites of *invigoration*, whereby the community attempts, by its own concerted and regimented effort, to galvanize its moribund condition and to procure that new lease on life which is imperative for the continuance of the topocosm. Last come the rites of *jubilation*, which bespeak men's sense of relief when the new year has indeed begun and the continuance of their own lives and that of the topocosm is thereby assured.[25]

In his *Muʿallaqah* Imruʾ al-Qays has metaphorically sublimated the blood vengeance paradigm to produce a poem that goes beyond the immediate tribal sacrificial level to assume mythic and cosmic proportions of Gaster's paradigm.

The Muʿallaqah of Imruʾ al-Qays opens with the traditional *istīqāf*: the poet implores his companions to stop and weep at the traces of an abode where his beloved once dwelt. The indefiniteness and lack of specificity of the first hemistich, "the memory of one beloved" and "an abode" should ambiguously suggest the recollection of a lost mistress and her abode or a deceased kinsman and his grave. This bivalency is intentional and the fact that the lost mistress is later specified should not delude us into a flat univocal reading of the opening verse, for it is perhaps a first hint that the theme of revenge underlies the poem. The second hemistich is as specific as the first is ambiguous: the location is pinpointed by proper names. Moreover we can expand upon Haydar's etymologies of these names[26] to discover an apposite expression of "mortification," in Gaster's terms—the failure of natural fertility—or, in terms closer to the qaṣīdah, the failed relationship between the poet and his erstwhile mistress or the death of the marthī. Thus *siqṭ* (*saqaṭa al-janīnu* = the fetus miscarried, aborted) suggests miscarriage between al-Dakhūl (*dakhl* = sexual penetration) and Ḥawmal (*ḥaml* = pregnancy). In these terms the opening hemistich conveys attempted revitalization through the

25. Ibid., 26.
26. Haydar, "*Muʿallaqa of Imruʾ al-Qays*, I," 238–40.

shedding of tears, through memory and recollection, counterbalanced by an etymological subtext of barrenness and failure (Gaster's mortification) in the second.

The failure of man/culture of the first verse is then juxtaposed in verses 2 and 3 to the vitalizing power of nature. The traces are not effaced but preserved by the weaving of the north and south winds. It is to be noted that, as in Labīd's *Muʿallaqah*, the preeminently cultural act of weaving is now assigned to nature; culture fails and fades while nature preserves and creates. The place-names of verse 2 suggest the fecundity of nature: Tūḍiḥ, from the root *w-ḍ-ḥ* (clarity), and al-Miqrāt, a pool where water gathers. The element of preservation, which is the essence of the differentiation between the raw and the cooked, is apparent too in verse 3, where the droppings of white antelope are likened to peppercorns, that is, the dung or decay of nature now serves as a preservative for nature as spice does for culture. Verse 4 describes the poet weeping on the day the tribe of his beloved loaded up and departed. Here, once again building on Haydar's suggestion, we can go beneath the surface simile—which suggests that the poet's emotional response of weeping is as direct as the physiological response to colocynth—to an etymological subtext: for *taḥammalū* hints at *ḥaml* (pregnancy), the red flowing sap of the *samurāt* trees is termed "menstruation" (*ḥāḍat al-samurāt*), and colocynth was traditionally employed as a drug to induce abortion.[27]

In sum, the opening four verses in a multivocity of symbol, allusion, etymology, and simile convey a message of the failure and fading of human fertility, of culture, the trace of which is preserved by nature, which in turn has assumed the attributes of culture—spices, weaving. If the absence of the beloved and the departure of her tribe offer a clear expression of the separation phase of the rite of passage, its counterpart in the mortification phase of the seasonal pattern "when one lease on life has drawn to a close and the next is not yet assured"[28] is given equally convincing expression.

The *wuqūf*, the halting at the ruined abode, of verse 5 provides the response to the *istīqāf* of verse 1. Here the poet's companions admonish him for weeping and bid him exercise some self-control. The poet's response in verse 6 exhibits most interesting diction—*wa inna shifāʾī ʿabratun muharāqatun* (surely my cure is tears poured forth)—for simply

27. Ibid., 239–40.
28. Gaster, *Thespis*, 26.

by substituting blood for tears we arrive at a traditional expression for blood vengeance, or rather, we should be reminded that the shedding of tears in mourning is metaphorically identified with the shedding of blood in avenging. In this light, the second hemistich takes on a double meaning; first, as a variant of Labīd's rhetorical question *wa kayfa suʾālunā*? (How do we question?): "At a worn-out trace is there a place for weeping?"; and second, implying, as in Muhalhil's poems, that the poet should be out shedding blood, not tears, and hence already anticipating the storm scene at the end of the poem. Once more, let us note that until this point the poem is ambiguous, the *ḥabīb* (beloved) of verse 1 could be equally a departed mistress, as in Labīd's *Muʿallaqah*, or a dead kinsman, as in the elegies of Muhalhil.

It is only in verse 7 that the beloved is identified as a woman, and the poet begins a recitation of his amorous exploits (7–43). The significance of these scenes in the context of the ritual paradigm can be elucidated by referring to the akhbār of Imruʾ al-Qays. There the poet is depicted as a wayward youth, a prodigal son who, on the one hand, refuses to give up poetry and the eroticism it implies to return to the innocence of childhood (premature eroticism) and, on the other hand, refuses to abandon his adolescent carousings to accept the challenge of manhood and fight at his father's side (arrested development). His state thus admirably fits Victor Turner's summation of the liminal stage as "betwixt and between the positions assigned and arrayed by law, custom, convention, and ceremonial."[29]

I propose that the extended erotic nasīb of *The Muʿallaqah of Imruʾ al-Qays* is likewise an expression of precocious sexuality and the arrested development of a prolonged adolescence. What we should then expect to find, in accordance with the rite of passage paradigm, are images expressive of the *disruption* of the expected process of passage, the *diversion* of the passenger from his proper course, of sexuality that is premature, nonserious and nonproductive, barren and dangerous—in a word, illicit. The eroticism of Imruʾ al-Qays's nasīb which is dangerous, frivolous, nonproductive, stands diametrically opposed to the sanctioned sexuality of marriage, which is safeguarded, serious, and productive. The erotic section breaks down into five episodes, all of which, according to the present analysis, express the concept of illicit, liminal sexuality.

The first is that of Umm al-Ḥuwayrith and her neighbor Umm al-

29. Turner, *Ritual Process*, 95.

Rabāb (verses 7–9). Verse 7 disabuses us of the notion that the poet is naive and lovestruck, hopelessly infatuated with his first love. To the contrary, he has had at least two mistresses before and, it would seem, simultaneously. Hardly cases of innocent infatuation, they consist rather of fornication with adulteresses, married women who have borne children (Umm = mother of), presumably to legal husbands and not the poet.[30] The fragrance of musk and clove that the two mistresses exude in verse 8 is, as Marcel Detienne has suggested of the spices and perfumes of the Adonis myth, an image of illicit eroticism, voluptuousness, and seduction, as opposed to the sanctioned sexuality of marriage.[31] These unions are ultimately failed and fruitless, their only product flowing tears (9).

The second episode is that of the slaughter of the poet's she-camel at Dārat Juljul (verses 10–12). The companions describe it as "a good day" (*yawmin ṣāliḥin*) that the poet had from "them" (women), and the scene is indeed one of delightful abandon: the poet has hocked his mount for the virgins (*ʿaqartu lil-ʿadhārā maṭiyyatī*), in preparation for slaughtering it, and they carry off his saddle and gear. The poet's slaughter of his mount at this juncture must be understood in terms of the usual place of camel slaughter (or sacrifice) in the Arabic qaṣīdah—that is, at the end of the poem, in the fakhr or madīḥ section when the poet has already completed his liminal journey. It can take the form of an unspecified *jazūr* (slaughter camel) to feed the clan and its dependents (as in *The Muʿallaqah of Labīd*) or, in a way more pertinent to the argument at hand, the poet's slaughter of his mount as a sort of votive offering at the end of the raḥīl, as if to mark the completion of the passage, or, in another case, the slaughter of a camel at a wedding. In all these cases, the camel slaughter is associated with the aggregation phase of the rite of passage or the communal feast of the plerosis (invigoration and jubilation) phase of Gaster's seasonal pattern. In the fakhr/aggregation section of Imruʾ al-Qays's *Muʿallaqah* itself, we find a clear expression of revitalization/invigoration in the hunt scene in which the prey—oryx that are likened to virgins—are slain and cooked (63–68).

30. The offspring of an illicit affair with a married woman would be reckoned to the paternity of her husband, according to the old Arab precept that lies behind the Islamic precept that the child is reckoned to the bed on which he is born (*al-walad lil-firāsh*). See Robertson Smith, *Kinship and Marriage*, 132; Ibn Qutaybah, *Al-Shiʿr wa al-Shuʿarāʾ*, 44–45.

31. Marcel Detienne, *The Gardens of Adonis: Spices in Greek Mythology*, trans. Janet Lloyd (Atlantic Highlands, N.J.: The Humanities Press, 1977), chap. 3.

In this light, the poet's slaughter of his she-camel in the nasīb for virgins—young girls not yet ready for marriage—appears to be a metaphor for premature sacrifice, immature sexuality. The she-camel is precisely the mount through whose endurance and fortitude the poet is normally able to complete his journey through the liminal wastes of the raḥīl. To hock the camel is to cripple it; to slaughter it for the frivolous entertainment of these playful maidens is to abandon the quest for mature manhood in pursuit of puerile pastimes—which is precisely how the akhbār present the poet. It thus stands quite opposed to the sacrifice that marks the end of the raḥīl, the completion of the liminal journey and aggregation, the cooking and commensal feast. Here, too, the meat is apparently raw, not cooked (*nayy* and *nāḍij* in Arabic mean raw and well-done, but also immature and mature), and the maidens are tossing it about and playing with it rather than eating it. The poet's relationship with the virgins is immature and unconsummate as the sacrificial meat is uncooked and unconsumed.[32] It is, in Freudian terms, perverse polymorphous infantile sexuality as opposed to genital, that is, generative, adult sexuality—in poetic terms, a frivolous silken fringe (verse 12) on the social fabric.

It is worth noting that the elaborate khabar concerning Imruʾ al-Qays's day at Dārat Juljul produces a narrative connection between this erotic episode (verses 10–12) and the next one, that of ʿUnayzah (13–15). Imruʾ al-Qays had fallen in love with his cousin ʿUnayzah and had pursued her unsuccessfully for some time, when, one day, the ladies of the tribe, along with the gear and servants, lagged behind the menfolk. The poet seized the opportunity and stayed lying in wait for them. When the ladies decided to stop at the pool at Dārat Juljul to bathe, Imruʾ al-Qays waited until they were all in the water, then stole up and took all their clothes. He refused to surrender their clothing until they emerged, naked, to claim it. They refused until it got late, when all but ʿUnayzah finally complied. When she, too, at last emerged, he gazed at her front and back. Once clothed, the irate women upbraided him for tormenting and starving them. Imruʾ al-Qays responded by hamstringing and slaughtering his camel for them. A huge fire was lit, the meat was cooked and the ladies ate. The poet ate, too, drank some wine he had with him, and entertained the ladies with song. When it was time to go, the women each took some of his gear to carry for him,

32. As Haydar puts it, "There is raw meat and no sexual contact." See Haydar, "*Muʿallaqa of Imruʾ al-Qays*, I," 242.

except ʿUnayzah. So to her Imru' al-Qays said, "You'll have to carry me!" She let him ride on the withers of her camel. The poet leaned toward her, stuck his head inside her howdah, and kissed her. When she pushed him away, her camel's load listed and she cried, "You have hocked my camel, so get down!"—whence the poet's lines.[33]

In the khabar the emphasis on the visual violation of the women, especially ʿUnayzah, and on the cooking and consumption of the meat suggests a carnal knowledge that is at odds with my (and Haydar's)[34] reading of the poetic verses. Likewise, I see in the poem no explicit association of ʿUnayzah with Dārat Juljul, and in fact, Ibn Qutaybah gives the cousin's name as Fāṭimah in the khabar cited earlier in this chapter. Thus although the khabar functions admirably in the context of the akhbār to depict the prodigal poet's life of wine, women, and song prior to the regicide of his father, to accept it as a straightforward fleshing-out of the poetic verses or as a paradigm of the full qaṣīdah would be misleading.

The third episode is a comical one of seduction, or attempted seduction, that takes place in the howdah of a certain ʿUnayzah (verses 13–15). The use of the phrase *dakhaltu al-khidra* (I entered the women's quarters)—here applied to ʿUnayzah's enclosed howdah (13)—already suggests in the Arabic context the success of the poet's venture (that is, sexual penetration, violation), and ʿUnayzah's cursing him for making her go on foot conveys the same message as his slaughtering of his mount at Dārat Juljul: that the illicit relationship is impeding, this time, *her* due course of progress. Verse 14 makes the point more emphatically in ʿUnayzah's accusation *ʿaqarta baʿīrī* (you have hocked my camel), which should mean for her the same thing as the poet's hocking of his own mount in the Dārat Juljul episode. The hilarity of the camel-top seduction scene, as well as the threat to the intended passage or liminal journey to maturity, is enhanced by the precarious swaying of the howdah, overburdened by the impetuous seducer (14). The hocking of the camel thus suggests, first of all, that the poet's advances are impeding ʿUnayzah's proper course or progress of passage, as well as the poet's own, and second as Louis ʿAwaḍ has suggested to me, a sexual allusion. The sexual interpretation is supported by the common metaphorical correspondence of animal sacrifice to the deflowering of a virgin and,

33. Ibn Qutaybah, *Al-Shiʿr wa al-Shuʿarā'*, 49–50. A full translation can be found in Arberry, *The Seven Odes*, 33–34.

34. Haydar, "*Muʿallaqa of Imru' al-Qays*, I," 242.

in *The Muʿallaqah of Imruʾ al-Qays* in particular, the metaphorical connection of virgins and the slaying of oryx cows in the hunt. Furthermore, it corroborates a sexual implication in the poet's hocking his mount for the virgins at Dārat Juljul: in both cases the verb *ʿaqara* is used. In other words, ʿUnayzah seems to have sacrificed her virginity prematurely and illicitly to the poet, rather than at marriage. The incorrigible poet's response is to tell her to loosen the reins, that is, again, to slow down her journey but also to relinquish control, "let yourself go," and not to drive him away from her fruit, which is (reading al-Zawzanī) *muʿallalī*, twice-tasted or ought to be twice-tasted, or (according to al-Anbārī and al-Ṭibrīzī) *muʿallilī*, diverting, distracting—that is, in my reading, from the proper course of passage. Like the swaying of the howdah and the stumbling of the overburdened camel, the relationship is unstable and precarious. Its very occurrence during a journey indicates its liminal, illicit character, as opposed to sanctioned sexuality within the tribal confines and tribal institutions.

The most explicit depiction of an illicit relationship that diverts its participants from their proper social roles is that of verses 16 and 17, considered among the most scandalous in the classical poetic canon. Here the poet goes by night to a pregnant woman with a one-year-old nursling from whom he diverts her. In the phrase *fa alhaytuhā* (then I diverted her) the verb *alhā* is synonymous with *ʿallala* of *muʿallilī* (15). It is from the root of *lahw* (pastime, diversion, play), again suggesting, as in the other erotic episodes, the nonseriousness and frivolity of the relationship. Just how diverted this woman is from her maternal duties, how divided she is in her loyalties (treacheries?) is made clear in verse 17: when, in the middle of their tryst, her one-year-old cries from behind her, she turns only the upper half of her body toward him to nurse him, while her lower half stays put beneath the poet. In light of the pre-Islamic belief that sexual intercourse with a nursing mother is harmful to the nursling,[35] she is endangering her children, born and unborn, as well as betraying her husband, the father, or *pater putativus* at least, of her nursling and unborn child. These details enhance the illicit and antisocial aspect of the liminal erotic encounter.

In the fifth episode, that with Fāṭimah (verses 18–22), the concept that illicit infatuation is ultimately barren and short-lived is expressed in a conceit that we are perhaps more familiar with from the Latin elegiac poets or, in the Arabic context, the ʿUdhrī poets of the Umayyad

35. Robertson Smith, *Kinship and Marriage*, 295.

period: love that kills or sacrifices its victim. Further, there is a subtext of sacrifice and passage, this time on the part of Fāṭimah, who swears an oath to reject her poet paramour and, it appears, sacrifices a victim—the poet himself. We should recall Walter Burkert's remark that in the classical world there was no oath without a sacrifice,[36] that is, no vow without a votive offering. Fāṭimah, it appears, has abandoned frivolity for seriousness. It is ironic that the poet's own lack of seriousness skews his perception of Fāṭimah, for in his infatuation he imagines that her seriousness is a jest, mere coquetry (19). He then declares that despite his apparent abject dependence upon her (20), he will not make their separation difficult, she need only withdraw her affection from him as if gently pulling her garments from his. The clothes here serve as the conventional metaphor for the soul and self. For her part, Fāṭimah has determined to proceed with her own passage, as it were, and the *jazūr* (slaughter camel) to be sacrificed to mark the completion of this journey, is *qalbin muqattalī* (a tractable, or slain, heart), the poet's. The sacrificial pattern is expressed in a most subtle way, relying on the nuances of a precisely selected diction to convey a subtextual, or subliminal, message: in verse 18, Fāṭimah swears an oath. This should remind us of the patterns we are already familiar with, that of the oath of blood vengeance from which the swearer is released only by slaying his victim or the votive offering of the poet's mount at the end of the journey. In verse 20 the poet says *anna ḥubbaki qātilī* (your love is my slayer), and in verse 22 Fāṭimah's oath is fulfilled with the figurative "slaying" of the poet or, as we would say, "breaking his heart." The expression used, that the "two shafts" of her eyes pierce *aʿshāri qalbin muqattalī* (the pieces of my slaughtered heart) is carefully crafted. For *aʿshāri qalbin*, as the commentators note, suggests *aʿshār al-qidr*, the shards of a pot or cauldron, but also *aʿshār al-jazūr*, the ten parts or cuts of the meat of the slaughter camel to be divided in *maysir* for the sustenance of the kin group and its clients. The two arrows or shafts can then be taken to be the two *maysir* arrows that between them win all ten cuts of the *jazūr*. Similarly, *qalbin muqattalī* not only means an oft-slain or oft-slaughtered heart, insinuating that the poet often finds himself in such amorous predicaments, but, according to the commentators, suggests the expression *baʿīr muqattal*—a tractable or submissive camel.[37]

36. Burkert, *Homo Necans*, 35.

37. Al-Zawzanī, *Sharḥ al-Muʿallaqāt al-Sabʿ*, 93; al-Tibrīzī, *Sharḥ al-Qaṣāʾid al-ʿAshr*, 36–37; al-Anbārī, *Sharḥ al-Qaṣāʾid al-Sabʿ*, 47–48.

The last and longest of the amorous episodes of the nasīb is Imruʾ al-Qays's description of *bayḍati khidrin* (an "egg" of the curtained quarters). This final episode reinforces, indeed sharpens, the point of the earlier episodes, that these erotic encounters are expressions of sexuality that is immature and premature, frivolous and illicit (Freud's perverse and polymorphous infantile sexuality), and that distracts and arrests the proper progress of the passenger/poet toward manhood and maturity.

The epithet "an egg of the curtained quarters" that opens this passage (verse 23) is an expression of delicacy and purity, as al-Anbārī states,[38] a description of the pale complexion of the woman who is constantly veiled and secluded. It is also, here at least, an expression of the immaturity of the poet's inamorata. It is a metaphor for another sort of incubation, the custom of confining pubescent girls until they are ready for marriage—the female counterpart of the male liminal expulsion. This practice recalls Turner's remark that liminality is often likened to being in the womb.[39] A girl's marriage, deflowering, then, constitutes the sacrifice/rebirth that marks her reentry into society (aggregation), now with the status of an adult woman. We are perhaps most familiar with the passive-confinement liminal phase of the adolescent girl from fairytales: Snow White's death and entombment after being tempted into biting the apple of carnal knowledge and Sleeping Beauty's one-hundred-year sleep in the palace overgrown with thorns after pricking her finger with a spindle—marking puberty, sexual awakening—on her sixteenth birthday. Both are awakened to new life by their suitors' kiss. This same principle is at work in the medieval Christian doctrine of the Dormition of the Virgin, according to which the mother of Jesus does not die but, after a period of dormition, appears in Heaven bearing such titles as Bride of Christ and Queen of Heaven, and is described as "espoused to God."[40] How appropriate it is, then, that this period of dormancy and growth, this "dormition of the virgin," which ends with the deflowering of the bride on her wedding night, should be likened to an egg that gestates until it is matured and then hatches. What an outrage it is when the poet interrupts this period of confinement and chastity to take his pleasure with the young girl at his leisure.

The diction of the rest of the verse is equally expressive of liminality and arrested development: the element of danger in *lā yurāmu khibāʾuhā*

38. Al-Anbārī, *Sharḥ al-Qaṣāʾid al-Sabʿ*, 48.

39. Turner, *Ritual Process*, 95.

40. See James Hall, *A History of Ideas and Images in Italian Art* (London: J. Murray, 1983), 181.

(none dares seek her tent—or ought to); the idea of play and diversion in *lahw* (pleasure, distraction); and finally in *ghayra muʿjalī* (unhurried) the poet's cavalier attitude toward danger and uninterest in hurrying along the road to manhood and maturity (responsibility). The metaphorical danger that was playfully suggested in the previous episode of Fāṭimah's lethal and heartbreaking tears and glances, becomes in this case a mortal one, for the girl's tent is surrounded by bloodthirsty guards and kinsmen (verse 24). The verb *tajāwaztu* (I stole past) means to exceed the bounds, to trespass, to transgress, to violate, and here the boundaries are not merely territorial but societal and moral. The preeminent liminal characteristic of being both in danger and dangerous is evident in these two verses.

In verse 25 a sense of dishabille and feminine unfolding is suggested in the likening of the arc of the Pleiades across the sky to the spread-out folds of a woman's gem-engrossed girdle. The time is thus propitious, as, in verse 26, the poet arrives at the virgin's tent to find that she is undressed for sleep, clad only in a loose sleeping gown. The lady seems to protest, as all ladies must, in verse 27, but at the same time she resigns herself, finding no way to dissuade her ardent suitor and no sign that the veil of his error is lifting. Once again, the use of *ghawāyah* (error, seduction) expresses deviation from the proper course. Having thus violated the sanctity of the women's quarters, the poet (28–29) leads his mistress out of the tribal enclosure, the train of her figured silk gown erasing their guilty tracks, to a trysting place in a hollow among the winding sand dunes. The unstable extrasocietal nature of the affair is thus conveyed by the locale, the shifting dunes outside the tribal enclosure.

Verse 30 opens an extended description of this "egg" of the curtained quarters. It begins with diction that suggests a relationship based on natural affinity rather than cultural sanction: her waist is hollow (*haḍīb*), that is, like a depressed hollow (*haḍb*), her ankle is plump (*rayyā*), a word used to describe a tender, well-watered green branch. She is further described in terms of feminine perfection: slender, fair-skinned, her collarbone like a polished mirror (31). There follow in verses 32 and 33 well-known motifs of the nasīb: the coquettish baring and covering of the cheek, the glance like that of the newly fawned doe at Wajrah, the long neck like that of the white antelope, except adorned with jewels. Thus to the floral similes of well-watered tenderness, purity, and fertility are added likenesses to the fecund fauna of the nasīb. The image of fructification and vegetable abundance continues in verses

34 to 36: her luxuriant hair, its locks and braids in lascivious disarray, is likened to bunches of dates, her waist to a slender bowstring, her lower leg, in an image recalling that of verse 30, to a papyrus reed, well-watered, tender.

The next few verses complete the description of the "egg" of the curtained quarters as the sort of pubescent beauty that stirs infatuation and erotic fantasy, not visions of connubial domesticity. She offers the seductive eroticism of Aphrodite, not the domesticity of Hera. Her bed is strewn with crumbs of musk, an expression of seduction and eroticism if we accept Detienne's interpretation of these elements in the Greek context[41] as applicable here, and she sleeps late into the forenoon, not rising or girding herself for work (verse 37). Her voluptuous indolence is further detailed in verse 38 in the description of her fingers, soft as the sandworms of Ẓaby, smooth and slender like the supple twigs of the *isḥil* tree, not calloused or roughened by work. In verse 39 her luminous complexion is compared to a monk's lamp illuminating the darkness, her sensual radiance to his radiant spirituality. So striking is the beauty of this girl who has reached full height but not full figure, captured here in the fleeting instant when the blossom has just barely bloomed and not yet begun to fade, that even the otherwise staid and forbearing pillars of mature manhood find themselves gazing with ardor (40). How then can our fickle and immature poet, already overly susceptible to adolescent fancies and infatuations, resist?!

The final description of the "egg" of the curtained quarters (verse 41) is richly polysemous, combining several semantic possibilities, all of which are metaphorical expressions for a single concept of feminine purity and sexuality/fertility. For *bikr* (virgin, first fruit), as the commentarists discuss at length, denotes equally the first-laid egg of an ostrich, an unbored pearl, and the blossom of the nenuphar (water lily).[42] The egg I have already discussed as a symbol of feminine purity and fertility; the unbored pearl is a traditional Arabic expression for a virgin, as is the lily, the unplucked blossom. In this regard we should note that the pearl and the lily, in medieval Christian iconography, are emblems of the Virgin Mary, that is, of combined female fertility and purity. Pictorially all three, as al-Anbārī points out, the egg, the pearl, and the lily, have in common the ideal hue of the feminine complexion,

41. Detienne, *Gardens of Adonis*, chap. 3.

42. Al-Zawzanī, *Sharḥ al-Muʿallaqāt al-Sabʿ*, 99–101; al-Anbārī, *Sharḥ al-Qaṣāʾid al-Sabʿ*, 70–72; al-Tibrīzī, *Sharḥ al-Qaṣāʾid al-ʿAshr*, 49–50.

which, in the Arab aesthetic canon, is white mixed with yellow.[43] In addition, all three are described as nurtured by limpid water, unmuddied by alighting travelers—muddied water being a traditional expression for sullied female virtue. Whether we select one denotation of *bikr* or accept all three, the connotations are such that the polysemy resolves into univocity: the unplucked blossom, the unbored pearl, the unhatched egg are all expressions of a delicate natural process of growth and development which should ultimately bear fruit and ought not to be untimely disturbed or interrupted.

The last two lines of the nasīb succinctly convey the poet's sense of his own arrested development. Whereas mature men are consoled or diverted from the foolish infatuations of their youth, the poet's heart remains bound to puerile passion (verse 42), antagonizing those who censure him and offer sound and sincere advice. In the *radd al-ʿajuz ʿalā al-ṣadr* (repetition of a word in the rhyme word) of verse 42—*tasallat* (be diverted, consoled) and *munsalī* (diverted, consoled)—the poet describes himself and his obsession tellingly. He does not say, from the mature, aggregate point of view, that his puerile passion for his mistress has diverted him from the pursuit of manhood and maturity; rather, in a curiously inverted expression,[44] he says that the pursuit of manhood has not diverted his heart or consoled him for his love for her. The societal goal has become for the poet a diversion and what society considers a diversion, the poet's goal.

The nasīb thus exhibits many of the characteristics of both the separation and liminal phases of the ritual paradigm, but it is nevertheless unusual in its lack of progression. It ends, as it began, with the poet disconsolate, still, it would seem, weeping over "the memory of one beloved" with no suggestion of departure or of resolve to depart. The air is rather one of stasis, even stagnation, and it is this mood or theme of arrested development that shapes the coming section, the description of the seemingly endless night (verses 44–48), followed by the description of the poet and the wolf (49–52). The night and wolf "scenes" are as close as Imruʾ al-Qays comes to a raḥīl section, for whereas both are adequately suited to our paradigmatic liminal phase, the explicit themes

43. Al-Anbārī, *Sharḥ al-Qaṣāʾid al-Sabʿ*, 70–72.

44. Al-Zawzanī remarks that some scholars claim that the expression in this verse is inverted (*qalb*). See al-Zawzanī, *Sharḥ al-Muʿallaqāt al-Sabʿ*, 105. The point here is that the inversion expresses the poet's distorted point of view. A literal rendering of the line would be something like: "The follies of men have been distracted / from their youth, / But my heart is not distracted from / its love for you."

or *topoi* of the traditional raḥīl, above all the she-camel, are lacking. They might be better understood as extensions of the nasīb, and the structure of the poem would then be binary, as are the blood-vengeance elegies of Muhalhil.

The night filled with cares (*humūm*) is a theme better known to us from the nasīb, or, in the context of the present argument, from the rithāʾ, especially that of blood vengeance, and it is of note that those poems, too, have no raḥīl, but rather an abrupt transition from adolescent, even effeminate, self-indulgence in tears to a manly resolve to avenge the slain kinsman. The care-filled night is first likened to an overwhelming, billowing sea (verse 44), but then, in an image suggestive of the poet's own delayed progress, the passing of the night is likened to the slow and ponderous rising of a bulky camel (45). The allusion behind the image is to a raḥīl very slow in getting under way. Verse 46, in which the poet calls upon the darkness to disperse and reveal the dawn of day, should remind us again of the night → day imagery of the poem of blood vengeance. But the poet here despairs, believing that day, when it breaks, will be no better for him. The plaintive lament of the verse is produced by the multiplications of the *l* and long *ā* sounds in the first hemistich: *a-lā ayyuhā al-laylu al-ṭawīlu a-lā injalī*, where *yā laylu al-ṭawīlu injali* would have carried the "meaning" in the limited sense. But the rest, far from being mere metrical filler (*ḥashw*), serves to give metrical weight and emotive force to the plaintive call (*nidāʾ*), an effect compounded by the rhymed hemistichs.

The night → day or lamenting → avenging dialectic or progression that we saw in Muhalhil, proceeds here at a much slower pace. The poet, desperate as he is for the temporal and psychological "night" to end, does not anticipate that the end of the temporal will effect the end of the psychological night. Meteorological darkness may disperse, but the poet's spiritual despondency will not. In any case, the darkness does not disperse, at least not yet. Moreover, in verses 47–48 the stars—time as measured by the rotation of the heavenly sphere or the nightly journey of the constellations—have come to a stop. The stars bound to the immovable and immutable Mount Yadhbul and the Pleiades stopped in midcourse, suspended by flaxen cords from immobile rock, present us once again with an image of arrested development, of a natural passage halted midway. The diction, too, is of interest. Mount Yadhbul is one of the *rawāsikh* (firmly rooted mountains), the foundations of the earth, as it were, and a byword for all that is fixed and immutable; *maṣām* (48) means the standing place of a horse, "stable" in both senses of the word, suggesting that the *noctis equi* are firmly tethered, not coursing through the firmament; but the verb *ṣāma/yaṣūmu* also means "to reach its midpoint," hence the stars are suspended in midcourse, and the rocks to which they are bound are termed *ṣumm* (obdurate, unchanging, mute), a term already familiar to us from the "mute immortals" (*ṣumman khawālida*) of Labīd. The image, like the words, has its "etymology" too, for the tightly twisted flaxen ropes that bind the stationary stars recall the *qaṭʿ al-waṣl* (severing of bonds) *topos* of the nasīb—the cutting of bonds and fraying of ropes—which expresses, in the present terms, the poet's separation from the affairs of youth and his setting out on his course toward manhood. The emphatic reiteration of unseverable ropes in this passage, then, indicates the opposite—excessive attachment to the affairs of youth, to the past, once more, arrested development.

The scene of the desert and the wolf (verses 49–52) should recall to the reader al-Shanfarā's treatment of the same theme. The imagery and diction are that of the ṣuʿlūk, the outcast, the passenger manqué: the desert crossing with no she-camel but only a shoulder submissive from much travel, the liminal waste, the wolf like an outcast, the images of hunger, privation, of a tilth that is barren. These are precisely the characteristics of the permanent liminal entity, the ṣuʿlūk, and should therefore have no place in the poem of completed passage, of ultimate aggregation. The reader will not then be surprised to read in al-Anbārī's commentary on verse 48: "One of the transmitters gives here four verses and mentions that they are from this qaṣīdah, but the rest of the transmitters disagree with him and claim that they are by Taʾabbaṭa Sharran."[45] The question to ask, however, is not so much whether the verses are authentically Imruʾ al-Qays's but why such archetypally ṣuʿlūk verses, regardless of their authorship, occur in *The Muʿallaqah of Imruʾ al-Qays*. Referring once again to Imruʾ al-Qays's akhbār, we note that in both the excesses of his youth and his obsession with extraordinary vengeance, which is wreaked against his own would-be or would-have-been subjects, he bears a striking resemblance to the ṣaʿālīk, as he does too in his ultimate demise. Al-Malik al-Ḍillīl (the errant/erring king) is, in terms of the rite of passage paradigm, precisely the passenger *ḍillīl*/manqué. In the context of the qaṣīdah itself, the passenger manqué of the wolf scene reiterates the immobilized or para-

45. Al-Anbārī, *Sharḥ al-Qaṣāʾid al-Sabʿ*, 80.

lyzed passenger of the night scene. It must then be this sense of Imru' al-Qays as not merely an ordinary initiate but a prodigal son, one almost lost in the liminal desert, whose return or aggregation is thus all the more dramatic and all the more valued, which explains the occurrence of these verses in the poem.

The two passages, read in light of my proposed paradigm, set up a contrary expectation: the passenger is lost, a permanent outcast at the liminal stage, as I read the wolf scene, or, as the night scene suggests, bound to the world of liminal night, or perhaps arrested at an even earlier stage, bound to all that is puerile, adolescent, and ultimately frivolous.

Before going further we must look again at verse 52. In terms of the rite of passage paradigm it reads as a closure to the liminal phase, the passenger is left a starving outcast likened first to the feral embodiment of antisociety, the wolf, and then to the tiller of a barren tilth. The second of these metaphors closes this section of the poem with an image and diction that cannot fail to suggest to us once more Gaster's seasonal pattern. The meaning is clearly metaphorical: the poet and wolf have been "sowing wild oats," or, in more biblical terms, "casting their seed in the wilderness" but the seasonal deep structure is stated explicitly and emphatically, first through the *jinās* (paronomasia) and *takrār* (repetition) of the root *ḥ-r-th* (to till, to sow) and finally in the rhyme word *yuhzalī* (is emaciated) from the same root as *mahāzilu* (unfruitful years—cf. the biblical "seven lean years"): *wa man yaḥtarith ḥarthī wa ḥarthaka yuhzalī* (verse 52). On the mythic level, the "barren tilth" is identical to the "wasteland" that Imru' al-Qays has inherited, the kingdom ravaged by regicide.

The endless night and barren waste suddenly, but from what we know from Muhalhil's poetry and Gaster's seasonal pattern, not unexpectedly, give way to dawn (verse 53) and the torrent (54) in the description of the poet's steed. The adolescent, antisocial, and unproductive liminal gives way to the productivity and maturity of aggregate manhood; the mortification and purgation of Gaster's kenosis (emptying) phase gives way to the invigoration and jubilation of the plerosis (filling) phase. By now it has become clear that the meaning of the qaṣīdah is borne more in the subtleties of metaphor and diction, of structure and pattern, than in the surface descriptive aspect of the poem. Adnan Haydar was the first to point out that what we are dealing with in the final two sections of the poem is not so much the description of the horse and the storm but rather an expression of "the tribe's regeneration" as evidenced in the "preponderance of cultural images."[46] The relation of the fakhr section to the preceding ones is analogous to the ephebe/hoplite antithesis formulated by Vidal-Naquet and, particularly in light of the amorous exploits of Imruʾ al-Qays's youth, the Adonis/Heracles antithesis noted by Marcel Detienne: "Adonis the seducer, who is attracted to the world of women and pleasure and attached to his mistresses by exaggerated bonds of a 'shameless passion,' is excluded from the world of war and of hunting. To the Greeks he is the perfect antithesis of a warrior hero such as Heracles."[47] Considering this remark in light of Vidal-Naquet's "law of symmetrical inversion," we can identify Adonis and Heracles not so much as two distinct types but as two distinct stages of development, ephebe/hoplite.

Inasmuch as the horse (*faras*), as I have established, is an embodiment of aggregate manhood, we can expect to find images of "nature civilized," that is, the taming of the wild to serve society, and the superiority of "culture" to "nature." In verse 53, *wa qad aghtadī* (I would ride forth early) signals aggregation, just as daybreak did in the poems of Muhalhil ibn Rabīʿah. The horse and hunter outdo nature by arising before the birds, nature's harbingers of dawn. The steed is described as *munjarid*, sleek and well-groomed, an aggregate characteristic already known to us from the description of the stripped (*jardāʾ*) palm tree of Labīd's *Muʿallaqah* (verse 66), a term antithetical to the liminal *ashʿath* (disheveled). We recall that it is not the object described that is the "subject" or bears the "meaning" of the qaṣīdah but rather its characteristics. In other words, in orally preserved poetry, abstract concepts—in this case "cultivation" or "domestication"—are expressed as physical attributes of concrete objects, so that whereas the object of attribution changes, from palm trunk to horse, for example, the attribute, which conveys ultimate meaning, remains the same. The steed bears the further epithet *qaydi al-awābidi* (a shackle for wild game), which likewise expresses the concept of cultural control or domination over nature. Verse 53 thus succinctly presents the first of the horse's functions and of the aggregate male's obligations: sustaining the tribe through the hunt. Verse 54 describes the other: defending the tribe in battle.

The tremendous skill and momentum of the battle steed is captured

46. Haydar, "Structure and Meaning," I: 255, II: 62; S. Stetkevych, "Structuralist Interpretations," 104–7.

47. Detienne, *Gardens of Adonis*, 67.

morphologically and acoustically in the justly famed first hemistich: *mikárrin mifárrin múqbilin múdbirin máʿan* (wheeling, charging, advancing, retreating all at once) through the pairs of intensive/reiterative *mifʿal* (*ism al-ālah* [noun of tool] used for habitual action) and *mufʿil* (form IV active participle) to create through assonance, alliteration, and the forward shift of the stress the effect of an accelerating gallop, precisely the sense of the visual image of the second hemistich. The boulder hurled down by the torrent (verse 54) and the raindrops slipping from hard rock (55) create images of male potency and fertility that serve as harbingers of the concluding storm scene, while underlining its semantic connection to the horse scene or, in terms of the seasonal pattern, identifying the "invigoration" of the horse and hunt (that is, of animal sacrifice) with the vegetable invigoration of rain, along with its suggestion of sexual potency.

The association of the horse/hunt revitalization with the seasonal pluvial invigoration of the land is apparent, too, in the diction of verse 57, where the steed at full gallop is described as *misaḥḥ* (pouring forth) (again the *mifʿal* form of verse 54) from the verb *saḥḥa* (to pour forth), as in *maṭar sāḥḥ* (pouring rain) and the use of the traditional epithet *sābiḥāt* (literally, swimmers) for horses, contrasted to the dry dust (*ghubār*). The metaphor or simile suggested by the etymology of the epithet *misaḥḥ* in Imruʾ al-Qays's poem is stated explicitly elsewhere, for example, in a verse by Quṭbah ibn Sayyār ibn Aznam:

From the strength of his gallop
  he stirred up a flood
As a rain shower pours forth [*saḥḥa*]
  from a storm cloud.[48] [48]

In verse 59 the steed is termed *darīr* (swift, streaming), and finally, verse 61 offers a second pluvial reading, for *ḍāfin* (full) also means "overflowing," and *aʿzal* (crooked) also means "a rainless cloud."[49]

Whatever the symbolic or mythic associations of the horse with the storm or water, what concerns is the function of this pluvial subtext in light of the ritual paradigms here employed. The insistence upon this

48. Anthony Ashley Bevan, ed., *Kitāb al-Naqāʾiḍ: Naqāʾiḍ Jarīr wa al-Farazdaq*, 3 vols. (Baghdad: Maktabat al-Muthannā, n.d.) [offset of Leiden: E. J. Brill, 1907], 2:586.

49. The association of the horse and water in this poem was first discussed in Haydar, "*Muʿallaqa of Imruʾ al-Qays*, I," 249. The predominance of water in the traditional Arabic epithets for the horse is discussed in J. Stetkevych, "Name and Epithet," 103–4.

association—in simile (verses 54, 55), in epithet (57, 59), in diction (61), and in the overall juxtaposition of the horse/hunt scene (53–70) to the concluding storm scene (71–82)—is unrelenting. I suggest that one function of this association in the context of a poetry that is oral and ritual is to ensure that the role of the horse, its sociomorphic function, within the qaṣīdah structure is not lost. The identification of the steed with water and rainfall identifies it with plerosis, fertility, and reinvigoration in terms of the seasonal paradigm and, in terms of the rite of passage paradigm, with the abundance and potency of aggregate manhood. The association of the steed with the mature manhood of aggregation as opposed to the immature youth (hoplite versus ephebe) is made explicit in verse 58: the slender youth cannot hold his seat, but when the full-grown and experienced man is mounted, the horse, despite his rider's weight, takes off at full gallop.

Complementing the images of rain and fertility are those of culture, the abundant and licit culture of the fakhr section, not the lost and illicit one of the nasīb or the privative anticulture of the raḥīl or, in this case, the night and wolf scenes. In verse 56 the steed's ebullience, in anticipation, as it were, of the success of the hunt (68), is likened to a boiling cauldron. Likewise, verse 59 describes the steed as *darīr* (streaming, swift), from a root especially associated with the abundant flow of milk, divine bounty, and pouring rain, and also with the whirling of a spindle. Here the whirling or spinning is that of a boy's *khudhrūf*, a stone on a string.

The superiority of culture to nature is implicit, too, in verse 60 in which the steed, the emblem of natural vigor subjugated to culture, subsumes the best qualities of gazelle, ostrich, wolf, and fox. The next two verses are particularly revealing of the ritual associations of the horse and hunt with sacrifice and redemption, with invigoration. In verse 62 the horse's rump is likened to a *madāk*, a stone with which (or on which),[50] a bride pounds perfume. Given the metaphorical association in Arabic poetry of perfume with female sexuality, this is an eminently phallic image, suggesting the identity of the invigoration of hunt and battle with that of marriage—that is, licit and procreative sexuality. The second simile, like a stone on which colocynth is pounded, suggests—especially in light of Haydar's discussion of the significance of colocynth in the nasīb as associated with bitterness, tears, and miscarriage[51]—death, sacrifice in the hunt or on the battlefield. The following image

50. See al-Anbārī, *Sharḥ al-Qaṣā'id al-Sab'*, 91.
51. Haydar, "*Mu'allaqa of Imru' al-Qays*, I," 239.

(63), in which the bloodstains on the hunting steed are likened to henna on an old man's hair, offers a more straightforward analogy: the simile on the surface is visual—white stained with red—but the intended similitude is that of the revitalizing effect of blood shed in the hunt to the rejuvenating effect of henna on hoary locks. It is this sacrificial association that renders the Islamic use of henna in accordance with the Sunnah of the Prophet a symbolic expression of the immortality conferred by Islam.[52]

Verses 64–68 express the invigoration and jubilation of the plerosis phase of Gaster's seasonal pattern through the hunt (64–67) and the ensuing cooking of meat for the feast (68). In terms of the passage paradigm the hunt and feast constitute the sacrifice that signals aggregation and the commensal meal that celebrates it. Again, cultural similes point to the ritual and structural role of this scene. In verse 64 the oryx cows are likened to virgins circumambulating a sacred stone. This simile alerts us first of all to the ritual perception of the hunt. As Robertson Smith demonstrated, in tribal societies all slaughter is sacrifice,[53] hence, every feast a commensal meal. The function of the hunt is therefore not merely alimentary but, above all, sociomorphic.[54] The hunter is, ipso facto, the aggregate male, sacrificing himself to serve the kin group and those under its protection; the partakers of the ensuing feast define the polity. The comparison (65) of the alternating black and white of the markings of the turning oryx herd to that of black and white beads on the neck of a boy with noble paternal and maternal uncles in the clan once more exploits a powerful visual image to express an abstract sociomorphic principle: the alternating male/female, maternal uncle/paternal uncle structure of the kinship system. In other words, each successful hunt and its following feast serve to reaffirm the tribal social structure. In the next two verses the distinctions of the social structure are mirrored, as it were, in the structure of the oryx herd: leaders/followers (66), male/female (67).

Furthermore, verses 64 and 68 in their virgins and roast meat offer an explicit contrast to the virgins and uncooked meat of the poet's earlier episode at Dārat Juljul (10–12).[55] If virgins playing with raw meat suggest premature sacrifice, that is, deviation from the prescribed

52. See S. Stetkevych, *Abū Tammām*, 190, 203–4.
53. Robertson Smith, *Religion of the Semites*, 281.
54. See Mary Douglas's remarks on the sacrificial ox as an image of the body politic in *Implicit Meanings*, 67–68.
55. Haydar, "Structure and Meaning, I," 242; S. Stetkevych, "Structuralist Analyses," 97–98.

ritual order, and immature, unconsummate sexuality, then surely the aggregate male hunt and consumption of cooked meat is likewise a sexual metaphor: that ritually sanctioned virgins are appropriate for sexual consumption as cooked (= cultivated) meat is for gastric. Illicit and immature sexuality is unproductive, and uncooked meat is unconsumable; licit mature sexuality reproduces the kin group just as cooked meat nourishes it. The metaphor of killing and sex, of gastric and sexual consumption, serves above all to emphasize the importance of the proper ritual progression for the perpetuation of the kin group.

Verses 69 and 70 seal the horse section with an image of the steed as an heraldic emblem of potent masculinity tamed to the service of tribal society. He is of dazzling beauty, but stands through the night in saddle and bridle, tethered by his master's tent, "not loose to graze."

Any discussion of the celebrated storm scene that forms the concluding section of Imru' al-Qays's *Muʿallaqah* must first address the question of why it occurs here in the first place, for the storm is not one of the common motifs of the fakhr-section of the classical qaṣīdah.[56] In the context of this particular qaṣīdah, however, and especially in light of the seasonal ritual pattern, we should have been at least subliminally prepared for the storm. In the kenosis/plerosis framework the wolf section concluded (verse 42) with an agrarian image—or at least diction—of drought, of wasteland, surely a "setup" for the coming downpour. Likewise, the pluvial subtext of the horse section (54, 55, 57, 59) prepares the way for an overt pluvial text. Moreover, the rite of passage paradigm proposes a reading of the storm scene in terms of mythic or ritual death and rebirth, pollution and purification already associated in the ancient Middle East with the flood and rain—thus revealing the ultimate identity of the seasonal and passage patterns—and the *prise du pouvoir*, accession to power, of the passenger/hero. Both ritual patterns, seasonal and passage, prepare us, too, for the metaphorical subtext of the storm scene: images of cultural regeneration, of reinvigoration and jubilation, of accession to manhood.

Ultimately, however, we have to attempt to place this scene within the larger qaṣīdah tradition, and it is perhaps here that the three parts of the akhbār of Imru' al-Qays can help to direct us. His prodigal and

56. Note, however, poem 5 in Imru' al-Qays's *dīwān* (attributed by some to Abū Du'ād al-Iyādī) which opens with a lightning and storm scene. See Imru' al-Qays, *Dīwān*, ed. Muḥammad Abū Faḍl Ibrāhīm, 3d ed. (Cairo: Dār al-Maʿārif: 1969), 72–73. Note too that ʿAbīd ibn al-Abraṣ, whose poetry as well as biography is associated with Imru' al-Qays's, is famous for his depictions of storms and rain. See Lyall, *Dīwān of ʿAbīd ibn al-Abraṣ*, 7, 9, and refs. 9 n. 3.

wayward youth finds an analogy in the extended erotic nasīb of his *Muʿallaqah*, but his quest to avenge the treacherous murder of his royal father, King al-Ḥujr, culminating in his bloody victory over the Banū Asad, and his demise through the intrigues of the Byzantine court are not mentioned. In light of the emphasis on the quest for blood vengeance that dominates his akhbār, it is curious, or suspicious, that there is no explicit reference to it in his most famous poem. On these grounds, I propose that the storm scene of *The Muʿallaqah of Imruʾ al-Qays* is a sublimated or metaphorical expression of the achievement of blood vengeance, that this is the root meaning from which this extended description and its particular imagery derive.

Before I analyze the verses themselves, let me posit a few considerations in support of this interpretation. First, the theme of the regicide of Ḥujr and Imruʾ al-Qays's quest for retribution dominates the akhbār and figures as well in several poems by ʿAbīd ibn al-Abraṣ and in a number of (mostly minor) poems in the *dīwān* of Imruʾ al-Qays.[57] Second, the standard poetic imagery of blood vengeance is that of thirsting and drinking: both the seekers of vengeance and the souls of the unavenged dead in the form of the owl that cries, *isqūnī* (Give me drink!) are described as thirsting. In the akhbār of Imruʾ al-Qays he and his men are "dying of thirst" and then take vengeance at a water hole. Conventionally, lances are described as "given to drink" the blood of vengeance; vultures drink the blood of the slain; and often concomitantly avengers drink wine. Related to these images and more precisely akin to Imruʾ al-Qays's storm scene are metaphors and similes that describe the battle as a rain storm. For example, ʿAlqamah in *Mufaḍḍaliyyah no. 119* describes the battle in which the Ghassanid al-Ḥārith ibn Jabalah defeated the Lakhmid Mundhir ibn Māʾ al-Samāʾ:

> As if there poured down upon them
>   a rain cloud
> Whose lightning bolts left the vultures
>   creeping on the ground.[58] [49]

57. Lyall provides a list of ʿAbīd ibn al-Abraṣ's poems wherein he boasts over the slaying of Ḥujr and taunts Imruʾ al-Qays, the would-be avenger. See refs. in Lyall, *Dīwān of ʿAbīd ibn al-Abraṣ*, 4, and Lyall's edition and translation of the texts. In the *Dīwān* of Imruʾ al-Qays, see no. 4, pp. 56–71, no. 11, pp. 97–100, no. 16, pp. 119–22, no. 21, pp. 134–35, no. 55, pp. 255–58, no. 58, pp. 251, no. 99, pp. 358–61. I am not addressing here the issue of the authenticity of these shorter poems attributed to Imruʾ al-Qays; my point is, rather, that they support my thesis that the murder and avenging of Ḥujr are dominant features of the poet's literary persona.

58. *Mufaḍḍaliyyah no. 119,* line 32, Lyall, *Al-Mufaḍḍalīyāt* 1:784. See also the discussion in S. Stetkevych, "Pre-Islamic Panegyric."

As I established in my reading of al-Fāriʿah bint Shaddād's marthiyah in Chapter 5, moreover, the "lightning-flashing cloud . . . pouring profuse rain" expresses in the elegiac tradition the taking of blood vengeance. Similarly, a short poem attributed to Imruʾ al-Qays on the regicide of Ḥujr opens:

Wakeful I spent the night
  for a thundering lightning bolt
Whose flash illumined
  the mountain's highest peak.[59] [50]

Within Imruʾ al-Qays's *Muʿallaqah* itself, it is suggestive in this respect that Mount Qaṭan, upon which the right flank of the downpour falls, is identified by al-Anbārī as a mountain in the territory of the Banū Asad.[60] Third, in both the ritual and thematic constructs of the qaṣīdah the storm scene occupies precisely the place where we would expect to find mimetic combat as an expression of invigoration followed by jubilation (the plerosis phase of Gaster's seasonal pattern), aggregation and accession to manhood and power (rite of passage), and the fakhr theme of defending the tribe (since the other dominant theme, providing for the tribe, has already been treated in the horse/hunt scene).

Thus, I read the storm scene in Imruʾ al-Qays's *Muʿallaqah*, in light of these observations, as a sublimation of or metaphor for the battle of blood vengeance. The effect of substituting the storm scene for the battle scene is to raise the level of poetic discourse from the heroic to the cosmic or mythic. In this we can perhaps detect a distinction between, on the one hand, the poetry of the *fursān al-ʿArab*, the knights of the Jāhiliyyah, such as Muhalhil ibn Rabīʿah and Durayd ibn al-Ṣimmah, and the *sādah*, lords or chieftains of tribes, such as Labīd, which operates on the tribal level and, on the other, the poetry by or for *mulūk*, kings or kinglets, which is elevated to the cosmic and soterial terms of ancient Near Eastern sacred kingship in which rites of sacrifice, combat, and sacred marriage guarantee the prosperity of the realm.[61] But Imruʾ al-Qays's discourse is sublimated beyond both the tribal fahkr and the royal, or courtly, panegyric. There is no mention of proper names of individuals, tribes, or kings. If I may speculate at this

59. Al-Iṣbahānī, *Kitāb al-Aghānī* 9:3208; Imruʾ al-Qays, *Dīwān*, no. 48, p. 261 (reading *ariqtu*).
60. Al-Anbārī, *Sharḥ al-Qaṣāʾid al-Sabʿ*, 102.
61. See S. Stetkevych, "Pre-Islamic Panegyric," passim.

point on the relation between the akhbār and the poem, it would appear to be precisely Imruʾ al-Qays's craving for vengeance exceeding what is acceptable by his kinsmen and their idol (Dhū al-Khalaṣah) which finds its poetic counterpart in the elevation of the qaṣīdah from the mortal to the mythic level.

Finally, however, our reading of the verses (71–82) themselves can alone convince us of their intent. A flash of lightning, suggesting, especially in the simile of the two hands shining, all the archetypal significations of Zeus's thunderbolt, heralds the storm (71). But the storm must also be read in close association with the elegiac conventions of its native tradition—the "lightning-flashing cloud" that for al-Fāriʿah signals the taking of vengeance. Spiritual illumination is added to meteorological in verse 72, in which the lightning flash is likened to the sudden flare of an anchorite's lamp after he has tilted it to soak the wick in oil. Here again the simile is on the surface a visual one, but its effect—and intent—is to alert us that the storm scene is meant to convey an abstract concept, that the poetic description of purification and revitalization of nature is to be understood in spiritual or symbolic, not literal, terms. The subtext of Imruʾ al-Qays's storm imagery is, as Haydar has established, "positive cultural symbols."[62] If the weaving of the south and north winds in the nasīb (2) constitutes the unraveling of the social fabric, then the textile imagery of the storm scene expresses its reweaving. This imagery must first be understood in terms of the traditional simile of the *istisqāʾ* (prayer for rain) of the nasīb, describing the herbage that shoots up after the spring rains as an embroidered cloth. In Imruʾ al-Qays's *Muʿallaqah*, then, the rains that are traditionally called down in the nasīb are, as it were, transferred to and intensified in the fakhr section. Textiles are first suggested in the etymology of the place-names Mount Sitār (veil) (74) and also in simile—the likening of Mount Thabīr to a chieftain clad in a striped cloak (78), of the ring of rubbish left by the torrent around Mount Mujaymir to the whorl of a spindle (79). Finally, taking the Yemeni's goods in verse 80, as al-Anbārī does, and as the imagery suggests, to be cloth, the image is that of the desert clothed in fresh herbage that has sprung up after the rain.[63] Thus, the savage desert is "clothed," nature is "civilized," and in terms of the rite of passage paradigm, the outcast socialized.

Along with the textile subtext, we find imagery of pollution and

62. Haydar, "Structure and Meaning, I," 254–55.
63. Al-Anbārī, *Sharḥ al-Qaṣāʾid al-Sabʿ*, 109.

purification, death and rebirth, which appears to convey the "mortification" of the older generation and concomitant *prise du pouvoir* of the younger. Recalling the use of the palm trunk as a male emblem in *The Muʿallaqah of Labīd*, the overturning of the lofty *kanahbal* trees "upon their beards" or "chins" (*adhqān*) (verse 75) and the uprooting of palm trees (77) suggests unmanning and military defeat, the overthrow of the older generation or vanquishing of the foe, as well as natural devastation. Purification is conveyed, too, in the image of the storm driving the mountain goats down from the heights (76) and the destruction of all edifices but those built of solid stone (77).

The poem is sealed with a couplet (verses 81–82) whose imagery subsumes all the levels of meaning I have discussed—death and rebirth, pollution and purification, the triumph of culture over nature—and at the same time elevates the whole to yet a higher level of sublimity. Verse 81 is, first of all, an image of nature civilized: the songbirds, emblems of sublimity and art, of poetry itself, are inebriated on man's most cultivated drink, peppered wine. Both spiced and fermented, the wine is, as it were, doubly "cooked." In the context of the Arabic qaṣīdah, however, we must inquire further, for however much its songbirds resemble Keats's skylark and share its pedigree, the Arabic tradition is not one of "profuse strains of unpremeditated art."

We must look for closer relatives within the Arabic tradition for similar associations of birds and wine. The only "blithe spirits" here are the stumbling vultures bloated with carrion, and the only wine that drunk by the avenger fresh from the kill. However improbable it may seem, these scavengers are the literary next of kin to Imruʾ al-Qays's inebriate songbirds. Moreover, the symbolic intent of the blood-drinking vultures of the poetry of blood vengeance—that of the revitalized soul, the ancestral spirits returned for the commensal feast and reincarnate with sacrificial flesh—and of the drinking of wine as an expression of achieving blood vengeance, aggregation, civilization, and even immortality, is confirmed by Imruʾ al-Qays's use here of a transmuted version of the same imagery. Let us recall, too, the association of the morning with the achievement of vengeance and drinking of wine. In other words, what Imruʾ al-Qays has achieved in the penultimate verse of his *Muʿallaqah* is an expression of blood vengeance sublimated into an image of sacrifice and redemption, of the soul purified and reborn to immortal life. Indeed, even the diction suggests the Qurʾānic imagery of the immortal garden, for Imruʾ al-Qays's *raḥīqin mufalfalī* (peppered wine) is quite close to the Qurʾānic *raḥīq makhtūm* (sealed wine)(Qurʾān 83:22).[64]

If verse 81 expresses salvation, then the closing line expresses perdition, the destruction of wild and savage nature, that aspect of the poet/passenger which has died in the ritual death and rebirth, that which is washed away and drowned in the ritual purification by water. Thus the corpses of the drowned wild beasts, symbols of man's baser nature, lie bloated on the edge of the floodwaters at nightfall and are likened to the plucked-out roots of wild onion (*anābīshu ʿunṣulī*). The first term derives from the verb *nabash*, which means to pull forth or draw out (as a leguminous plant), but also to disinter a corpse.[65] The second, which would appear to be related to the triliteral *aṣl* (root, origin), is said to mean wild onion (*baṣal barrī*), and thus, like the wild beasts, a symbol of what is savage and uncivilized as opposed to the tame and cultivated. The sense of perdition already apparent in the wild beasts' corpses, the oncoming darkness, and image of extirpation, takes on, too, in light of the idioms associated with *ʿunṣul*, a moral dimension. For *akhadha fī ṭarīqi al-ʿunṣuli* or *al-ʿunṣulayn* (take up the road of the wild onion, or two wild onions) means "to go astray," and *salaka ṭarīqa al-ʿunṣulayn* (travel the road of the two wild onions) means "to pursue that which is false, vain, futile."[66]

The greatness of *The Muʿallaqah of Imruʾ al-Qays* lies in the process of sublimation, most evident perhaps in the closing storm scene, which allows the qaṣīdah to transcend the specific to the mythic. The substitution, as it were, of the storm scene for the battle of blood vengeance that our *Formgefühl* for the qaṣīdah and our reading of the akhbār had led us to expect has the effect of elevating the poem from the tribal to the universal. A military triumph has given way to a poetic one.

The Damnation of Imruʾ al-Qays

The relation of Imruʾ al-Qays's *Muʿallaqah* to his akhbār is such as to undermine the working premise of this entire book. If his *Muʿallaqah*

64. See the discussion of these two lines in S. Stetkevych, "Intoxication and Immortality," 42–43.
65. Lane, *n-b-sh*.
66. Lane, *ʿ-n-ṣ-l*.

is a qaṣīdah that concludes with what is perhaps the most powerfully achieved image of spiritual rebirth, even immortality, in the classical Arabic poetic tradition, why do the akhbār of Imruʾ al-Qays conclude with such incontrovertible insignia of damnation and perdition—the abandoning of his ancestral coats of arms, the sloughing off of his skin, his death in exile unavenged, like Oedipus, the last of his royal line? The answers to this question are both literary-archetypal and more specifically Arab-Islamic. As for the first, Imruʾ al-Qays is more a tragic than a heroic figure. His tale is one of hubris, of pride and excess; he is akin to Oedipus or Achilles, not Odysseus. In this respect the storm scene, the elevation of the tribal obligation of blood vengeance to mythic proportions, is the appropriate expression of his obsessive exaggeration in avenging his royal father. It thus represents the moment of heroic glory before the tragic demise.

From the Islamic point of view, Imruʾ al-Qays embodies the *jahl* (impetuosity) that was for Islam the essence of the pagan past, the seed of its moral and political undoing, and hence embraces all in the Jāhiliyyah that was anti-Islamic. Imruʾ al-Qays is thus the counterpart or opposite of Labīd, who embodies the highest of Jāhilī virtues, *ḥilm*, forbearance, the opposite of *jahl*, and all that is proto-Islamic. For Islam is above all submission (*islām*), to God and to His Prophet, and if Labīd was willing to forswear poetry for Muḥammad's prophecy, one shudders to think, in light of Imruʾ al-Qays's reply to Dhū al-Khalaṣah, how he might have responded to the Prophet of Islam. In this regard, Imruʾ al-Qays's sobriquet al-Malik al-Ḍillīl (usually translated as "the wandering, or errant, king") both predicts and confirms the Islamic judgment of the poet. For although on the surface it derives from Imruʾ al-Qays's period of traveling from tribe to tribe and court to court in search of support for his vengeful venture, the verb *ḍalla*, of which *ḍillīl* is the intensive adjectival form, means to be lost, or go astray. On the mythic and archetypal level it thus connotes the disinherited "errant" monarch who has lost his patrimony and even, as the sloughing off of his skin suggests, his self and soul, who, dying in a Byzantine robe, has abandoned his Arab identity. On the specifically Arab-Islamic level, however, *al-ḍillīl* inevitably evokes *al-ḍāllīn* of the opening of the Qurʾān, Sūrat al-Fātiḥah, those who have strayed from the path of righteousness (*al-ṣirāṭ al-mustaqīm*) and have incurred God's wrath (Qurʾān 1:6–7). In this context the greatest of the Jāhilī poets is, above all, morally misguided, lacking the guiding light of Islam.

It was the very power of pre-Islamic poetry that prepared the Arabs culturally and linguistically for the literary miracle of the Qurʾān, but it was precisely that power, too, which, if it did not submit to Islam, would challenge it and therefore be condemned. It comes as no surprise, then, that the greatest of the Jāhilī poets was, ipso facto, also the "damnedest"—or, in the words of the Prophet Muḥammad, that Imruʾ al-Qays is "the leader of the poets into hellfire."[67]

67. Ibn Qutaybah, *Al-Shiʿr wa al-Shuʿarāʾ*, 51.

Appendix of Arabic Texts

[1] قَالَ لَبِيدُ بْنُ رَبِيعَةَ الْعَامِرِيُّ

١ عَفَتِ الدِّيَارُ مَحَلُّهَا فَمُقَامُهَا   بِمِنًى تَأَبَّدَ غَوْلُهَا فَرِجَامُهَا

٢ فَمَدَافِعُ الرَّيَّانِ عُرِّيَ رَسْمُهَا   خَلَقًا كَمَا ضَمِنَ الْوُحِيَّ سِلَامُهَا

٣ دِمَنٌ تَجَرَّمَ بَعْدَ عَهْدِ أَنِيسِهَا   حِجَجٌ خَلَوْنَ حَلَالُهَا وَحَرَامُهَا

٤ رُزِقَتْ مَرَابِيعَ النُّجُومِ وَصَابَهَا   وَدْقُ الرَّوَاعِدِ جَوْدُهَا فَرِهَامُهَا

٥ مِنْ كُلِّ سَارِيَةٍ وَغَادٍ مُدْجِنٍ   وَعَشِيَّةٍ مُتَجَاوِبٍ إِرْزَامُهَا

٦ فَعَلَا فُرُوعُ الْأَيْهُقَانِ وَأَطْفَلَتْ   بِالْجَلْهَتَيْنِ ظِبَاؤُهَا وَنَعَامُهَا

٧ وَالْعِينُ سَاكِنَةٌ عَلَى أَطْلَائِهَا   عُوذًا تَأَجَّلُ بِالْفَضَاءِ بِهَامُهَا

٨ وَجَلَا السُّيُولُ عَنِ الطُّلُولِ كَأَنَّهَا   زُبُرٌ تُجِدُّ مُتُونَهَا أَقْلَامُهَا

٩ أَوْ رَجْعُ وَاشِمَةٍ أُسِفَّ نَؤُورُهَا   كِفَفًا تَعَرَّضَ فَوْقَهُنَّ وِشَامُهَا

١٠ فَوَقَفْتُ أَسْأَلُهَا وَكَيْفَ سُؤَالُنَا   صُمًّا خَوَالِدَ مَا يَبِينُ كَلَامُهَا

١١ عَرِيَتْ وَكَانَ بِهَا الْجَمِيعُ فَأَبْكَرُوا   مِنْهَا وَغُودِرَ نُؤْيُهَا وَثُمَامُهَا

١٢ شَاقَتْكَ ظُعْنُ الْحَيِّ حِينَ تَحَمَّلُوا   فَتَكَنَّسُوا قُطُنًا تَصِرُّ خِيَامُهَا

١٣ مِنْ كُلِّ مَحْفُوفٍ يُظِلُّ عِصِيَّهُ   زَوْجٌ عَلَيْهِ كِلَّةٌ وَقِرَامُهَا

١٤ زُجَلاً كَأَنَّ نِعَاجَ تُوضِحَ فَوقَهَا   وَظِبَاءَ وَجْرَةَ عُطَّفًا آرَامُهَا

١٥ حُفِزَتْ وَزَايَلَهَا السَّرَابُ كَأَنَّهَا   أَجْزَاعُ بِيشَةَ أَثْلُهَا وَرِضَامُهَا

١٦ بَلْ مَا تَذَكَّرُ مِنْ نَوَارَ وَقَدْ نَأَتْ   وَتَقَطَّعَتْ أَسْبَابُهَا وَرِمَامُهَا

١٧ مُرِّيَّةٌ حَلَّتْ بِفَيْدَ وَجَاوَرَتْ   أَهْلَ الْحِجَازِ فَأَيْنَ مِنْكَ مَرَامُهَا

١٨ بِمَشَارِقِ الْجَبَلَيْنِ أَوْ بِمُحَجَّرٍ   فَتَضَمَّنَتْهَا فَرْدَةٌ فَرُخَامُهَا

١٩ فَصُوَائِقٌ إِنْ أَيْمَنَتْ فَمَظِنَّةٌ   فِيهَا وِحَافُ الْقَهْرِ أَوْ طِلْخَامُهَا

٢٠ فَاقْطَعْ لُبَانَةَ مَنْ تَعَرَّضَ وَصْلُهُ   وَلَخَيْرُ وَاصِلِ خُلَّةٍ صَرَّامُهَا

٢١ وَاحْبُ الْمُجَامِلَ بِالْجَزِيلِ وَصَرْمُهُ   بَاقٍ إِذَا ظَلَعَتْ وَزَاغَ قِوَامُهَا

٢٢ بِطَلِيحِ أَسْفَارٍ تَرَكْنَ بَقِيَّةً   مِنْهَا فَأَحْنَقَ صُلْبُهَا وَسَنَامُهَا

٢٣ وَإِذَا تَغَالَى لَحْمُهَا وَتَحَسَّرَتْ   وَتَقَطَّعَتْ بَعْدَ الْكَلَالِ خِدَامُهَا

٢٤ فَلَهَا هِبَابٌ فِي الزِّمَامِ كَأَنَّهَا   صَهْبَاءُ خَفَّ مَعَ الْجَنُوبِ جَهَامُهَا

٢٥ أَوْ مُلْمِعٌ وَسَقَتْ لِأَحْقَبَ لَاحَهُ   طَرْدُ الْفُحُولِ وَضَرْبُهَا وَكِدَامُهَا

٢٦ يَعْلُو بِهَا حَدَبَ الْإِكَامِ مُسَحَّجٌ   قَدْ رَابَهُ عِصْيَانُهَا وَوِحَامُهَا

٢٧ بِأَحِزَّةِ الثَّلَبُوتِ يَرْبَأُ فَوْقَهَا   قَفْرَ الْمَرَاقِبِ خَوْفُهَا آرَامُهَا

٢٨ حَتَّى إِذَا سَلَخَا جُمَادَى سِتَّةً   جَزْآ فَطَالَ صِيَامُهُ وَصِيَامُهَا

٢٩ رَجَعَا بِأَمْرِهِمَا إِلَى ذِي مِرَّةٍ   حَصِدٍ وَنُجْحُ صَرِيمَةٍ إِبْرَامُهَا

٣٠ وَرَمَى دَوَابِرَهَا السَّفَا وَتَهَيَّجَتْ   رِيحُ الْمَصَايِفِ سَوْمُهَا وَسَهَامُهَا

٣١ فَتَنَازَعَا سَبِطًا يَطِيرُ ظِلَالُهُ   كَدُخَانِ مُشْعَلَةٍ يُشَبُّ ضِرَامُهَا

٣٢ مَشْمُولَةٍ غُلِثَتْ بِنَابِتِ عَرْفَجٍ   كَدُخَانِ نَارٍ سَاطِعٍ أَسْنَامُهَا

٣٣ فَمَضَى وَقَدَّمَهَا وَكَانَتْ عَادَةً   مِنْهُ إِذَا هِيَ عَرَّدَتْ إِقْدَامُهَا

٣٤ فَتَوَسَّطَا عُرْضَ السَّرِيِّ وَصَدَّعَا   مَسْجُورَةً مُتَجَاوِرًا قُلاَّمُهَا
٣٥ مَحْفُوفَةً وَسْطَ الْيَرَاعِ يُظِلُّهَا   مِنْهُ مُصَرَّعُ غَابَةٍ وَقِيَامُهَا
٣٦ أَفَتِلْكَ أَمْ وَحْشِيَّةٌ مَسْبُوعَةٌ   خَذَلَتْ وَهَادِيَةُ الصِّوَارِ قِوَامُهَا
٣٧ خَنْسَاءُ ضَيَّعَتِ الْفَرِيرَ فَلَمْ يَرِمْ   عُرْضَ الشَّقَائِقِ طَوْفُهَا وَبُغَامُهَا
٣٨ لِمُعَفَّرٍ قَهْدٍ تَنَازَعَ شِلْوَهُ   غُبْسٌ كَوَاسِبُ لاَ يُمَنُّ طَعَامُهَا
٣٩ صَادَفْنَ مِنْهَا غِرَّةً فَأَصَبْنَهَا   إِنَّ الْمَنَايَا لاَ تَطِيشُ سِهَامُهَا
٤٠ بَاتَتْ وَأَسْبَلَ وَاكِفٌ مِنْ دِيمَةٍ   يُرْوِي الْخَمَائِلَ دَائِمًا تَسْجَامُهَا
٤١ يَعْلُو طَرِيقَةَ مَتْنِهَا مُتَوَاتِرٌ   فِي لَيْلَةٍ كَفَرَ النُّجُومَ غَمَامُهَا
٤٢ تَجْتَافُ أَصْلاً قَالِصًا مُتَنَبِّذًا   بِعُجُوبِ أَنْقَاءٍ يَمِيلُ هَيَامُهَا
٤٣ وَتُضِيءُ فِي وَجْهِ الظَّلاَمِ مُنِيرَةً   كَجُمَانَةِ الْبَحْرِيِّ سُلَّ نِظَامُهَا
٤٤ حَتَّى إِذَا ٱنْحَسَرَ الظَّلاَمُ وَأَسْفَرَتْ   بَكَرَتْ تَزِلُّ عَنِ الثَّرَى أَزْلاَمُهَا
٤٥ عَلِهَتْ تَرَدَّدُ فِي نِهَاءِ صُعَائِدٍ   سَبْعًا تُؤَامًا كَامِلاً أَيَّامُهَا
٤٦ حَتَّى إِذَا يَئِسَتْ وَأَسْحَقَ حَالِقٌ   لَمْ يُبْلِهِ إِرْضَاعُهَا وَفِطَامُهَا
٤٧ فَتَوَجَّسَتْ رِزَّ الْأَنِيسِ فَرَاعَهَا   عَنْ ظَهْرِ غَيْبٍ وَالْأَنِيسُ سَقَامُهَا
٤٨ فَغَدَتْ كِلاَ الْفَرْجَيْنِ تَحْسَبُ أَنَّهُ   مَوْلَى الْمَخَافَةِ خَلْفُهَا وَأَمَامُهَا
٤٩ حَتَّى إِذَا يَئِسَ الرُّمَاةُ وَأَرْسَلُوا   غُضْفًا دَوَاجِنَ قَافِلاً أَعْصَامُهَا
٥٠ فَلَحِقْنَ وَٱعْتَكَرَتْ لَهَا مَدَرِيَّةٌ   كَالسَّمْهَرِيَّةِ حَدُّهَا وَتَمَامُهَا
٥١ لِتَذُودَهُنَّ وَأَيْقَنَتْ إِنْ لَمْ تَذُدْ   أَنْ قَدْ أَحَمَّ مِنَ الْحُتُوفِ حِمَامُهَا
٥٢ فَتَقَصَّدَتْ مِنْهَا كَسَابِ فَضُرِّجَتْ   بِدَمٍ وَغُودِرَ فِي الْمَكَرِّ سُخَامُهَا
٥٣ فَبِتِلْكَ إِذْ رَقَصَ اللَّوَامِعُ بِالضُّحَا   وَٱجْتَابَ أَرْدِيَةَ السَّرَابِ إِكَامُهَا
٥٤ أَقْضِي اللُّبَابَةَ لاَ أُفَرِّطُ رِيبَةً   أَوْ أَنْ يَلُومَ بِحَاجَةٍ لُوَّامُهَا

٥٥ أَوَ لَمْ تَكُنْ تَدْرِي نَوَارُ بِأَنَّنِي   وَصَّالُ عَقْدِ حَبَائِلٍ جَذَّامُهَا
٥٦ تَرَّاكُ أَمْكِنَةٍ إِذَا لَمْ أَرْضَهَا   أَوْ يَعْتَلِقْ بَعْضَ النُّفُوسِ حِمَامُهَا
٥٧ بَلْ أَنْتِ لاَ تَدْرِينَ كَمْ مِنْ لَيْلَةٍ   طَلْقٍ لَذِيذٍ لَهْوُهَا وَنِدَامُهَا
٥٨ قَدْ بِتُّ سَامِرَهَا وَغَايَةِ تَاجِرٍ   وَافَيْتُ إِذْ رُفِعَتْ وَعَزَّ مُدَامُهَا
٥٩ أُغْلِي السِّبَاءَ بِكُلِّ أَدْكَنَ عَاتِقٍ   أَوْ جَوْنَةٍ قُدِحَتْ وَفُضَّ خِتَامُهَا
٦٠ وَصَبُوحِ صَافِيَةٍ وَجَذْبِ كَرِينَةٍ   بِمُوَتَّرٍ تَأْتَالُهُ إِبْهَامُهَا
٦١ بَادَرْتُ حَاجَتَهَا الدَّجَاجَ بِسُحْرَةٍ   لِأُعَلَّ مِنْهَا حِينَ هَبَّ نِيَامُهَا
٦٢ وَغَدَاةِ رِيحٍ قَدْ وَزَعْتُ وَقِرَّةٍ   قَدْ أَصْبَحَتْ بِيَدِ الشَّمَالِ زِمَامُهَا
٦٣ وَلَقَدْ حَمَيْتُ الْحَيَّ تَحْمِلُ شِكَّتِي   فُرُطٌ وِشَاحِي إِذْ غَدَوْتُ لِجَامُهَا
٦٤ فَعَلَوْتُ مُرْتَقَبًا عَلَى ذِي هَبْوَةٍ   حَرِجٍ إِلَى أَعْلاَمِهِنَّ قَتَامُهَا
٦٥ حَتَّى إِذَا أَلْقَتْ يَدًا فِي كَافِرٍ   وَأَجَنَّ عَوْرَاتِ الثُّغُورِ ظَلاَمُهَا
٦٦ أَسْهَلْتُ وَٱنْتَصَبَتْ كَجِذْعِ مُنِيفَةٍ   جَرْدَاءَ يَحْصَرُ دُونَهَا جُرَّامُهَا
٦٧ رَفَّعْتُهَا طَرْدَ النَّعَامِ وَشَلَّهُ   حَتَّى إِذَا سَخُنَتْ وَخَفَّ عِظَامُهَا
٦٨ قَلِقَتْ رِحَالَتُهَا وَأَسْبَلَ نَحْرُهَا   وَٱبْتَلَّ مِنْ زَبَدِ الْحَمِيمِ حِزَامُهَا
٦٩ تَرْقَى وَتَطْعُنُ فِي الْعِنَانِ وَتَنْتَحِي   وِرْدَ الْحَمَامَةِ إِذْ أَجَدَّ حَمَامُهَا
٧٠ وَكَثِيرَةٍ غُرَبَاؤُهَا مَجْهُولَةٍ   تُرْجَى نَوَافِلُهَا وَيُخْشَى ذَامُهَا
٧١ غُلْبٌ تَشَذَّرُ بِالذُّحُولِ كَأَنَّهَا   جِنُّ الْبَدِيِّ رَوَاسِيًا أَقْدَامُهَا
٧٢ أَنْكَرْتُ بَاطِلَهَا وَبُؤْتُ بِحَقِّهَا   عِنْدِي وَلَمْ يَفْخَرْ عَلَيَّ كِرَامُهَا
٧٣ وَجَزُورِ أَيْسَارٍ دَعَوْتُ لِحَتْفِهَا   بِمَغَالِقٍ مُتَشَابِهٍ أَجْسَامُهَا
٧٤ أَدْعُو بِهِنَّ لِعَاقِرٍ أَوْ مُطْفِلٍ   بُذِلَتْ لِجِيرَانِ الْجَمِيعِ لِحَامُهَا
٧٥ فَالضَّيْفُ وَالْجَارُ الْجَنِيبُ كَأَنَّمَا   هَبَطَا تَبَالَةَ مُخْصِبًا أَهْضَامُهَا

٧٦ تَأْوِي إِلَى الأَطْنَابِ كُلُّ رَذِيَّةٍ مِثْلِ الْبَلِيَّةِ قَالِصٍ أَهْدَامُهَا
٧٧ وَيُكَلِّلُونَ إِذَا الرِّيَاحُ تَنَاوَحَتْ خُلُجًا تُمَدُّ شَوَارِعًا أَيْتَامُهَا
٧٨ إِنَّا إِذَا الْتَقَتِ الْمَجَامِعُ لَمْ يَزَلْ مِنَّا لِزَازُ عَظِيمَةٍ جَشَّامُهَا
٧٩ وَمُقَسِّمٌ يُعْطِي الْعَشِيرَةَ حَقَّهَا وَمُغَذْمِرٌ لِحُقُوقِهَا هَضَّامُهَا
٨٠ فَضْلاً وَذُو كَرَمٍ يُعِينُ عَلَى النَّدَى سَمْحٌ كَسُوبُ رَغَائِبٍ غَنَّامُهَا
٨١ مِنْ مَعْشَرٍ سَنَّتْ لَهُمْ آبَاؤُهُمْ وَلِكُلِّ قَوْمٍ سُنَّةٌ وَإِمَامُهَا
٨٢ لاَ يَطْبَعُونَ وَلاَ يَبُورُ فَعَالُهُمْ إِذْ لاَ يَمِيلُ مَعَ الْهَوَى أَحْلاَمُهَا
٨٣ فَاقْنَعْ بِمَا قَسَمَ الْمَلِيكُ فَإِنَّمَا قَسَمَ الْخَلاَئِقَ بَيْنَنَا عَلاَّمُهَا
٨٤ وَإِذَا الأَمَانَةُ قُسِّمَتْ فِي مَعْشَرٍ أَوْفَى بِأَوْفَرِ حَظِّنَا قَسَّامُهَا
٨٥ فَبَنَى لَنَا بَيْتًا رَفِيعًا سَمْكُهُ فَسَمَا إِلَيْهِ كَهْلُهَا وَغُلاَمُهَا
٨٦ وَهُمُ السُّعَاةُ إِذَا الْعَشِيرَةُ أُفْظِعَتْ وَهُمُ فَوَارِسُهَا وَهُمْ حُكَّامُهَا
٨٧ وَهُمُ رَبِيعٌ لِلْمُجَاوِرِ فِيهِمُ وَالْمُرْمِلاَتِ إِذَا تَطَاوَلَ عَامُهَا
٨٨ وَهُمُ الْعَشِيرَةُ أَنْ يُبَطِّئَ حَاسِدٌ أَوْ أَنْ يَمِيلَ مَعَ الْعَدُوِّ لِئَامُهَا

[2] قَالَ لَبِيدُ بْنُ رَبِيعَةَ

١ بَلِينَا وَمَا تَبْلَى النُّجُومُ الطَّوَالِعُ وَتَبْقَى الْجِبَالُ بَعْدَنَا وَالْمَصَانِعُ
٤ وَمَا النَّاسُ إِلاَّ كَالدِّيَارِ وَأَهْلُهَا بِهَا يَوْمَ حَلُّوهَا وَغَدْوًا بَلاَقِعُ

[3] قَالَ الأَعْشَى بْنُ مَيْمُونٍ

٣٨ وَإِذَا غَاضَتْ رَفَعْنَا زِقَّنَا طَلَّقَ الأَوْدَاجِ فِيهَا فَانْسَفَحْ

[4] قَالَ لَبِيدُ بْنُ رَبِيعَةَ

١ أَكُلَّ يَوْمٍ هَامَتِي مُقَزَّعَهْ يَا رُبَّ هَيْجَا هِيَ خَيْرٌ مِنْ دَعَهْ

٢ نَحْنُ بَنِي أُمِّ الْبَنِينَ الْأَرْبَعَهْ   سُيُوفُ حَزٍّ وَجِفَانٌ مُتْرَعَهْ
٣ نَحْنُ خِيَارُ عَامِرِ بْنِ صَعْصَعَهْ   اَلضَّارِبُونَ الْهَامَ تَحْتَ الْخَيْضَعَهْ
٤ وَالْمُطْعِمُونَ الْجَفْنَةَ الْمُدَعْدَعَهْ   مَهْلاً أَبَيْتَ اللَّعْنَ لاَ تَأْكُلْ مَعَهْ
٥ إِنَّ ٱسْتَهُ مِنْ بَرَصٍ مُلَمَّعَهْ   وَإِنَّهُ يُدْخِلُ فِيهَا إِصْبَعَهْ
٦ يُدْخِلُهَا حَتَّى يُوَارِي أَشْجَعَهْ   كَأَنَّهُ يَطْلُبُ شَيْئًا ضَيَّعَهْ

[5] قال النُّعْمَانُ

١ شَرِّدْ بِرَحْلِكَ عَنِّي حَيْثُ شِئْتَ وَلاَ   تُكْثِرْ عَلَيَّ وَدَعْ عَنْكَ الْأَبَاطِيلاَ
٢ فَقَدْ ذُكِرْتَ بِشَيْءٍ لَسْتُ نَاسِيَهُ   مَا جَاوَرَتْ مِصْرُ أَرْضَ الشَّامِ وَالنِّيلاَ
٤ قَدْ قِيلَ ذَلِكَ إِنْ حَقًّا وَإِنْ كَذِبًا   فَمَا ٱعْتِذَارُكَ مِنْ قَوْلٍ إِذَا قِيلاَ

[6] قال لَبِيدُ بْنُ رَبِيعَةَ

* الْحَمْدُ لِلَّهِ إِذْ لَمْ يَأْتِنِي أَجَلِي   حَتَّى كَسَانِي مِنَ الإِسْلَامِ سِرْبَالاَ

[7] قال تَأَبَّطَ شَرًّا

١ إِنَّ بِالشِّعْبِ الَّذِي دُونَ سَلْعٍ   لَقَتِيلاً دَمُهُ مَا يُطَلُّ
٢ خَلَّفَ الْعِبْءَ عَلَيَّ وَوَلَّى   أَنَا بِالْعِبْءِ لَهُ مُسْتَقِلُّ
٣ وَوَرَاءَ الثَّأْرِ مِنِّي ٱبْنُ أُخْتٍ   مَصِعٌ عُقْدَتُهُ مَا تُحَلُّ
٤ مُطْرِقٌ يَرْشَحُ سَمًّا كَمَا أَطْـ   ـرَقَ أَفْعَى يَنْفِثُ السَّمَّ صِلُّ
٥ خَبَرٌ مَا نَابَنَا مُصْمَئِلٌّ   جَلَّ حَتَّى دَقَّ فِيهِ الْأَجَلُّ
٦ بَزَّنِي الدَّهْرُ وَكَانَ غَشُومًا   بِأَبِيٍّ جَارُهُ مَا يُذَلُّ
٧ شَامِسٌ فِي الْقُرِّ حَتَّى إِذَا مَا   ذَكَتِ الشِّعْرَى فَبَرْدٌ وَظِلُّ
٨ يَابِسُ الْجَنْبَيْنِ مِنْ غَيْرِ بُؤْسٍ   وَنَدَى الْكَفَّيْنِ شَهْمٌ مُدِلُّ

٩ ظَاعِنٌ بِالْحَزْمِ حَتَّى إِذَا مَا   حَلَّ حَلَّ الْحَزْمُ حَيْثُ يَحُلُّ

١٠ غَيْثُ مُزْنٍ غَامِرٌ حَيْثُ يُجْدِي   وَإِذَا يَسْطُو فَلَيْثٌ أَبَلُّ

١١ مُسْبِلٌ فِي الْحَيِّ أَحْوَى رِفَلٌّ   وَإِذَا يَغْزُو فَسِمْعٌ أَزَلُّ

١٢ وَلَهُ طَعْمَانِ أَرْيٌ وَشَرْيٌ   وَكِلاَ الطَّعْمَيْنِ قَدْ ذَاقَ كُلُّ

١٣ يَرْكَبُ الْهَوْلَ وَحِيداً وَلاَ يَصْـ   ـحَبُهُ إِلاَّ الْيَمَانِي الْأَفَلُّ

١٤ وَفُتُوٍّ هَجَّرُوا ثُمَّ أَسْرَوْا   لَيْلَهُمْ حَتَّى إِذَا ٱنْجَابَ حَلُّوا

١٥ كُلُّ مَاضٍ قَدْ تَرَدَّى بِمَاضٍ   كَسَنَى الْبَرْقِ إِذَا مَا يُسَلُّ

١٦ فَٱدَّرَكْنَا الثَّأْرَ مِنْهُمْ وَلَمَّا   يَنْجُ مِلْحَيَّيْنِ إِلاَّ الْأَقَلُّ

١٧ فَٱحْتَسَوْا أَنْفَاسَ نَوْمٍ فَلَمَّا   هَوَّمُوا رُعْتَهُمُ فَٱشْمَعَلُّوا

١٨ فَلَئِنْ فَلَّتْ هُذَيْلٌ شَبَاهُ   لَبِمَا كَانَ هُذَيْلاً يَفُلُّ

١٩ وَبِمَا أَبْرَكَهَا فِي مُنَاخٍ   جَعْجَعٍ يَنْقَبُ فِيهِ الْأَظَلُّ

٢٠ وَبِمَا صَبَّحَهَا فِي ذَرَاهَا   مِنْهُ بَعْدَ الْقَتْلِ نَهْبٌ وَشَلُّ

٢١ صَلِيَتْ مِنِّي هُذَيْلٌ بِخِرْقٍ   لاَ يَمَلُّ الشَّرَّ حَتَّى يَمَلُّوا

٢٢ يُنْهِلُ الصَّعْدَةَ حَتَّى إِذَا مَا   نَهِلَتْ كَانَ لَهَا مِنْهُ عَلُّ

٢٣ حَلَّتِ الْخَمْرُ وَكَانَتْ حَرَاماً   وَبِلأْيٍ مَا أَلَمَّتْ تَحِلُّ

٢٤ فَٱسْقِنِيهَا يَا سَوَادَ بنَ عَمْرٍو   إِنَّ جِسْمِي بَعْدَ خَالِي لَخَلُّ

٢٥ تَضْحَكُ الضَّبْعُ لِقَتْلَى هُذَيْلٍ   وَتَرَى الذِّئْبَ لَهَا يَسْتَهِلُّ

٢٦ وَعِتَاقُ الطَّيْرِ تَغْدُو بِطَاناً   تَتَخَطَّاهُمْ فَمَا تَسْتَقِلُّ

[8] قَالَ دُرَيْدُ بْنُ الصِّمَّةِ

٦ فَإِنَّا لَلَحْمُ السَّيْفِ غَيْرَ نَكِيرَةٍ   وَنُلْحِمُهُ حِيناً وَلَيْسَ بِذِي نُكْرِ

٧ يُغَارُ عَلَيْنَا وَاتِرِينَ فَيُشْتَفَى   بِنَا إِنْ أُصِبْنَا أَوْ نُغِيرُ عَلَى وِتْرِ
٨ قَسَمْنَا بِذَاكَ الدَّهْرَ شَطْرَيْنِ بَيْنَنَا   فَمَا يَنْقَضِي إِلاَّ وَنَحْنُ عَلَى شَطْرِ

[9] قال دُرَيْدُ بْنُ الصِّمَّةِ

١ تَأَبَّدَ مِنْ أَهْلِهِ مَعْشَرُ   فَجَوُّ سُوَيْقَةَ فَالْأَصْفَرُ
٢ فَجِزْعُ الْحُلَيْفِ إِلَى وَاسِطٍ   فَذَٰلِكَ مَبْدًى وَذَا مَحْضَرُ
٣ فَأَبْلِغْ سُلَيْمًا وَأَلْفَافَهَا   وَقَدْ يَعْطِفُ النَّسَبُ الْأَكْبَرُ
٤ بِأَنِّي ثَأَرْتُ بِإِخْوَانِكُمْ   وَكُنْتُ كَأَنِّي بِهِمْ مُخْفِرُ
٥ صَبَحْنَا فَزَارَةَ سُمْرَ الْقَنَا   فَمَهْلاً فَزَارَةُ لاَ تَضْجَرُوا
٦ وَأَبْلِغْ لَدَيْكَ بَنِي مَازِنٍ   فَكَيْفَ الْوَعِيدُ وَلَمْ تَقْرِرُوا
٧ فَإِنْ تَقْتُلُوا فِتْيَةً أُفْرِدُوا   أَصَابَهُمُ الْحَيْنُ أَوْ تَظْفَرُوا
٨ فَإِنَّ حِزَامًا لَدَى مَعْرَكٍ   وَإِخْوَتَهُ حَوْلَهُمْ أَنْسُرُ
٩ وَيَوْمَ يَزِيدِ بَنِي نَاشِبٍ   وَقَبْلُ يَزِيدُكُمُ الْأَكْبَرُ
١٠ أَثَرْنَا صَرِيخَ بَنِي نَاشِبٍ   وَرَهْطَ لَقِيطٍ فَلاَ تَفْخَرُوا
١١ تَجُرُّ الضِّبَاعُ بِأَوْصَالِهِمْ   وَيَلْقَحْنَ مِنْهُمْ وَلَمْ يُقْبَرُوا

[10] قال زَيْدُ بْنُ بِشْرٍ التَّغْلِبِيُّ

١ لاَ يَجُوزَنَّ أَرْضَنَا مُضَرِيٌّ   بِخَفِيرٍ وَلاَ بِغَيْرِ خَفِيرِ
٢ طَحَنَتْ تَغْلِبٌ هَوَازِنَ طَحْنًا   وَأَلَحَّتْ عَلَى بَنِي مَنْصُورِ
٣ يَوْمَ تَرْدِي الْكُمَاةُ حَوْلَ عُمَيرٍ   حَجَلاَنَ النُّسُورِ حَوْلَ جَزُورِ

[11] قال تَأَبَّطَ شَرًّا

١ وَقَالُوا لَهَا لاَ تَنْكِحِيهِ فَإِنَّهُ   لَأَوَّلُ نَصْلٍ أَنْ يُلاَقِيَ مَجْمَعَا

٢ فَلَمْ تَرَ مِنْ رَأْيٍ فَتِيلاً وَحَاذَرَتْ   تَأَيُّمَهَا مِنْ لاَبِسِ اللَّيْلِ أَرْوَعَا
٣ قَلِيلُ غِرَارِ النَّوْمِ أَكْبَرُ هَمِّهِ   دَمُ الثَّأْرِ أَوْ يَلْقَى كَمِيًّا مُقَنَّعَا
٤ قَلِيلُ آدِّخَارِ الزَّادِ إِلاَّ تَعِلَّةً   وَقَدْ نَشَزَ ٱلشُّرْسُوفُ وَٱلْتَصَقَ الْمِعَى
٥ يُنَاضِلُهُ كُلُّ يُشَجِّعُ نَفْسَهُ   وَمَا طِبُّهُ فِي طَرْقِهِ أَنْ يُشَجَّعَا
٦ يَبِيتُ بِمَغْنَى الْوَحْشِ حَتَّى أَلِفْنَهُ   وَيُصْبِحُ لاَ يَحْمِي لَهَا الدَّهْرَ مَرْتَعَا
٧ رَأَيْنَ فَتًى لاَ صَيْدُ وَحْشٍ يُهِمُّهُ   فَلَوْ صَافَحَتْ إِنْسًا لَصَافَحْنَهُ مَعَا
٨ وَلٰكِنَّ أَرْبَابَ الْمَخَاضِ يُشِفُّهُمْ   إِذَا ٱفْتَقَرُوهُ أَوْ رَأَوْهُ مُشَيَّعَا
٩ وَإِنِّي وَإِنْ عُمِّرْتُ أَعْلَمُ أَنَّنِي   سَأَلْقَى سِنَانَ الْمَوْتِ يُبْرِقُ أَصْلَعَا
١٠ عَلَى غِرَّةٍ أَوْ جَهْرَةٍ مِنْ مُكَاثِرٍ   أَطَالَ نِزَالَ الْمَوْتِ حَتَّى تَسَعْسَعَا
١١ فَكَيْفَ أَظُنُّ الْمَوْتَ فِي الْحَيِّ أَوْ أَرَى   أَلَذُّ وَأَكْرَى أَوْ أَمُوتَ مُقَنَّعَا
١٢ وَلَسْتُ أَبِيتُ الدَّهْرَ إِلاَّ عَلَى فَتًى   أُسَلِّبُهُ أَوْ أَذْعَرُ السِّرْبَ أَجْمَعَا
١٣ وَمَنْ يَضْرِبِ الأَبْطَالَ لاَ بُدَّ أَنَّهُ
سَيَلْقَى بِهِمْ مِنْ مَصْرَعِ الْمَوْتِ مَصْرَعَا

[12] قال تَأَبَّطَ شَرًّا

١ أَلاَ مَنْ مُبْلِغٌ فِتْيَانَ فَهْمٍ   بِمَا لاَقَيْتُ عِنْدَ رَحَى بِطَانِ
٢ بِأَنِّي قَدْ لَقِيتُ الْغُولَ تَهْوِي   بِسَهْبٍ كَالصَّحِيفَةِ صَحْصَحَانِ
٣ فَقُلْتُ لَهَا كِلاَنَا نِضْوُ أَيْنٍ   أَخُو سَفَرٍ فَخَلِّي لِي مَكَانِي
٤ فَشَدَّتْ شَدَّةً نَحْوِي فَأَهْوَى   لَهَا كَفِّي بِمَصْقُولٍ يَمَانِي
٥ فَأَضْرِبُهَا بِلاَ دَهَشٍ فَخَرَّتْ   صَرِيعًا لِلْيَدَيْنِ وَلِلْجِرَانِ
٦ فَقَالَتْ عُدْ فَقُلْتُ لَهَا رُوَيْدًا   مَكَانَكِ إِنَّنِي ثَبْتُ الْجَنَانِ

٧ فَلَمْ أَنفَكّ مُنْكِبًا عَلَيْهَا لِأَنْظُرَ مُصْبِحًا مَاذَا أَتَانِي
٨ إِذَا عَيْنَانِ فِي رَأْسٍ قَبِيحٍ كَرَأْسِ الْهِرّ مَشْقُوقِ اللّسَانِ
٩ وَسَاقَا مُخْدَجٍ وَسَرَاةُ كَلْبٍ وَثَوْبٌ مِنْ عَبَاءٍ أَوْ شِنَانِ

[13] قال تَأَبَّطَ شَرًّا

١ تَقُولُ سُلَيْمَى لِجَارَاتِهَا أَرَى ثَابِتًا يَفَنًا حَوْقَلاَ
٢ لَهَا الْوَيْلُ مَا وَجَدَتْ ثَابِتًا أَلَفّ الْيَدَيْنِ وَلاَ زُمَّلاَ
٣ وَلاَ رَعِشَ السَّاقِ عِنْدَ الْجِرَاءِ إِذَا بَادَرَ الْحَمْلَةُ الْهَيْضَلاَ
٤ يَفُوتُ الْجِيَادَ بِتَقْرِيبِهِ وَيَكْسُو هَوَادِيَهَا الْقَسْطَلاَ
٥ وَأَدْهَمَ قَدْ جُبْتُ جِلْبَابَهُ كَمَا ٱجْتَابَتِ الْكَاعِبُ الْخَيْعَلاَ
٦ إِلَى أَنْ حَدَا الصُّبْحُ أَثْنَاءَهُ وَمَزَّقَ جِلْبَابَهُ الْأَلْيَلاَ
٧ عَلَى شَيْمِ نَارٍ تَنَوَّرْتُهَا فَبِتُّ لَهَا مُدْبِرًا مُقْبِلاَ
٨ فَأَصْبَحْتُ وَالْغُولُ لِي جَارَةٌ فَيَا جَارَتَا أَنْتِ مَا أَهْوَلاَ
٩ وَطَالَبْتُهَا بُضْعَهَا فَٱلْتَوَتْ بِوَجْهٍ تَهَوَّلَ فَٱسْتَغْوَلاَ
١٠ فَقُلْتُ لَهَا يَا ٱنْظُرِي كَيْ تَرَيْ فَوَلَّتْ فَكُنْتُ لَهَا أَغْوَلاَ
١١ فَطَارَ بِقَحْفِ ٱبْنَةِ الْجِنّ ذُو سَفَاسِقَ قَدْ أَخْلَقَ الْمِحْمَلاَ
١٢ إِذَا كَلَّ أَمْهَيْتُهُ بِالصَّفَا فَحَدّ وَلَمْ أُرِهِ صَيْقَلاَ
١٣ عَظَاءَةَ قَفْرٍ لَهَا حُلَّتَا نِ مِنْ وَرَقِ الطَّلْحِ لَمْ تُغْزَلاَ
١٤ فَمَنْ سَالَ أَيْنَ ثَوَتْ جَارَتِي فَإِنَّ لَهَا بِاللِّوَى مَنْزِلاَ
١٥ وَكُنْتُ إِذَا مَا هَمَمْتُ ٱعْتَزَمْتُ وَأَحْرِ إِذَا قُلْتُ أَنْ أَفْعَلاَ

[14] قال تَأَبَّطَ شَرًّا

١ يَا عِيدُ مَا لَكَ مِنْ شَوْقٍ وَإِيرَاقِ   وَمَرِّ طَيْفٍ عَلَى الْأَهْوَالِ طَرَّاقِ
٢ يَسْرِي عَلَى الْأَيْنِ وَالْحَيَّاتِ مُحْتَفِيًا   نَفْسِي فِدَاؤُكَ مِنْ سَارٍ عَلَى سَاقِ
٣ إِنِّي إِذَا خُلَّةٌ ضَنَّتْ بِنَائِلِهَا   وَأَمْسَكَتْ بِضَعِيفِ الْوَصْلِ أَحْذَاقِ
٤ نَجَوْتُ مِنْهَا نَجَائِي مِنْ بَجِيلَةَ إِذْ   أَلْقَيْتُ لَيْلَةَ خَبْتِ الرَّهْطِ أَرْوَاقِي
٥ لَيْلَةَ صَاحُوا وَأَغْرَوْا بِي سِرَاعَهُمُ   بِالْعَيْكَتَيْنِ لَدَى مَعْدَى ٱبْنِ بَرَّاقِ
٦ كَأَنَّمَا حَثْحَثُوا حُصًّا قَوَادِمُهُ   أَوْ أُمَّ خِشْفٍ بِذِي شَثٍّ وَطُبَّاقِ
٧ لَا شَيْءَ أَسْرَعُ مِنِّي لَيْسَ ذَا عُذَرٍ   أَوْ ذَا جَنَاحٍ بِجَنْبِ الرَّيْدِ خَفَّاقِ
٨ حَتَّى نَجَوْتُ وَلَمَّا يَنْزِعُوا سَلَبِي   بِوَالِهٍ مِنْ قَبِيضِ الشَّدِّ غَيْدَاقِ
٩ وَلَا أَقُولُ إِذَا مَا خُلَّةٌ صَرَمَتْ   يَا وَيْحَ نَفْسِيَ مِنْ شَوْقٍ وَإِشْفَاقِ
١٠ لٰكِنَّمَا عَوَلِي إِنْ كُنْتُ ذَا عَوَلٍ   عَلَى بَصِيرٍ بِكَسْبِ الْحَمْدِ سَبَّاقِ
١١ سَبَّاقِ غَايَاتِ مَجْدٍ فِي عَشِيرَتِهِ   مُرَجِّعِ الصَّوْتِ هَدًّا بَيْنَ أَرْفَاقِ
١٢ عَارِي الظَّنَابِيبِ مُمْتَدٍّ نَوَاشِرُهُ   مِدْلَاجِ أَدْهَمَ وَاهِي الْمَاءِ غَسَّاقِ
١٣ حَمَّالِ أَلْوِيَةٍ شَهَّادِ أَنْدِيَةٍ   قَوَّالِ مُحْكَمَةٍ جَوَّابِ آفَاقِ
١٤ فَذَاكَ هَمِّي وَغَزْوِي أَسْتَغِيثُ بِهِ   إِذَا ٱسْتَغَثْتُ بِضَافِي الرَّأْسِ نَغَّاقِ
١٥ كَالْحِقْفِ حَدَّأَهُ النَّامُونَ قُلْتُ لَهُ   ذُو ثَلَّتَيْنِ وَذُو بَهْمٍ وَأَرْبَاقِ
١٦ وَقُلَّةٍ كَسِنَانِ الرُّمْحِ بَارِزَةٍ   ضَحْيَانَةٍ فِي شُهُورِ الصَّيْفِ مِحْرَاقِ
١٧ بَادَرْتُ قُنَّتَهَا صَحْبِي وَمَا كَسِلُوا   حَتَّى نَمَيْتُ إِلَيْهَا بَعْدَ إِشْرَاقِ
١٨ لَا شَيْءَ فِي رَيْدِهَا إِلَّا نَعَامَتُهَا   مِنْهَا هَزِيمٌ وَمِنْهَا قَائِمٌ بَاقِ
١٩ بِشَرْثَةٍ خَلَقٍ يُوقَى الْبَنَانُ بِهَا   شَدَدْتُ فِيهَا سَرِيحًا بَعْدَ إِطْرَاقِ

٢٠ بَلْ مَنْ لِعَذَّالَةٍ خَذَّالَةٍ أَشِبٍ   حَرَّقَ بِاللَّوْمِ جِلْدِي أَيَّ تَحْرَاقِ

٢١ يَقُولُ أَهْلَكْتَ مَالاً لَوْ قَنِعْتَ بِهِ   مِنْ ثَوْبِ صِدْقٍ وَمِنْ بَزٍّ وَأَعْلاَقِ

٢٢ عَاذِلَتِي إِنَّ بَعْضَ اللَّوْمِ مَعْنَفَةٌ   وَهَلْ مَتَاعٌ وَإِنْ أَبْقَيْتُهُ بَاقِ

٢٣ إِنِّي زَعِيمٌ لَئِنْ لَمْ تَتْرُكُوا عَذَلِي   أَنْ يَسْأَلَ الْحَيُّ عَنِّي أَهْلَ آفَاقِ

٢٤ أَنْ يَسْأَلَ الْقَوْمُ عَنِّي أَهْلَ مَعْرِفَةٍ   فَلاَ يُخَبِّرُهُمْ عَنْ ثَابِتٍ لاَقِ

٢٥ سَدِّدْ خِلاَلَكَ مِنْ مَالٍ تُجَمِّعُهُ   حَتَّى تُلاَقِي الَّذِي كُلُّ آمْرِئٍ لاَقِ

٢٦ لَتَقْرَعِنَّ عَلَيَّ السِّنَّ مِنْ نَدَمٍ   إِذَا تَذَكَّرْتَ يَوْمًا بَعْضَ أَخْلاَقِي

[15] قال الشَّنْفَرَى الأَزْدِيُّ

* قَتَلْتُ حَرَامًا مُهْدِيًا بِمُلَبَّدٍ
بِبَطْنِ مِنًى وَسْطَ الْحَجِيجِ الْمُصَوِّتِ

[16] قال الشَّنْفَرَى الأَزْدِيُّ

١ لاَ تَقْبُرُونِي إِنَّ قَبْرِي مُحَرَّمٌ   عَلَيْكُمْ وَلَكِنْ أَبْشِرِي أُمَّ عَامِرِ

٢ إِذَا آحْتَمَلُوا رَأْسِي وَفِي الرَّأْسِ أَكْثَرِي
وَغُودِرَ عِنْدَ الْمُلْتَقَى ثَمَّ سَائِرِي

٣ هُنَالِكَ لاَ أَرْجُو حَيَاةً تَسُرُّنِي   سَجِيسَ اللَّيَالِي مُبْسَلاً بِالْجَرَائِرِ

[17] قال الشَّنْفَرَى الأَزْدِيُّ

١ أَلاَ أُمُّ عَمْرٍو أَجْمَعَتْ فَآسْتَقَلَّتِ   وَمَا وَدَّعَتْ جِيرَانَهَا إِذْ تَوَلَّتِ

٢ وَقَدْ سَبَقَتْنَا أُمُّ عَمْرٍو بِأَمْرِهَا   وَكَانَتْ بِأَعْنَاقِ الْمَطِيِّ أَظَلَّتِ

٣ بِعَيْنَيَّ مَا أَمْسَتْ فَبَاتَتْ فَأَصْبَحَتْ   فَقَضَّتْ أُمُورًا فَآسْتَقَلَّتْ فَوَلَّتِ

٤ فَوَا كَبِدَا عَلَى أُمَيْمَةَ بَعْدَمَا   طَمِعْتُ فَهَبْهَا نِعْمَةَ الْعَيْشِ زَلَّتِ

٥ فَيَا جَارَتِي وَأَنْتِ غَيْرُ مُلِيمَةٍ   إِذَا ذُكِرَتْ وَلاَ بِذَاتِ تَقَلَّتِ

٦ لَقَدْ أَعْجَبَتْنِي لاَ سُقُوطًا قِنَاعُهَا   إِذَا مَا مَشَتْ وَلاَ بِذَاتِ تَلَفُّتِ

٧ تَبِيتُ بُعَيْدَ النَّوْمِ تُهْدِي غَبُوقَهَا   لِجَارَتِهَا إِذَا الْهَدِيَّةُ قَلَّتِ

٨ تَحُلُّ بِمَنْجَاةٍ مِنَ اللَّوْمِ بَيْتَهَا   إِذَا مَا بُيُوتٌ بِالْمَذَمَّةِ حُلَّتِ

٩ كَأَنَّ لَهَا فِي الْأَرْضِ نِسْيًا تَقُصُّهُ   عَلَى أَمِّهَا وَإِنْ تُكَلِّمْكَ تَبْلَتِ

١٠ أُمَيْمَةُ لاَ يُخْزِي نَثَاهَا حَلِيلَهَا   إِذَا ذُكِرَ ٱلنِّسْوَانُ عَفَّتْ وَجَلَّتِ

١١ إِذَا هُوَ أَمْسَى آبَ قُرَّةَ عَيْنِهِ   مَآبَ السَّعِيدِ لَمْ يَسَلْ أَيْنَ ظَلَّتِ

١٢ فَدَقَّتْ وَجَلَّتْ وَٱسْبَكَرَّتْ أُكْمِلَتْ   فَلَوْ جُنَّ إِنْسَانٌ مِنَ الْحُسْنِ جُنَّتِ

١٣ فَبِتْنَا كَأَنَّ الْبَيْتَ حُجِّرَ فَوْقَهَا   بِرَيْحَانَةٍ رِيحَتْ عِشَاءً وَطُلَّتِ

١٤ بِرَيْحَانَةٍ مِنْ بَطْنِ حَلْيَةَ نَوَّرَتْ   لَهَا أَرَجٌ مَا حَوْلَهَا غَيْرُ مُسْنِتِ

١٥ وَبَاضِعَةٍ حُمْرِ الْقِسِيِّ بَعَثْتُهَا   وَمَنْ يَغْزُ يَغْنَمْ مَرَّةً وَيُشَمَّتِ

١٦ خَرَجْنَا مِنَ الْوَادِي الَّذِي بَيْنَ مِشْعَلٍ
وَبَيْنَ الْجَبَا هَيْهَاتَ أَنْشَأْتُ سُرْبَتِي

١٧ أُمَشِّي عَلَى الْأَرْضِ الَّتِي لَنْ تَضُرَّنِي   لِأَنْكِيَ قَوْمًا أَوْ أُصَادِفَ حُمَّتِي

١٨ أُمَشِّي عَلَى أَيْنِ الْغَزَاةِ وَبُعْدِهَا   يُقَرِّبُنِي مِنْهَا رَوَاحِي وَغُدْوَتِي

١٩ وَأُمِّ عِيَالٍ قَدْ شَهِدْتُ تَقُوتُهُمْ   إِذَا أَطْعَمَتْهُمْ أَوْتَحَتْ وَأَقَلَّتِ

١٩-١ وَمَا إِنْ بِهَا ضَنٌّ بِمَا فِي وِعَائِهَا   وَلٰكِنَّهَا مِنْ خِيفَةِ الْجُوعِ أَبْقَتِ

٢٠ تَخَافُ عَلَيْنَا الْعَيْلَ إِنْ هِيَ أَكْثَرَتْ   وَنَحْنُ جِيَاعٌ أَيَّ آلٍ تَأَلَّتِ

٢١ مُصَعْلِكَةٌ لاَ يَقْصُرُ السِّتْرُ دُونَهَا   وَلاَ تُرْتَجَى لِلْبَيْتِ إِنْ لَمْ تُبَيِّتِ

٢٢ لَهَا وَفْضَةٌ فِيهَا ثَلاَثُونَ سَيْحَفًا   إِذَا آنَسَتْ أُولَى الْعَدِيِّ ٱقْشَعَرَّتِ

٢٣ وَتَأْتِي الْعَدِيَّ بَارِزًا نِصْفُ سَاقِهَا   تَجُولُ كَعَيْرِ الْعَانَةِ الْمُتَلَفِّتِ

٢٤ إِذَا فَزِعُوا طَارَتْ بِأَبْيَضَ صَارِمٍ   وَرَامَتْ بِمَا فِي جَفْرِهَا ثُمَّ سَلَّتِ

٢٥ حُسَامٍ كَلَوْنِ الْمِلْحِ صَافٍ حَدِيدُهُ   جُرَازٍ كَأَقْطَاعِ الْغَدِيرِ الْمُنَعَّتِ

٢٦ تَرَاهَا كَأَذْنَابِ الْحَسِيلِ صَوَادِرًا   وَقَدْ نَهِلَتْ مِنَ الدِّمَاءِ وَعَلَّتِ

٢٧ قَتَلْنَا قَتِيلاً مُهْدِيًا بِمُلَبِّدٍ   جِمَارَ مِنًى وَسْطَ الْحَجِيجِ الْمُصَوِّتِ

٢٨ جَزَيْنَا سَلاَمَانَ بْنَ مُفْرِجَ قَرْضَهَا   بِمَا قَدَّمَتْ أَيْدِيهِمُ وَأَزَلَّتِ

٢٩ وَهُنِّئَ بِي قَوْمٌ وَمَا إِنْ هَنَأْتُهُمْ   وَأَصْبَحْتُ فِي قَوْمٍ وَلَيْسُوا بِمَنْبِتِي

٣٠ شَفَيْنَا بِعَبْدِ اللهِ بَعْضَ غَلِيلِنَا   وَعَوْفٍ لَدَى الْمَعْدَى أَوَانَ ٱسْتَهَلَّتِ

٣١ إِذَا مَا أَتَتْنِي مِيتَتِي لَمْ أُبَالِهَا   وَلَمْ تُذْرِ خَالاَتِي الدُّمُوعَ وَعَمَّتِي

٣٢ أَلاَ لاَ تَعُدْنِي إِنْ تَشَكَّيْتُ خُلَّتِي   شَفَانِي بِأَعْلَى ذِي الْبُرَيْقَيْنِ عَدْوَتِي

٣٣ وَإِنِّي لَحُلْوٌ إِنْ أُرِيدَتْ حَلاَوَتِي   وَمُرٌّ إِذَا نَفْسُ الْعَزُوفِ ٱسْتَمَرَّتِ

٣٤ أَبِيٌّ لِمَا آبَى سَرِيعٌ مَبَاءَتِي   إِلَى كُلِّ نَفْسٍ تَنْتَحِي فِي مَسَرَّتِي

٣٤-أ وَلَوْ لَمْ أَرِمْ فِي أَهْلِ بَيْتِيَ قَاعِدًا   أَتَتْنِي إِذًا بَيْنَ الْعَمُودَيْنِ حُمَّتِي

[18] قَالَ الشَّنْفَرَى الْأَزْدِيُّ

١ أَقِيمُوا بَنِي أُمِّي صُدُورَ مَطِيِّكُمْ   فَإِنِّي إِلَى قَوْمٍ سِوَاكُمْ لَأَمْيَلُ

٢ فَقَدْ حُمَّتِ الْحَاجَاتُ وَاللَّيْلُ مُقْمِرٌ   وَشُدَّتْ لِطِيَّاتٍ مَطَايَا وَأَرْحُلُ

٣ وَفِي الْأَرْضِ مَنْأًى لِلْكَرِيمِ عَنِ الْأَذَى   وَفِيهَا لِمَنْ خَافَ الْقِلَى مُتَعَزَّلُ

٤ لَعَمْرُكَ مَا فِي الْأَرْضِ ضِيقٌ عَلَى ٱمْرِئٍ   سَرَى رَاغِبًا أَوْ رَاهِبًا وَهُوَ يَعْقِلُ

٥ وَلِي دُونَكُمْ أَهْلُونَ سِيدٌ عَمَلَّسٌ   وَأَرْقَطُ زُهْلُولٌ وَعَرْفَاءُ جَيْأَلُ

٦ هُمُ الْأَهْلُ لاَ مُسْتَوْدَعُ السِّرِّ ذَائِعٌ   لَدَيْهِمْ وَلاَ الْجَانِي بِمَا جَرَّ يُخْذَلُ

٧ وَكُلٌّ أَبِيٌّ بَاسِلٌ غَيْرَ أَنَّنِي   إِذَا عَرَضَتْ أُولَى الطَّرَائِدِ أَبْسَلُ

٨ وَإِنْ مُدَّتِ الْأَيْدِي إِلَى الزَّادِ لَمْ أَكُنْ   بِأَعْجَلِهِمْ إِذْ أَجْشَعُ الْقَوْمِ أَعْجَلُ
٩ وَمَا ذَاكَ إِلاَّ بَسْطَةٌ عَنْ تَفَضُّلٍ   عَلَيْهِمْ وَكَانَ الْأَفْضَلَ الْمُتَفَضِّلُ
١٠ وَإِنِّي كَفَانِي فَقْدَ مَنْ لَيْسَ   جَازِيًا بِحُسْنَى وَلاَ فِي قُرْبِهِ مُتَعَلَّلُ
١١ ثَلاَثَةُ أَصْحَابٍ فُؤَادٌ مُشَيَّعٌ   وَأَبْيَضُ إِصْلِيتٌ وَصَفْرَاءُ عَيْطَلُ
١٢ هَتُوفٌ مِنَ الْمُلْسِ الْمُتُونِ يَزِينُهَا   رَصَائِعُ قَدْ نِيطَتْ إِلَيْهَا وَمِحْمَلُ
١٣ إِذَا زَلَّ عَنْهَا السَّهْمُ حَنَّتْ كَأَنَّهَا   مُرَزَّأَةٌ عَجْلَى تَرِنُّ وَتُعْوِلُ
١٤ وَلَسْتُ بِمِهْيَافٍ يُعَشِّي سَوَامَهُ   مُجَدَّعَةً سُقْبَانُهَا وَهْيَ بُهَّلُ
١٥ وَلاَ جُبَّاءٍ أَكْهَى مُرِبٍّ بِعِرْسِهِ   يُطَالِعُهَا فِي شَأْنِهِ كَيْفَ يَفْعَلُ
١٦ وَلاَ خَرِقٍ هَيْقٍ كَأَنَّ فُؤَادَهُ   يَظَلُّ بِهِ الْمُكَّاءُ يَعْلُو وَيَسْفُلُ
١٧ وَلاَ خَالِفٍ دَارِيَّةٍ مُتَغَزِّلٍ   يَرُوحُ وَيَغْدُو دَاهِنًا يَتَكَحَّلُ
١٨ وَلَسْتُ بِعَلٍّ شَرُّهُ دُونَ خَيْرِهِ   أَلَفَّ إِذَا مَا رُعْتَهُ اهْتَاجَ أَعْزَلُ
١٩ وَلَسْتُ بِمِحْيَارِ الظَّلاَمِ إِذَا انْتَحَتْ
هُدَى الْهَوْجَلِ الْعِسِّيفِ يَهْمَاءُ هَوْجَلُ
٢٠ إِذَا الْأَمْعَزُ الصَّوَّانُ لاَقَى مَنَاسِمِي   تَطَايَرَ مِنْهُ قَادِحٌ وَمُفَلَّلُ
٢١ أُدِيمُ مِطَالَ الْجُوعِ حَتَّى أُمِيتَهُ   وَأَضْرِبُ عَنْهُ الذِّكْرَ صَفْحًا فَأُذْهَلُ
٢٢ وَأَسْتَفُّ تُرْبَ الْأَرْضِ كَيْلاَ يَرَى لَهُ   عَلَيَّ مِنَ الطَّوْلِ امْرُؤٌ مُتَطَوِّلُ
٢٣ وَلَوْلاَ اجْتِنَابُ الذَّأْمِ لَمْ يُلْفَ مَشْرَبٌ   يُعَاشُ بِهِ إِلاَّ لَدَيَّ وَمَأْكَلُ
٢٤ وَلٰكِنَّ نَفْسًا مُرَّةً لاَ تُقِيمُ بِي   عَلَى الذَّأْمِ إِلاَّ رَيْثَمَا أَتَحَوَّلُ
٢٥ وَأَطْوِي عَلَى الْخَمْصِ الْحَوَايَا كَمَا انْطَوَتْ
خُيُوطَةُ مَارِيٍّ تُغَارُ وَتُفْتَلُ
٢٦ وَأَغْدُو عَلَى الْقُوتِ الزَّهِيدِ كَمَا غَدَا   أَزَلُّ تَهَادَاهُ التَّنَائِفُ أَطْحَلُ

٢٧ غَدَا طَاوِيًا يُعَارِضُ الرِّيحَ هَافِيًا ... يَخُوتُ بِأَذْنَابِ الشِّعَابِ وَيَعْسِلُ

٢٨ فَلَمَّا لَوَاهُ القُوتُ مِنْ حَيْثُ أَمَّهُ ... دَعَا فَأَجَابَتْهُ نَظَائِرُ نُحَّلُ

٢٩ مُهَلْهَلَةٌ شِيبُ الوُجُوهِ كَأَنَّهَا ... قِدَاحٌ بِكَفَّيْ يَاسِرٍ تَتَقَلْقَلُ

٣٠ أَوِ الخَشْرَمُ المَبْعُوثُ حَثْحَثَ دَبْرَهُ ... مَحَا بِيضُ أَرْدَاهُنَّ سَامٍ مُعَسِّلُ

٣١ مُهَرَّتَةٌ فُوهٌ كَأَنَّ شُدُوقَهَا ... شُقُوقُ العِصِيِّ كَالِحَاتٌ وَبُسَّلُ

٣٢ فَضَجَّ وَضَجَّتْ بِالبَرَاحِ كَأَنَّهَا ... وَإِيَّاهُ نُوحٌ فَوْقَ عَلْيَاءَ ثُكَّلُ

٣٣ وَأَغْضَى وَأَغْضَتْ وَاتَّسَى وَاتَّسَتْ بِهِ ... مَرَامِيلُ عَزَّاهَا وَعَزَّتْهُ مُرْمِلُ

٣٤ شَكَا وَشَكَتْ ثُمَّ ارْعَوَى بَعْدُ وَارْعَوَتْ

وَلَلصَّبْرُ إِنْ لَمْ يَنْفَعِ الشَّكْوُ أَجْمَلُ

٣٥ وَفَاءَ وَفَاءَتْ بَادِرَاتٍ وَكُلُّهَا ... عَلَى نَكَظٍ مِمَّا يُكَاتِمُ مُجْمِلُ

٣٦ وَتَشْرَبُ أَسْآرِي القَطَا الكُدْرُ بَعْدَمَا ... سَرَتْ قَرَبًا أَحْنَاؤُهَا تَتَصَلْصَلُ

٣٧ هَمَمْتُ وَهَمَّتْ وَابْتَدَرْنَا وَأَسْدَلَتْ ... وَشَمَّرَ مِنِّي فَارِطٌ مُتَمَهِّلُ

٣٨ فَوَلَّيْتُ عَنْهَا وَهْيَ تَكْبُو لِعَقْرِهِ ... يُبَاشِرُهُ مِنْهَا ذُقُونٌ وَحَوْصَلُ

٣٩ كَأَنَّ وَغَاهَا حَجْرَتَيْهِ وَحَوْلَهُ ... أَضَامِيمُ مِنْ سَفْرِ القَبَائِلِ نُزَّلُ

٤٠ تَوَافَيْنَ مِنْ شَتَّى إِلَيْهِ فَضَمَّهَا ... كَمَا ضَمَّ أَذْوَادَ الأَصَارِيمِ مَنْهَلُ

٤١ فَعَبَّتْ غِشَاشًا ثُمَّ مَرَّتْ كَأَنَّهَا ... مَعَ الصُّبْحِ رَكْبٌ مِنْ أُحَاظَةَ مُجْفِلُ

٤٢ وَآلَفُ وَجْهَ الأَرْضِ عِنْدَ افْتِرَاشِهَا ... بِأَهْدَأَ تُنْبِيهِ سَنَاسِنُ قُحَّلُ

٤٣ وَأَعْدِلُ مَنْحُوضًا كَأَنَّ فُصُوصَهُ ... كِعَابٌ دَحَاهَا لَاعِبٌ فَهْيَ مُثَّلُ

٤٤ فَإِنْ تَبْتَئِسْ بِالشَّنْفَرَى أُمُّ قَسْطَلِ ... لَمَا اغْتَبَطَتْ بِالشَّنْفَرَى قَبْلُ أَطْوَلُ

٤٥ طَرِيدُ جِنَايَاتٍ تَيَاسَرْنَ لَحْمَهُ ... عَقِيرَتُهُ لِأَيِّهَا حُمَّ أَوَّلُ

٤٦ تَنَامُ إِذَا مَا نَامَ يَقْظَى عُيُونُهَا ... حِثَاثًا إِلَى مَكْرُوهِهِ تَتَغَلْغَلُ

٤٧ وَإِلْفُ هُمُومٍ مَا تَزَالُ تَعُودُهُ   عِيَادًا كَحُمَّى الرِّبْعِ أَوْهِيَ أَثْقَلُ
٤٨ إِذَا وَرَدَتْ أَصْدَرْتُهَا ثُمَّ إِنَّهَا   تَثُوبُ فَتَأْتِي مِنْ تُحَيْتُ وَمِنْ عَلُ
٤٩ فَإِمَّا تَرَيْنِي كَٱبْنَةِ الرَّمْلِ ضَاحِيًا   عَلَى رِقَّةٍ أَحْفَى وَلاَ أَتَنَعَّلُ
٥٠ فَإِنِّي لَمَوْلَى الصَّبْرِ أَجْتَابُ بَزَّهُ   عَلَى مِثْلِ قَلْبِ السِّمْعِ وَالْحَزْمَ أَنْعَلُ
٥١ وَأُعْدِمُ أَحْيَانًا وَأَغْنَى وَإِنَّمَا   يَنَالُ الْغِنَى ذُو الْبُعْدَةِ الْمُتَبَذِّلُ
٥٢ فَلاَ جَزِعٌ مِنْ خَلَّةٍ مُتَكَشِّفٌ   وَلاَ مَرِحٌ تَحْتَ الْغِنَى أَتَخَيَّلُ
٥٣ وَلاَ تَزْدَهِي ٱلْأَجْهَالُ حِلْمِي وَلاَ أُرَى   سَؤُولاً بِأَعْقَابِ ٱلْأَقَاوِيلِ أُنْمِلُ
٥٤ وَلَيْلَةِ نَحْسٍ يَصْطَلِي الْقَوْسَ رَبُّهَا   وَأَقْطُعَهُ اللاَّتِي بِهَا يَتَنَبَّلُ
٥٥ دَعَسْتُ عَلَى غَطْشٍ وَبَغْشٍ وَصُحْبَتِي
سُعَارٌ وَإِرْزِيزٌ وَوَجْرٌ وَأَفْكَلُ
٥٦ فَأَيَّمْتُ نِسْوَانًا وَأَيْتَمْتُ إِلْدَةً   وَعُدْتُ كَمَا أَبْدَأْتُ وَاللَّيْلُ أَلْيَلُ
٥٧ وَأَصْبَحَ عَنِّي بِالْغُمَيْصَاءِ جَالِسًا   فَرِيقَانِ مَسْؤُولٌ وَآخَرُ يَسْأَلُ
٥٨ فَقَالُوا لَقَدْ هَرَّتْ بِلَيْلٍ كِلاَبُنَا   فَقُلْنَا أَذِئْبٌ عَسَّ أَمْ عَسَّ فُرْعُلُ
٥٩ فَلَمْ تَكُ إِلاَّ نَبْأَةٌ ثُمَّ هَوَّمَتْ   فَقُلْنَا قَطَاةٌ رِيعَ أَمْ رِيعَ أَجْدَلُ
٦٠ فَإِنْ يَكُ مِنْ جِنٍّ لَأَبْرَحُ طَارِقًا   وَإِنْ يَكُ إِنْسًا مَا كَهَا ٱلْإِنْسُ تَفْعَلُ
٦١ وَيَوْمٍ مِنَ الشِّعْرَى يَذُوبُ لُوَابُهُ   أَفَاعِيهِ فِي رَمْضَائِهِ تَتَمَلْمَلُ
٦٢ نَصَبْتُ لَهُ وَجْهِي وَلاَ كِنَّ دُونَهُ   وَلاَ سِتْرَ إِلاَّ ٱلْأَتْحَمِيُّ الْمُرَعْبَلُ
٦٣ وَضَافٍ إِذَا هَبَّتْ لَهُ الرِّيحُ طَيَّرَتْ   لَبَائِدَ عَنْ أَعْطَافِهِ مَا تُرَجَّلُ
٦٤ بَعِيدٌ بِمَسِّ الدُّهْنِ وَالْفَلْيِ عَهْدُهُ   لَهُ عَبَسٌ عَافٍ مِنَ الْغِسْلِ مُحْوِلُ
٦٥ وَخَرْقٍ كَظَهْرِ التُّرْسِ قَفْرٍ قَطَعْتُهُ   بِعَامِلَتَيْنِ ظَهْرُهُ لَيْسَ يُعْمَلُ
٦٦ وَأَلْحَقْتُ أُولاَهُ بِأُخْرَاهُ مُوفِيًا   عَلَى قُنَّةٍ أُقْعِي مِرَارًا وَأَمْثُلُ

٦٧ تَرُودُ الْأَرَاوِي الصُّحْمُ حَوْلِي كَأَنَّهَا عَذَارَى عَلَيْهِنَّ الْمُلَاءُ الْمُذَيَّلُ
٦٨ وَيَرْكُدْنَ بِالْآصَالِ حَوْلِي كَأَنَّنِي
مِنَ الْعُصْمِ أَدْفَى يَنْتَحِي الْكِيحَ أَعْقَلُ

[19] قالت الْخِرْنِقُ بنتُ بَدْرِ بْنِ هِفَّانَ

١ لاَ يَبْعَدَنْ قَوْمِي الَّذِينَ هُمُ سُمُّ الْعُدَاةِ وَآفَةُ الْجُزْرِ
٢ اَلنَّازِلُونَ بِكُلِّ مُعْتَرَكٍ وَالطَّيِّبُونَ مَعَاقِدَ الْأُزْرِ
٣ اَلضَّارِبُونَ بِحَوْمَةٍ نَزَلَتْ وَالطَّاعِنُونَ بِأَذْرُعٍ شُعْرِ
٤ وَالْخَالِطُونَ لُجَيْنَهُمْ بِنُضَارِهِمْ وَذَوِي الْغِنَى مِنْهُمْ بِذِي الْفَقْرِ
٥ إِنْ يَشْرَبُوا يَهَبُوا وَإِنْ يَذَرُوا يَتَوَاعَظُوا عَنْ مَنْطِقِ الْهُجْرِ
٦ قَوْمٌ إِذَا رَكِبُوا سَمِعْتَ لَهُمْ لَغْطًا مِنَ التَّأْيِيهِ وَالزَّجْرِ
٧ مِنْ غَيْرِ مَا فُحْشٍ يَكُونُ بِهِمْ فِي مُنْتَجِ الْمُهُرَاتِ وَالْمُهْرِ
٨ [لَاقَوْا غَدَاةَ قُلَابَ حَتْفَهُمُ سَوْقَ الْعَتِيرِ يُسَاقُ لِلْعَتْرِ]
٩ هٰذَا ثَنَائِي مَا بَقِيتُ لَهُمْ فَإِذَا هَلَكْتُ أَجَنَّنِي قَبْرِي

[20] قال زُهَيْرُ بْنُ أَبِي سُلْمَى

١ يَقُولُونَ حِصْنٌ ثُمَّ تَأْبَى نُفُوسُهُمْ وَكَيْفَ بِحِصْنٍ وَالْجِبَالُ جُنُوحُ
٢ وَلَمْ تَلْفِظِ الْمَوْتَى الْقُبُورُ وَلَمْ تَزُلْ نُجُومُ السَّمَاءِ وَالْأَدِيمُ صَحِيحُ

[21] قال الحَادِرَةُ

* فَأَثْنُوا عَلَيْنَا لاَ أَبَا لِأَبِيكُمُ بِأَفْعَالِنَا إِنَّ الثَّنَاءَ هُوَ الْخُلْدُ

[22] قال الشَّاعِرُ

* فَإِنْ تَكُ أَفْنَتْهُ اللَّيَالِي فَأَوْشَكَتْ فَإِنَّ لَهُ ذِكْرًا سَيُفْنِي اللَّيَالِيَا

[23] قَالَ الْمُتَنَبِّي

* ذِكْرُ الْفَتَى عُمْرُهُ الثَّانِي وَحَاجَتُهُ   مَا قَاتَهُ وَفُضُولُ الْعَيْشِ أَشْغَالُ

[24] قَالَ مَالِكُ بْنُ الرَّيْبِ الْمَازِنِيُّ

* يَقُولُونَ لاَ تَبْعَدْ وَهُمْ يَدْفِنُونَنِي   وَأَيْنَ مَكَانُ الْبُعْدِ إِلاَّ مَكَانِيَا

[25] قَالَ الْفَرَّارُ السُّلَمِيُّ

* مَا كَانَ يَنْفَعُنِي مَقَالُ نِسَائِهِمْ   وَقُتِلْتُ دُونَ رِجَالِهِمْ لاَ تَبْعَدِ

[26] قَالَ عَنْتَرَةُ بْنُ شَدَّادٍ

* دَارَتْ عَلَى الْقَوْمِ رَحًا طَحُونُ *

[27] قَالَ زُهَيْرُ بْنُ أَبِي سُلْمَى

* فَتَعْرُكْكُمُ عَرْكَ الرَّحَا بِثِفَالِهَا   وَتَلْقَحْ كِشَافاً ثُمَّ تَحْمِلْ فَتَفْطِمِ

[28] قَالَتِ الْفَارِعَةُ بِنْتُ شَدَّادٍ الْمُرِّيَّةُ

١ يَا عَيْنُ جُودِي لِمَسْعُودِ بْنِ شَدَّادِ   بِكُلِّ ذِي عَبَرَاتٍ شَجْوُهُ بَادِي
٢ يَا مَنْ رَأَى بَارِقًا قَدْ بِتُّ أَرْمُقُهُ   جَوْدًا عَلَى الْحَرَّةِ السَّوْدَاءِ بِالْوَادِي
٣ أَسْقِي بِهِ قَبْرَ مَنْ أَعْنِي وَحَبَّ بِهِ   قَبْرًا إِلَيَّ وَلَوْ لَمْ يَفْدِهِ فَادِي
٤ شَهَّادُ أَنْدِيَةٍ رَفَّاعُ أَبْنِيَةٍ   شَدَّادُ أَلْوِيَةٍ فَتَّاحُ أَسْدَادِ
٥ نَحَّارُ رَاغِيَةٍ قَتَّالُ طَاغِيَةٍ   حَلاَّلُ رَابِيَةٍ فَكَّاكُ أَقْيَادِ
٦ قَوَّالُ مُحْكَمَةٍ نَقَّاضُ مُبْرَمَةٍ   فَرَّاجُ مُبْهَمَةٍ حَبَّاسُ أَوْرَادِ
٧ حَلاَّلُ مُمْرِعَةٍ حَمَّالُ مُضْلِعَةٍ   فَرَّاجُ مُفْظِعَةٍ طَلاَّعُ أَنْجَادِ
٨ جَمَّاعُ كُلِّ خِصَالِ الْخَيْرِ قَدْ عَلِمُوا   زَيْنُ الْقِرَى وَنَكَالُ الظَّالِمِ الْعَادِي

٩ أَبَا زُرَارَةَ لاَ تَبْعَدْ فَكُلُّ فَتًى   يَوْمًا رَهِينُ صَفِيحَاتٍ وَأَعْوَادِ
١٠ هَلاَّ سَقَيْتُمْ بَنِي جَرْمٍ أَسِيرَكُمُ   نَفْسِي فِدَاؤُكَ مِنْ ذِي غُلَّةٍ صَادِ
١١ اَلطَّاعِنُ الطَّعْنَةَ النَّجْلاَءَ يَتْبَعُهَا   مُثْعَنْجِرٌ بَعْدَمَا يَغْلِي بِإِزْبَادِ
١٢ وَيَتْرُكُ الْقِرْنَ مُصْفَرًّا أَنَامِلُهُ   كَأَنَّ أَثْوَابَهُ مُجَّتْ بِفِرْصَادِ
١٣ والسَّابِئُ الزِّقَّ لِلأَضْيَافِ إِنْ نَزَلُوا   إِلَى ذَرَاهُ وَغَيْثُ الْمُحْوِجِ الْغَادِي

[29] قال الشَّاعِرُ

* أُولٰئِكَ عَيْنُ الْمَاءِ فِيهِمْ وَعِنْدَهُمْ   مِنَ الْخِيفَةِ الْمَنْجَاةُ وَالْمُتَحَوَّلُ

[30] قال عَلْقَمَةُ بْنُ عَبَدَةَ

* كَأَنَّهُمُ صَابَتْ عَلَيْهِمْ سَحَابَةٌ   صَوَاعِقُهَا لِطَيْرِهِنَّ دَبِيبُ

[31] قالت أُخْتُ عَمْرِو بْنِ عَاصِيَةَ السُّلَمِيِّ

١ هَلاَّ سَقَيْتُمْ بَنِي سَهْمٍ أَسِيرَكُمُ   نَفْسِي فِدَاؤُكَ مِنْ ذِي غُلَّةٍ صَادِي
٢ اَلطَّاعِنُ الطَّعْنَةَ النَّجْلاَءَ يَتْبَعُهَا   مُضَرَّجٌ بَعْدَ مَا جَادَتْ بِإِزْبَادِ

[32] قال عَبِيدُ بْنُ الأَبْرَصِ

* قَدْ أَتْرُكُ الْقِرْنَ مُصْفَرًّا أَنَامِلُهُ   كَأَنَّ أَثْوَابَهُ مُجَّتْ بِفِرْصَادِ

[33] قالت رَيْطَةُ أُخْتُ عَمْرٍو ذِي الْكَلْبِ

١ كُلُّ امْرِئٍ بِمِحَالِ الدَّهْرِ مَكْذُوبُ   وَكُلُّ مَنْ غَالَبَ الأَيَّامَ مَغْلُوبُ
٢ وَكُلُّ حَيٍّ وَإِنْ عَزُّوا وَإِنْ سَلِمُوا   يَوْمًا طَرِيقُهُمُ فِي الشَّرِّ دُعْبُوبُ
٣ أَبْلِغْ هُذَيْلاً وَأَبْلِغْ مَنْ يُبَلِّغُهَا   عَنِّي رَسُولاً وَبَعْضُ الْقَوْلِ تَكْذِيبُ
٤ بِأَنَّ ذَا الْكَلْبِ عَمْرًا خَيْرَهُمْ نَسَبًا   بِبَطْنِ شِرْيَانَ يَعْوِي حَوْلَهُ الذِّيبُ

٥ اَلطَّاعِنُ الطَّعْنَةَ النَّجْلاَءَ يَتْبَعُهَا مُثْعَنْجِرٌ مِنْ نَجِيعِ الْجَوْفِ أُسْكُوبُ
٦ وَالتَّارِكُ الْقِرْنَ مُصْفَرًّا أَنَامِلُهُ كَأَنَّهُ مِنْ نَجِيعِ الْجَوْفِ مَخْضُوبُ
٧ اَلْمِخْرَجُ الْعَاتِقَ الْعَذْرَاءَ مُذْعِنَةً فِي السَّبْيِ يَنْفَحُ مِنْ أَرْدَانِهَا الطِّيبُ
٨ تَمْشِي النُّسُورُ عَلَيْهِ وَهْيَ لاَهِيَةٌ مَشْيَ الْعَذَارَى عَلَيْهِنَّ الْجَلاَبِيبُ

[34] قالت كَبْشَةُ بنتُ مَعْدِيكَرِبَ

١ أَرْسَلَ عَبْدُ اللّٰهِ إِذْ حَانَ يَوْمُهُ إِلَى قَوْمِهِ لاَ تَعْقِلُوا لَهُمُ دَمِي
٢ وَلاَ تَأْخُذُوا مِنْهُمْ إِفَالاً وَأَبْكُرًا وَأُتْرَكَ فِي بَيْتٍ بِصَعْدَةَ مُظْلِمِ
٣ وَدَعْ عَنْكَ عَمْرًا إِنَّ عَمْرًا مُسَالِمٌ وَهَلْ بَطْنُ عَمْرٍو غَيْرُ شِبْرٍ لِمَطْعَمِ
٤ فَإِنْ أَنْتُمُ لَمْ تَثْأَرُوا وَٱتَّدَيْتُمُ فَمَشُّوا بِآذَانِ النَّعَامِ الْمُصَلَّمِ
٥ وَلاَ تَرِدُوا إِلاَّ فُضُولَ نِسَائِكُمْ إِذَا ٱرْتَمَلَتْ أَعْقَابُهُنَّ مِنَ الدَّمِ

[35] قال جَرِيرُ بْنُ عَطِيَّةَ

* لاَ تَذْكُرُوا حَالَ الْمُلُوكِ فَإِنَّكُمْ بَعْدَ الزُّبَيْرِ كَحَائِضٍ لَمْ تَغْسِلِ

[36] قالت أُمُّ عَمْرٍو بنتُ وَقْدَانٍ

١ إِنْ أَنْتُمُ لَمْ تَطْلُبُوا بِأَخِيكُمُ فَذَرُوا السِّلاَحَ وَوَحِّشُوا بِالْأَبْرَقِ
٢ وَخُذُوا الْمَكَاحِلَ وَالْمَجَاسِدَ وَالْبَسُوا
نُقَبَ النِّسَاءِ فَبِئْسَ رَهْطُ الْمُرْهَقِ
٣ أَلْهَاكُمُ أَنْ تَطْلُبُوا بِأَخِيكُمُ أَكْلُ الْخَزِيرِ وَلَعْقُ أَجْرَدَ أَمْحَقِ

[37] قالت هِنْدُ بنتُ حُذَيْفَةَ

١ تَطَاوَلَ لَيْلِي لِلْهُمُومِ الْحَوَاضِرِ وَشَيَّبَ رَأْسِي يَوْمُ وَقْعَةِ حَاجِرِ
٢ لَعَمْرِي وَمَا عَمْرِي عَلَيَّ بِهَيِّنٍ وَلاَ حَالِفٌ بَرٌّ كَآخَرَ فَاجِرِ

٣ لَقَدْ نَالَ كُرْزٌ يَوْمَ حَاجِرَ وَقْعَةً   كَفَتْ قَوْمَهُ أُخْرَى اللَّيَالِي الْغَوَابِرِ

٤ فَلِلَّهِ عَيْنَا مَنْ رَأَى مِثْلَهُ فَتًى   تَنَاوَلَهُ بِالرُّمْحِ كُرْزُ بْنُ عَامِرِ

٥ فَيَا لَبَنِي ذُبْيَانَ بَكُّوا عَمِيدَكُمْ   بِكُلِّ رَقِيقِ الْحَدِّ أَبْيَضَ بَاتِرِ

٦ وَكُلِّ رُدَيْنِيٍّ أَصَمَّ كُعُوبُهُ   يَنُوءُ بِنَصْلٍ كَالْعَقِيقَةِ زَاهِرِ

٧ وَكُلِّ أَسِيلِ الْخَدِّ طَاوٍ كَأَنَّهُ   ظَلِيمٌ وَجَرْدَاءَ النَّسَالَةِ ضَامِرِ

٨ فَإِنْ أَنْتُمُ لَمْ تَصْبِحُوا الْقَوْمَ غَارَةً   يُحَدِّثُ عَنْهَا وَارِدٌ بَعْدَ صَادِرِ

٩ وَتَرْمُوا عُقَيْلاً بِالَّتِي لَيْسَ بَعْدَهَا   بَقَاءٌ فَكُونُوا كَالْإِمَاءِ الْعَوَاثِرِ

[38] قال أَبُو طَالِبٍ

* وَنُسْلِمُهُ حَتَّى نُصَرَّعَ حَوْلَهُ   وَنَذْهَلَ عَنْ أَبْنَائِنَا وَالْحَلَائِلِ

[39] قالت هِنْدُ بِنتُ عُتْبَةَ

١ نَحْنُ جَزَيْنَاكُمْ بِيَوْمِ بَدْرِ   وَالْحَرْبُ بَعْدَ الْحَرْبِ ذَاتُ سُعْرِ

٢ مَا كَانَ عَنْ عُتْبَةَ لِي مِنْ صَبْرِ   وَلاَ أَخِي وَعَمِّهِ وَبِكْرِي

٣ شَفَيْتُ نَفْسِي وَقَضَيْتُ نَذْرِي   شَفَيْتَ وَحْشِيُّ غَلِيلَ صَدْرِي

٤ فَشُكْرُ وَحْشِيٍّ عَلَيَّ عُمْرِي   حَتَّى تَرِمَّ أَعْظُمِي فِي قَبْرِي

[40] قالت هِنْدُ بِنتُ أُثَاثَةَ

١ خَزِيتِ فِي بَدْرٍ وَبَعْدَ بَدْرِ   يَا بِنْتَ وَقَّاعٍ عَظِيمِ الْكُفْرِ

٢ صَبَّحَكِ اللَّهُ غَدَاةَ الْفَجْرِ   مِلْهَاشِمِيِّينَ الطِّوَالِ الزُّهْرِ

٣ بِكُلِّ قَطَّاعٍ حُسَامٍ يَفْرِي   حَمْزَةُ لَيْثِي وَعَلِيٌّ صَقْرِي

٤ إِذْ رَامَ شَيْبٌ وَأَبُوكِ غَدْرِي   فَخَضَّبَا مِنْهُ ضَوَاحِي النَّحْرِ

٥ وَنَذْرُكِ السُّوءَ فَشَرُّ نَذْرِ   أَعْطَيْتِ وَحْشِيَّ ضَمِيرَ الصَّدْرِ

٦ هَتَكَ وَحْشِيٌّ حِجَابَ السِّتْرِ   مَا لِلْبَغَايَا بَعْدَهَا مِنْ فَخْرِ

[41] قالت أُمَامَةُ بنتُ كُلَيْبٍ

١ أَتَلْهُو بِالْمَلَاهِي وَالْخُمُورِ   وَلَا تَدْرِي بِعَاقِبَةِ الْأُمُورِ
٢ وَلَا تَدْرِي بِأَنَّ كُلَيْبَ أَضْحَى   قَتِيلاً عِنْدَ جَسَّاسَ الْغَدُورِ

[42] قال مُهَلْهِلُ بْنُ رَبِيعَةَ

١ كُنَّا نَغَارُ عَلَى الْعَوَاتِقِ أَنْ تُرَى   بِالْأَمْسِ خَارِجَةً عَنِ الْأَوْطَانِ
٢ فَخَرَجْنَ حِينَ ثَوَى كُلَيْبٌ حُسَّرًا   مُسْتَيْقِنَاتٍ بَعْدَهُ بِهَوَانِ
٣ فَتَرَى الْكَوَاعِبَ كَالظِّبَاءِ عَوَاطِلاً   إِذْ حَانَ مَصْرَعُهُ مِنَ الْأَكْفَانِ
٤ يَخْمِشْنَ مِنْ أَدَمِ الْوُجُوهِ حَوَاسِرًا   مِنْ بَعْدِهِ وَيَعِدْنَ بِالْأَزْمَانِ
٥ مُتَسَلِّبَاتٍ نُكْدَهُنَّ وَقَدْ وَرَى   أَجْوَافَهُنَّ بِحُرْقَةٍ وَرَوَانِي
٦ وَيَقُلْنَ مَنْ لِلْمُسْتَضِيقِ إِذَا دَعَا   أَمْ مَنْ لِخَضْبِ عَوَالِي الْمُرَّانِ
٧ أَمْ لَاتِّسَارٍ بِالْجَزُورِ إِذَا غَدَا   رِيحٌ يُقَطِّعُ مَعْقِدَ الْأَشْطَانِ
٨ أَمْ مَنْ لِأَسْبَاقِ الدِّيَاتِ وَجَمْعِهَا   وَلِفَادِحَاتِ نَوَائِبِ الْحِدْثَانِ
٩ كَانَ الذَّخِيرَةَ لِلزَّمَانِ فَقَدْ أَتَى   فِقْدَانُهُ وَأَخَلَّ رُكْنَ مَكَانِي
١٠ يَا لَهْفَ نَفْسِي مِنْ زَمَانٍ فَاجِعٍ   أَلْقَى عَلَيَّ بِكَلْكَلٍ وَجِرَانِ
١١ بِمُصِيبَةٍ لَا تُسْتَقَالُ جَلِيلَةٍ   غَلَبَتْ عَزَاءَ الْقَوْمِ وَالنِّسْوَانِ
١٢ هَدَّتْ حُصُونًا كُنَّ قَبْلُ مَلَاوِذًا   لِذَوِي الْكُهُولِ مَعًا وَلِلشُّبَّانِ
١٣ أَضْحَتْ وَأَضْحَى سُورُهَا مِنْ بَعْدِهِ   مُتَهَدِّمَ الْأَرْكَانِ وَالْبُنْيَانِ
١٤ فَابْكِينَ سَيِّدَ قَوْمِهِ وَانْدُبْنَهُ   شُدَّتْ عَلَيهِ قَبَاطِيَ الْأَكْفَانِ
١٥ وَابْكِينَ لِلْأَيْتَامِ لَمَّا أَقْحَطُوا   وَابْكِينَ عِنْدَ تَخَاذُلِ الْجِيرَانِ

١٦ وَٱبْكِينَ مَصْرَعَ جِيدِهِ مُتَزَمِّلاً … بِدِمَائِهِ فَلَذَاكَ مَا أَبْكَانِي
١٧ فَلَأَتْرُكَنَّ بِهِ قَبَائِلَ تَغْلِبٍ … قَتْلَى بِكُلِّ قَرَارَةٍ وَمَكَانِ
١٨ قَتْلَى تُعَاوِرُهَا ٱلنُّسُورُ أَكُفَّهَا … يَنْهَشْنَهَا وَحَوَاجِلُ ٱلْغِرْبَانِ

[43] قَالَ مُهَلْهِلُ بْنُ رَبِيعَةَ

١ أَهَاجَ قَذَاءَ عَيْنِي ٱلِاذِّكَارُ … هُدُوًّا فَٱلدُّمُوعُ لَهَا ٱنْحِدَارُ
٢ وَصَارَ ٱللَّيْلُ مُشْتَمِلاً عَلَيْنَا … كَأَنَّ ٱللَّيْلَ لَيْسَ لَهُ نَهَارُ
٣ وَبِتُّ أُرَاقِبُ ٱلْجَوْزَاءَ حَتَّى … تَقَارَبَ مِنْ أَوَائِلِهَا ٱنْحِدَارُ
٤ أُصَرِّفُ مُقْلَتِي فِي إِثْرِ قَوْمٍ … تَبَايَنَتِ ٱلْبِلَادُ بِهِمْ فَغَارُوا
٥ وَأَبْكِي وَٱلنُّجُومُ مُطَلِّعَاتٌ … كَأَنْ لَمْ تَحْوِهَا عَنِّي ٱلبِحَارُ
٦ عَلَى مَنْ لَوْ نُعِيتُ وَكَانَ حَيًّا … لَقَادَ ٱلْخَيْلَ يَحْجُبُهَا ٱلْغُبَارُ
٧ دَعَوْتُكَ يَا كُلَيْبُ فَلَمْ تُجِبْنِي … وَكَيْفَ يُجِيبُنِي ٱلْبَلَدُ ٱلْقِفَارُ
٨ أَجِبْنِي يَا كُلَيْبُ خَلَاكَ ذَمٌّ … ضَنِينَاتُ ٱلنُّفُوسِ لَهَا مَزَارُ
٩ أَجِبْنِي يَا كُلَيْبُ خَلَاكَ ذَمٌّ … لَقَدْ فُجِعَتْ بِفَارِسِهَا نِزَارُ
١٠ سَقَاكَ ٱلْغَيْثُ إِنَّكَ كُنْتَ غَيْثًا … وَيُسْرًا حِينَ يُلْتَمَسُ ٱلْيَسَارُ
١١ أَبَتْ عَيْنَايَ بَعْدَكَ أَنْ تَكُفَّا … كَأَنَّ غَضَا ٱلْقَتَادِ لَهَا شِفَارُ
١٢ وَإِنَّكَ كُنْتَ تَحْلُمُ عَنْ رِجَالٍ … وَتَعْفُو عَنْهُمُ وَلَكَ ٱقْتِدَارُ
١٣ وَتَمْنَعُ أَنْ يَمَسَّهُمُ لِسَانٌ … مَخَافَةَ مَنْ يُجِيرُ وَلَا يُجَارُ
١٤ وَكُنْتُ أَعُدُّ قُرْبِي مِنْكَ رِبْحًا … إِذَا مَا عَدَّتِ ٱلرِّبْحَ ٱلتِّجَارُ
١٥ فَلَا تَبْعَدْ فَكُلٌّ سَوْفَ يَلْقَى … شَعُوبًا يَسْتَدِيرُ بِهَا ٱلْمَدَارُ
١٦ يَعِيشُ ٱلْمَرْءُ عِنْدَ بَنِي أَبِيهِ … وَيُوشِكُ أَنْ يَصِيرَ بِحَيْثُ صَارُوا

١٧ أَرَى طُولَ الْحَيَاةِ وَقَدْ تَوَلَّى   كَمَا قَدْ يُسْلَبُ الشَّيْءُ الْمُعَارُ

١٨ كَأَنِّي إِذْ نَعَى النَّاعِي كُلَيْبًا   تَطَايَرَ بَيْنَ جَنْبَيَّ الشَّرَارُ

١٩ فَدُرْتُ وَقَدْ عَشِيَ بَصَرِي عَلَيْهِ   كَمَا دَارَتْ بِشَارِبِهَا الْعُقَارُ

٢٠ سَأَلْتُ الْحَيَّ أَيْنَ دَفَنْتُمُوهُ   فَقَالُوا لِي بِسَفْحِ الْحَيِّ دَارُ

٢١ فَسِرْتُ إِلَيْهِ مِنْ بَلَدِي حَثِيثًا   وَطَارَ النَّوْمُ وَٱمْتَنَعَ الْقَرَارُ

٢٢ وَحَادَتْ نَاقَتِي عَنْ ظِلِّ قَبْرٍ   ثَوَى فِيهِ الْمَكَارِمُ وَالْفَخَارُ

٢٣ لَدَى أَوْطَانِ أَرْوَعَ لَمْ يَشِنْهُ   وَلَمْ يَحْدُثْ لَهُ فِي النَّاسِ عَارُ

٢٤ أَتَغْدُو يَا كُلَيْبُ مَعِي إِذَا مَا   جَبَانُ الْقَوْمِ أَنْجَاهُ الْفِرَارُ

٢٥ أَتَغْدُو يَا كُلَيْبُ مَعِي إِذَا مَا   حُلُوقُ الْقَوْمِ يَشْحَذُهَا الشِّفَارُ

٢٦ أَقُولُ لِتَغْلِبٍ وَالْعِزُّ فِيهَا   أَثِيرُوهَا لَذٰلِكُمُ ٱنْتِصَارُ

٢٧ تَتَابَعَ إِخْوَتِي وَمَضَوْا لِأَمْرٍ   عَلَيْهِ تَتَابَعَ الْقَوْمُ الْحِسَارُ

٢٨ خُذِ الْعَهْدَ الْأَكِيدَ عَلَيَّ عُمْرِي   بِتَرْكِي كُلَّ مَا حَوَتِ الدِّيَارُ

٢٩ وَهَجْرِي الْغَانِيَاتِ وَشُرْبَ كَأْسٍ   وَلُبْسِي جُبَّةً لَا تُسْتَعَارُ

٣٠ وَلَسْتُ بِخَالِعٍ دِرْعِي وَسَيْفِي   إِلَى أَنْ يَخْلَعَ اللَّيْلَ النَّهَارُ

٣١ وَإِلَّا أَنْ تَبِيدَ سَرَاةُ بَكْرٍ   فَلَا يَبْقَى لَهَا أَبَدًا أَثَارُ

[44] قَالَ مُهَلْهِلُ بْنُ رَبِيعَةَ

١ أَلَيْلَتَنَا بِذِي حُسُمٍ أَنِيرِي   إِذَا أَنْتِ ٱنْقَضَيْتِ فَلَا تَحُورِي

٢ فَإِنْ يَكُ بِالذَّنَائِبِ طَالَ لَيْلِي   فَقَدْ يُبْكَى مِنَ اللَّيْلِ الْقَصِيرِ

٣ فَلَوْ نُبِشَ الْمَقَابِرُ عَنْ كُلَيْبٍ   فَيُخْبَرَ بِالذَّنَائِبِ أَيُّ زِيرِ

٤ بِيَوْمِ الشَّعْثَمَيْنِ لَقَرَّ عَيْنًا   وَكَيْفَ لِقَاءُ مَنْ تَحْتَ الْقُبُورِ

٥ فَإِنِّي قَدْ تَرَكْتُ بِوَارِدَاتٍ   بُجَيْرًا فِي دَمٍ مِثْلِ الْعَبِيرِ
٦ وَهَمَّامَ بْنَ مُرَّةَ قَدْ تَرَكْنَا   عَلَيْهِ الْقَشْعَمَانِ مِنَ النُّسُورِ
٧ وَصَبَّحْنَا الْوُخُومَ بِيَوْمِ سَوْءٍ   يُدَافِعْنَ الْأَسِنَّةَ بِالنُّحُورِ
٨ كَأَنَّا غُدْوَةً وَبَنِي أَبِينَا   بِجَوفِ عُنَيْزَةٍ رَحَيَا مُدِيرِ
٩ فَلَوْلَا الرِّيحُ أُسْمِعَ أَهْلُ حَجْرٍ   صَلِيلَ الْبَيْضِ يُقْدَعُ بِالذُّكُورِ

[45] قال مُهَلْهِلُ بْنُ رَبِيعَةَ

١ لَمَّا نَعَى النَّاعِي كُلَيْبًا أَظْلَمَتْ   شَمْسُ النَّهَارِ فَمَا تُرِيدُ طُلُوعَا
٢ قَتَلُوا كُلَيْبًا ثُمَّ قَالُوا أَرْتِعُوا   كَذَبُوا لَقَدْ مَنَعُوا الْجِيَادَ رُتُوعَا
٣ كَلَّا وَأَنْصَابٍ لَنَا عَادِيَّةٍ   مَعْبُودَةٍ قَدْ قُطِّعَتْ تَقْطِيعَا
٤ حَتَّى أُبِيدَ قَبِيلَةً وَقَبِيلَةً   قَبِيلَةً وَقَبِيلَتَيْنِ جَمِيعَا
٥ وَتَذُوقَ حَتْفًا آلُ بَكْرٍ كُلُّهَا   وَنَهُدَّ مِنْهَا سَمْكَهَا الْمَرْفُوعَا
٦ حَتَّى نَرَى أَوْصَالَهُمْ وَجَمَاجِمًا   مِنْهُمْ عَلَيْهَا الْخَامِعَاتُ وُقُوعَا
٧ وَنَرَى سِبَاعَ الطَّيْرِ تَنْقُرُ أَعْيُنًا   وَتَجُرُّ أَعْضَاءً لَهُمْ وَضُلُوعَا
٨ وَالْمَشْرَفِيَّةَ لَا تُعَرِّجُ عَنْهُمُ   ضَرْبًا يَقُدُّ مَغَافِرًا وَدُرُوعَا
٩ وَالْخَيْلَ تَقْتَحِمُ الْغُبَارَ عَوَابِسًا   يَوْمَ الْكَرِيهَةِ مَا يُرِدْنَ رُجُوعَا

[46] قال مُهَلْهِلُ بْنُ رَبِيعَةَ

١ بَاتَ لَيْلِي بِالْأَنْعَمَيْنِ طَوِيلَا   أَرْقُبُ النَّجْمَ سَاهِرًا لَنْ يَزُولَا
٢ كَيْفَ أُمْدِي وَلَا يَزَالُ قَتِيلٌ   مِنْ بَنِي وَائِلٍ يُنَادِي قَتِيلَا
٣ أَزْجُرُ الْعَيْنَ أَنْ تُبَكِّي الطُّلُولَا   إِنَّ فِي الصَّدْرِ مِنْ كُلَيْبٍ فَلِيلَا
٤ إِنَّ فِي الصَّدْرِ حَاجَةً لَنْ تُقَضَّى   مَا دَعَا فِي الْغُصُونِ دَاعٍ هَدِيلَا

٥ كَيْفَ أَنْسَاكَ يَا كُلَيْبُ وَلَمَّا   أَقْضِ حُزْنًا يَنُوبُنِي وَغَلِيلاَ
٦ أَيُّهَا الْقَلْبُ أَنْجِزِ الْيَوْمَ نَحْبًا   مِنْ بَنِي الْحِصْنِ إِذْ غَدَوْا وَذُحُولاَ
٧ كَيْفَ يَبْكِي الطُّلُولَ مَنْ هُوَ رَهْنٌ   بِطِعَانِ الأَنَامِ جِيلاً فَجِيلاَ
٨ اِنْتَضَوْا مَعْجِسَ الْقِسِيِّ وَأَبْرَقْ   نَا كَمَا تُوْعِدُ الْفُحُولُ الْفُحُولاَ
٩ وَصَبَرْنَا تَحْتَ الْبَوَارِقِ حَتَّى   دَكْدَكَتْ فِيهِمِ السُّيُوفُ طَوِيلاَ
١٠ لَمْ يُطِيقُوا أَنْ يَنْزِلُوا وَنَزَلْنَا   وَأَخُو الْحَرْبِ مَنْ أَطَاقَ النُّزُولاَ

[47] قال امْرُؤُ الْقَيْسِ بْنُ حُجْرٍ

١ قِفَا نَبْكِ مِنْ ذِكْرَى حَبِيبٍ وَمَنْزِلِ   بِسِقْطِ اللِّوَى بَيْنَ الدَّخُولِ فَحَوْمَلِ
٢ فَتُوضِحَ فَالْمِقْرَاةِ لَمْ يَعْفُ رَسْمُهَا   لِمَا نَسَجَتْهَا مِنْ جَنُوبٍ وَشَمْأَلِ
٣ تَرَى بَعَرَ الأَرْآمِ فِي عَرَصَاتِهَا   وَقِيعَانِهَا كَأَنَّهُ حَبُّ فُلْفُلِ
٤ كَأَنِّي غَدَاةَ الْبَيْنِ يَوْمَ تَحَمَّلُوا   لَدَى سَمُرَاتِ الْحَيِّ نَاقِفُ حَنْظَلِ
٥ وُقُوفاً بِهَا صَحْبِي عَلَيَّ مَطِيَّهُمْ   يَقُولُونَ لاَ تَهْلِكْ أَسًى وَتَجَمَّلِ
٦ وَإِنَّ شِفَائِي عَبْرَةٌ مُهَرَاقَةٌ   فَهَلْ عِنْدَ رَسْمٍ دَارِسٍ مِنْ مُعَوَّلِ
٧ كَدَأْبِكَ مِنْ أُمِّ الْحُوَيْرِثِ قَبْلَهَا   وَجَارَتِهَا أُمِّ الرَّبَابِ بِمَأْسَلِ
٨ إِذَا قَامَتَا تَضَوَّعَ الْمِسْكُ مِنْهُمَا   نَسِيمَ الصَّبَا جَاءَتْ بِرَيَّا الْقَرَنْفُلِ
٩ فَفَاضَتْ دُمُوعُ الْعَيْنِ مِنِّي صَبَابَةً   عَلَى النَّحْرِ حَتَّى بَلَّ دَمْعِيَ مِحْمَلِي
١٠ أَلاَ رُبَّ يَوْمٍ لَكَ مِنْهُنَّ صَالِحٍ   وَلاَ سِيَّمَا يَوْمٌ بِدَارَةِ جُلْجُلِ
١١ وَيَوْمَ عَقَرْتُ لِلْعَذَارَى مَطِيَّتِي   فَيَا عَجَبًا مِنْ كُورِهَا الْمُتَحَمَّلِ
١٢ فَظَلَّ الْعَذَارَى يَرْتَمِينَ بِلَحْمِهَا   وَشَحْمٍ كَهُدَّابِ الدِّمَقْسِ الْمُفَتَّلِ
١٣ وَيَوْمَ دَخَلْتُ الْخِدْرَ خِدْرَ عُنَيْزَةٍ   فَقَالَتْ لَكَ الْوَيْلاَتُ إِنَّكَ مُرْجِلِي

١٤ تَقُولُ وَقَدْ مَالَ الْغَبِيطُ بِنَا مَعًا   عَقَرْتَ بَعِيرِي يَا ٱمْرَأَ ٱلْقَيْسِ فَٱنْزِلِ
١٥ فَقُلْتُ لَهَا سِيرِي وَأَرْخِي زِمَامَهُ   وَلاَ تُبْعِدِينِي مِنْ جَنَاكِ الْمُعَلَّلِ
١٦ فَمِثْلِكِ حُبْلَى قَدْ طَرَقْتُ وَمُرْضِعٍ   فَأَلْهَيْتُهَا عَنْ ذِي تَمَائِمَ مُحْوِلِ
١٧ إِذَا مَا بَكَى مِنْ خَلْفِهَا ٱنْصَرَفَتْ لَهُ   بِشِقٍّ وَتَحْتِي شِقُّهَا لَمْ يُحَوَّلِ
١٨ وَيَوْمًا عَلَى ظَهْرِ ٱلْكَثِيبِ تَعَذَّرَتْ   عَلَيَّ وَآلَتْ حَلْفَةً لَمْ تَحَلَّلِ
١٩ أَفَاطِمَ مَهْلاً بَعْضَ هٰذَا التَّدَلُّلِ
وَإِنْ كُنْتِ قَدْ أَزْمَعْتِ صَرْمِي فَأَجْمِلِي
٢٠ أَغَرَّكِ مِنِّي أَنَّ حُبَّكِ قَاتِلِي   وَأَنَّكِ مَهْمَا تَأْمُرِي الْقَلْبَ يَفْعَلِ
٢١ وَإِنْ تَكُ قَدْ سَاءَتْكِ مِنِّي خَلِيقَةٌ   فَسُلِّي ثِيَابِي مِنْ ثِيَابِكِ تَنْسُلِ
٢٢ وَمَا ذَرَفَتْ عَيْنَاكِ إِلاَّ لِتَضْرِبِي   بِسَهْمَيْكِ فِي أَعْشَارِ قَلْبٍ مُقَتَّلِ
٢٣ وَبَيْضَةِ خِدْرٍ لاَ يُرَامُ خِبَاؤُهَا   تَمَتَّعْتُ مِنْ لَهْوٍ بِهَا غَيْرَ مُعْجَلِ
٢٤ تَجَاوَزْتُ أَحْرَاسًا إِلَيْهَا وَمَعْشَرًا   عَلَيَّ حِرَاصًا لَوْ يُسِرُّونَ مَقْتَلِي
٢٥ إِذَا مَا الثُّرَيَّا فِي السَّمَاءِ تَعَرَّضَتْ   تَعَرُّضَ أَثْنَاءِ الْوِشَاحِ الْمُفَصَّلِ
٢٦ فَجِئْتُ وَقَدْ نَضَتْ لِنَوْمٍ ثِيَابَهَا   لَدَى السِّتْرِ إِلاَّ لِبْسَةَ الْمُتَفَضِّلِ
٢٧ فَقَالَتْ يَمِينَ اللّٰهِ مَا لَكَ حِيلَةٌ   وَمَا إِنْ أَرَى عَنْكَ الْغَوَايَةَ تَنْجَلِي
٢٨ خَرَجْتُ بِهَا أَمْشِي تَجُرُّ وَرَاءَنَا   عَلَى أَثَرَيْنَا ذَيْلَ مِرْطٍ مُرَحَّلِ
٢٩ فَلَمَّا أَجَزْنَا سَاحَةَ الْحَيِّ وَٱنْتَحَى   بِنَا بَطْنُ خَبْتٍ ذِي حِقَافٍ عَقَنْقَلِ
٣٠ هَصَرْتُ بِفَوْدَيْ رَأْسِهَا فَتَمَايَلَتْ   عَلَيَّ هَضِيمَ الْكَشْحِ رَيَّا الْمُخَلْخَلِ
٣١ مُهَفْهَفَةٌ بَيْضَاءُ غَيْرُ مُفَاضَةٍ   تَرَائِبُهَا مَصْقُولَةٌ كَالسَّجَنْجَلِ
٣٢ تَصُدُّ وَتُبْدِي عَنْ أَسِيلٍ وَتَتَّقِي   بِنَاظِرَةٍ مِنْ وَحْشِ وَجْرَةَ مُطْفِلِ
٣٣ وَجِيدٍ كَجِيدِ الرِّئْمِ لَيْسَ بِفَاحِشٍ   إِذَا هِيَ نَصَّتْهُ وَلاَ بِمُعَطَّلِ

٣٤ وَفَرْعٍ يَزِينُ الْمَتْنَ أَسْوَدَ فَاحِمٍ أَثِيثٍ كَقِنْوِ النَّخْلَةِ الْمُتَعَثْكِلِ
٣٥ غَدائِرُهُ مُسْتَشْزِرَاتٌ إِلَى الْعُلاَ تَضِلُّ الْعِقَاصُ فِي مُثَنًّى وَمُرْسَلِ
٣٦ وَكَشْحٍ لَطِيفٍ كَالْجَدِيلِ مُخَصَّرٍ وَسَاقٍ كَأُنْبُوبِ السَّقِيِّ الْمُذَلَّلِ
٣٧ وَتُضْحِي فَتِيتُ الْمِسْكِ فَوْقَ فِرَاشِهَا
نَؤُومُ الضُّحَى لَم تَنْتَطِقْ عَنْ تَفَضُّلِ
٣٨ وَتَعْطُو بِرَخْصٍ غَيْرِ شَثْنٍ كَأَنَّهُ أَسَارِيعُ ظَبْيٍ أَوْ مَسَاوِيكُ إِسْحِلِ
٣٩ تُضِيءُ الظَّلاَمَ بِالْعِشَاءِ كَأَنَّهَا مَنَارَةُ مُمْسَى رَاهِبٍ مُتَبَتِّلِ
٤٠ إِلَى مِثْلِهَا يَرْنُو الْحَلِيمُ صَبَابَةً إِذَا مَا ٱسْبَكَرَّتْ بَيْنَ دِرْعٍ وَمِجْوَلِ
٤١ كَبِكْرِ الْمُقَانَاةِ الْبَيَاضِ بِصُفْرَةٍ غَذَاهَا نَمِيرُ الْمَاءِ غَيْرُ الْمُحَلَّلِ
٤٢ تَسَلَّتْ عَمَايَاتُ الرِّجَالِ عَنِ الصِّبَا وَلَيْسَ فُؤَادِي عَنْ هَوَاكِ بِمُنْسَلِ
٤٣ أَلاَ رُبَّ خَصْمٍ فِيكِ أَلْوَى رَدَدْتُهُ نَصِيحٍ عَلَى تَعْذَالِهِ غَيْرِ مُؤْتَلِ
٤٤ وَلَيْلٍ كَمَوْجِ الْبَحْرِ أَرْخَى سُدُولَهُ عَلَيَّ بِأَنْوَاعِ الْهُمُومِ لِيَبْتَلِي
٤٥ فَقُلْتُ لَهُ لَمَّا تَمَطَّى بِصُلْبِهِ وَأَرْدَفَ أَعْجَازًا وَنَاءَ بِكَلْكَلِ
٤٦ أَلاَ أَيُّهَا اللَّيْلُ الطَّوِيلُ أَلاَ ٱنْجَلِ بِصُبْحٍ وَمَا الإِصْبَاحُ مِنْكَ بِأَمْثَلِ
٤٧ فَيَا لَكَ مِنْ لَيْلٍ كَأَنَّ نُجُومَهُ بِكُلِّ مُغَارِ الْفَتْلِ شُدَّتْ بِيَذْبُلِ
٤٨ كَأَنَّ الثُّرَيَّا عُلِّقَتْ فِي مَصَامِهَا بِأَمْرَاسِ كَتَّانٍ إِلَى صُمِّ جَنْدَلِ
٤٩ وَقِرْبَةِ أَقْوَامٍ جَعَلْتُ عِصَامَهَا عَلَى كَاهِلٍ مِنِّي ذَلُولٍ مُرَحَّلِ
٥٠ وَوَادٍ كَجَوْفِ الْعَيْرِ قَفْرٍ قَطَعْتُهُ بِهِ الذِّئْبُ يَعْوِي كَالْخَلِيعِ الْمُعَيَّلِ
٥١ فَقُلْتُ لَهُ لَمَّا عَوَى إِنَّ شَأْنَنَا قَلِيلُ الْغِنَى إِنْ كُنْتَ لَمَّا تَمَوَّلِ
٥٢ كِلاَنَا إِذَا مَا نَالَ شَيْئًا أَفَاتَهُ وَمَنْ يَحْتَرِثْ حَرْثِي وَحَرْثَكَ يُهْزَلِ
٥٣ وَقَدْ أَغْتَدِي وَالطَّيْرُ فِي وُكُنَاتِهَا بِمُنْجَرِدٍ قَيْدِ الْأَوَابِدِ هَيْكَلِ

٥٤ مِكَرٍّ مِفَرٍّ مُقْبِلٍ مُدْبِرٍ مَعًا
كَجُلْمُودِ صَخْرٍ حَطَّهُ السَّيْلُ مِنْ عَلِ

٥٥ كُمَيْتٍ يَزِلُّ اللِّبْدُ عَنْ حَالِ مَتْنِهِ　　كَمَا زَلَّتِ الصَّفْوَاءُ بِالْمُتَنَزَّلِ

٥٦ عَلَى الذَّبْلِ جَيَّاشٍ كَأَنَّ ٱهْتِزَامَهُ　　إِذَا جَاشَ فِيهِ حَمْيُهُ غَلْيُ مِرْجَلِ

٥٧ مِسَحٍّ إِذَا مَا السَّابِحَاتُ عَلَى الْوَنَى　　أَثَرْنَ الْغُبَارَ بِالْكَدِيدِ الْمُرَكَّلِ

٥٨ يُزِلُّ الْغُلَامَ الْخِفَّ عَنْ صَهَوَاتِهِ　　وَيُلْوِي بِأَثْوَابِ الْعَنِيفِ الْمُثَقَّلِ

٥٩ دَرِيرٍ كَخُذْرُوفِ الْوَلِيدِ أَمَرَّهُ　　تَتَابُعُ كَفَّيْهِ بِخَيْطٍ مُوَصَّلِ

٦٠ لَهُ أَيْطَلَا ظَبْيٍ وَسَاقَا نَعَامَةٍ　　وَإِرْخَاءُ سِرْحَانٍ وَتَقْرِيبُ تَتْفُلِ

٦١ ضَلِيعٍ إِذَا ٱسْتَدْبَرْتَهُ سَدَّ فَرْجَهُ　　بِضَافٍ فُوَيْقَ الأَرْضِ لَيْسَ بِأَعْزَلِ

٦٢ كَأَنَّ عَلَى الْمَتْنَيْنِ مِنْهُ إِذَا ٱنْتَحَى　　مَدَاكَ عَرُوسٍ أَوْ صَلَايَةَ حَنْظَلِ

٦٣ كَأَنَّ دِمَاءَ الْهَادِيَاتِ بِنَحْرِهِ　　عُصَارَةُ حِنَّاءٍ بِشَيْبٍ مُرَجَّلِ

٦٤ فَعَنَّ لَنَا سِرْبٌ كَأَنَّ نِعَاجَهُ　　عَذَارَى دَوَارٍ فِي مُلَاءٍ مُذَيَّلِ

٦٥ فَأَدْبَرْنَ كَالْجَزْعِ الْمُفَصَّلِ بَيْنَهُ　　بِجِيدِ مُعَمٍّ فِي الْعَشِيرَةِ مُخْوَلِ

٦٦ فَأَلْحَقَنَا بِالْهَادِيَاتِ وَدُونَهُ　　جَوَاحِرُهَا فِي صَرَّةٍ لَمْ تُزَيَّلِ

٦٧ فَعَادَى عِدَاءً بَيْنَ ثَوْرٍ وَنَعْجَةٍ　　دِرَاكًا وَلَمْ يَنْضَحْ بِمَاءٍ فَيُغْسَلِ

٦٨ فَظَلَّ طُهَاةُ اللَّحْمِ مِنْ بَيْنِ مُنْضِجٍ　　صَفِيفَ شِوَاءٍ أَوْ قَدِيرٍ مُعَجَّلِ

٦٩ وَرُحْنَا يَكَادُ الطَّرْفُ يَقْصُرُ دُونَهُ　　مَتَى مَا تَرَقَّ الْعَيْنُ فِيهِ تَسَفَّلِ

٧٠ فَبَاتَ عَلَيْهِ سَرْجُهُ وَلِجَامُهُ　　وَبَاتَ بِعَيْنِي قَائِمًا غَيْرَ مُرْسَلِ

٧١ أَصَاحِ تَرَى بَرْقًا أُرِيكَ وَمِيضَهُ　　كَلَمْعِ الْيَدَيْنِ فِي حَبِيٍّ مُكَلَّلِ

٧٢ يُضِيءُ سَنَاهُ أَوْ مَصَابِيحُ رَاهِبٍ　　أَمَالَ السَّلِيطَ بِالذُّبَالِ الْمُفَتَّلِ

٧٣ قَعَدْتُ لَهُ وَصُحْبَتِي بَيْنَ ضَارِجٍ　　وَبَيْنَ الْعُذَيْبِ بَعْدَ مَا مُتَأَمَّلِي

٧٤ عَلَى قَطَنٍ بِالشَّيْمِ أَيْمَنُ صَوْبِهِ وَأَيْسَرُهُ عَلَى السِّتَارِ فَيَذْبُلِ

٧٥ فَأَضْحَى يَسُحُّ الْمَاءَ حَوْلَ كُتَيْفَةٍ يَكُبُّ عَلَى الْأَذْقَانِ دَوْحَ الْكَنَهْبَلِ

٧٦ وَمَرَّ عَلَى الْقَنَانِ مِنْ نَفَيَانِهِ فَأَنْزَلَ مِنْهُ الْعُصْمَ مِنْ كُلِّ مُنْزَلِ

٧٧ وَتَيْمَاءَ لَمْ يَتْرُكْ بِهَا جِذْعَ نَخْلَةٍ وَلَا أُطُمًا إِلَّا مَشِيدًا بِجَنْدَلِ

٧٨ كَأَنَّ ثَبِيرًا فِي عَرَانِينِ وَبْلِهِ كَبِيرُ أُنَاسٍ فِي بِجَادٍ مُزَمَّلِ

٧٩ كَأَنَّ ذُرَا رَأْسِ الْمُجَيْمِرِ غُدْوَةً مِنَ السَّيْلِ وَالْغُثَاءِ فَلْكَةُ مِغْزَلِ

٨٠ وَأَلْقَى بِصَحْرَاءِ الْغَبِيطِ بَعَاعَهُ نُزُولَ الْيَمَانِي ذِي الْعِيَابِ الْمُحَمَّلِ

٨١ كَأَنَّ مَكَاكِيَّ الْجِوَاءِ غُدَيَّةً صُبِحْنَ سُلَافًا مِنْ رَحِيقٍ مُفَلْفَلِ

٨٢ كَأَنَّ السِّبَاعَ فِيهِ غَرْقَى عَشِيَّةً بِأَرْجَائِهِ الْقُصْوَى أَنَابِيشُ عُنْصُلِ

[48] قال قُطْبَةُ بْنُ سَيَّارِ بْنِ أَزْنَمَ

* يَجِيشُ بِطُوفَانٍ مِنَ الشَّدِّ جَرْيُهَا كَمَا سَحَّ شُؤْبُوبٌ مِنَ الْوَبْلِ مَاطِرُ

[49] قال عَلْقَمَةُ بْنُ عَبَدَةَ

* كَأَنَّهُمْ صَابَتْ عَلَيْهِمْ سَحَابَةٌ صَوَاعِقُهَا لِطَيْرِهِنَّ دَبِيبُ

[50] قال امْرُؤُ الْقَيْسِ بْنُ حُجْرٍ

* أَرِقْتُ لِبَرْقٍ بِلَيْلٍ أَهَلْ يُضِيءُ سَنَاهُ بِأَعْلَى الْجَبَلْ

Works Cited

Abu-Deeb, Kamal. "Studies in Arabic Literary Criticism: The Concept of Organic Unity." *Edebiyât* 2, no. 1 (1977): 57–89.

——. "Towards a Structural Analysis of Pre-Islamic Poetry." *International Journal of Middle Eastern Studies* 6 (1975): 148–84.

——. "Towards a Structural Analysis of Pre-Islamic Poetry (II): The Eros Vision." *Edebiyât* 1 (1976): 3–69.

Ahlwardt, Wilhelm. *Chalef elahmars Qasside*. Greifswald: C. A. Koch, 1859.

al-Ālūsī, Maḥmūd Shukrī. *Bulūgh al-Arab fī Maʿrifat Aḥwāl al-ʿArab*. Ed. Muḥammad Bahjat al-Atharī. 3 vols. 2d ed. Beirut: Dār al-Kutub al-ʿIlmiyyah, n.d.

al-Anbārī, Abū Bakr Muḥammad ibn al-Qāsim. *Sharḥ al-Qaṣāʾid al-Sabʿ al-Ṭiwāl al-Jāhiliyyāt*. Ed. ʿAbd al-Salām Muḥammad Hārūn. 2d ed. Cairo: Dār al-Maʿārif, 1969.

Arberry, A. J., trans. *The Koran Interpreted*. 2 vols. in 1. New York: Macmillan, 1969.

——. *The Seven Odes: The First Chapter in Arabic Literature*. London: George Allen and Unwin, 1957.

al-Asad, Nāṣir al-Dīn. *Maṣādir al-Shiʿr al-Jāhilī wa Qīmatuhā al-Tārīkhiyyah*. Cairo: Dār al-Maʿārif, 1962.

al-Aʿshā, Maymūn ibn Qays. *Sharḥ Dīwān al-Aʿshā*. Beirut: Dār al-Kātib al-ʿArabī, 1968.

al-Aṣmaʿī, Abū Saʿīd ʿAbd al-Malik ibn Qurayb. *Al-Aṣmaʿiyyāt*. Ed. Aḥmad Muḥammad Shākir and ʿAbd al-Salām Hārūn. 3d ed. Cairo: Dār al-Maʿārif, 1967.

al-Baghdādī, ʿAbd al-Qādir ibn ʿUmar. *Khizānat al-Adab wa Lubb Lubāb Lisān al-ʿArab*. Ed. ʿAbd al-Salām Hārūn. 13 vols. 2d ed. Cairo: Maktabat al-Khānjī, 1984.

Bellamy, J. A. "Some Observations on the Arabic *Rithāʾ* in the *Jāhilīyah* and Islam." *Jerusalem Studies in Arabic and Islam* 13 (1990): 44–61.

Bettelheim, Bruno. *The Uses of Enchantment: The Meaning and Importance of Fairy Tales*. New York: Random House, 1977.
Bevan, Anthony Ashley, ed. *Kitāb al-Naqā'iḍ: Naqā'iḍ Jarīr wa al-Farazdaq*. 3 vols. Baghdad: Maktabat al-Muthannā, n.d. [offset of Leiden: E. J. Brill, 1907].
Blachère, Régis. *Histoire de la littérature arabe des origines à la fin du XVe siècle de J.-C.*. 3 vols. Paris: Maisonneuve, 1952, 1964, 1966.
Bloch, Alfred. "Qaṣīda." *Etudes Asiatiques: Revue de la Société Suisse d'études asiatiques* 2 (1948): 106–32.
Bodkin, Maud. *Archetypal Patterns in Poetry: Psychological Studies of Imagination*. London: Oxford University Press, 1963.
Boustany, S. "Imru' al-Ḳays b. Ḥudjr." *The Encyclopaedia of Islam*. 2d ed.
al-Buḥturī, al-Walīd Abū ʿUbādah. *Al-Ḥamāsah*. Ed. Kamāl Muṣṭafā. Cairo: al-Maṭbaʿah al-Raḥmāniyyah, 1929.
al-Bukhārī, Abū ʿAbd Allāh. *Ṣaḥīḥ Abī ʿAbd Allāh al-Bukhārī bi-Sharḥ al-Kirmānī*. 25 vols. Cairo: al-Maṭbaʿah al-Bahiyyah al-Miṣriyyah, 1933–62.
Burkert, Walter. *Homo Necans: The Anthropology of Ancient Greek Ritual and Myth*. Trans. Peter Bing. Berkeley: University of California Press, 1983 [*Homo Necans*, 1972].
Bynum, Caroline Walker. *Holy Feast and Holy Fast: The Religious Significance of Food to Medieval Women*. Berkeley: University of California Press, 1987.
Campbell, Joseph. *The Hero with a Thousand Faces*. New York: Pantheon Books, 1949.
Chelhod, Joseph. *Le sacrifice chez les Arabes: Recherches sur l'évolution, la nature, et la fonction des rites sacrificiels en Arabie occidentale*. Paris: Presses Universitaires de France, 1955.
Delcourt, Marie. *Oedipe; ou, La légende du conquérant*. Paris: E. Droz, 1944.
Detienne, Marcel. *The Gardens of Adonis: Spices in Greek Mythology*. Trans. Janet Lloyd. Atlantic Highlands, N.J.: Humanities Press, 1977.
Diel, Paul. *Symbolism in Greek Mythology: Human Desire and Its Transformations*. Boulder, Colo.: Shambhala, 1980.
Douglas, Mary. *Implicit Meanings: Essays in Anthropology*. London: Routledge and Kegan Paul, 1975.
——. *Purity and Danger: An Analysis of Concepts of Pollution and Taboo*. London: Routledge and Kegan Paul, 1966.
The Encyclopaedia of Islam. 1st ed. Ed. M. Th. Houtsma et al. Leiden: E. J. Brill, 1913–36. 2d ed. Ed. H. A. R. Gibb et al. Leiden: E. J. Brill, 1960–.
Gabrieli, Francesco. "Sull'autenticità della *Lāmiyyat al-ʿarab*." *Revista degli Studi Orientali* 15 (1935): 358–61.
——. "Ta'abbaṭa Šarran, Šanfarà, Ḫalaf al-Aḥmar." *Atti della Accademia Nazionale dei Lincei*, ser. 8 (1946): 40–69.
Gaster, Theodor H. *Thespis: Ritual, Myth, and Drama in the Ancient Near East*. New York: W. W. Norton, 1977.
Gelder, G. J. H. van. *Beyond the Line: Classical Arabic Literary Critics on the Coherence and Unity of the Poem*. Leiden: E. J. Brill, 1982.
Gennep, Arnold van. *The Rites of Passage*. Trans. Monika B. Vizedom and Gabrielle L. Caffee. Chicago: University of Chicago Press, 1960 [*Les rites de passage*, 1908].

Ghayth, Muḥammad Ṣiddīq. "Al-Taḥlīl al-Dirāmī lil-Aṭlāl bi Muʿallaqat Labīd." *Fuṣūl* 4 (Jan. 1984): 165–77.
Girard, René. *Violence and the Sacred.* Trans. Patrick Gregory. Baltimore: Johns Hopkins University Press, 1979 [*La violence et le sacré*, 1972].
Goldziher, Ignaz. *Gesammelte Schriften.* Ed. Joseph Desomogyi. Hildesheim: G. Olms, 1970.
——. *Muslim Studies.* Ed. S. M. Stern. Trans. C. M. Barber and Stern. 2 vols. Vol. 1: Albany, N.Y.: State University of New York Press, 1967. Vol. 2: Chicago: Aldine, 1970.
Grunebaum, G. E. von. *Muhammaden Festivals.* New York: Schuman, 1951.
Guillaume, Alfred, trans. *The Life of Muhammad: A Translation of Isḥāq's "Sīrat Rasūl Allāh."* Lahore: Oxford University Press, Pakistan Branch, 1974.
Hall, James. *A History of Ideas and Images in Italian Art.* London: J. Murray, 1983.
Hamori, Andras. *On the Art of Medieval Arabic Literature.* Princeton, N.J.: Princeton University Press, 1974.
Hava, J. G. *Al-Faraid Arabic-English Dictionary.* Beirut: Catholic Press, 1964.
Havelock, Eric A. *The Muse Learns to Write: Reflections on Orality and Literacy from Antiquity to the Present.* New Haven, Conn.: Yale University Press, 1986.
Haydar, Adnan. "*The Muʿallaqa of Imruʾ al-Qays*: Its Structure and Meaning." Part I: *Edebiyât* 2 (1977): 227–61; Part II: *Edebiyât* 3 (1978): 51–82.
Hesiod, the Homeric Hymns, Fragments of the Epic Cycle, and Homerica. Trans. Hugh G. Evelyn-White. Loeb Classicial Library, 57. Cambridge: Harvard University Press, 1982.
Homerin, Th. E. "Echoes of a Thirsty Owl." *Journal of Near Eastern Studies* 44, no. 3 (1985): 165–84.
Hubert, Henri, and Marcel Mauss. *Sacrifice: Its Nature and Function.* Trans. W. D. Halls. Chicago: University of Chicago Press, 1981 [*Essai sur la nature et la fonction du sacrifice*, 1898].
al-Hudhaliyyūn, *Dīwān al-Hudhaliyyīn.* Cairo: Dār al-Qawmiyyah, 1965. [Photo offset of Cairo: Dār al-Kutub, 1945–50.]
al-Ḥūfī, Aḥmad Muḥammad. *Al-Marʾah fī al-Shiʿr al-Jāhilī.* 2d ed. Cairo: Dār al-Fikr al-ʿArabī, 1963.
Hurgronje, Snouck. "Le droit Musluman." Trans. Arnold van Gennep. In G. H. Bousquet and Joseph Schacht, eds. *Selected Works of C. Snouck Hurgronje.* Leiden: E. J. Brill, 1957
al-Ḥuṣrī, Ibrāhīm ibn ʿAlī. *Zahr al-Ādāb wa Thamar al-Albāb.* Ed. ʿAlī Muḥammad al-Bijāwī. 2 vols. 2d ed. Cairo: ʿĪsā al-Bābī al-Ḥalabī, 1969.
Ibn ʿAbd Rabbih, Abū ʿUmar Aḥmad ibn Muḥammad. *Kitāb al-ʿIqd al-Farīd.* Ed. Aḥmad Amīn, Aḥmad al-Zayn, and Ibrāhīm al-Abyārī. 7 vols. 3d ed. Cairo: Maṭbaʿat Lajnat al-Taʾlīf wa al-Tarjamah wa al-Nashr, 1969.
Ibn al-Athīr, ʿIzz al-Dīn. *Al-Kāmil fī al-Taʾrīkh.* 13 vols. Beirut: Dār Ṣādir/Dār Bayrūt, 1965.
Ibn Hishām, Abū Muḥammad ʿAbd al-Malik. *Al-Sīrah al-Nabawiyyah.* 4 vols. Cairo: Dār al-Fikr, n.d..
Ibn Manẓūr, Muḥammad ibn Mukarram. *Lisān al-ʿArab.* 15 vols. Beirut: Dār Ṣādir, 1955–56.

Ibn Qutaybah, ʿAbd Allāh ibn Muslim. *Kitāb al-Shiʿr wa al-Shuʿarāʾ*. Ed. M. J. de Goeje. Leiden: E. J. Brill, 1904.

Ibn Rashīq al-Qayrawānī, Abū ʿAlī al-Ḥasan. *Al-ʿUmdah fī Maḥāsin al-Shiʿr wa Ādābih wa Naqdih*. Ed. Muḥammad Muḥyī al-Dīn ʿAbd al-Ḥamīd. 2 vols. in 1. 4th ed. Beirut: Dār al-Jīl, 1972.

Imruʾ al-Qays. *Dīwān*. Ed. Muḥammad Abū Faḍl Ibrāhīm. 3d ed. Cairo: Dār al-Maʿārif, 1969.

al-Iṣbahānī, Abū al-Faraj. *Kitāb al-Aghānī*. Ed. Ibrāhīm al-Abyārī. 32 vols. Cairo: Dār al-Shaʿb, 1970.

ʿIzz al-Dīn, Ḥasan al-Bannā. *Al-Kalimāt wa al-Ashyāʾ: Baḥth fī al-Taqālīd al-Fanniyyah lil-Qaṣīdah al-Jāhiliyyah*. Cairo: Dār al-Fikr al-ʿArabī, 1988.

——. *Al-Ṭayf wa al-Khayāl fī al-Shiʿr al-ʿArabī al-Qadīm*. Cairo: Dār al-Nadīm, 1988.

Jacob, Georg. *Schanfarà-Studien*, parts 1 and 2. In *Abhandlungen der Königlich bayerischen Akademie der Wissenschaften, philosophisch-philologische und historische Klasse*, 1914, no. 8, and 1915, no. 4. Munich, 1914, 1915.

Jacobi, Renate. "The Camel-Section of the Panegyrical Ode." *Journal of Arabic Literature* 8 (1982): 1–22.

——. *Studien zur Poetik der altarabischen Qaṣide*. Wiesbaden: Franz Steiner, 1971.

al-Jāḥiẓ, Abū ʿUthmān ʿAmr ibn Baḥr. *Al-Ḥayawān*. Ed. ʿAbd al-Salām Muḥammad Hārūn. 8 vols. Cairo: Muṣṭafā al-Bābī al-Ḥalabī, 1965–69.

Jamison, Stephanie W. *The Ravenous Hyenas and the Wounded Sun: Myth and Ritual in Ancient India*. Ithaca, N.Y.: Cornell University Press, 1991.

Juynboll, Th. W. "Ḥadīth." *The Encyclopaedia of Islam*. 1st ed.

Kaḥḥālah, ʿUmar Riḍā. *Aʿlām al-Nisāʾ fī ʿĀlamay al-ʿArab wa al-Islām*. 5 vols. Damascus: Muʾassasat al-Risālah, 1977.

Kerenyi, Karl. *The Heroes of the Greeks*. Trans. H. J. Rose. London: Thames and Hudson, 1959.

al-Khalīl ibn Aḥmad al-Farāhīdī. *Kitāb al-ʿAyn*. Ed. ʿAbd Allāh Darwīsh. Baghdad: Maṭbaʿat al-ʿĀnī, 1968.

al-Khirniq. *Dīwān al-Khirniq Ukht Ṭarafah*. Ed. Luwīs Shaykhū. Beirut: Maṭbaʿat al-Ābāʾ al-Yasūʿiyyīn, 1899.

——. *Dīwān Shiʿr al-Khirniq bint Badr ibn Hiffān*. Ed. Ḥusayn Naṣṣār. [Cairo,] U.A.R.: Maṭbaʿat Dār al-Kutub, 1969.

Khulayyif, Yūsuf. *Al-Shuʿarāʾ al-Ṣaʿālīk fī al-ʿAṣr al-Jāhilī*. Cairo: Dār al-Maʿārif, 1966.

Krenkow, Fritz. "Al-Shanfarā." *The Encyclopaedia of Islam*. 1st. ed.

Labīd ibn Rabīʿah al-ʿĀmirī. *Dīwān*. Beirut: Dār Ṣādir, n.d.

Lammens, Henri. "Le caractère religieux du *ṯār* ou vendetta chez les Arabes préislamistes." *Bulletin de l'Institut Français d'Archéologie Orientale* 26 (1926): 83–127.

Lane, Edward William. *Arabic-English Lexicon*. 8 vols. New York: Frederick Ungar, 1958 [London, 1863].

Laylā al-Akhyaliyyah. *Dīwān*. Ed. Khalīl Ibrāhīm al-ʿAṭiyyah and Jalīl al-ʿAṭiyyah. Baghdad: Dār al-Jumhūriyyah, 1967.

Leach, Edmund. "Against Genres: Are Parables Lights Set in Candlesticks or Put under a Bushel?" In Leach and D. Alan Aycock, *Structuralist Interpretations of Biblical Myth*. Cambridge: Cambridge University Press, 1983.

Lyall, Charles James, ed. and trans. *The Dīwāns of ʿAbīd ibn al-Abraṣ, of Asad, and ʿĀmir ibn aṭ-Ṭufail, of ʿĀmir ibn Ṣaʿṣaʿah*. Cambridge: Cambridge University Press, 1980 [Reprint of E. J. W. Gibb Memorial Series, vol. 21, 1913].

——. *The Mufaḍḍalīyāt: An Anthology of Ancient Arabian Odes Compiled by al-Mufaḍḍal Son of Muḥammad according to the Recension and with the Commentary of Abū Muḥammad al-Qāsim ibn Muḥammad al-Anbārī*. Vol. 1: Arabic text. Vol. 2: translation and notes. Oxford: Clarendon Press, 1921.

——. *Translations of Ancient Arabian Poetry, Chiefly Prae-Islamic, with Introduction and Notes*. New York: Columbia University Press, 1930.

Madelung, W. "Imāmah." *The Encyclopaedia of Islam*. 2d ed.

Malti-Douglas, Fedwa. "Structure and Organization in a Monographic *Adab* Work: *Al-Taṭfīl* of al-Khaṭīb al-Baghdādī." *Journal of Near Eastern Studies* 40, no. 3 (1981): 227–45.

al-Marzūqī, Abū ʿAlī Aḥmad ibn Muḥammad al-Ḥasan. *Sharḥ Dīwān al-Ḥamāsah*. Ed. Aḥmad Amīn and ʿAbd al-Salām Hārūn. 4 vols. 2d ed. Cairo: Maṭbaʿat Lajnat al-Taʾlīf wa al-Tarjamah wa al-Nashr, 1967.

Mauss, Marcel. *The Gift: The Forms and Functions of Exchange in Archaic Societies*. Trans. Ian Cunnison. New York: Norton, 1967 [*Essai sur le don, form archaïque de l'échange*, 1925].

al-Maymanī, ʿAbd al-ʿAzīz. *Al-Ṭarāʾif al-Adabiyyah*. Cairo: Maṭbaʿat Lajnat al-Taʾlīf wa al-Tarjamah wa al-Nashr, 1937.

Monroe, J. T. "Oral Composition in Pre-Islamic Poetry." *Journal of Arabic Literature* 3 (1972): 1–53.

al-Mubarrad, Abū al-ʿAbbās Muḥammad ibn Yazīd. *Al-Kāmil fī al-Lughah wa al-Adab*. 2 vols. Beirut: Muʾassasat al-Maʿārif, n.d.

al-Mufaḍḍal al-Ḍabbī, Abū al-ʿAbbās. *Dīwān al-Mufaḍḍaliyyāt*. Commentary by Abū Muḥammad al-Qāsim ibn Muḥammad al-Anbārī. Ed. Charles James Lyall. Beirut: Maṭbaʿat al-Ābāʾ al-Yasūʿiyyīn, 1920 [= vol. 1 of Lyall, ed. *The Mufaḍḍalīyāt*].

——. *Al-Mufaḍḍaliyyāt*. Ed. Aḥmad Muḥammad Shākir and ʿAbd al-Salām Muḥammad Hārūn. 5th ed. Cairo: Dār al-Maʿārif, 1976.

Müller, Gottfried. *Ich bin Labīd und das ist mein Ziel: Zum Problem der Selbstbehauptung in der altarabischen Qaside*. Wiesbaden: Franz Steiner, 1981.

Nagy, Gregory. *Greek Mythology and Poetics*. Ithaca, N.Y.: Cornell University Press, 1990.

Nicholson, Reynold A. *A Literary History of the Arabs*. Cambridge: Cambridge University Press, 1956.

Nöldeke, Theodor. *Beiträge zur Kenntnis der Poesie des alten Araber*. Hildesheim: Georg Olms, 1967. [Photo rpr. of Hanover, 1864]

al-Nuwayrī, Shihāb al-Dīn Aḥmad ibn ʿAbd al-Wahhāb. *Nihāyat al-Arab fī Funūn al-Adab*. 18 vols. Cairo: al-Muʾassasah al-Miṣriyyah al-ʿĀmmah lil-Taʾlīf wa al-Tarjamah wa al-Ṭibāʿah wa al-Nashr, 1964.

Ong, Walter J. *Orality and Literacy: The Technologizing of the Word*. London: Methuen, 1982.
Onians, Richard Broxton. *The Origins of European Thought about the Body, the Mind, the Soul, the World, Time, and Fate*. Cambridge: Cambridge University Press, 1951.
Pedersen, Johannes. *Der Eid bei den Semiten in seinem Verhältnis zu verwandten Erscheinungen sowie die Stellung des Eides im Islam*. Strassburg: Karl J. Trübner, 1914.
Procksch, Otto. *Über die Blutrache bei den vorislamischen Arabern und Mohammeds Stellung zu ihr*. Leipzig: B. G. Teubner, 1899.
Propp, Vladimir. *Morphology of the Folktale*. Trans. Laurence Scott. 2d ed. Austin, Tex.: University of Texas Press, 1968.
al-Qālī, Abū ʿAlī Ismāʿīl ibn al-Qāsim. *Kitāb al-Amālī wa yalīh al-Dhayl wa al-Nawādir lil-Muʾallif wa Kitāb al-Tanbīh li Abī ʿUbayd al-Bakrī*. 4 vols. in 2. Beirut: al-Maktab al-Tijārī, 1965.
Roberts, Nancy N. "Voice and Gender: An Annotated Translation of Three Passages from Aḥmad Ibn Abī Ṭāhir Ṭayfūr's *Balāghāt al-Nisāʾ*." *Al-ʿArabiyya*. Forthcoming.
Robertson Smith, W. *Kinship and Marriage in Early Arabia*. Oosterhout N.B., Netherlands: Anthropological Publications, 1966. [Reprint of 2d ed., 1907]
——. *The Religion of the Semites: The Fundamental Institutions*. New York: Meridian Books, 1957 [London, 1889].
Rückert, Friedrich. *Hamasa; oder, Die ältesten arabischen Volkslieder, gesammelt von Abu Temmâm*. 2 vols. Stuttgart: S. G. Liesching, 1846.
Sacy, Sylvestre de. *Chrestomathie arabe*. 3 vols. Paris: Imprimerie royale, 1926.
al-Sandūbī, Ḥasan. *Akhbār al-Marāqisah wa Ashʿāruhum fī al-Jāhiliyyah wa Ṣadr al-Islām*. Cairo: Maṭbaʿat al-Istiqāmah, 1939.
Ṣaqr, ʿAbd al-Badīʿ. *Shāʿirāt al-ʿArab*. N.p.: Manshūrāt al-Maktab al-Islāmī, n.d.
Sells, Michael A. *Desert Tracings: Six Classical Arabian Odes*. Middletown, Conn.: Wesleyan University Press, 1989.
——. "The *Qaṣīda* and the West: Self-Reflective Stereotype and Critical Encounter." *Al-ʿArabiyya* 20 (1987): 307–24.
Sezgin, Fuat. *Geschichte des arabischen Schrifttums*, vol. 2: *Poesie bis ca. 430 H.* Leiden: E. J. Brill, 1975.
Shahîd, I. "Kinda." *The Encyclopaedia of Islam*. 2d ed.
Shākir and Hārūn. *See* al-Mufaḍḍal al-Ḍabbī, Abū al-ʿAbbas.
Shaykhū, Luwīs. *Kitāb Shuʿarāʾ al-Naṣrāniyyah*. 2 vols. 2d ed. Beirut: al-Maṭbaʿah al-Kāthūlīkiyyah, 1967.
——. *Riyāḍ al-Adab fī Marāthī Shawāʿir al-ʿArab: Al-juzʾ al-awwal fī Shawāʿir al-Jāhiliyyah*. Beirut: Al-Maṭbaʿah al-Kāthūlīkiyyah, lil-Ābāʾ al-Yasūʿiyyah, 1897.
Slochower, Harry. *Mythopoesis: Mythic Patterns in the Literary Classics*. Detroit: Wayne State University Press, 1970.
Smith, W. Robertson. *See* Robertson Smith, W.
Sperl, Stefan. "Islamic Kingship and Arabic Panegyric Poetry in the Early 9th Century." *Journal of Arabic Literature* 8 (1977): 20–35.
——. *Mannerism in Arabic Poetry: A Structuralist Analysis of Selected Texts (3rd Century*

A.H./9th Century A.D.–5th Century A.H./11th Century A.D.). Cambridge: Cambridge University Press, 1989.

Stetkevych, Jaroslav. "Arabic Hermeneutical Terminology: Paradox and the Production of Meaning." *Journal of Near Eastern Studies* 48, no. 2 (1989): 81–96.

——. "Name and Epithet: The Philology and Semiotics of Animal Nomenclature in Early Arabic Poetry." *Journal of Near Eastern Studies* 45, no. 2 (1986): 112–25.

——. Sīniyyat Aḥmad Shawqī wa ʿIyār al-Shiʿr al-ʿArabī al-Kilāsīkī." *Fuṣūl* 7 (Oct. 1986–Mar. 1987): 12–29.

——. "Toward an Arabic Elegiac Lexicon: The Seven Words of the Nasīb." In S. Stetkevych, ed. *Reorientations.*

——. *The Zephyrs of Najd: The Poetics of Nostalgia in the Classical Arabic Nasīb.* Chicago: University of Chicago Press, 1993.

Stetkevych, Suzanne Pinckney. *Abū Tammām and the Poetics of the ʿAbbāsid Age.* Studies in Arabic Literature, 13. Leiden: E. J. Brill, 1991.

——. "Archetype and Attribution in Early Arabic Poetry: al-Shanfarā and the *Lāmiyyat al-ʿArab.*" *International Journal of Middle Eastern Studies* 18 (1986): 361–90.

——. "Durayd ibn al-Ṣimmah and the Passing of the Heroic Age." Unpublished paper presented at the annual meeting of the American Oriental Society; Baltimore, 1983.

——. "Intoxication and Immortality: Wine and Associated Imagery in al-Maʿarrī's Garden." In Fedwa Malti-Douglas, ed., *Critical Pilgrimages: Studies in the Arabic Literary Tradition* [= *Literature East and West* 25 (1989)], 29–48.

——. "The Nature of Narrative in the *Kitāb al-Aghānī.*" Unpublished paper presented at the annual meeting of the Middle East Studies Association, Philadelphia, 1982.

——. "Pre-Islamic Panegyric and the Poetics of Redemption: *Mufaḍḍaliyyah 119* of ʿAlqamah and *Bānat Suʿād* of Kaʿb ibn Zuhayr." In S. Stetkevych, ed. *Reorientations.*

——. *"Al-Qaṣīdah al-ʿArabiyyah wa Ṭuqūs al-ʿUbūr." Majallat Majmaʿ al-Lughah al-ʿArabiyyah bi-Dimashq* 60, no. 1 (1985): 55–85.

——. "*The Rithā' of Ta'abbaṭa Sharran*: A Study of Blood-Vengeance in Early Arabic Poetry." *Journal of Semitic Studies* 31, no. 1 (1986) 27–45.

——. "Ritual and Sacrificial Elements in the Poetry of Blood-Vengeance: Two Poems by Durayd ibn al-Ṣimmah and Muhalhil ibn Rabīʿah." *Journal of Near Eastern Studies* 45, no. 1 (1986): 31–43.

——. "Sarah and the Hyena: Laughter, Menstruation, and the Genesis of a Double Entendre." Unpublished paper presented at the annual meeting of the American Oriental Society, Berkeley, Calif., 1991.

——. "Structuralist Analyses of Pre-Islamic Poetry: Critique and New Directions." *Journal of Near Eastern Studies* 42, no. 2 (1983): 85–107.

——. "The Ṣuʿlūk and His Poem: A Paradigm of Passage Manqué." *Journal of the American Oriental Society* 104, no. 4 (1984): 661–78.

——, ed. *Reorientations/Arabic and Persian Poetry.* Bloomington: Indiana University Press, 1993.

al-Suyūṭī, ʿAbd al-Raḥmān Jalāl al-Dīn. *Al-Muzhir fī ʿUlūm al-Lughah wa Anwāʿihā.* Ed. Muḥammad Aḥmad Jād al-Mawlā Bek. 2 vols. Cairo: ʿĪsā al-Bābī al-Ḥalabī, 1945.

Svenbro, Jesper. *Phrasikleia: Anthropologie de la lecture en Grèce ancienne.* Paris: la Découverte, 1988.

al-Ṭabarī, Abū Jaʿfar Muḥammad ibn Jarīr. *The History of al-Ṭabarī (Taʾrīkh al-rusul waʾl-mulūk)*, Vol. 7: *The Foundation of the Community.* Ed. and trans. W. Montgomery Watt and M. V. McDonald. Albany: State University of New York Press, 1987.

——. *Jāmiʿ al-Bayān ʿan Āy al-Qurʾān.* 30 vols. 3d ed. Cairo: Muṣṭafā al-Bābī al-Ḥalabī, 1968.

——. *Taʾrīkh al-Rusul wa al-Mulūk.* = Abū Djafar Mohammed ibn Djarir at-Tabari. *Annales.* Ed. M. J. de Goeje. 15 vols. Leiden: E. J. Brill, 1964–65 [Photo edition of 1879–1901].

Ṭayfūr, Aḥmad ibn Abī Ṭāhir. *Balāghāt al-Nisāʾ wa Ṭarāʾif Kalāmihinna wa Mulaḥ Nawādirihinna wa Akhbār Dhawāt al-Raʾy minhunna wa Ashʿāruhunna fī al-Jāhiliyyah wa al-Islām.* Ed. Aḥmad al-Alfī. Tunis: al-Maktabah al-ʿAtīqah, 1985 [reprint of Cairo, 1326/1908].

al-Tibrīzī, Abū Zakariyyā Yaḥyā ibn ʿAlī al-Shaybānī. *Sharḥ al-Mufaḍḍaliyyāt.* Ed. ʿAlī Muḥammad al-Bijāwī. 3 vols. Cairo: Dār Nahḍat Miṣr lil-Ṭabʿ wa al-Nashr, 1977.

——. *Sharḥ al-Tibrīzī ʿalā Dīwān Ashʿār al-Ḥamāsah.* 2 vols. Cairo: Būlāq, 1879.

Turner, Victor. *The Forest of Symbols: Aspects of Ndembu Ritual.* Ithaca, N.Y.: Cornell Univeristy Press, 1967.

——. *The Ritual Process: Structure and Anti-Structure.* Ithaca, N.Y.: Cornell University Press, 1977.

Vermeule, Emily. *Aspects of Death in Early Greek Art and Poetry.* Berkeley: University of California Press, 1979.

Vernant, Jean-Pierre. "The Lame Tyrant: From Oedipus to Periander." In Vernant and Pierre Vidal-Naquet. *Myth and Tragedy in Ancient Greece.* Trans. Janet Lloyd. New York: Zone Books, 1988.

Vidal-Naquet, Pierre. "The Black Hunter and the Origin of the Athenian Ephebeia." In R. L. Gordon, ed., *Myth, Religion, and Society: Structuralist Essays by M. Detienne, L. Gernet, J.-P. Vernant, and P. Vidal-Naquet.* Cambridge: Cambridge University Press, 1981.

——. "Sophocles' *Philoctetes* and the Ephebeia." In Jean-Pierre Vernant and Vidal-Naquet, *Tragedy and Myth in Ancient Greece.* Trans. Janet Lloyd. Sussex: Harvester Press, 1981.

Wensinck, A. J. "Sunnah." *The Encyclopaedia of Islam.* 1st ed.

Wright, William. *A Grammar of the Arabic Language.* 2 vols. 3d ed. Cambridge: Cambridge University Press, 1955.

al-Yūsuf, Yūsuf. "Taḥlīl Muʿallaqat Imriʾ al-Qays." *Al-Maʿrifah* 163 (1975): 62–91.

al-Zamakhsharī, Muḥammad ibn ʿUmar. *Aʿjab al-ʿAjab fī Sharḥ Lāmiyyat al-ʿArab.* In al-Shanfarā, *Qaṣīdat Lāmiyyat al-ʿArab wa yalīhā. . . .* Istanbul: Maṭbaʿat al-Jawāʾib, 1300 H. [includes the al-Mubarrad/Thaʿlab commentary].

al-Zawzanī, Abū ʿAbd Allāh al-Ḥusayn ibn Aḥmad. *Sharḥ al-Muʿallaqāt al-Sabʿ*. Ed. Muḥammad ʿAlī Ḥamd Allāh. Damascus: al-Maktabah al-Umawiyyah, 1963.

Zwettler, Michael. *The Oral Tradition of Classical Arabic Poetry: Its Character and Implications*. Columbus: Ohio State University Press, 1972.

Index

ʿAbd Allāh ibn ʿAbd al-Muṭṭalib, 38
ʿAbd al-Muṭṭalib, 38, 163n
ʿAbīd ibn al-Abraṣ, 186, 242n, 243, 279
abomination, 99, 140–41, 192, 199–205, 208–9, 223, 244
Abu-Deeb, K., 4, 6n, 9n, 241n
Abū Tammām. *See Al-Ḥamāsah*
aggregation, 33–42, 52, 71–72, 273–83; metaphorical, 156–57. *See also* rite of passage
ʿAlqamah, 180, 279
al-Ālūsī, Maḥmūd Shukrī, 24, 28n, 38n, 39n, 98n, 174n, 175n, 192n
ʿĀmir ibn al-Ṭufayl, 50, 53–54
al-Anbārī, Abū Bakr, 18n, 67n, 257n, 267, 280
al-Anbārī, Abū Muḥammad, 31n, 107n, 108, 127, 136n
ʿAntarah, 172
Arbad ibn Qays, 50, 52–54
Arberry, A. J., 9n, 24n, 241n
archetypal criticism, 6
arrested development, 74, 261, 264, 267–73
al-Asad, N., 123n
al-Aʿshā, Maymūn ibn Qays, 34–35
al-Aṣmaʿī, Abū Saʿīd/*Al-Aṣmaʿiyyāt*: *ʿAṣm. no. 53*, 225
aṭlāl (ruined abodes), 18, 76–77, 215, 221–23, 236–37, 259–61
authenticity of pre-Islamic poetry, 57–58, 119–25
ʿAwaḍ, L., 264

Badr, Battle of, 199–205
al-Baghdādī, ʿAbd al-Qādir, 169–71, 173n, 175, 186, 189
al-Basūs: she-camel of, 207–10; War of, 206–38 passim
Bellamy, J. A., 162n, 164
Bettelheim, B., 37n, 53n
Bible: *Job 29:30*, 68; *Luke 17:37*, 68; *Matthew 24:28*, 68
Blachère, R., 119, 122–23, 124n, 132
Bloch, A., 82n
blood: drinking of, 66, 68–70, 186; and henna, 277; and immortality, 68–70; and milk, 208; and mulberry, 186–87; polluted, 194; sacrifice of, 34–35; washing blood with, 174, 227. *See also* menstrual blood
blood-stained clothes, 186–87, 191
blood vengeance, 55–83; excessive, 223–24, 244–48, 272, 281, 284; as inheritance, 61, 244–45, 248; as inverted sacrifice, 69–70, 80–81, 202–3; as rite of passage/initiation, 73–75, 80; ritual pattern of, 70–73, 75, 244–45, 258–59; as sacrifice, 187; as sacrilege, 140–41
bloodwite, 27, 38, 193–94, 196–97, 210
Boustany, S., 241n
brigand-poet. *See ṣuʿlūk*
al-Bukhārī, Abū ʿAbd Allāh, 173n
Burkert, W., 55, 56n, 82–83, 266
Bynum, C. W., 174n

camel, 271. *See also* she-camel
camel slaughter, 37–41, 66, 154, 208–10, 262–66. *See also maysir*; sacrifice
cannibalism, 202–3
Chelhod, J., 21–22, 55, 57, 62n, 65n, 69, 72n, 80, 130, 156n
chiastic pattern of rites, 56–57, 64, 70

Christ as sacrifice, 68–69, 174
circumambulation, 156–57, 277
cloth, 25, 281. *See also* weaving
commensal feast, 37, 187, 277; blood vengeance as inverted form, 65, 69–70, 80–81; and return of dead, 69–70. *See also* sacrifice
consecration. *See iḥrām*
crow, 215, 233

damnation, 52–54, 283–85
dār al-qarār, 41–42, 52
Dārat Juljul, 246, 258, 262–64, 277
death and rebirth, 7, 34, 219, 278, 282–83
Delcourt, M., 6, 95, 98–99
Detienne, M., 262n, 269, 274
Dhū al-Khalaṣah, 247, 284
diametrical oppposition, 150. *See also* symmetrical inversion
Diel, P., 99–101, 130
dormition of the virgin, 267
Douglas, M., 7–8, 26–27, 55, 89, 91, 116, 141–42, 155, 174, 195, 277n
dove, 236–37
Durayd ibn al-Ṣimmah, 63, 73–83; *akhbār*, 73–75; *Maʿshar Has Been Deserted*, 76–81, 227

effeminacy, 196, 218–20, 237
egg, 267–70
elegy. *See rithāʾ*
ephebe manqué, 89. *See also* rite of passage: manqué
epistolary function of poem, 82
equal of dead kinsman, slaying of, 63, 141, 223, 229, 238
equals in combat, 200, 229, 238. *See also inṣāf*
eroticism, 245–46; illicit, 261–70; immature, 245, 261; perverted *(ghūl)*, 93–104; poetry, 245–46
exchange, ritual, 55, 64
exegetical function of poems, 231–32, 234
eye, 177–79, 234

faʿʿāl-form (intensive adjective), 108, 115, 117–18, 183–84
fakhr (boast), 4, 33–42, 274–83
faras. *See* horse
al-Fāriʿah bint Shaddād, 176–88
al-Farrār al-Sulamī, 171
feralization/anthropomorphization, 151–53, 156
foot, 99–101, 130, 138. *See also* gait
formula, oral-elegiac, 169–71, 177–87, 190, 220–22

Gabrieli, F., 121–22, 143
gait, special/irregular, 99–101, 130, 192, 233
gambling. *See maysir*
Gaster, T., seasonal pattern, 69–70, 77n, 180n, 233, 258–62, 273, 277–78, 280
Gelder, G. J. H. van, 4
gender distinction in *rithāʾ*, 167, 175–76, 197–99, 211–12, 213–15, 237
gender inversion, 138–40
gender-linked imagery, 194–96, 198–99
generosity, 34–43 passim, 46, 51–52, 139, 177–79, 187–88, 214, 221, 277
Gennep, A. van, 6–8, 55–56, 88
Ghayth, M. Ṣ., 9n
ghūl, 93–104
Girard, R., 55, 56n, 64, 157
Goldziher, I., 69n, 123–24, 162, 163n, 169n, 182n
Guillaume, A., 199n–205n

al-Ḥādirah, 170
ḥadīth collection, 123–24
ḥajj, 140–41, 156
ḥalāl/ḥarām, 62, 71–72, 228, 234
Hall, J., 267n
al-Ḥamāsah of Abū Tammām: *The Rithāʾ of Taʾabbaṭa Sharran*, 58–60; *Ḥam. no. 52*, 193; *no. 164*, 129; *no. 272*, 63; *no. 671*, 196
Hamori, A., 6n, 258n
Ḥamzah ibn ʿAbd al-Muṭṭalib, 200–205
handmill, 172, 229
Harīdī, A., 87
Ḥassān ibn Thābit, 201, 203n
Havelock, E., 22, 81n, 122
Haydar, A., 4, 6n, 63n, 241n, 242n, 259–60, 263n, 264n, 273–74, 275n, 277n, 281
Hesiod, 99n
hijāʾ (invective), 4
ḥilm (forbearance), 45, 284
Hind bint Athāthah, 203–5
Hind bint Ḥudhayfah, 197–99
Hind bint ʿUtbah, 199–205
Homerin, Th. E., 69–70, 186n
horse, 35–36, 231–34, 273–78; lack of, 109, 150
hospitality, 39; breaking law of, 112–13. *See also* generosity
Hubert, H., 55–56, 75, 258

al-Ḥūfī, A. M., 161n, 162n, 164–66, 182n, 202n
Ḥujr ibn al-Ḥārith, 242–46, 280
humūm (cares), 154, 198, 271
hunger, 91, 138–40, 152–53
hunt, 277–78
Hurgronje, S., 124n
al-Ḥuṣrī, Ibrāhīm, 177n
hyena, 66–67, 79–80, 130, 151, 233

Ibn ʿAbd Rabbih, 120, 204n, 227n
Ibn al-Athīr, ʿIzz al-Dīn, 211n, 213n
Ibn Durayd, 120–21
Ibn Hishām, Abū Muḥammad, 164n, 199–205
Ibn Manẓūr, Muḥammad, 94, 97, 120, 172n, 177–79
Ibn Qutaybah, 3n, 19n, 46, 50–51, 52n, 102n, 104n, 257, 262n, 264n, 285
Ibn Rashīq al-Qayrawānī, 4, 82
Ibrāhīm, 66–67
iḥrām (consecration), 62, 72, 80, 140, 155–56, 227
ijmāʿ (consensus), 123–24
imām, 41, 44
immaturity, 218, 221, 226, 237, 258
immortality, 21, 35, 40, 52–54, 69–70, 282; praise/poetry as, 170–71, 175, 188
Imruʾ al-Qays: ancestry, 242–43; avenging father, 244–49; damnation of, 283–85; death, 248–49; *Muʿallaqah of*, 249–83; wandering king, 247, 282, 284; wayward youth, 244–46
incubation, 276
inṣāf (equal treatment of enemy), 63, 229, 238
instigation to vengeance. *See taḥrīḍ*
intensified contextuality, 181–85
intensive adjectives. *See faʿʿāl*-form; *ism al-ālah*
al-Iṣbahānī, Abū al-Faraj, *Kitāb al-Aghānī*: on Durayd, 73–76; on al-Fāriʿah, 185; on Imruʾ al-Qays, 241–48; on Labīd, 46–51; on Muhalhil, 206n, 208, 210n; on al-Shanfarā, 141–48; on Taʾabbaṭa Sharran, 90–96, 109–13
Isis, 192
Islam, 42–45, 50–54, 199–205, 284–85. *See also* Qurʾān
ism al-ālah (noun of tool), 115, 191, 275
ism al-mubālaghah. *See faʿʿāl*-form
ʿItr, 175
ʿIzz al-Dīn, Ḥ., 18n, 103n, 108n

Jacob, G., 119, 121
Jacobi, R., 3, 27n, 150n
al-Jāḥiẓ, 31, 67n, 68n, 79, 81n, 233n
jahl (impetuosity), 45, 205, 223–24, 245–48, 284
Jamison, S., 79n
jazūr (slaughter camel), 39, 154, 209, 262, 266. *See also* camel slaughter; *maysir*; she-camel
al-Jurjānī, ʿAbd al-Qāhir, 4

Kaʿbah, 24
Kabshah bint Maʿdī Karib, 192–97
Khalaf al-Aḥmar, 58, 120–22, 157
al-Khalīl ibn Aḥmad, 178, 183
al-Khansāʾ, 161, 164
al-Khirniq bint Badr, 168–76, 181, 184
Khulayyif, Y., 58n, 120, 143, 150n
kin/kinship: confusion of, 208–10; and elegy, 161–63, 167–68, 187, 219; in *fakhr*, 40; inverted status of *ṣuʿlūk*, 92, 98, 117–18, 127–31, 142, 150–51, 155, 157; and non-kin, 65–66, 71–73, 78, 83, 229
Kindah, 242, 249
kingship ritual, Ancient Middle Eastern, 4, sacred, 280
Krenkow, F., 121
Kulayb Wāʾil, 207–11, 214, 222

Labīd: biographical anecdotes, 45–54; etymology, 45–46; *Muʿallaqah of*, 9–45
lameness, 100–101. *See also* gait
lament, female ritual, 164–67, 213–15, 219, 236–37
Lāmiyyat al-ʿArab, 143–57; authenticity of, 119–25
Lammens, H., 55, 57, 61n, 62n, 63n, 72n, 80n, 81, 161–62, 168n, 169n, 185n, 229n
Laylā al-Akhyaliyyah, 164
Leach, E., 55–56, 68
Lévi-Strauss, C., 88
lightning, 179–80, 238, 280–82. *See also* rain cloud; rain storm
lily, 269–70
liminal erotic encounter, 261–70
liminality, 7–8, 26–33, 62, 270–73; perpetual, 87–89, 93, 130–31, 137–39, 154–55
liquid soul, 168, 179
liver, 202–3
longevity, 46, 52–54; of vulture, 67–68
Lyall, C. J., 62, 64, 69n, 107n, 114n, 115n, 116n, 128, 134n, 135n, 136, 139n, 141n, 142n, 180n, 186n, 242n–43, 278n–79n

Madelung, W., 44n
madḥ/madīḥ (panegyric), 4

Mālik ibn al-Rayb, 171
Malti-Douglas, F., 37n
marginality. *See* liminality
Ma'rib, Dam of, 23–24
marthiyah. *See rithā'*
al-Marzūqī, Abū ʿAlī, 58, 60, 63n, 68, 72n, 112n, 129n, 156n, 193n, 194, 196n
Mauss, M., 55, 258
al-Maymanī, ʿAbd al-ʿAzīz, 125n
maysir (gambling), 37–44, 153–54, 214, 266
menstrual blood, 66–67, 172–75, 194–96, 227
milk, 196, 208–10
mnemonic features of poetry, 81, 167, 172, 181–85, 231–32
Monroe, J. T., 4, 122
morning. *See* night: to day
Al-Muʿallaqāt: *Muʿ. of Imru' al-Qays*, 149–57; *Muʿ. of Labīd*, 9–18
al-Mubarrad, 119, 163n, 226n
al-Mufaḍḍal al-Ḍabbī, *Al-Mufaḍḍaliyyāt*: *Muf. no. 1*, 105–7; *no. 20*, 132–36
Muhalhil ibn Rabīʿah, 63n, 78n, 206–38 passim, 274; *Aṣmaʿiyyah no. 53*, 224–30; *Long Was My Night*, 234–38; *Memory Inflamed*, 216–25; *Once We Used to Guard*, 212–16; *When the Herald Cried*, 230–34
Muḥammad, the Prophet, 199–205, 285
Müller, G., 9n
al-Mutanabbī, 170–71
mute rocks, 21–23, 272

al-Nābighah al-Dhubyānī, 50
Nagy, G., 21–22
nāqah. *See* she-camel
nasīb, 4, 18–26, 136–37; and *rithā'*, 171, 180, 220–22, 226, 235–36
nature/culture dialectic, 4, 18–26, 36, 111, 130, 157, 260, 274–83
Nicholson, R. A., 3
night: to day, 228, 231, 271–73, 282–83; sleepless, 198, 219–20, 235, 270–72; as unavenged blood, 198, 228, 271–73
niyāḥah, 162, 163n
Nöldeke, T., 119, 121
al-Nuʿmān, Lakhmid king, 47–50
al-Nuwayrī, Shihāb al-Dīn, 28n, 46n, 67n, 79, 208n, 209n, 210, 224n, 233n

Odyssey 11, 69–70
oedipal relation to mother, 95, 99
oedipal tension, 74, 210, 226, 244–45
oedipal violence, 64, 226, 246
Oedipus, 93–104, 157, 245, 284
onager, 29–30, 33
one hundred, vengeance of, 129–30, 245–46
Ong, W. J., 22, 81n, 122
Onians, R. B., 202n
orality, 4, 81, 122, 161–238 passim. *See also* formula, oral-elegiac; mnemonic features of poetry
oryx, 31–33, 262–63, 265
owl, 69, 186; and dove, 236–37

Parry-Lord theory, 4
passenger manqué, 89, 272. *See also* rite of passage: manqué
pearl, 32, 269–70
Pedersen, J., 72n
perfume, 172–75, 191, 202, 227–28, 276
pilgrim, slaying of, 140–42
pilgrimage. *See ḥajj*
pollution, and purification, 4, 66, 78–79, 172–75, 194–96, 215, 223, 227–28, 278, 281–82; of corpse, 67, 79
Procksch, O., 55
Propp, V., 4, 6
proto-Islamic, 42–45, 284–85

al-Qālī, Abū ʿAlī, 120, 193
qaṣīdah form/structure, 3–6, 73, 80, 89, 109, 117–18, 156, 164, 206, 228
Qur'ān: *1:6–7*, 284; *2:168*, 42; *2:173*, 43; *4:40*, 43; *7:71–77*, 27–28; *11:71*, 66; *11:95*, 170; *22:114*, 19n; *34:15–19*, 23–24; *76:5–17*, 43; *83:21–29*, 43; *83:22*, 283; relation to poetry, 51, 284–85; Sūrat al-Baqarah, 51; Sūrat Āl ʿImrān, 51

raḥīl (journey section), 4, 26–33; of *ṣuʿlūk*, 138, 150–51, 270–73
rain: as generosity, 178–80, 187–88, 221; and horse, 275
rain cloud, 179–80
rain storm, 199, 278–83. *See also* lightning
raw vs. cooked, 263, 277–78, 282
Rayṭah Ukht ʿAmr, 188–92
regicide, 242–45, 279–80
revitalization/devitalization, 65, 78–83, 187, 191–92, 196, 226, 229, 282–83
rite of celebration, 192
rite of passage/initiation: in *akhbār* of Durayd, 73–75; in *akhbār* of Imru' al-Qays, 244–47; in *akhbār* of Labīd, 47–50; and blood vengeance, 73–75, 80; female, 267; from Jāhiliyyah to Islam, 42; manqué, 104–18; and *qaṣīdah*, 6–8, 18–42 passim, 72, 80, 164, 215, 226, 228, 258–

rite of passage/initiation (cont.)
83 passim. *See also* aggregation; liminality; separation
rite of sacrifice, 56, 72, 73, 258. *See also* sacrifice
rithā'(elegy): and blood vengeance, 58–83; men's, 205–38; ritual structure of, 219; women's, 161–205; women's for male kin, 163. *See also* formula, oral-elegiac; lament, female ritual; sacrifice; *taḥrīḍ*
Roberts, N., 205n
Robertson Smith, W., 27n, 35, 42n, 55–57, 65, 66n, 67n, 69n, 116n, 233, 262n, 265n
Rückert, F., 119
ruse, 88, 109–14, 130–31

Saba', 23–24
sacred month, killing during, 112–13, 140–41
sacrifice, 55–83; animal, 34–35, 37–41, 175, 191; blood vengeance as, 55–83; blood vengeance as inversion of, 65–66, 80–81; cereal, 172–74; human, 57; improper, 202–3, 207–10, 262–66; place of, 116–17; premature, 262–70; and redemption, 4, 168, 172, 179, 185–88, 199, 282; *rithā'* as, 168, 175–76, 179; self-, 172, 188, 222, 230; of tears, 179–80. *See also* camel slaughter; rite of sacrifice
sacrificial dance, 233
sacrificial victim, 63, 140–41, 172; poet as, 154, 266
de Sacy, S., 119
al-Sandūbī, Ḥ., 206n, 245n
Ṣaqr, ʿA., 163n
scapegoat, 157
scavengers eating dead, 65, 232–33. *See also* hyena; vulture; wolf
seasonal pattern. *See* Gaster, T.
Sells, M. A., 4n, 9n, 98n
separation, 18–26; *ṣuʿlūk*, 150. *See also* rite of passage
sexual defilement, 198–99, 202–5; of corpse, 66–67, 79–80, 192
Shahîd, I., 242n, 249n
al-Shanfarā, 57–58, 119–57; ambiguous identity, 125–31; *Do Not Bury Me!*, 129–31; *Lāmiyyat al-ʿArab*, 119–25, 143–57; *Muf. no. 20*, 132–42
Shaykhū, L., 63n; Muhalhil, 206–35 passim; women's *rithā'*, 163n, 169, 177n, 179, 197–98n
Sheba, 23–24
she-camel, 26–31; absence of, 109, 138, 150, 271; of al-Basūs, 28, 207–10; as bloodwite, 38, 210; and sacrifice, 29, 37–41, 207–10; of Ṣāliḥ, 27–28, 207. *See also jazūr*
signs, 20–23
Sīrah of the Prophet, 199–205
slaughter camel. *See jazūr*
Sperl, S., 4, 6n
Sphinx, 93–104
spices, 260, 262, 282
Stetkevych, J., 3n, 6n, 20n, 21n, 26, 30n, 53n, 82n, 233n, 235n, 275n
storm. *See* rain storm
Structuralism, 4, 111. *See also* nature/culture dialectic; raw vs. cooked; symmetrical inversion
sublimation of blood vengeance paradigm, 259, 280, 283
ṣuʿlūk (brigand-poet), 57–58, 87–157 passim; definition, 87–90. *See also* liminality: perpetual; rite of passage: manqué; al-Shanfarā; Ta'abbaṭa Sharran
ṣuʿlūk qaṣīdah, 88–90, 117–18
Sunnah, 41, 44
Svenbro, J., 22–23
symmetrical inversion, 91–92, 109, 130–31, 139–42, 152, 213–14, 226, 234; Vidal-Naquet's law of, 88–89, 91n, 109n, 139, 274

Ta'abbaṭa Sharran, 87–118, 139; *Do Not Marry Him*, 90–93; etiology of surname, 93–107; *How I Met the Ghūl*, 96–101; *Muf. no. 1*, 105–18; *Rithā' of*, 57–73; *Sulaymā Says*, 101–4
al-Ṭabarī, Abū Jaʿfar, 66n, 199–205
taḥrīḍ (instigation to vengeance), 161–62, 166, 180, 189, 192–99, 201, 214
tarṣīʿ (internal rhyme), 182–85
tattoo, 20–23
ṭayf al-khayāl, 103, 108
Ṭayfūr, Aḥmad, 163n, 198n, 204–5n
tears, 219–20, 261; vs. blood, 198–99, 211–15; metaphor for elegy, 179; reviving dead, 180n, 221; as sacrifice, 179–80
Thaʿlab, 119
Thamūd, 24, 27–28, 207
tha'r. *See* blood vengeance
thirst, for blood/water, 69, 185–86, 237, 246, 279
al-Tibrīzī, Abū Zakariyyā, 58, 60n, 66, 68n, 95, 107n, 114, 115, 119, 137n, 193n, 194–95, 196n, 257n, 266n, 269n
Turner, V., 7, 25, 37, 55, 62, 71, 261, 267

ʿUdhrī *ghazal*, 157
Uḥud, Battle of, 199–205
Umāmah bint Kulayb, 210–11
ummu ʿiyālin (mater familias), 138–40, 152

Vermeule, E., 78n
Vernant, J.-P., 100–101, 130
Vidal-Naquet, P., 88–89, 91n, 109n, 113–14, 139, 274
virgin, 191–92, 267–70, 277
vow to vengeance, 62, 72, 211, 223, 230–32, 244–45; and sacrifice, 266
vulture, 67–70, 78–79, 180, 190–92, 215, 227, 233–34, 279

Waḥshī, 201–4
wasteland, 221, 273, 278
weaving, 260, 281
Wellhausen, 69n
Wensinck, A. J., 44n
wild ass. *See* onager
wine, 34, 42–43, 64, 71–73, 211, 228, 245, 279, 282–83
wolf, 151–53, 233, 272–73
women: concealment vs. exposure of, 165–66, 175–76, 189, 191–92; free vs. captive/slave, 165, 191, 198–99; status of, 161–68, 191, 194–96, 198–99
women's elegy, 161–205
Wright, W., 115n, 148n, 168n
writing, 20–23

al-Yūsuf, Y., 241n–42n

al-Zamakhsharī, Muḥammad, 64n, 150n, 151n, 152
ẓaʿn (tribal departure), 24–25, 220
al-Zawzanī, Abū ʿAbd Allāh, 18n, 35, 257n, 266n, 269n, 270n
Zayd ibn Bishr al-Taghlibī, 81
Zuhayr ibn Abī Sulmā, 170, 172–73
Zwettler, Michael, 4, 122, 123n

MYTH AND POETICS

A series edited by

GREGORY NAGY

Masks of Dionysus
edited by Thomas W. Carpenter and Christopher A. Faraone

Poet and Hero in the Persian Book of Kings
by Olga M. Davidson

The Ravenous Hyenas and the Wounded Sun: Myth and Ritual in Ancient India
by Stephanie W. Jamison

Poetry and Prophecy: The Beginnings of a Literary Tradition
edited by James Kugel

The Traffic in Praise: Pindar and the Poetics of Social Economy
by Leslie Kurke

Epic Singers and Oral Tradition
by Albert Bates Lord

The Language of Heroes: Speech and Performance in the Iliad
by Richard P. Martin

Heroic Sagas and Ballads
by Stephen A. Mitchell

Greek Mythology and Poetics
by Gregory Nagy

Myth and the Polis
edited by Dora C. Pozzi and John M. Wickersham

Knowing Words:
Wisdom and Cunning in the Classical Traditions of China and Greece
by Lisa Raphals

Homer and the Sacred City
by Stephen Scully

The Mute Immortals Speak: Pre-Islamic Poetry and the Poetics of Ritual
by Suzanne Pinckney Stetkevych

Phrasikleia: An Anthropology of Reading in Ancient Greece
by Jesper Svenbro
translated by Janet Lloyd

Library of Congress Cataloging-in-Publication Data

Stetkevych, Suzanne Pinckney.
The mute immortals speak : pre-Islamic poetry and the poetics of ritual / by Suzanne Pinckney Stetkevych.
p. cm. — (Myth and poetics)
Includes bibliographical references and index.
ISBN 0-8014-2764-9 (alk. paper)
1. Qasidas—Themes, motives. 2. Arabic poetry—To 622—History and criticism. 3. Rites and ceremonies in literature. I. Title. II. Series.
PJ7542.Q3S75
892′.71109—dc20 93-18173